Information Systems
for you
SECOND EDITION

Stephen Doyle

STANLEY THORNES (PUBLISHERS) LTD

First published in 1995 by
Stanley Thornes (Publishers) Ltd
Ellenborough House
Wellington Street
CHELTENHAM GL50 1YW

Revised edition published 1996

Second edition published 1999

00 01 02 03 / 10 9 8 7 6 5 4 3

A catalogue record for this book is available from the British Library
ISBN 0 7487 4459 2
Cartoons by Shaun Williams
Typeset by GreenGate Publishing Services, Tonbridge, Kent
Printed and bound in Italy by STIGE, Turin

Contents

Introduction   vii

Acknowledgements   x

1 What is an Information System?   1

Data • Information • The three stages of doing tasks • Manual information systems • Computerised information systems • Examples of computerised information systems

2 The Components of an Information System   7

Hardware and software • Why use computers? • Are there any drawbacks in using computers? • Processing data • Types of computer • Peripheral devices • Microprocessors

3 The 'Ins' and 'Outs' of Systems: Input and Output   14

The 'ins' and 'outs' of a video library • Input devices • Output devices

4 Storing Data   29

The storage of data • Memory (main store) • Magnetic media • Optical disks

5 Software   34

What is software? • Operating systems (systems software) • Multitasking • Multiuser • User interfaces • Applications software • Programming languages • Translation programs

6 Collecting Your Data   42

The problems with college enrolments • Coding data • Putting the details into the computer • Flood warning: an example of automatic data capture • Automatic data capture using signals • Turnaround documents

7 Checking Data   53

Reasons for errors • Consequences of errors • How are errors avoided? • Types of error • How to avoid errors

8 How Data Is Stored: Databases   61

The parts of a database • A card box filing system • Record design • Manual filing systems • Computerised databases

9 Types of Computer Operation   72

Life in the fast lane • Real-time processing • Doing all the processing in one go: batch processing • Multitasking and multiprogramming • Transaction processing • Multi-access and timesharing

10 Data Transfer 77

File conversion • ASCII Files • Transferring files between wordprocessors • Data/file compression • Digital and analogue computers

11 Ways of Presenting Your Data 82

Hard copy • Presentation graphics • Multimedia • CD-ROM • Sound • MIDI • Virtual reality

12 How to Describe an Information System 87

Describing systems • Structure diagrams • Data flow diagrams • Systems flowcharts

13 Systems Analysis: Sounds Hard, What is it? 95

Harlequin Aquatics • Fact finding • Feasibility study • Analysis phase • System design • Testing the system • Implementing (or introducing) the new system • Documentation • System evaluation

14 Weather Forecasting: An Application of Data Logging 105

Weather reporting: the old way • Problem • The solution • Weather reporting • The sensors • Analogue-to-digital conversion • Advantages of data logging • Transferring weather data to another package • Weather satellites

15 Transferring Data Around: A Company with a Communication Problem 113

Problems with the existing system • The solution to Binscope's problem • Networks • Local area networks • Wide area networks • Network topologies • Modems • The bits which make up a network • ISDN (Integrated Services Digital Network) • Telecommunications • Internet Service Provider (ISP) • The Internet • Electronic mail • Message sending • Protocols and handshakes • File compression • Speed of access • Bandwidth • Cost of installation • Electronic data interchange (EDI)

16 System Security 128

Computer security • Physical security • Computer theft • Protection from fires • Protection from dust and extremes of temperature • Software security • Protecting your files • Project advice • The difference between security and integrity

17 Data and You: The Data Protection Act 135

Computers and privacy • Loyalty cards • The reasons behind the Data Protection Act • The 1998 Data Protection Act • Data subjects and data controllers

18 Computers and the Law 146

Computer crime • Credit card use • Automated teller machines (ATMs) • Credit card fraud • Electronic fraud • Phantom withdrawals • Smart cards • Software piracy • The Copyright, Designs and Patents Act 1989 • The Computer Misuse Act 1990

19 The Social Effects of Information Systems 152

Social and economic effects of IT • Is information technology a good thing? • Changing employment patterns • Identity cards move a step closer • The shape of things to come • Environmental, ethical, moral and social issues raised by information technology

20 Controlling Things 160

Robots • Computers in control • Process control • Pseudo-code • Computers in greenhouses • Computers and safety of cars • Data logging

21 Computers and your Health 171

The problems • Protecting the workforce • Things to consider when designing an office

22 The Electronic Office 176

The paper chase • Equipment and facilities in an electronic office

23 Simulations: Almost as Good as the Real Thing 181

Modelling • Games • Model Builder • Expert systems • Expert Builder • Simulations • An example IT task

24 Bulmer's: A Case Study 190

H P Bulmer Ltd (cider makers) • Bulmer's information systems • Process control by computers • Computers in the laboratory • Using computers to help with presentations • Possible new developments

25 Computer Applications 198

Information technology: helping to solve crime • Information technology in the supermarket • Information technology in the music industry • IT and the TV/video industry • Information technology and medicine • Information technology and banking • Traffic control systems • Pollution monitoring

SKILLS FOR COURSEWORK

26 Advice on Coursework 211

What software can I use? • Hints and tips • How much do I write? • Can my teacher help me? • Do you get marks for your English? • What is entailed in the coursework? • Coursework for your examination board

27 Wordprocessing and Wordprocessing Exercises 219

Hardware and software for wordprocessing • The advantages of
wordprocessing • What can you do with wordprocessing software? •
Choosing a wordprocessing package

28 Spreadsheets and Spreadsheet Exercises 229

What is a spreadsheet? • Entering data correctly • Let the spreadsheet do
the work for you • Tips for building a spreadsheet • Mathematical
operators • Using conditions in spreadsheets • Printing spreadsheets •
Graphs • Business decisions • Finding the maximum volume of a box
made from a sheet of metal • Lookup tables • Testing a spreadsheet •
Documenting your spreadsheet

29 Desktop Publishing 246

Equipment needed • Some features of desktop publishing • Advantages
of desktop publishing • When to use a DTP package • Basic techniques
used in DTP • Summary of the main features of a DTP package • Glossary
of terms used in desktop publishing

30 Database Coursework 255

Creating a database • Using the database • Sorting and indexing • Comma
separated variables • Creating an information system using a database

31 Measurement and Control 271

Turtle graphics • Monitoring physical quantities (temperature, pressure,
etc.) using a computer • Other examples of computer control

32 Modelling 281

Modelling coursework • Modelling a supermarket queue • Break-even
analysis

33 Graphics Packages 292

Graphics • Graphics packages • Clip art • Presentation software •
Multimedia (hypermedia) presentations • Colour • Computer aided
design

34 Exam Preparation 302

Revising • The exam

Examination Questions 307

Glossary 335

Names, Addresses and Internet Sites 342

Appendix: The Old (1984) Data Protection Act 344

Index 346

Introduction

The aim of this book

The aim of this book is to build up your knowledge of information technology and to develop your skills in this area. By the time you reach the end of the course you should know about IT and be able to use the skills and knowledge you have acquired to solve your own problems. It is not necessary to study the chapters in the sequence they are presented in the book. However, if you study them in another order you may encounter unfamiliar terms that have been explained in previous chapters.

The starting point

Since many of the questions, tasks, projects, etc. presented in the book involve a knowledge of wordprocessing, spreadsheets, graphics, desktop publishing, multimedia, control, measurement and database software, you should make sure that you know what these are and how to use such software at a basic level.

Syllabus coverage

This book has been written to cover all the Information Technology syllabuses in the UK. The book covers both the full course and short course in Information Technology at GCSE. Some of the text also provides useful background material for students taking the Intermediate GNVQ in Information Technology.

The full course and the short course

You can approach Information Technology by taking either:

- GCSE Information Technology full course
- GCSE Information Technology short course

What are the differences between the full and the short courses?

The short course involves less work than the full course and when passed is the equivalent of a half GCSE. You can, at a later date, do further work to convert this into a full GCSE. Completing the short course GCSE shows that you are a skilled user of IT but you have not studied the subject to the depth of the full course.

The full course includes all the requirements of the short course but requires you to extend your knowledge of IT. For some of the examination boards, this means that you have to be able to design, create, analyse and evaluate the use of computers, software and related equipment in the real world.

Tiers of entry

As well as the two types of course (full and short) there are two tiers of entry for each course. (The Northern Ireland course is slightly different in its approach and you will need to ask your teacher about this.)

For all examination boards other than Northern Ireland the tiers and grades are summarised in the table below.

Tier	Grade range
Foundation	C to G
Higher	A* to D

How to use this book

The book is divided into two sections, the first part dealing with the material for the examination and the second part covering coursework. Chapters 1 to 25 cover the theoretical part of the syllabus, although they also include a variety of practical tasks. Chapters 27 to 34 are coursework chapters, the aim of which is to help you gain skills and knowledge about software and apply these to your own coursework. All GCSE marking schemes show a certain percentage of the marks allocated to coursework and this book gives you useful advice in this respect. If you want to know more about what the coursework involves, look at Chapter 26, Advice on Coursework.

At the end of most chapters there is a 'test yourself' section which tests on the material presented in the chapter.

Boxes marked 'Things to do' are also included. These contain a variety of problems including some examination-style questions.

Some chapters contain projects, entitled 'Investigations', and these encourage you to do some research on a particular topic and use your skills to present your findings. Such projects will add to your overall knowledge of information technology.

Questions within the text

Questions have been included within the text to help you understand concepts as you come to them. In this way you do not have to wait until the end of a chapter before testing your understanding.

'Skills Building' exercises

These exercises are scattered throughout the book and provide opportunities to build your hardware and software skills in solving real problems.

Investigations

'Investigations' provide an opportunity to carry out a project on a particular topic (or topics). The aim of such investigations is to reinforce your knowledge of the subject as well as developing a variety of skills in finding the information and then presenting it.

Making use of IT in other subjects

In many schools and colleges IT is not taught as a separate subject but included in other lessons. For instance, you may learn about how to access information held on CD-ROM while doing GCSE History coursework, or you might learn about sensors while performing an experiment to measure the heat liberated during a chemical reaction. If you are approaching the IT course in this way you will need to make sure that you cover all the parts of the syllabus. You are advised to get a copy of your syllabus and use it as a checklist. You should not just consider IT as a subject in its own right, since knowledge and skills in IT can be usefully applied to all subject areas and all aspects of your everyday life.

Advice on coursework

Chapter 26 provides hints and tips as well as answers to questions you might have such as:

What software can I use?
How much do I write?
Can my teacher help me?
Do you get marks for your English?
What is entailed in the coursework?

Also included are some suggestions (from several examination boards) for each type of task.

Examination questions

At the back of the book there is a section of actual examination questions which you can use for practice. These exam questions cover foundation and higher tiers. Also shown is whether a particular question is from the full or the short course. Use this information to help you choose the questions best suited for the course you are studying.

Glossary

There is a glossary at the back of the book; it is a sort of dictionary of computer words showing their meanings. If you come across a term that you do not understand you can do one of two things to help you find out what it means. You can turn to the glossary, where you will find a brief explanation of what it means. However, if you want a fuller explanation, use the index to find the relevant pages.

Looking up words in the glossary will reinforce your knowledge of the subject. You will find that several of the smaller examination questions ask what is meant by certain computer terms. It is a good idea to try to learn some of the words in the glossary along with their meanings. One approach to this is described next.

Learning the glossary

Find some paper or cardboard and cut it into rectangular pieces about the size of a playing card. Taking two cards at once, write a computer term on one card and its meaning on the other (see Figure 1). Shuffle all the cards and then try to match the terms with their meanings. Once you have done this, check your answers using the glossary.

Program

A set of instructions that the computer can understand

Figure 1 *Make up revision cards like these*

Acknowledgements

Thanks to Rick Jackman, Rachel Warner and Steve Mead of Stanley Thornes for their encouragement and help in producing this book.

Thanks are due to the following for permission to use material:

- George Thomas and Dr Martin Wynn of HP Bulmer Ltd
- Philip Harris Education
- DRS Data & Research Services plc
- SIMS Education Services Ltd
- Cambridgeshire Software House
- GST Software Products
- Liverpool Community College
- The Data Protection Commissioner
- IBM
- Driver and Vehicle Licensing Agency
- Global Software Publishing, Tel: 01480 496575
- Avon Cosmetics
- Tracon Systems Ltd
- AOL
- Dundee Satellite Receiving Station
- Sainsbury's Supermarkets Ltd

Microsoft Office screenshots reprinted with permission from Microsoft Corporation. Microsoft and its products are registered trademarks or trademarks of Microsoft Corporation in the United States and/or other countries.

Thank you also to the following examination boards which gave permission for the use of their questions:

- OCR
- Midland Examining Group
- Northern Examinations & Assessment Board
- Northern Ireland Council for the Curriculum, Examinations and Assessment. Questions reproduced from NI 1997 Specimen Papers 1 and 3, 1997 Papers 1 and 3, 1998 Papers 1 and 3, ©1997, 1998, with the permission of the Northern Ireland Council for the Curriculum, Examinations and Assessment.
- Royal Society of Arts
- Southern Examining Group
- London Examinations, a division of Edexcel Foundation
- Welsh Joint Education Committee

A full list of examinations boards and their addresses is given on page 342.

Photo credits

- Images Colour Library (p.294, left)
- Martin Sookias (p.200, right)

1 What is an Information System?

Data

We call raw facts and figures **data**. Facts and figures often have little meaning until they are sorted or until we calculate something from them. This sorting or calculation is called **data processing**. When data is processed, it provides **information** (see Figure 1.1).

Figure 1.1 *Processing data produces information*

Information

Information is the meaning we attach to the data. For instance, a red traffic light is a form of data. The meaning we attach to this data (i.e. STOP) is the information. Sometimes data can give rise to ambiguous information. If you are driving a car and a car travelling in the opposite direction flashes its lights at you, what does it mean? It could just mean that a friend has spotted you and is saying hello; it could also mean that there is an accident further up the road. The information that may be obtained from data depends on the way that the data is interpreted and the context in which it is used.

Data is often meaningless. For instance consider the number 250299. We could interpret this in any number of ways. For example it might be:

- your video club membership number
- the date, e.g. 25th February 1999
- the number of cars going down a certain road in a week.

The three stages of doing tasks

All tasks can be broken down into three stages: input, process and output. These are shown in Figure 1.2.

Figure 1.2 *The three stages of doing tasks*

Manual information systems

We are all used to dealing with some sort of manual information system. A telephone directory is an example. There may be several hundred thousand entries, but if we know the surname and address of the person we are trying to contact, we can find the number provided that it is in the directory.

Manual information systems have many disadvantages. Let's look at an example.

Suppose you have a friend whose phone number and surname you know but whose address you need to find. You do not know their parent's initial and their surname is, unfortunately, Jones. You could find the address by taking the following steps:

1 Look up the section for Jones.
2 Start from the beginning and work through the phone numbers, looking for the area code, e.g. look for 928 and see if the rest of the number coincides.
3 Once the phone number has been found you can read off the address.

An even worse problem might be if you had a phone number of a person scribbled down on a piece of paper and you wanted to find out who you were ringing first. The telephone directory is ordered alphabetically according to surname and not in numerical order according to telephone number, so to find the number would prove an immense and time-consuming task.

Computerised information systems

Computerised information systems are much more flexible than manual ones and a lot faster. With a computerised system you could type in a phone number and, if the number was stored in the system, the name and address could be provided immediately.

Examples of computerised information systems

The Driver Vehicle Licensing Authority
The Driver Vehicle Licensing Authority (DVLA) keeps a huge collection of information concerning every driver and every vehicle in the country. Such a huge collection of data is called a database. Summarised details of this database are passed to the Police National Computer (PNC).

Suppose there has been a hit and run accident and a witness is able to remember only part of the registration number, e.g. _704 N___. Imagine trying to search through the thousands of car registrations having those letters or numbers in them. Even a computer can take some time doing these sorts of searches. Even worse, what would happen if we only knew that the car was a Ford Mondeo with partial registration L___ N___. This type of situation happens all the time when the police are trying to trace cars. Computerised information systems are one of the main weapons in the fight against crime.

A computerised school management system
Consider your school or college. In the secretaries' office there will be a computer containing information on all the students in the school. What are the requirements of a school information system?

Here are some of the tasks that the system would need to deal with.

1 The system must record the attendance details twice a day for all the pupils. It must be able to identify pupils who have poor attendance records so that they may be investigated.
2 It must list a pupil's personal details. This would include such things as name, address, date of birth, name of parent or guardian, daytime contact numbers and addresses, sex, religion, medical problems, form, form teacher's name, mode of travel to school, whether students stay for school dinners and so on.
3 It must be easy to produce the various lists such as lists of pupils for registration groups, teaching groups, parents' evenings and school trips.
4 It must be possible to get information easily from the system so that letters may be generated and sent to certain pupils.
5 The system must be able to cope with the administration of examination entries.
6 It must cope with all the financial aspects of running a school.
7 The system should be able to help organise a timetable, making the best use of the teachers and the rooms.

As you can see from the above list, a lot of work goes on behind the scenes in a school.

Figure 1.3 *Pupil profile forms are read automatically using an optical mark reader*

Advantages of a computerised information management system
1 You don't need lots of filing cabinets to hold all the pupils' files and other forms. A single computer can store all the information needed.

2 Terminals can be used, so that many people can access the information in different places at the same time. Whenever data is updated it is instantly available to all the people using the system.

3 There is no duplication of information. The pupils' details need only be entered once and then used for different tasks. It is possible to produce year lists, class lists, option lists etc. using the data from the pupil file.

4 The system can be used in conjunction with a wordprocessor to produce mail shots to pupils' homes.

5 Some information can be transferred to the system without using the keyboard. For instance, Figure 1.3 shows marks on a document being read by an optical mark reader.

will be lost and new staff will need to be trained.

3 Security will need to be provided to protect personal pupil and staff information from prying eyes.

Figure 1.5 *A computer being used to view a pupil's personal details. Notice that it can even include a photograph*

Figure 1.4 *With manual systems, large numbers of filing cabinets are often needed to store records. With a computerised system, one computer could store all this information*

Disadvantages of a computerised information management system

1 Everything depends on the computer system. If there is a power failure, or if the system breaks down then an alternative system will need to be used.

2 To use the system, the staff will need to be trained. When staff leave their expertise

Pupils' personal details need only be recorded once on the system. Even a photograph can be put onto it as shown in Figure 1.5. The system is easy for everyone to use and can use the **Windows** style of menus as shown in Figure 1.6. All aspects of the school's administration can be dealt with by the system, from running the school library to recording pupils' option choices. The form shown in Figure 1.7 is used to record pupil option choices. Each option has a different barcode, which can be stuck to the form. The details can be read by using an optical character reader.

The Schools Information Management System enables the head teacher of the school to run the school as efficiently as possible for the benefit of all the pupils. Tasks that would have taken a long time now can be done quickly.

Figure 1.7 *This form is used to record pupil option details. Each option has a different barcode, which is stuck to the form. The details can be extracted using an optical mark reader or a barcode reader*

Figure 1.6 *A Windows screen from the Schools Information Management System*

The SIMS Approach — OPTION SELECTION SHEET

STUDENT NUMBER

Name:

Reg. Grp.

INSTRUCTIONS
Mark like this ▬
NOT like ✓ or ✗ or ◯

POPULATION

Enter option choices OR **Place barcode labels**

A   E   I

B   F   J

C   G   K

D   H   L

A

B

C

D — Mark below if this sheet starts with choice 10

E — Mark below if this sheet starts with choice 13

F

G

H

I

E60G20693/TAHD

© Joint Copyright SIMS Ltd & DRS Data & Research Services plc

Things to do

1 Write a list of manual information systems that you use in your everyday life.
   Here are a few to start you off:
   - Dictionary
   - Library catalogue
   - Mail order catalogue
   - Guinness Book of Hit Singles
   - Bus timetable

   See how many more you can think up.
   When you have finished, compare your list with your friends' lists.

2 You have been asked to produce a geography project on a particular country such as Iceland.
   You intend to do this using traditional reference books. What manual information sources
   would you use? Write a list.

3 Find out about the information systems (manual or computerised) used in your school office.
   You need to investigate each of the following:
   (a) How does the data get into the system?
        If the school uses a manual system, explain how the system deals with the various tasks
        mentioned in the text. If a computerised system is used, how is the data entered into the
        system? Also, what information does the system provide?
   (b) Find out what sort of information needs to be held about each pupil, including you. Write
        a list of the information and explain for each one, why it is held.

4 A school uses a database to store details about each pupil.
   (a) The details stored about each pupil include the following items:
        - Pupil number
        - Name
        - Address
        - Date of birth
        - Class
        - Sex
        (i)   Write down three more items of information the database would probably store about
              each pupil.
        (ii) Each pupil is given a unique pupil number when they join the school. What is the rea-
              son for this?
   (b) At the start of the year (or when a new pupil joins the school) pupils are asked to fill in a
        form which gives the school information to be put on the pupil database. Using an A4
        sized piece of paper, design such a form.
   (c) Many pupil database systems, as well as displaying the personal details about each pupil,
        also display a recent photograph of the pupil. Why might this be useful to the school staff?

INVESTIGATIONS

CD-ROMs are able to hold huge amounts of data which previously could only be found with great difficulty in huge sets of encyclopaedias, atlases, dictionaries and other reference books. Material held on CD can provide many things that books can't. If you are interested in a particular composer, such as Mozart, you can see a picture of him, read the text and hear his music all at the same time. It is important to be able to access reference material held on CD-ROMs.

1 Find out the titles of any CD-ROMs your school or college has. List the titles and what sort of information they contain (you can usually get this information from the piece of paper inside the sleeve). Have a look at any which seem interesting.

2 Taking a disk whose subject matter interests you, see if you can access information by:
   (a) using the main index
   (b) using the word search facility
   (c) using any sound sequences if available
   (d) using any animations (moving diagrams)
   (e) using any video clips.

3 Select an article that contains both a photograph and some text referring to the photograph and print it out.

The Components of an Information System

Hardware and software

There are two parts to all computer systems: the hardware and the software. Hardware is the term used for the parts of the computer that you can touch and handle. Hardware is the collective name given to all the devices that make up a computer system. Some examples of computer hardware are shown in Figure 2.1. Basically these devices may be split into:

- **input devices**, which are used to get the data into the computer
- the **central processing unit**, which is the brain of the computer
- the **backing storage**, which consists of the disk drives used to store data when the power is switched off
- the **output devices**, which include such units as printers and VDUs, which are used to provide output in the form of printouts, screen displays, etc.

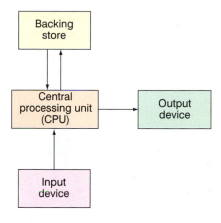

Figure 2.2 *A simple computer system*

The arrangement of these in a typical computer system is shown in Figure 2.2.

Software is the word used for the actual programs that allow the hardware to do a useful job. Without software, hardware is useless. Software is made up of a series of instructions that tell the computer what to do.

To understand the difference between hardware and software, think of a tape recorder and a blank tape. The tape recorder and the tape are the 'hardware' because we can actually pick them up. But if we recorded some music onto the tape, then the music would be the 'software'.

Why use computers?

Computers are extremely fast
A large computer used for producing weather forecasts is able to perform over one million calculations per second. This may appear to be excessive, but many millions of calculations are needed to produce a weather forecast, and forecasts need to be produced quickly.

Computer systems used by the gas and electricity companies have to produce bills to be sent out every three months. Without fast and powerful computers this would be impossible.

Figure 2.1 *The parts of a typical microcomputer*

Computers are very accurate

We have to remember when we see stories in newspapers about computers making huge mistakes that it is the people who have programmed them or entered the data that have made the mistakes. Computers only do what they are told to do. We often use the saying 'garbage in, garbage out' (GIGO for short): what it means is that if incorrect data is put into a computer, the computer won't realise that it is incorrect so it will produce a strange answer. If the computer is given the right information, then provided the hardware and software are working correctly, it will always produce the right output.

Computers can keep large amounts of information in a small space

Keeping all the information we need written on paper in files is an enormous task. Once you have gone through the tedious task of making up the files and cataloguing them, there is the problem of finding the file you want; sometimes you may have millions of them to hunt through! But if you use computerised storage you can keep millions of files in a very small space and get the information from them in seconds. You can also have a spare copy in case of accidents – imagine having duplicate written files (Figure 2.3).

Computers can work continuously for 24 hours a day

Computers don't become ill, they don't take lunch breaks or tea breaks and they don't go on strike (Figure 2.4). Computers can easily work 24 hours per day, 365 days per year. There are many things that are probably best left to humans though (Figure 2.5).

Computers can do some jobs that would be impossible without them

Airline booking, the use of credit cards and Switch cards, weather forecasting and space exploration would all be much more difficult without computers.

The clerical cost of filling a three drawer filing cabinet is reckoned to be about £1500. In addition, annual maintenance of the files would cost about £1200

Some 70% of paper filed is lost. However, the average document is copied seven times and this increases the chances of finding it again. What a waste!

Figure 2.3 *Manual filing systems can take up a lot of space and are difficult to organise*

Figure 2.4 *Computers don't have tea breaks and they don't go on strike*

Figure 2.5 *Many things are best left to humans*

Are there any drawbacks in using computers?

Computers can replace people
There is no doubt that the use of computers has lead to unemployment.

Computers hold personal information which may be misused
It is very easy to misuse the personal information held about individuals on computers. This will be looked at more closely in Chapter 18.

Problems arise when computers cannot be used
Sometimes a computer system breaks down, so things have to be done manually or postponed until it is fixed.

Staff need to be trained
Training can be expensive and if the staff leave new staff will need to be trained.

Processing data

Computers are used to process data. What we mean by 'processing' is doing something to the data. Processing includes:

- **calculating** – for example working out how much pay an employee gets
- **sorting** – your teacher may require a class list arranged in alphabetical order
- **searching** – your head teacher may want to produce a list of all pupils who stay for school dinners
- **storing** – information may be stored on the computer instead of using a paper-based system; old letters or memos may never be needed again but it might still be worth keeping them for a few years
- **drawing** – you might use a paint package in your art lesson or a computer aided design (CAD) package in your technology lesson to design a product.

The central processing unit

The central processing unit (often called the CPU or simply the processing unit) processes the raw data and turns it into information. We need not look too deeply into how it works because, as you can imagine, it is quite complicated. If you ever need to open up the case of a microcomputer you will see that there is a series of circuit boards containing the main processor along with various memory chips.

You will also find a transformer and sometimes a fan which is responsible for the hum that you get from a computer. Chips give out quite a bit of heat during operation, so a fan is used to cool them down.

There are three main elements of the central processing unit:

- the **control unit**, responsible for co-ordinating the input and output devices
- the **arithmetic and logic unit** in which all the calculations and logical decisions are made
- the **immediate access store**, which provides immediate memory for holding data and programs.

The immediate access store (IAS) is on a chip or a series of chips inside the computer. Data held here can be accessed immediately, unlike data held on disk, which can take some time to load.

Figure 2.6 shows how these three main parts of a computer are arranged. In this diagram the solid lines are the data signals passing between the various sections or units. The dotted lines show the signals that are used to control the peripheral devices.

Figure 2.6 *Central processing unit with peripherals*

Processing units for large mainframe computers look like metal cabinets. Smaller microcomputers, as shown in Figure 2.7, come in a variety of types, such as desktop, notebook and palm top computers.

The two types of signal

There are two kinds of signals that pass between the main processor and the other hardware. These are:

- **Control signals** – these include signals sent out by the main processor to the printer to tell it to be ready to receive some data.
- **Data signals** – these are the groups of binary digits that are used to represent characters (letters of the alphabet, numbers, punctuation marks, etc.).

Figure 2.7 *A desktop, B mini-tower, C tower, D notebook, E palm top, and F personal digital assistants (PDAs)*

Types of computer

There are three types of computer: micro-computers, mainframe computers and mini computers. We will look at each of these in turn.

Microcomputers

Microcomputers are the computers that you are most likely to encounter at home or in school or college. Different types include Apples, Acorns and PCs.

Personal digital assistants (PDAs)

Personal digital assistants (PDAs) are small, hand-held devices which you can use to organise a busy schedule. Their main advantage over a small PC, such as a laptop, is their small size. Most of them are little bigger than a diary or large calculator.

Using a PDA you can do the following:

- You can keep track of appointments and things you have to do on certain days.
- You can store the names and addresses of your contacts and friends.
- Many PDAs are able to download e-mail from your personal computer that you can then read offline on the PDA.
- They have calculating facilities similar to those of a fully featured calculator.
- You can prepare, edit and send faxes, and also receive them.

Palmtop computers

These are small computers that usually contain a limited number of applications. Their main advantage is their size which allows them to be carried around in a briefcase or even a pocket. They are useful mainly to occasional computer users such as sales reps who can organise their visits and can enter customers' orders. When reps get back to the office they can then download the data onto a personal computer or the company's network. In their offices, many reps now use infra-red links to communicate with their office networks; connecting in this way is much simpler than using cables.

Palm top computers can also be attached to mobile phones enabling them to receive and send e-mail.

Notebook computers

These computers are bigger than PDAs and palmtops and have a set of facilities almost identical to the larger PCs. They normally come with a battery, which needs to be charged up before the computer can be used away from the power supply. They also have LCDs (liquid crystal displays) instead of the conventional VDU. LCDs are not as bright as conventional VDUs but they are necessary because the whole unit needs to be kept small and power consumption minimised.

Portability does have drawbacks:

- Because of the way in which portable computers are used in public places (on trains, in hotel receptions, etc.) they are highly visible, and often stolen.
- Staff will take them home where their children may be tempted to play games on them with the corresponding risks of introducing viruses.

Mainframe computers

A mainframe computer is a large, powerful computer which is capable of supporting large numbers of terminals (typically 500+). The larger mainframe computers carry out 250 million instructions per second (MIPS). An instruction is the equivalent of adding two numbers together, and these machines can do that 250 million times per second. Because of their immense power they produce considerable amounts of heat, so computer rooms have to be air conditioned and some mainframes are water-cooled.

Banks, building societies, large insurance companies, the utility companies (i.e. gas, electricity, water) all make use of these powerful mainframe computers.

Mini computers

Mini computers have a size, power and cost somewhere between those of microcomputers and mainframes. With the rapid advances in technology, it is common to find modern minicomputers which are much more powerful than some of the mainframes still in use.

Peripheral devices

Peripheral devices are devices outside the central processing unit but under its control. They may be input devices, such as keyboards, used to get the data into the computer, output devices, such as printers, or storage devices, such as disk drives.

Microprocessors

A microprocessor is a single chip that performs the functions of a central processing unit. A chip consists of millions of tiny electronic components etched on a piece of silicon. A microcomputer comprises a microprocessor, together with other chips such as memory chips.

Microprocessors are used to control devices such as washing machines, video recorders, burglar alarms and microwave ovens. In fact, it is hard to think of any electrical or electronic device that could not employ a microprocessor to help control it.

TEST YOURSELF

Using the words in the list below, copy out and complete sentences A to H, underlining the words you have inserted. The words may be used once, more than once or not at all.

> programs   GIGO   hardware   information
>
> software   searching   quick   peripheral
>
> backing   microprocessor

A A computer system consists of two parts: _____ and _____.

B Software is the name given to the _____ which enable a computer to perform a useful task.

C A simple computer system consists of a CPU, input and output devices and some external storage called _____ storage.

D Gas and electricity boards use computers because they are very _____ at producing bills.

E A computer will give the wrong result if you feed it incorrect information to start with. This is often referred to as _____.

F Computers are often used because they are able to hold lots of _____ in a very small space. They are also quick at _____ for this information.

G A _____ device is the name given to a device that is outside the CPU but still under the control of it.

H A single chip which performs the functions of a CPU is called a _____.

Things to do

1 Tick one box for each of the items below to show whether it is hardware or software. If you get stuck use the index or the glossary at the back of the book to help.

	Hardware	Software
(a) Keyboard	☐	☐
(b) Floppy disk	☐	☐
(c) Visual display unit	☐	☐
(d) Mouse	☐	☐
(e) Central processing unit	☐	☐
(f) Wordprocessor	☐	☐
(g) Operating system	☐	☐
(h) Joystick	☐	☐
(i) Spreadsheet	☐	☐
(j) Database	☐	☐

2 (a) Give the name of the chip that carries out the functions of a central processing unit.
   (b) If you buy a floppy disk with a computer game on it, have you bought hardware, software or both?
   (c) Give three reasons why a computer is more efficient than a human being.

3 (a) Name two jobs that it would be impossible to perform without computers.
   (b) For the two jobs you have named, give reasons why it would be impossible to perform them manually (by hand).

4 Not all aspects of using computers are good but their good points far outweigh their bad points; otherwise we would not use them.

   Write a short paragraph on any disadvantages in using computers.

The 'Ins' and 'Outs' of Systems

Input and Output

The 'ins' and 'outs' of a video library

When designing any information system, you need first to consider what information you want to get out of the system. The output depends on the type of job (application). If you were considering a video library, you could decide that the following output is needed:

1 screen displays of videos out on loan and those that should be on the shelves
2 printouts containing details of members who have not returned their videos
3 letters to send to members reminding them to return their videos
4 membership lists
5 letters telling members they have to pay for videos they have failed to return (if the reminder in 3 above has had no response).

Then you need to consider what you should put into the system to get the above output. These **inputs** to the system might include:

1 membership details, such as membership number, name, address, etc.
2 details of all the videos kept, such as video number, title, category, etc.
3 details of the videos lent (these will link the membership numbers to the video numbers)
4 details of when videos are returned.

On the face of it, it looks as though you could use a visual display unit (VDU) and a printer for the output, and a keyboard for the input. This is only one solution. You should look at other alternatives so that you are able to choose the best one. You could use a barcode reader to read a barcode on the member's card and link it with the barcode on the video. This may prove more accurate and quicker than having to type in the membership and video numbers, but it

may prove too expensive. You must always consider all the options and then choose the best.

If there aren't many members or too many videos, a manual card boxed system may even be more cost effective than a computer system.

Input devices

Input devices are used to get data into a system. The ideal input device would be able to get data into a system as accurately as possible, in the least amount of time and preferably without human intervention. The device would also be relatively cheap. Unfortunately, no perfect input device is available and the choice is always a compromise. The fastest input devices are suitable only for a narrow range of applications. Here are some of the main input devices in use today.

Keyboard

The keyboard is the oldest and most familiar of all input devices. Keyboards are intelligent devices and contain their own chips. Basically each key acts as a switch which closes when the key is pressed. The microprocessor scans the keyboard hundreds of times a second to see if a key has been pressed; if it has, a code that depends on which key has been pressed is sent to the processing unit. The CPU translates this code into an ASCII code (the code that computers use to represent characters on the computer keyboard), which is then used by the computer program.

Concept keyboard

The arrangement of keys on a traditional computer keyboard is very similar to that on a typewriter keyboard. On a typewriter this arrangement was chosen for its slowness. New keyboards, called concept keyboards, have been developed which make use of the latest research into ergonomics. Concept keyboards are less tiring to use and higher typing speeds can be achieved. They do mean that people have to get used to them and this has prevented their widescale acceptance.

Figure 3.1 *These concept keyboards are very different from traditional keyboards*

Mouse

A mouse is an input device that translates its movements on the desktop into digital information; this is fed to the computer which in

The cat's swallowed a mouse – so what's new?

Figure 3.2

turn causes the cursor to move on the screen. Underneath the mouse is a ball which rotates as the mouse is moved on the desk, and sensors pick up this movement. Mice usually have one, two or three buttons, which are used to make selections on the screen.

Tracker ball

A tracker ball is like an upside down mouse. The ball is rotated by the user but in this case the 'mouse' stays still. The advantage of a tracker ball compared with a conventional mouse, is that it takes up much less space, and this is why tracker balls are often seen on laptop computers.

Touch sensitive pad

Touch sensitive pads or track pads are commonly found on notebook computers. You move a stylus (or your finger) across a pad and this moves the cursor on the screen. Figure 3.3 shows a laptop featuring a track pad.

Track pad

Figure 3.3 *A laptop computer*

Joystick

A joystick is similar to a tracker ball. Whenever the stick is moved, the cursor moves in a similar direction on the screen. Joysticks are mainly used for games (Figure 3.4), but you can also see them being used with, for example, scanners in hospitals.

15

Figure 3.4

Light pen

A screen cursor can be moved by touching the screen with a light pen. Light pens are mainly used for design work and need special software to make them work.

Touch screen

A touch screen is a special kind of screen which is sensitive to touch. A selection is made from a menu on the screen by touching part of it. These screens are ideal for use in banks and building societies, where customers who are not used to keyboards can obtain information about the services offered. You can also see touch screens in restaurants and bars.

Graphics tablets (digitisers)

Graphics tablets are rather like electronic tracing paper and, like paper, they come in all sizes from a modest A4 size to a very large A0 size which will occupy the best part of a desk. A cursor or puck is used on a graphics tablet to trace over technical drawings put on the screen using a computer aided design package such as AutoCAD.

Magnetic stripe reader

You can see magnetic stripe readers at the side of computerised tills (often called electronic point-of-sale (EPOS) terminals). Figure 3.5 shows one being used to read information contained in the magnetic stripe of a credit card.

Figure 3.5 *A magnetic stripe reader*

Barcode readers

If you think that barcodes are used only in supermarkets, take another look. Barcodes are used in library systems, luggage handling systems at airports and for warehouse stock control. Barcode systems are now at an advanced stage and readers can record barcodes at distances of five metres or more. This has increased the number of applications. In America, researchers have painstakingly glued barcodes to the backs of some bees (Figure 3.6). These barcodes are scanned every time a bee enters or leaves its hive thus providing valuable information about pollination. Imagine the chaos this could cause if a

Figure 3.6 *A bee with a barcode!*

swarm of bees entered a supermarket (see Figure 3.7)!

Figure 3.8 *Recognising some characters is not easy*

Figure 3.7 *Bees on the bill!*

Optical character readers and optical character recognition (OCR)

Optical character recognition is a method of inputting text using a scanner along with special software to turn the scanned image into standard ASCII code. In other words, the text is no longer treated as a picture, since each individual letter is recognised on its own and can therefore be edited using wordprocessing software.

Since OCR software must be able to distinguish between an S and a 5 or a B and an 8, the original text really needs to be typed. As well as recognising the different characters, optical character readers must be able to read different fonts (i.e. different patterns of letters), different type sizes and upper and lower case letters.

OCR software can also be used to scan financial documents such as company accounts directly into spreadsheets, as well as to scan text directly into wordprocessors.

Magnetic ink character reader and optical character recognition (MICR)

Magnetic ink characters are the rather strange looking numbers that you see at the bottom of cheques, as shown in Figure 3.9. The characters are printed using an ink which contains iron and may be magnetised. The magnetic pattern of the numbers is read by a special reader called a magnetic ink character reader.

Figure 3.9 *A cheque showing the magnetic ink characters*

When a cheque is printed, the account number, branch code and cheque number are all printed in magnetic ink. When someone writes a cheque, the receiver takes it to their bank and pays it into their account. The bank then has to type the amount onto the cheque using magnetic ink before the cheque is dealt with.

Magnetic ink character recognition uses expensive equipment and is suitable only for very large scale applications. The expense of the system is an advantage in banking since it is unlikely that people would be able to build the equipment and start to print their own cheques.

Optical mark readers and optical mark recognition (OMR)

Optical mark readers are able to sense marks made on a special form in certain places. Figure 3.10 shows a typical example of such a form used to collect details regarding student enrolments. Notice that just to collect a single letter, 26 marks have to be used.

Uses for optical mark readers include multiple choice answersheet marking, capturing data from questionnaires and enrolment forms, and the checking of football pools coupons.

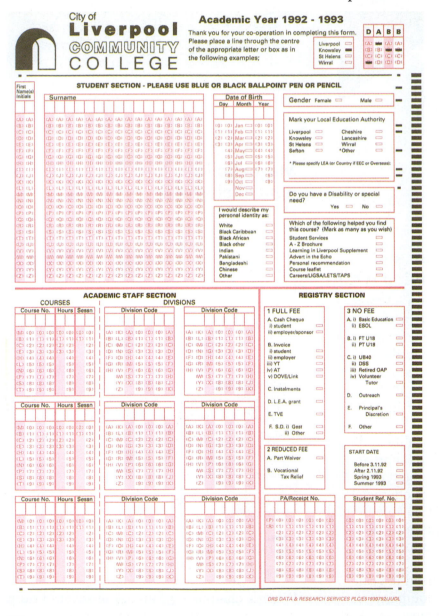

Figure 3.10 *An OMR form used by a college to collect student details for enrolment*

People who have never completed optical mark reading sheets can have problems filling them in. For instance, in a questionnaire to find out people's opinions of television programmes, the following 'variations' were obtained, despite the correct method of shading in the complete box being explained.

Just some of the variations were:

Did you enjoy the programme? YES NO

Did you enjoy the programme? YES NO

Did you enjoy the programme? YES NO

Did you enjoy the programme? YES NO

Disadvantages

1 If the forms are being filled in by the general public then very clear instructions are needed. A couple of examples should be chosen as an illustration. No matter how clear your instructions are you will find that a high proportion of forms are filled in incorrectly. The rejection rate is found to be around 30%.
2 If the forms are creased or folded then they may be rejected or foul the machine. This will add to the time needed to read the forms. Badly damaged forms will need to be rewritten or keyed in manually.

Advantages

1 The use of OMR means that details do not have to be typed in; typing could introduce errors and takes time.
2 OMR reduces the cost of inputting large volumes of data because people do not need to type the details.
3 The method is useful when results of tests are needed very quickly, e.g. with an aptitude test for a job.

Punched card

Punched cards contain holes in different positions which mean something when they are read by a reader. Before screens and keyboards were widely used, punched cards

were the main method of entering data into computers. They are seldom used now but two uses still remain: the Kimball tag mentioned in the next section and the clock card which is used to record the hours a person works so that wages can be calculated.

Kimball tag

Kimball tags are the small cards with holes punched in them that you see attached to clothing in certain shops. When you buy the goods, one of the tags is removed and sent for processing to a computer centre. A card reader there reads the information contained in the holes such as stock number, size, colour, etc. This information is used to keep stock records and to re-order stock. Figure 3.11 shows a Kimball tag.

Figure 3.11 *A Kimball tag*

Voice recognition

With voice recognition you speak directly to the computer. It is particularly useful for handicapped people with limited movement. It is now popular for inputting data into word-processing or database packages. A microphone is the input device for such systems.

Microphone

A microphone is used as the input device for a speech recognition system. The voice pattern of the user is then converted into instructions to the operating system or applications software, or into text on the screen.

A microphone may also be used as an input device to a voice mail system. Voice mail uses the Internet to send, store and receive voice messages. The system works in a similar way to the e-mail system but instead of a text message being stored on disk, the user's voice is stored instead. The company providing the connection to the Internet, called the Internet service provider (ISP) stores the voice message on its server and when the user logs on the system informs them that they have a voice mail message. The user can then play the message back using a loudspeaker as the output device.

Figure 3.12 *Voice recognition*

Electronic point of sale (EPOS) terminal

EPOS terminals are the cash registers which also act as terminals to a main computer system. As well as providing customers with itemised bills, these systems also give useful management information.

Electronic fund transfer at point of sale (EFTPOS)

EFTPOS terminals are similar to EPOS terminals but with some additional features. For instance, they are able to transfer funds from your bank account directly to a store's account using a card called a debit card. A Switch card is an example of such a card. If you have a debit card you can use it instead

of a cheque and it is a faster method of payment. The advantage to a store is that the money is instantly transferred into its account, whereas with cheques and credit cards there is a delay before the money reaches the shop's account.

There are some disadvantages with such cards: they may be stolen or forged and they are said to encourage people to spend more money.

Video digitiser

A video digitiser is a combination of hardware and software that converts an analogue video signal into a digital signal in the computer's memory. Each frame from a video is converted, using the video digitiser and it may be played back in any required sequence. Taking a video frame and digitising it is often called image grabbing or frame grabbing.

Grabbed video images take up a lot of main memory and when stored use a large amount of disk space.

Video digitising is used to convert a frame from a video sequence into a picture, which can be printed in isolation in a magazine or document. Digitising is also used to make television adverts and to produce pop videos.

Scanner

Scanners are used to scan text or pictures into a computer's memory where they can then be manipulated in some way before being printed. They can be cheap hand held ones, or flatbed A4 size or larger.

Optical character recognition (OCR) involves scanning in the image of a page of text with a scanner and then using special software to recognise each of the characters separately, so that they can be altered, if needed, using a wordprocessor. Scanners often have OCR software included in the price.

Scanners are also used to scan in photographs and pictures for use in desktop publishing. One of the main problems you encounter when scanning images is the amount of space they take up on the disk.

However, special file compression software, can be used to reduce file sizes.

Digital cameras

Digital cameras are becoming very popular for a number of reasons:

- No film is needed.
- There are no expensive developing costs.
- You can put photographic images directly into a document without the need for a scanner.
- The pictures, since they are in digital form, can be sent immediately over the Internet.
- You can size (enlarge and reduce) the image as well as crop it (cut out the part of the photograph you want) yourself using software without the need for professional dark room work.

Digital cameras look just like traditional cameras except they have no film as such. Instead they have a memory which stores the image and many of them have special memory cards to give extra storage. The more memory they have, the greater the number of pictures which can be taken before downloading. Storage varies widely between cameras from 40 to 100 pictures.

The amount of memory taken up by a picture depends on its resolution. The resolution is determined by the number of dots which make the picture; the greater the number of dots, the crisper the image. Higher resolution photographs take up more memory so the camera will store fewer of them.

As well as the camera, you also need special software to edit, store and display your pictures on a computer. Using this software you can also remove things which you did not spot when taking the photograph. You could for instance, remove a telegraph pole which looks as though it is sticking out of someone's head, correct red-eye and adjust the colour and contrast. It is even possible to take the outline of a person and put them into an entirely different picture or background.

Touch tone telephones

Modern telephones work by having a different tone for each number key pressed, so for example a number five has a slightly different tone from a number six and it is by using these different tones that the numbers dialled are recognised and routed to the correct telephone. Once connected, a touch tone telephone can be used as a data entry device. For instance, in some home banking systems the customer keys in their identification number using the phone keys. Once connected, the customer can select certain services, such as statement requests, using the same keypad.

Which input device?

Here are some situations where you have to decide which would be the best input device to use. You should give reasons for your choice:

1 Your teacher would like to keep a bank of past GCSE questions on a certain subject such as history. She does not want to have to type them all in but she may want to alter them slightly using her wordprocessor. What do you suggest?

2 A firm runs an aptitude test with multiple choice style answers for all job applicants. The applicants first take the test and if they pass they are given an interview. The whole test (usually around 50 sheets) needs to be marked quickly and accurately whilst the applicants are having a coffee break. Which input device could be used?

3 A video library would like to have a new way of recording the membership number and video number when a video is rented. At present the six digit number of the member and video are typed in and this causes a lot of errors. Which alternative method could they use?

4 A building society is thinking of introducing a new cheque book account. Which input method would be best for the process of cheque clearing?

Data from sensors

Sensors are used to obtain data automatically. For instance, traffic lights have a sensor which records the frequency of the traffic. A microprocessor can then alter the sequencing of the lights to improve the flow of the traffic. Burglar alarms and central heating thermostats both contain sensors. We will be looking at sensors in a later chapter.

Output devices

Output devices provide results in a suitable form after data processing. In many cases this will be in the form of a hard copy (printout) or on a screen. The widespread use of electronic mail means output is now often in the form of an electronic message to another computer.

Visual display units (VDUs) or monitors

VDUs or monitors are almost taken for granted as output devices. They are ideal for showing the results from an enquiry where no printout is needed. For instance, if you go into a travel agency and ask if a particular holiday is available on a certain date all you need to know is yes or no so it is not necessary to print this out. VDUs come in many different sizes and resolutions. The quoted size of the screen actually indicates the length of the diagonal, so a 17 inch screen has a 17 inch diagonal. The resolution is determined by the number of dots of light (pixels) displayed on the screen. If the screen is being used for computer aided design (CAD) work or for desktop publishing, then a large screen with high resolution is required.

Liquid crystal display (LCD) screens

LCD screens are most often seen on portable or laptop computers. They are used in these applications because they are small and light. LCD screens are also used where space is at a premium. You can now see them in banks and building societies where a traditional monitor would take up too much space.

Graphical display units

Graphical display units are usually larger than normal VDUs and have greater resolutions so that the lines on the screen don't look as though they are made up of lots of tiny dots. Graphical display units are often used in conjunction with light pens.

Laser printers

Laser printers offer both high speed and excellent print quality for text and graphics. Laser printers have toner cartridges which contain a fine powdered black plastic called toner.

Figure 3.13 shows a laser printer. As you can see it looks very much like a small photocopier.

Figure 3.13 *A laser printer*

Ink-jet printers

Ink-jet printers are also commonly called bubble-jet printers. The print head of an ink-jet printer consists of nozzles (usually 64). The ink flows through the appropriate nozzle, where it is heated and a bubble forms. This expands and breaks, releasing a very small ink droplet. The dots so formed are much smaller (and there are more of them) than in a dot-matrix printer. This means that ink-jet printers can print high quality text and graphics, almost comparable to that produced by laser printers. They are almost silent in operation.

Ink-jet printers are cheaper to buy than laser printers. However, they are quite expensive to run, because the ink cartridges are expensive and need frequent replacement. If you do not do a large amount of printing, an ink-jet printer could be the best type to buy.

Figure 3.14 *An ink-jet printer*

Another advantage of ink-jets is that they can print satisfactorily in colour. Dot-matrix printers can print in colour but the colour produced is not as uniform as that produced by ink-jets.

Dot-matrix printers

Dot-matrix printers have been almost completely replaced by ink-jet and laser printers. There are some uses however for which dot-matrix printers are ideal.

Dot-matrix printers are impact printers, which can transfer print through layers of paper. This means that they are able to print multi-part stationery. So if you want to print a multi-part sheet where, for example, the white topsheet goes to the customer, the yellow goes to accounts, the blue to the stores, then you will need to use a dot-matrix printer.

Colour printers

Colour printing is useful for improving the appearance of the output from a computer system. Imagine how much more interesting financial reports, posters, brochures, business letters, etc. are when in colour.

Colour ink-jet printers

These are the cheapest colour printers and are generally the ones chosen for home use where they find a variety of uses such as printing birthday cards, invitations, menus and producing colour photographs from digital cameras. In order to produce high quality colour, ink-jet printers need special glossy paper which is quite expensive. When the image quality is not so crucial, then ordinary paper can be used.

Although ink-jets are cheap to buy (typically £150), their running costs are quite high because the ink cartridges are quite expensive.

Colour laser printers

Colour laser printers are much clearer than their ink-jet counterparts but considerably more expensive. Because of their high initial cost (typically at least £1500), their use is restricted to commercial organisations. Although colour laser printers cost more to buy their running costs are less than those of colour ink-jet printers.

Figure 3.15 *A dot-matrix printer*

QUESTIONS

Explain how a colour printer might be useful to:
(a) an estate agent
(b) a curtain design and fitting company
(c) a person who stores all their family photographs on their computer
(d) a pupil at school producing GCSE project work.

Advantages and disadvantages of laser printers

If you look at each type of printer you can see that the laser printer is probably the best overall printer with the ink-jet printer a close second. There are some advantages and disadvantages of laser printers as we will see here.

Figure 3.16 *Toner cartridges are messy to change and can make you look as though you've been to a fingerprinting session at the local police station*

Advantages of laser printers

1 Since they are page printers they are able to print a page at a time so this means they are very fast. The speed of a laser printer is typically about 10 ppm (pages per minute).
2 They produce high quality text and graphics. Typically laser printers print at 600 or 1200 dpi (dots per inch). This improves the quality (called the resolution) of the image compared with other types of printer.
3 They are quiet in operation compared with dot-matrix printers, which are very noisy. The only sound laser printers make is the sound of the cooling fans and the paper moving.

4 Laser printers are equipped with paper trays for both the input and the output paper and this means that once the printer has been set up it does not need supervision.

Disadvantages of laser printers

1 Laser printers are more expensive than dot-matrix or ink-jet printers.
2 They are quite large and can take up a lot of desk space.
3 They are quite complex, so the repair bills can be high.
4 Because they are non-impact printers, multi-part stationery cannot be used. With a dot-matrix printer, the impact can make marks on several sheets of paper at the same time. These thin sheets can then be sent to different departments within a company.
5 Laser printers are page printers, so they cannot be used with continuous stationery.

Graph plotters

Graph plotters enable accurate line diagrams to be produced on paper. They are ideal for plans, maps, line diagrams and three-dimensional drawings. Graph plotters use pens to produce images and different pens may be used containing different coloured inks. There are two types of graph plotter. The flat bed plotter is shown in Figure 3.17 and the drum plotter in Figure 3.18. The drum plotter

Figure 3.17 *A flat bed plotter*

has the advantage that very large drawings can be produced.

Figure 3.18 *A drum plotter*

Voice output

Visually handicapped people find the spoken word from a computer invaluable. For instance, when special software is used with a wordprocessor they can hear each letter on headphones as it is typed and if they go to the start of a word then this is also indicated.

Electrical signals

Sometimes the output from one computer system can simply be a series of electrical signals. This is the case if one computer is being used as a terminal and the work that is done sent as electrical signals to a main computer, remote from the terminals.

Electrical signals can be output and used to control all kinds of devices, such as central heating systems or burglar alarms.

Robots

Electrical signals from a computer can be used to control a robot arm like the one shown in Figure 3.19. Robots are dealt with in Chapter 20.

Figure 3.19 *Electrical signals can be used to control a robot arm*

Actuators

An actuator is a device which responds when signalled to do so by the computer. An example of an actuator is an electric motor.

TEST YOURSELF

Using the words in the list below, copy out and complete sentences A to L, underlining the words you have inserted. The words may be used once, more than once or not at all.

mouse   optical mark recognition   keyboard

laser   optical character reader   Kimball tags

joysticks   light pens   barcode readers   ink-jet

magnetic ink character recognition   retail

A The commonest input device, which comes with all computers is the _____.

B A _____ is used to move the pointer around the screen and to make selections.

C _____ are used primarily with games.

D _____ _____ are used with computer aided design packages to produce technical drawings on the screen.

E _____ _____ are used in supermarkets for recording the details of goods as they are passed over the laser scanner.

F Text may be read directly into a computer using a device called an _____ _____ _____.

G The method used by banks when inputting the details contained on cheques during the clearing process is called _____ _____ _____ _____.

H Optical mark readers are able to read the marks made on special forms. The process is called _____ _____ _____.

I The punched card is an old fashioned input device which can still be found in the form of _____ _____.

J EPOS and EFTPOS are systems that are used extensively in _____ outlets.

K The type of printer that produces the highest quality print and uses a toner cartridge is called a _____ printer.

L A cheaper printer, which squirts a jet of ink at the paper is called an _____ _____ printer.

Things to do

1 A bathroom design company uses a computer to help plan new bathrooms. The company sends a salesperson out who measures up the bathroom and makes certain suggestions regarding the arrangement of the toilet, bath, basin, shower, etc. When the client is happy with the arrangement, the salesperson returns to the shop where the bathroom design is transferred to the screen. The client is then sent a three-dimensional diagram of what their bathroom will look like.
(a) Name a device, other than a keyboard, that the designer could use as an input device and say why it is suitable.
(b) A very accurate and high quality printout is needed for the installers to work from. Name an output device that could produce a high quality plan.
(c) What other tasks could the computer perform other than those already mentioned?

2 The following diagrams show a variety of input or output devices.
For each one:
(a) name it
(b) say how it is used
(c) give an application for it (e.g. you need to mention the type of job each is suited to).

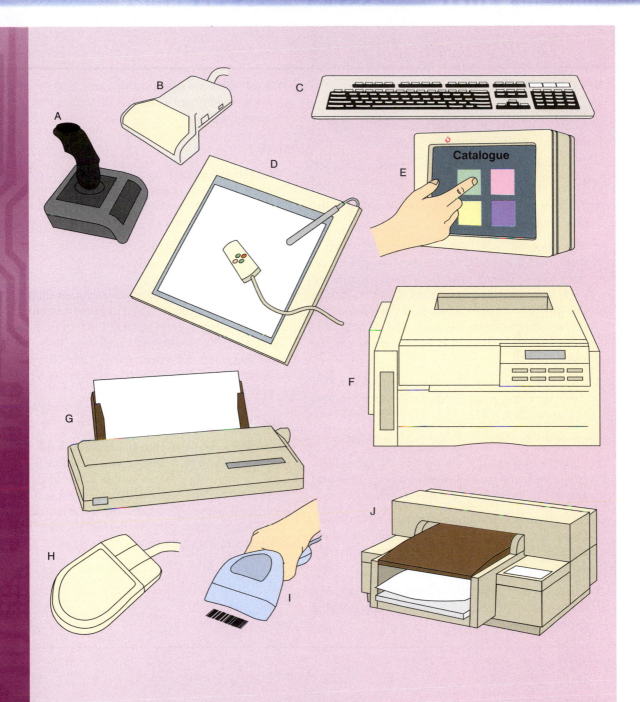

3 A great many printers are now available, ranging from small slow devices to versatile fast printers. Describe various types of printer that are now in use, giving an indication of their comparative speeds and paying particular attention to:

(a) the different facilities that they provide

(b) typical applications for which they are appropriate.

(It is best to get your information for this question from recent copies of any computer magazine).

4 A friend has asked you for your advice on buying a suitable printer. Write down a list of questions that you would need to ask them, before advising them.

INVESTIGATIONS

BETTERBUYS

Betterbuys is a small chain of food supermarkets. At present there are 20 shops scattered throughout Britain.

The present manual system at the checkout is as follows:

1 The customer brings their basket or trolley to the checkout.

2 The price of each item is on a ticket which is stuck onto the goods when they are placed on the shelves. The till operator keys in the price of each item, presses a key to tell the till to display the total when ready and keys in the amount of money the customer has paid. The till automatically calculates how much change should be given.

3 The stock is checked each day by a person with a stock list going around the shelves and counting the stock of each item.

Some of the problems with the existing system are:

1 Sometimes goods are brought to the till with no label on them. Looking them up takes time and angers the shoppers in the queue behind.

2 All the main competitors are now using EPOS systems, where an itemised bill is produced, which gives all the names of the goods, along with their prices.

3 Changing prices for special offers is difficult, since it is necessary to stick new price stickers over the existing labels.

4 Customers are often complaining that the supermarkets frequently run out of certain items such as bread.

Task 1

Visit a large supermarket (e.g. Tesco, Sainsbury, Asda, Safeway, etc.) which uses EPOS terminals. Produce a wordprocessed report outlining the way in which EPOS terminals are used in the supermarket you have visited.

Task 2

Mr C Watts, the recently appointed managing director of Betterbuys, wants to know what the main advantages are in using EPOS terminals compared with the existing manual system. In a wordprocessed document, explain what these advantages are. Are there any disadvantages to the supermarket or to the customers?

Task 3

It is eventually decided to go ahead with the EPOS system and you have been asked to produce a leaflet explaining how the system works and how it will be better for shoppers. This leaflet should be produced using wordprocessing or (better) desktop publishing software. This leaflet will be given to shoppers to help explain the new system.

Storing Data

Computers store data either in chips inside the main processor, in what is called memory (main store), or on other media such as magnetic disk, in what is called backing store.

The storage of data

The number of instructions and amount of data a computer can store in its memory is measured in **bytes**. One byte contains 8 bits (short for binary digits, 0 and 1). Computers work by using pulses of voltage which represent either 0 or 1. A low voltage pulse represents a 0 and a high voltage pulse a 1. In most cases, 8 bits are needed to store one character. So, a single character (letter, number or symbol on the keyboard) can be stored in one byte. We normally refer to storage capacities in terms of kilobytes (KB) or megabytes (MB).

    1 KB = 1 kilobyte = 1024 bytes
    1 MB = 1 048 576 bytes
    1 GB = 1 gigabyte = 1000 MB

From this you can see that for each megabyte we could store 1 048 576 characters.

Memory (main store)

There are two types of memory or main store:

- read-only memory (ROM)
- random-access memory (RAM).

Memory (or main store) is the name given to the group of chips inside the processing unit where data is held temporarily whilst processing takes place. The data held in the memory is instantly available to the computer, unlike backing storage which has to be accessed on disk or tape. The memory needed to run programs has increased enormously over the last few years as they have employed more icons and other graphics. Even laser

printers now have more memory than computers did only a few years ago (Figure 4.1).

Figure 4.1 *Most computers have expansion slots for extra memory chips*

Memory is used to hold the following:

1. programs – these may be the operating system (programs which control the hardware) or applications programs (programs to do a particular task such as wordprocessing)
2. input data – this is put into the memory before processing
3. working area – this is used to store the data that is currently being processed
4. output data – this is put into the part of the store ready to be output to the printer.

Read-only memory (ROM)

ROM is held on a chip inside the processor and is used to hold data which cannot be changed by the user. Programs are stored on ROM chips when a computer is manufactured. Usually, the data held on ROM will be the software that tells the computer how to load the operating system (called the boot program). Since data is permanently stored on ROM it will still stay stored even if the power is switched off. ROM is often referred to as non-volatile memory.

EPROM

EPROM stands for erasable programmable read-only memory. This is a memory chip whose contents are normally fixed. However, the chip may have its contents erased by the action of ultra-violet light and may then be reprogrammed.

Random access memory (RAM)

RAM is again held on a chip but data in RAM is held only temporarily, which means that the data disappears when the power is switched off. For this reason, RAM is often called volatile memory. RAM is used to hold both data and programs during processing.

Both RAM and ROM are often referred to as immediate access store (IAS).

Magnetic media

Magnetic media storage devices include floppy disks and hard disks.

Floppy disks

Most computers come with a 3.5 inch disk drive. The 3.5 inch disks are used to transfer small amounts of data between computers. Although the floppy disk is in a hard case the disk inside is floppy.

Magnetic disks store binary (a series of 0s and 1s) data as a magnetic pattern on the disk surface. The anatomy of a 3.5 inch disk is shown in Figure 4.2. Disks must be looked after and some things to avoid are illustrated in Figure 4.3.

Figure 4.2 *The anatomy of a 3.5 inch floppy disk*

Figure 4.3 *How not to treat your floppy disks!*

A typical 3.5 inch floppy disk holds 1.44 MB of data. Before data is stored on a disk, the disk needs to be formatted. This creates a magnetic map of the disk surface to enable the data to be either read from the disk or written onto the disk, quickly.

Hard drives

Hard drives usually consist of several disks on a single spindle. Each disk surface is able to store data and this has the advantage that each surface can have its own read/write head as shown in Figure 4.4. This enables the read/write heads to operate simultaneously, which means that the data can be transferred more quickly than by using a single larger disk. Hard disks are available in all sorts of sizes and bigger sizes are becoming available all the time. A typical personal computer will have a hard disk capacity of around 10 GB (10 000 MB).

Figure 4.4 *The inside of a hard disk drive showing the arrangement of disks and read/write heads*

Magnetic tape

Large spools of tape are used by very large computer systems that need to hold huge amounts of data. They are not as common as they used to be. Tapes in cartridges as shown in Figure 4.5 are now becoming much more common. These look similar to audio cassettes, except they are larger. Their main use is for making backup (security) copies of hard disks. Backing up a hard disk is not feasible with floppy disks because of the number of disks needed and the time it would take. A 3.5 inch floppy disk can hold 1.44 MB of data

while a large hard disk holds in excess of 10 000 MB. A simple calculation (10 000/1.44) shows that to back up such a hard disk when it is full of data would need nearly 7000 floppy disks and a correspondingly large amount of time.

Optical disks

CD-ROM drives

CD-ROM drives use the same technology as music CDs and CD players. The data is stored on the disk digitally and a laser beam is used to read the data off the disk. Because light is used to read the disk, the data may be packed closely and the disk therefore has a huge capacity. CD-ROM drives are included in multimedia systems. Because of their huge storage capacities they are very useful for distributing software on a single disk where normally many floppy disks would be needed. CD-ROMs can be filled with clip art (pictures you can use in your documents), encyclopaedias, photographs and all sorts of reference material.

CD-ROMs are read-only disks, which means that you can read the data off the disk but not alter it or store new data. Figure 4.5 shows the backing storage media, including a CD-ROM drive, used in a typical multimedia system. A typical CD holds around 600 MB of data.

Figure 4.5 *Backup storage devices for a multimedia system*

CD-R

A CD recordable (CD-R) drive has a read/write capability. Using this device you can write around 650 MB of data in around 15 minutes. CD-R can be used to back up hard drives.

Standard CD-R disks can be written to only once, but there is a type of disk called CD-RW. With suitable drives, these disks can be written, erased and rewritten. They are more expensive than CD-R disks.

Digital versatile disks (DVDs)

DVDs are similar to CD-ROMs in that they look identical and are used to store lots of data. Like CD-ROMs, they can be used to store computer application software, multimedia programs (encyclopaedias) and full length movies. Any application software that needs six to seven CD-ROMs for installation could be replaced by a single DVD. This is because CD-ROMs typically store 650 MB of data whereas a DVD stores up to 4.7 GB (4700 MB).

The latest generation of DVDs allows users to write data to the disk so they may be used in much the same way as a normal hard disk. DVD drives (the hardware you need to read the DVD disks) look the same as CD-ROM drives. Eventually all computers will come with a DVD drive.

DVDs also are used to store movies where they produce much better quality pictures and sound compared to a normal video tape. A film stored on DVD can even be made to offer the viewer a choice of several languages in which it can be played back.

Backup devices

It is important to take regular backups of both data and programs for security purposes. Floppy disks do not have a very high storage capacity and so are seldom used for backup. Instead higher capacity and faster storage devices are used and the main ones are as follows.

Tape streamers

Tape streamers are devices used to back up the data contained on hard drives.

Zip drives

Zip drives are useful for backing up hard drives. They use high storage capacity floppy disks which are slightly larger and twice as thick as normal floppies. They can typically store 100 MB compared with the 1.44 MB of the normal floppy. Both the drives and the removable disks are inexpensive and are used for backing up the data on hard disks and also to transfer large files between machines.

Figure 4.6 *Examples of backup devices (a Zip drive and a Jaz drive)*

Jaz drives

A Jaz drive is a removable disk drive which is very fast at transferring data. Each disk can hold up to 2 GB (2000 MB) of data. The high data transfer rate means that they can be used to back up data in a very short time. They can also be used for everyday storage, just like an ordinary disk drive.

TEST YOURSELF

Using the words in the list below, copy out and complete sentences A to I, underlining the words you have inserted. The words may be used more than once.

character   one   byte   kilobytes   memory

megabytes   floppy   CD-ROMs   magnetic tape

RAM   ROM   hard

A A bit is the smallest unit of storage and may be nought or _____.

B A group of 8 bits is called a _____.

C One byte is used to store one _____.

D Storage is usually measured in _____ or the larger unit _____.

E Data and program instructions currently being dealt with are held in _____.

F There are two types of storage: one retains data when the power is removed and is called _____; the other loses data when the power is turned off and is called _____.

G The commonest backing storage media are _____ disks and hard disks.

H Optical disks, called _____ are used in multi-media systems and can store around 600 megabytes of data.

I Because _____ disks store so much information, taking back-up copies using floppy disks takes too long and uses too many disks, so data is best transferred to _____ _____.

Things to do

1 The words RAM and ROM are often used when computer memory is discussed.
   (a) What do the following abbreviations stand for?
       (i) RAM
       (ii) ROM.
   (b) What are the main differences between RAM and ROM?
   (c) Backing storage is storage outside the central processing unit. Why is backing storage needed?

2 A general practitioner's surgery contains a personal computer on which all the patients' records are stored. What type of backing storage would it be most likely to have?

3 Data may be stored by a computer either in memory (internal storage) or backing store (external storage). For each of the following, say whether they are used for internal or external storage.

RAM   hard disk   3.5 inch floppy disk   ROM   CD-ROM   magnetic tape   DVD.

Software

What is software?

Software is the general name given to all the programs that can be run on computer hardware. There are two main categories of software: operating systems (systems software) and applications software.

Operating systems (systems software)

An operating system is a program that controls the hardware directly. Operating systems perform the following tasks:

- They provide a way for applications software to communicate with the hardware. For example, in your wordprocessing package (an application), if you click on the printer icon, the operating system gives an instruction to the printer to start printing.
- They manage the system resources such as memory and also allocate CPU time to the task being run.
- They manage the transfer of data to and from the various peripherals (keyboards, mice, scanners, printers, etc.)
- They manage system security. Many operating systems allocate certain rights to users. A user can only do certain things on entering a password.

Examples of operating systems include Windows 98, Windows NT, UNIX and OS/2.

The operating system provides an interface between the user and the computer hardware. Figure 5.1 helps to explain this. Without an operating system, a computer would be useless, so the first thing a computer looks for when it is switched on is the operating system. Once the operating system has been found, the computer loads it from disk.

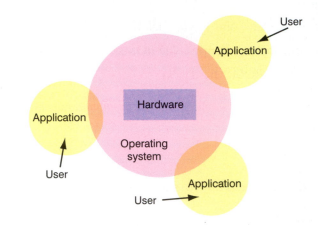

Figure 5.1 *The operating system acts as a 'shell' around the hardware. For programs to work, they need an operating system. For users to get useful work out of the computer they have to use applications programs and the operating system to communicate with the hardware*

Multitasking

Multitasking means the ability of a computer to run two or more programs at the same time. As a user it may be hard to see how you can do two things at once. One way would be to print out a large document (say 20 pages) whilst continuing to use the wordprocessor to type in a new letter. The operating system takes care of the printing and the wordprocessing at the same time.

Other examples could include sending a fax or transferring a large file over the Internet whilst working on another task.

Multiuser

Multiuser software allows several users to access the same data at the same time. A multiuser operating system needs to be used with most networks.

User interfaces

The user interface is what you see when you turn on the computer; it consists of the cursors, prompts, icons, menus, etc. which allow you to get something done using your computer. Ideally the user interface should be as easy to use as possible, so it is obvious to someone who has never used the software before, what they have to do.

User interfaces may be:

1 command-driven
2 menu-driven
3 graphical (referred to as a graphical user interface or GUI).

Command-driven interface

With a command-driven interface, you type in an instruction, which is usually abbreviated, in order to get something done. Command-driven user interfaces are not easy to use. If you are new to the software you have to remember many commands in order to be able to use the software quickly. Commands for different software packages are rarely the same, so people often get the commands mixed up. Some people, mainly those who are used to using them, prefer command-driven menus because they can be faster to use once you have learnt all the commands.

Menu-driven interface

This type of user interface produces a list of commands or options available within a pro-

gram and the user can make a selection by using either a mouse or a keyboard. Both Microsoft Windows and Apple Macintosh programs are menu driven.

Graphical user interface

A graphical user interface (GUI) provides a way for the user to communicate with the computer through pictures (icons) and through pull-down menus. Windows is an example of a GUI. Windows provides a common way of using programs, which makes them easier to learn. It also takes care of some common chores such as working with the printer and the disk drive.

Apple Macintosh computers were amongst the first to use a GUI (Figure 5.2).

Figure 5.2 *Wordprocessing on a Macintosh computer*

Figure 5.3

WIMP

WIMP stands for windows, icons, menus and pointing devices. The term describes the features of a graphical user interface (GUI) which make it easier for the user to get things done.

Designing a user interface

To make an interface as user friendly as possible it is necessary to take care when designing it and take into account the following.

- **Consistency** – each part of the software should behave in the same way as another, making the program easier to learn and use.
- **Positioning of items on the screen** – icons, menus, etc. should be consistent, again making software easier to learn and use.
- **Use of colour** – some colours are easier for the eye while others make things harder to see; colours should be chosen carefully.
- **Use of sound** – sound can be annoying to some people so it is best to make sound an option which a user can turn off if desired.
- **Availability of help** – most software has on-line help which means that it is often not necessary to refer to a manual; the user simply accesses the help screen for a particular function or topic.

Utility programs

Utility programs are often provided as part of the operating system, although they may be bought separately. A utility program is a program that performs a task which is often needed (e.g. a sort routine or providing a list of files).

Tasks carried out by utility programs include:

- renaming files
- listing files on a disk
- deleting files
- copying files
- sending files to a printer
- sorting data
- repairing damaged files
- backing up files.

Other utility programs can be bought to supplement those supplied by the operating system. One of these utilities is shown in Figure 5.4.

Figure 5.4 *One of the most widely used and essential utility programs is a virus checker*

Translation programs

Translation programs are also part of the systems software and we will look at these in more detail later.

Applications software

Applications software is used to perform specific tasks. Some applications software needs to be used within a particular operating system. Three broad types of applications software are described below.

Applications packages

There are many different types of applications software, ranging from the wordprocessing packages used widely to write letters and reports, to specialist packages that are only used within one industry. Examples of applications packages are:

- wordprocessing software, such as Word and WordPerfect
- spreadsheet software, such as Lotus 1-2-3 and Excel
- database software, such as Access.

Integrated software

Integrated software consists of a collection of application packages which share a common set of commands. Putting it simply, an integrated package may be a wordprocessor, spreadsheet, database and graphics package, all in one. One advantage of having such a package is that the commands are common throughout so it is easier to get used to than several different packages. Also, moving data from one program to another is easier. For instance, if you wanted to print out details of amounts outstanding from your database you could transfer the data to your wordprocessor. This would be easier to do with the integrated package than with the two separate programs.

Integrated packages tend to be much cheaper than separate packages and this is a major reason for their popularity.

There are some disadvantages. Integrated packages tend to be strong in one area and weak in others. For instance, a package may have a good database but a poor wordprocessor. If you want the best wordprocessor, database, etc. and are prepared to pay a higher price, then it is best to buy the separate packages.

Tailor-made software

An organisation may write its own software or employ an outside company to write it. This tailor-made software can be very expensive and is used only by companies with large computer departments, or where applications packages are not available.

General purpose packages

Much applications software is not specific to a particular type of business. For instance, a wordprocessing package can be used by any business. Some database packages such as Microsoft Access can be used to develop tailor-made software. General purpose packages are very popular because their documentation (manuals, tutorials, etc.) tends to be very good, the programs are well tested and they are relatively cheap. Sometimes general purpose software is called 'content free software'.

Programming languages

A program is a set of instructions that the computer can understand. Since the computer can understand only binary code (a series of 1s and 0s), all computer languages must be eventually reduced to binary code and the way this is done depends on the type of language used. Humans can use different languages to communicate and computers are no different. There is a variety of computer languages and the one that is chosen for a particular job depends on the job that is being done.

Low-level languages

Low-level languages are languages that are easy for the computer to understand but more difficult for the programmer to understand. Assembly language and machine code are collectively called low-level languages.

Machine language (or machine code)

Machine language is the language directly understood by the machine. In other words, it consists of a series of 1s and 0s. All other languages must be translated into machine code before the instructions can be carried out unless the program is already written in machine code. Machine code is often machine specific, which means that one computer's machine code will not be understood by a different type of computer. A program written in machine code needs no translation and is therefore very fast. A lot of games or simulation programs are written in machine code for this reason.

Assembly language

An assembly language is a language that uses simple instructions such as ADD, SUB and LDA and is used in preference to machine code, since it is easier for the programmer to use and to debug (debugging means removing any mistakes from the program). Once a program has been written in assembly language it needs translating into machine code by software called an assembler before it can be understood by a computer.

Figure 5.5

High-level language

A high-level language is developed with the programmer in mind rather than the computer. Such languages have the advantage that they are not as machine-dependent as machine codes or assembly language, so once a program has been written it can be used on different computers with very little alteration.

High-level language instructions are similar to English, which means that programming is made easier. Instructions in BASIC, a high-level language, include such commands as PRINT, GOTO and READ which are easy for us to understand and remember.

Advantages of high-level languages

1 Simple instructions similar to English make high-level languages easy to understand.
2 It is easy to correct errors and test programs.

3 Programs written in high-level languages can be used on different makes of computer.

Some high-level languages have been developed with a particular problem in mind. Here are some along with their main uses.

- **COBOL** is used mainly for business data processing because of its excellent file handling.
- **BASIC** is mainly used as a teaching language.
- **FORTRAN** is used mainly in scientific applications.
- **C++** is an increasingly popular language. It is very good for graphics and good for developing commercial software.
- **LOGO** is used primarily for teaching children about programming and using computers. Children are taught to write a series of instructions to control the movement of a 'turtle', which draws a line behind it on the screen.
- **JAVA** A language especially suited for writing software used to search for things on the Internet.
- **HTML** Hypertext Markup language. A language used for the development of websites.

Translation programs

Translation programs are part of the systems software and are used to convert the program commands into machine code. There are three types of translation programs: compilers, interpreters and assemblers.

Compilers and interpreters

Compilers and interpreters are both programs that change high-level language instructions into machine code, although the way they do this is different.

An **interpreter** takes each instruction in turn, converts it to machine code and then carries it out. It is rather like a person who cannot read French taking a word in a document, looking it up in a dictionary, translating it and then moving on to the next word. If the document needs to be read at a later date then the same process will need to be performed.

A **compiler** is software that converts the whole of a program written in a high-level language into machine code in one go. Provided that there are no mistakes in the program, the complete program is converted to machine code. Suppose an original disk contains a program written in a high-level language (called the source code), then after compilation another disk with the program written in machine code will be produced (called the object code). Whenever the program needs to be run the disk with the program converted to machine code is used. This is like a person translating the whole of the document from French to English in one go and then using the English version if the document needs to be read again. If a program needs to be altered at a later date, the original source code is altered and the program recompiled.

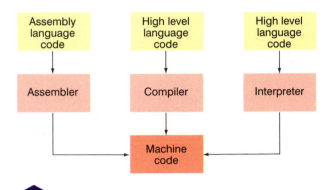

Figure 5.6 *The relationship between assemblers, compilers and interpreters*

Assemblers

Assemblers translate assembly language instructions into machine code. This translation is easy because one instruction in assembly language usually corresponds to one machine code instruction.

TEST YOURSELF

Using the words in the list below, copy out and complete sentences A to G, underlining the words you have inserted. The words may be used more than once.

hardware   software   systems   operating

compilers   utility   assembler

A Programs that may be run on a computer are called _____.

B Software may be classed into two groups: _____ software and applications software.

C Another name for the systems software is the _____ system.

D Without systems software the _____ would be useless.

E A program that performs such tasks as deleting or copying files is called a _____ program.

F Translation programs which convert high-level language instructions into machine code are of two types: interpreters or _____.

G A translation program used to convert a low-level language instruction into machine code is called an _____.

1 Systems software can be divided into three types: the operating system, utility programs and translation programs.

    (a) (i) Give the name of the system software that your computer uses.

       (ii) Give two jobs performed by the operating system.

    (b) Give two examples of a utility program and explain what each does.

    (c) Two types of translation program are used for translating high-level languages into machine code. Explain the differences in the way that compilers and interpreters translate instructions.

    (d) There is another type of program used to translate assembly language into machine code. Give the name of it.

    (e) There are many high-level languages to choose from. Name two of them and for each give the type of job for which they are particularly suited.

2 The following is a list of types of general purpose package:

    wordprocessing   spreadsheet
    database   graphics
    desktop publishing.

Find out, using computer magazines to help you, which of the above categories each of the following packages falls into:

    Microsoft Word   Microsoft Access
    Lotus 1-2-3   Excel
    CorelDraw   Lotus Approach
    Microsoft Publisher   PageMaker
    Microsoft Powerpoint

3 LOGO is a computer program which may be used to control an arrow on the screen. When the arrow moves forward, it leaves a line on the screen. To control the movement of the arrow, commands are typed in. Some of the commands that may be used are as follows:

    FORWARD distance   (in mm)
    RIGHT angle   (in degrees)
    LEFT angle   (in degrees)

For instance, the command FORWARD 20 would move the arrow forward 20 mm and the command RIGHT 30 would turn the arrow through an angle of 30° with the angle measured from the line drawn straight ahead from the arrow. Write down the instructions needed to draw the following shape.

4 You have been made treasurer of your local athletics club. As the treasurer, you have to perform a variety of tasks and the members of the club have decided to buy a computer to help you. You have decided that it will be necessary to purchase the following software: word-processor, spreadsheet, database and graphics package.

(a) Explain what is meant by
   (i) an applications package
   (ii) an integrated package.

(b) Someone at the club has suggested that an integrated package is bought 'because it will be cheaper'. Look through recent computer magazines at the adverts for software and say whether you think they are right.

(c) Another member has suggested that 'we go along to night-school to learn how to write our own programs and therefore save money'. Is this a sensible suggestion? Give your comments.

Collecting Your Data

The problems with college enrolments

Every year new students enrol on courses in colleges and each college needs to record the student details onto its computer system. Because the enrolments all happen at the same time, the main problem is with the time and the number of staff needed to enter the student details. Let's look at what details need to be recorded.

QUESTIONS

Write down a list of the details that a college would need to keep about each of its students. Show your list to a friend to see if you missed any items. It is a good idea to think about who is likely to use the details. Not everyone gets their fees paid for them. For example, some part-time students may have full-time jobs so they have to pay their own fees or their employers pay for them. So you need to distinguish between full- and part-time students.

Form design

In the student enrolment problem discussed above, students would have been asked to fill in a form. The students completed details that only they would know, such as name, date of birth, address, etc. and the college added details such as course codes, fees, etc. The design of forms is very important, as most of the information from forms will be placed on a computer system.

We all have to fill in forms sooner or later. Some forms, if they have been carefully thought out and designed, are very good but others are appalling. Important information is left out while irrelevant information is included. Often, not enough space is left for the important information. How do we

design a good form? To do this, we should bear in mind the following points.

Have people been consulted who will be using the form?

Some users of the form should be asked what the form should contain. Design of an important form is best not left to one person, who may forget to include something.

Headings

The title of the form should describe its use. Too much information on a form will clutter its appearance.

Instructions

Instructions should be in a prominent position and should be clear. If they are not clear, many forms will be returned with items missing or filled in incorrectly. For special types of form, such as those used by optical mark readers like that shown in Figure 6.1, you have to remember that people may not have seen such a form before. It is therefore a good idea to include an example of the way to fill in the form on the form itself.

Layout

The layout should be simple and follow a logical sequence. The items should be spaced out and the form made an appropriate size.

Sections

Many forms have a part which is filled in by the subject and another part which is filled in by the person who distributed the form. Sometimes the latter part says 'for official use only'. If you design such a form, make sure that you place all the parts to be filled in by the subject together and make sure that it is clear which parts have to be completed.

Testing

It is always a good idea after you have designed a form to ask people to fill it in and then to ask them whether they found it easy

Figure 6.1 *Enrolment form to be filled in by a student writing and shading in boxes*

to understand. Doing this will also give you an idea about whether you have left enough space for users to write in.

QUESTIONS

At the time of enrolment students are required to fill in an application form. Some of the form will be preprinted; part of it will be filled in by the student and another part will be filled in by the tutor when the correct courses have been decided on. Using your answer to the question earlier in this chapter, design a form that could be used to hold details about the student and the courses they are following.

Coding data

In many instances codes are used to represent information, and these are useful provided we know how to interpret them. Why do we use codes? Well there are several reasons and these include the following.

1 Codes are quicker to type in, both initially and for subsequent searches.
2 Using codes reduces the sizes of the files, which in turn increases the speed of searches and any processes performed on the data.
3 Codes are often unique. For instance, if we gave each student a unique code number

we could use this to search for a student's details. Using a surname for a search might reveal several students with the same name.

Designing codes

There are certain points to remember when designing a coding system. These are:

1 Codes should always be the same length. This is a useful check (called a validation check). If the code is too long or too short, then we know a mistake has been made.
2 Codes must be easy to use. People will not use them if they are too cumbersome.
3 Codes must not be too short. Although they are easier to type in if they are short, there is the possibility of running out of codes.

Codes may be used in a student enrolment system for the course details. When the code is either typed in or scanned using a barcode reader, the computer obtains the full details of the course, such as name of course, hours of attendance, fee payable, directly from the course file stored on disk by the computer.

Figure 6.2 Self-adhesive label containing course

Putting the details into the computer

Getting the information into a structure in which it can be processed by the computer is called **data capture**.

There are various methods that can be used and we will look at each one with its advantages and disadvantages.

QUESTIONS

1 The self-adhesive label shown in Figure 6.2 contains a course code.
   (a) Why has a barcode been used?
   (b) If the information has been stored in a barcode why is it then written underneath?
   (c) Someone has suggested that all the information contained on the student enrolment form could be put on a series of barcodes. What problems are there in doing this?

2 Your head teacher has asked you to come up with a coding system for options taken in year 8. You will need first to investigate the options. The head teacher would like some sort of coding system where the code refers to option, year, etc. Make sure that you fully explain how your coding system was developed. You should also mention any other systems that you developed along the way and the reasons for arriving at your final choice.

3 Design a form to be read by an optical mark reader, that you could give to the members of your class to record their names, addresses and dates of birth.

Key to disk

The student enrolment form can be used as the source document and the details that it contains typed into the computer. The main problem with this is that it takes some time. Typing can also introduce many errors. This method may be used if the number of students is small, but if a college has about, say, 8000 students, then this could take too long.

Alternative methods of data capture

The use of keyboard entry has been dismissed because of the time it takes. If more staff were to be employed then they would not be fully occupied for the rest of the year, so this method has been discounted. It would be ideal to have some way of the computer automatically reading data from the forms. Several direct input methods can be considered and these are detailed below.

QUESTIONS

You have been appointed to be in charge of student enrolments in a college with 5000 full-time and 6000 part-time students (11 000 altogether). All the students need to be enrolled in the first two weeks of term so that the college receives funding and the tutors can be given class lists.

(a) Using the enrolment form you have already designed, work out how many characters (letters, numbers, punctuation marks and spaces) there would be in the details supplied by the student and the tutor for an average student. Remember that you do not need to include the information that is preprinted on the form.

(b) Using the total obtained from part (a) and using the fact that a keyboard operator could input data at a rate of 50 characters per minute, find the total number of hours it would take for a single operator to key in all 11 000 student details using a keyboard.

(c) From your answer to part (b) report back to the college principal outlining the problems of using keyboard input for this number of students.

Magnetic ink character

Figure 6.3 *A bank cheque*

Magnetic ink character recognition (MICR)

With MICR the reader detects characters written in magnetic ink. The problem here is that these characters are usually preprinted (as on a cheque) and only a small amount of data is typed onto the form before processing. Because of the volume of data that needs to be input, this method would be no quicker than typing the data normally. In addition, the equipment needed is very expensive so it is used only by banks for clearing cheques (Figure 6.3).

Optical mark reading (OMR)

With OMR the student would make marks on a form similar to that shown in Figure 6.1. A machine called an optical mark reader is then able to read the marks and convert them into characters in the student file. The instructions on such a form have to be made extremely clear, since many students will not have seen one before, although some may have come across this system with multiple choice answer sheets. One of the main problems with optical mark forms is that they have a high rejection rate (see Chapter 3). Optical mark readers are not too expensive to buy and the reading speeds are quite high although the forms are difficult to design. Nevertheless, the use of OMR is a distinct possibility for our enrolment system.

Barcode readers

Barcodes are really suitable only for preprinted information. You could not have a barcode for a student's details since you would not know these in advance. Although barcodes can be printed by laser or ink-jet printers using special software (Figure 6.4), data would still have to be typed into a computer, so this would offer no advantage over keying to disk. However, barcode readers are cheap and accurate. We could use them to solve part of the problem. Each course could have its own barcode so that when a student enrols, barcodes for each of their courses are added to the form. With this method, student details such as name, address, date of birth, etc. would still have to be keyed in, but for a student doing say six GCSEs, just six barcodes could be used instead of all the course information being typed in for each course.

First the bars must be related to the data that needs to be captured for each of the courses. Either an ink-jet printer or a laser printer can then be used to print the barcodes. When the barcodes for each course are read with a scanner, time can be saved keying information.

Optical character recognition (OCR)

With OCR, the computer scans a page containing text, looks at each character in turn and compares it with characters it has previously stored. Although the reading speed is high, this method suffers from high rates of rejection and is really suitable only for reading material that has already been typed. For student enrolment the rejection rate would be high, so this method may be rejected.

Taking orders quickly

You can use a special package which, when you type a postcode and house number, provides all the address details automatically togther with the customer's full name. The system makes use of all 26 million Royal Mail postal addresses and the 44 million names on the Electoral Role (a file of everyone eligible to vote in local and general elections).

The system has advantages:

- It saves around 80% of the keystrokes that would normally be needed.
- There are no problems with the operator having to understand a strange accent.
- It saves time with difficult spellings.
- Spellings are always accurate.

Talking to your computer – speech recognition

Many people are unable to type at high speed and this slows them down when entering data. Rather than type data in using the keyboard we can now use speech recognition to dictate data into the computer. A speech recognition system usually consists of a multimedia computer with a microphone headset and special speech recognition software. When you talk into the microphone your words are turned into commands or text on the screen. Before the system can be used

First the bars must be linked to the data you want to capture

The barcode can then be printed out, using either an ink jet printer (as here) or using a laser printer

The barcode may then be read with a scanner

Figure 6.4 *Designing, printing and reading a barcode*

Figure 6.5

can cost insurance companies hundreds of thousands of pounds as householders put in claims for the damage caused by the water. If it is known that a river is likely to burst its banks, then remedial action may be taken to divert the water or use sand bags to build up the banks. The problem is that the river could burst its banks at any time of the day or night, not just during working hours! It is not feasible for a river's water level to be constantly monitored by human staff. Instead sensors are used to measure the water level. Radio links send the data from the sensors to the main computer and if there is a danger of flooding, the emergency services can be alerted and a flood warning issued.

you have to allow the computer to get used to your voice. It may make mistakes at first, but like a child it will learn by its mistakes. Once you have told the computer about the mistakes it has made and corrected them, it starts to make fewer mistakes. The more you talk to your computer the better it gets at understanding you.

As well as dictating text into a word-processor, you can also issue commands using your voice. By saying 'dictate to Word' you could let the computer know that it needs to load the wordprocessing package Word.

Once you have dictated a document into the computer, you can get the system to speak it back to you via the loudspeakers.

More information on this can be obtained from the following web sites:

- www.software.ibm.com/is/voicetype/
- www.dragonsystems.com/

Flood warning: an example of automatic data capture

Where there is low lying land near to a large river there is always a danger that, after prolonged heavy rain, the river could burst its banks and cause extensive flooding. Flooding

Automatic data capture using signals

Not all data has to be entered using a keyboard or special forms. Some data can be entered directly into a computer in the form of electronic signals. This data usually comes from sensors which produce a signal that depends on a physical property. For instance, components passing along a production line could break a beam of light as they pass. A sensor detects that the light is absent when each component passes and a signal is sent to a computer which enables the computer to count the components. Because a sensor receives data from the outside world it may be considered as an input device.

If local authorities wanted to know about the traffic flow along a certain road they used to employ people (usually students) to stand at the side of the road monitoring and recording the traffic flow. With the flow of traffic we now have on many roads, this is not feasible. Instead pressure sensors are used which record a pulse every time a vehicle passes over them. You may have seen these; they look like thick black wires running across the road and there is sometimes a box at the side of the road to house the recording system. A diagram of this arrangement is shown in Figure 6.6.

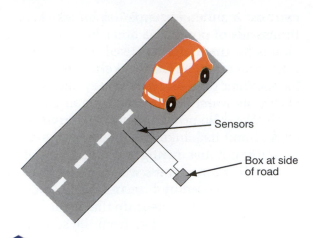

Figure 6.6 *System to automatically monitor traffic flow along a road*

Remote sensing

Remote sensing means sensing at a distance. The electronic signals from remote sensors can be sent through telephone wires or via radio transmitters to a computer in another part of the country or even in another part of the world. Such a system is ideal for remote weather stations, where temperature, pressure and wind speed can be detected at thousands of remote weather stations which send the data to a central computer.

As well as using remote sensing to detect when a river is likely to burst its banks, river authorities also use sensors to monitor the water quality in our rivers and to give a pollution alert should the quality change.

Turnaround documents

Problem

A gas company sends out bills for payment. The customers can pay the bill in various ways: they can take the bill and payment to the local gas showroom and pay, or write a cheque and put it in the post. There are other ways to pay but we will concentrate on the postal method. When a payment is made, it has to be linked to the customer and this is done using the customer reference number. Given that the reference number is 15 digits long a mistake could easily be typed, resulting in the wrong person being credited with the cheque.

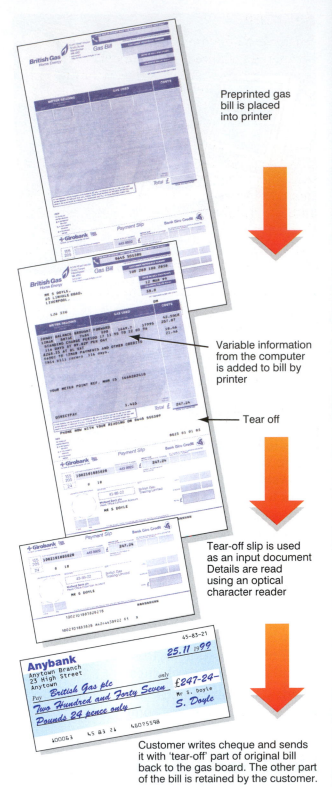

Preprinted gas bill is placed into printer

Variable information from the computer is added to bill by printer

Tear off

Tear-off slip is used as an input document Details are read using an optical character reader

Customer writes cheque and sends it with 'tear-off' part of original bill back to the gas board. The other part of the bill is retained by the customer.

Figure 6.7 *Using a turnaround document to record payment of a gas bill*

Solution

Turnaround documents are used by most companies who receive payment by post. Credit card companies, water, electricity and gas companies all use these documents.

Turnaround documents are documents produced by a computer which are subsequently used as input documents by the computer. For instance, electricity or gas bills contain some preprinted information on them and the variable information (name, address, number of units used, etc.) is added by the computer. Figure 6.7 shows these processes.

The bills are sent to customers for payment. If a customer writes a cheque to pay for electricity supply, this is sent back to the electricity board with part of the bill. The tear-off slip is used as an input document with an optical character reader. The computer then notes that the payment has been received and there has been no need to key in account or reference numbers.

TEST YOURSELF

Using the words in the list below, copy out and complete sentences A to G, underlining the words you have inserted. The words may be used more than once.

MICR   key-to-disk   OMR   turnaround

sensors   data capture   laser   scanner

A Typing the details contained on a form into a computer using a keyboard and then storing the data on disk is called _____-____-_____.

B _____ _____ is the name given to the process of getting the details into a form that can be processed by the computer.

C Banks use _____ for data capture because it is extremely quick and very difficult to forge.

D _____ involves using a form with boxes that are shaded in. Multiple choice answer sheets are an example of the use of this method.

E Barcode reading involves using a _____ _____ to read a number or code contained in the barcode.

F Data may also be captured using electric signals from _____.

G Documents which are output by the computer and are subsequently used for input into the system are called _____ documents.

Things to do

1 A motoring organisation uses a computer to work out routes for its members when they go on holiday in Britain.

The computer takes into account:

- date of travel
- type of route required (shortest, quickest, scenic, avoiding motorways)
- whether the car is towing a caravan
- the starting and finishing points
- the names of two places the route may go through.

Design a data capture form that could be sent to a member wanting to use this service.

(GCSE IS SEG HT Spec)

2 The form in Figure 6.8 has been poorly designed. The person who designed the form has asked you for your opinion.
   (a) The purpose of the form is to capture the information so that the form can be used as a source document for keying into the computer system. Explain what is meant by
      (i) data capture
      (ii) source document.
   (b) Figure 6.9 on the next page shows the form after it has been handed to a parent for filling in. The blank parts of the form are then filled in by the headteacher. Examine the form carefully and say what is wrong with it.
   (c) The headteacher has asked you to redesign the form. Redesign it, paying attention to making sure that it is arranged in a logical order, that the spaces left are long enough to accommodate the information, and that there is a clearly marked section to be filled in only by the headteacher.

```
Application form for entry into the 6th form

DOB_____ Pupil number_____

Name_____ Sex (M/F)_____

Address_____

_____

Postcode_____
GCSEs passed with grades
(for 6th form applicants)_____

_____

Ethnicity_____ Religion_____

Home language_____

Mode of travel to school_____

Parents and contacts_____

_____

_____

Arrangements for lunch_____

_____

Form_____ Name of form teacher_____

Name and address of previous school_____

_____

Admission date_____

Hobbies_____

_____

Any special medical problems_____

_____

_____
```

Figure 6.8 *A blank application form*

```
Application form for entry into the 6th form
DOB   26th March 83   Pupil number____7____
Name_____Joanne Davis_____ Sex (M/F)_____
Address_____5 Cartbridge Lane,_____
_____Crosby, Liverpool_____
Postcode____L23 67A_____
GCSEs passed with grades
(for 6th form applicants)___Mathematics (B)
English Language (C), English Literature (B), History (C),
Geography (C), Art (A), Biology (C), French (E)
Ethnicity___British___ Religion___Christian___
Home language____English_____
Mode of travel to school___School bus_____
Parents and contacts___Mother: Jackie Davis___
5 Cartbridge Lane, Crosby, Liverpool  L23 67A
_____
Arrangements for lunch____School Lunch_____
_____
Form___7___ Name of form teacher_____7_____
Name and address of previous school_____
____Same school_____
Admission date_____7_____
Hobbies____Tennis, Swimming, Disco Dancing__
_____
Any special medical problems___Has Asthma.__
Always needs to carry an inhaler. Has permission to
miss school games if she feels unwell.
```

Figure 6.9   *The application form after it has been completed by a parent but before the headteacher has added information*

3   The driver number on a driving licence codes the date of birth and sex of the driver in the following way:

        digits 1 to 5 – first five letters of surname
        digits 6 and 11 – year of birth
        digits 7 and 8 – month of birth (if female 50 is added)
        digits 9 and 10 – day of month of birth
        digits 12 and 13 – initials of first names or 9 if none.

   (a)   What information can you obtain from this coded driver number?
       KENNE409209SE9IB

   (b)   By referring to the driver licence code above, briefly explain the difference between data and information.

4   You are a junior systems analyst and you are working on an order processing and sales invoicing system. You have been instructed by your boss to draft the invoice/advice note which will be printed out by the computer. On this advice note will be a variety of items, along with a space, called a data field, for the data to be inserted. You will need to decide how much space should be left for insertion of the data in each field. Your draft design should provide for the computer to print out the following data fields:

   (i)   invoice address
   (ii)   delivery address
   (iii)   customer order number
   (iv)   supplier order number
   (v)   sales district code

(vi)   salesperson's code
(vii) invoice date
(viii) product code
(ix)   product description
(x)   quantity
(xi)   unit price
(xii) total price for each product
(xiii) carriage and packing charge
(xiv) invoice total.

(a) Use a full A4 page to show the design of this document and state any assumptions that you have made. For the purpose of simplicity we will ignore the VAT calculations, which would normally be present on such a form.

(b) In order to prepare a usable document, you would need to obtain further information about the 14 data fields shown above. What further information would you need?

IT TASKS

Task 1

The local newspaper has asked a record store to provide it with a list of the 10 top selling CDs each week. The record store uses only an ordinary till so there is no way of counting the sales, other than manually. To make things easier for the shop assistants, the shop manager would like to design a form which could be filled in each time a CD is sold.

(a) The manager comes up with the form shown in Figure 6.10 and has asked you for your comments.

Bearing in mind that the shop sells around 800 CDs each week, explain why you think the form would be unsuitable.

There are other problems with the form. Imagine that you are trying to record the sale of CDs using this form: can you think of any additional problems you might have? Explain these.

(b) Design an alternative form and explain how it could be used to obtain the chart.

Name of CD	Artist/Artists	Number sold

Figure 6.10 *Manager's suggested form for recording CD sales*

7 *Checking Data*

Reasons for errors

Computers can produce accurate results (e.g. payslips, bills, invoices, etc.) only if the data put into them is accurate. In many systems an input document may be used and the data on this document keyed in to the computer. In other systems, this document is input directly to the computer, thus avoiding the need for typing which frequently introduces errors. Incorrect data can have serious or not so serious consequences! (See Figure 7.1.)

Consequences of errors

1 Customers become angry if they are sent bills that are too large and companies lose money if bills are too small.
2 Wrong decisions are made by the managers because the decisions are based on wrong information.
3 A company could be prosecuted under the Data Protection Act 1998 if the incorrect information causes the person concerned some kind of loss. For instance if someone lost a job because a computer contained wrong information about a criminal record, the unsuccessful applicant could claim compensation.

How are errors avoided?

Verification

Let us look at a situation with which we are all probably familiar. Suppose that you go to buy goods at a catalogue-based shop such as Index or Argos. You first look up the goods required using the latest catalogue and then fill in an order form, as shown in Figure 7.2. This order form is taken to the point-of-sale terminal for the operator to type in the details provided on the form. The process is shown in Figure 7.3.

If you were to use an old catalogue, the catalogue number may no longer coincide with the goods required. When the operator keys in this catalogue number there are two possibilities: it may no longer be a valid number or it may be the catalogue number corresponding to different goods. Or, suppose the operator made a typing mistake with the catalogue

Figure 7.1 *Incorrect data can have serious or not so serious consequences*

Check digits

When any large number is input to a computer, either using a keyboard or using a direct input device such as a barcode reader, there is always a chance of error. These large numbers are important, since they could be product numbers in a supermarket, employee numbers for a payroll or account numbers in a bank; it is essential that they are input correctly. For this reason an additional number is usually included, placed at the end of the original number. This additional number is called a check digit and is calculated from the other numbers.

When an account number is input the computer cuts off the last digit, which is the check digit. It then uses the rest of the numbers to recalculate the check digit, which it then compares with the removed digit. If the numbers are the same then the account number has been input correctly.

Calculating a check digit

If you look at any book, including this one, you will see a number on the back and inside the book, called the International Standard Book Number (ISBN). This is a unique number and is used by bookshops and libraries to identify a particular book.

The computer calculates the check digit in the following way.

Suppose a book with the ISBN 0 09 172981 5 is input to a computer.

1 The computer removes the last number which is the check digit, so that it is left with

0 09 172981

2 We now have nine numbers. Working from the left hand side, the first number (i.e. 0) is multiplied by ten, the second number (also 0) is multiplied by nine, the third number (9) is multiplied by eight and so on. The total is then found:
$$0 \times 10 + 0 \times 9 + 9 \times 8 + 1 \times 7 + 7 \times 6 + 2 \times 5 + 9 \times 4 + 8 \times 3 + 1 \times 2 = 193$$

3 The total (193) is then divided by 11 (it is always divided by 11) and the remainder is noted. 11 divides into 193 17 times, with a remainder of 6.

4 The remainder is then subtracted from 11 to give the check digit:
$$11 - 6 = 5$$
so 5 is the check digit.

5 The check digit will sometimes be 10, in which case an X is used.

This may seem quite a complicated procedure to follow, but the method has to be able to detect where digits have been swapped around. Remember that a computer can perform millions of calculations each second, so a little calculation like this is very quick.

Spelling checkers

Spelling checkers are not just used in word-processing software. Any software where accurate text needs to be entered can have a spell checker facility.

Custom dictionaries

Despite having a huge dictionary, most word-processors still fail to recognise certain words. Generally these words are of two types:

- proper names – names of people or places for example
- specialist words used in a narrow field – medical terms, legal terms, computer jargon, new slang words, etc.

It is possible to purchase supplementary dictionaries for foreign languages, medical terms, etc. Another alternative is to create your own customised dictionary with the terms correctly spelt. Once these words have been added to the dictionary, the spell checker will not question the words again unless they are misspelled.

Length checks

Sometimes a certain item of information is always of a certain length: it contains a set number of characters. A national insurance number such as YY232425A always has nine characters. If a national insurance number has more or fewer characters than this, then the length check will alert you to the fact that it has been entered incorrectly.

Lookup tables

Stock items are given a unique code to identify them. Whenever this code is used, it is checked against a table stored by the computer to make sure that it is a valid stock code. If the code is not in the table it is rejected, thus preventing any processing using incorrect codes.

Parity errors

When data is passed along a communication line it is important that the data is not corrupted in any way and if it is, it is equally important that this is detected and the data re-transmitted.

The checking of data after it has passed along a communication line is performed by using a parity bit. Parity checking works in the following way. The computer adds up the number of bits in one byte and if the parity is different to the parity setting the computer will report an error. It is possible to use either even or odd parity. Taking odd parity for instance, suppose we are sending the letter C along a communication line. In ASCII code, the series of bits used to represent C is 1000011. Since there are three 1s in this code and odd parity is being used, then a 0 is added to the left-hand side of the group of bits so that the total for the byte is odd. If even parity were being used, a 1 would need to be added so that total for the byte would then be an even number.

Modems have a chip inside them to deal with parity checks: the sending modem adds the parity bits and the receiving unit calculates what the parity bit should be. If an error has occurred, transmission parity will no longer be observed, and the corruption is detected. The problem with parity checks is that if more than one error occurs and the errors compensate for each other, parity can still appear to be correct.

Types of error

Transcription errors

Transcription errors occur due to misreading or mistyping data. This may be caused by bad handwriting or confusing, for instance, the number 5 with the letter S or 0 with O.

Transposition errors

Transposition errors occur when two digits or letters are swapped around. If you are typing in data at high speed you do not always look at the screen and it is very common to end up with say 'ot' instead of 'to' or 5124 instead of 5214. It is estimated that about 70% of all errors are transposition errors.

How to avoid errors

Despite all the checks that we can perform on the 'raw' data before it is accepted into a system some errors are bound to occur.

If data is entered into a system via a keyboard, the simplest way of reducing errors is for the person who is entering the data to proof read it carefully against the original document. This simple method reduces the chances of the keyboard operator introducing new errors.

Checking for errors in a wordprocessed document

There are two different situations to consider:

1   The first situation is where the typist has been given a copy of a document or where a document is on an audio tape. All the typist has to do is to key in the document.

    In this situation the typist will be working at high speed (often in excess of 70 words per minute) and will be looking at the document or listening to the tape. They will not look at the keyboard and will only occasionally look at the screen. At such high speed, mistakes are not noticed and any mistakes not corrected as the document is typed. Instead the typist can leave all the corrections until the document is typed. The spell checking facility on the wordprocessor can then be used. Secondly the typist will carefully proof read the document. Any mistakes spotted are corrected and a copy then printed out.

2   The second situation is where someone types their own document. This is generally a much slower process, since the person has to think about the meaning of

what is being typed. Also, such a person is likely to type more slowly than a fully trained typist. A slow typist will probably correct any typing mistakes as the text is typed. The document will still need spell checking and proof reading at the end. In some cases, an important document goes through a series of drafts. Each draft is printed out, corrected and the corrections keyed in until a final copy is obtained.

Automatic spell checking as you type

With newer programs like Word and WordPerfect, errors such as 'ot' and 'teh'

instead of 'to' and 'the' can be corrected automatically by the program.

Using direct input methods

To completely avoid keying in errors alternative methods of inputting the data are needed, other than a keyboard. Such methods include OCR (optical character recognition), OMR (optical mark recognition), MICR (magnetic ink character recognition) and barcode recognition. The input documents for these methods are shown in Figure 7.6. Although all of these methods can introduce errors, they are so fast they leave plenty of time for the errors to be corrected.

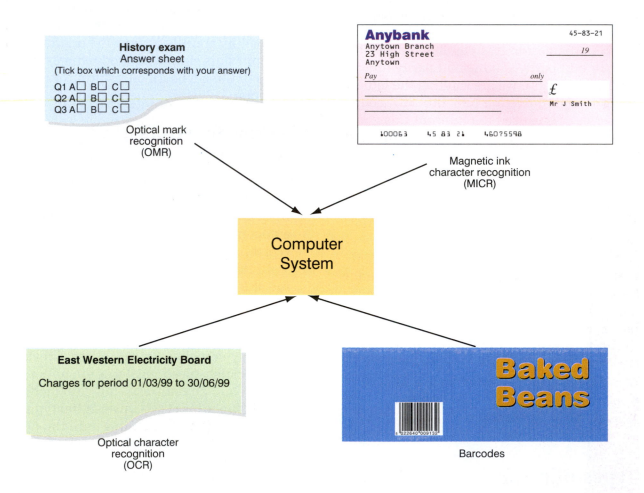

Figure 7.6 *Direct methods of data input reduce errors and are much quicker*

TEST YOURSELF

Read the chapter carefully. The following sentences are incomplete. Copy out and complete the sentences using the words in the list below.

transposition   range   verification   check digit

proof reading   character type   validation

processing

A One method of _____ is to let two people type in the same data. Only if they make identical keystrokes will the data be accepted for _____.

B Another, more feasible method involves getting someone to check carefully what has been typed in. This is called _____ _____.

C _____ is performed by a computer program. Validation checks include the following: _____ _____. To make sure the right type of character has been entered, _____ checks to make sure that the data lies within a certain range.

D When a large number is entered, mistakes often occur, so an extra number is added at the end which is calculated from the other numbers. This extra number is called a _____ _____.

E The commonest type of error is the _____ error which is caused by letters or numbers being typed in the wrong order.

Things to do

1 One type of error that could be made when data is typed into a computer system is a transcription error.
   (a) A transcription error can be detected by a verification check. Explain how this check is carried out. (3 marks)
   (b) A date can be validated as well as verified. A date is to be input in the form 25 APR 1999 (a two digit day, followed by a three letter month, followed by a four digit year). Describe the validation checks that could be carried out on dates in this form. (4 marks)

(SEG IS IT Spec)

2 The following is a list of International Standard Book Numbers. Some of these numbers are correct and some are incorrect. Using the method shown in this chapter, check each of the ISBNs and, showing your working out, say whether each is correct or not.
   (a) 0 582 05179 6
   (b) 0 582 05165 7
   (c) 0 09 182438 9

3 Each of the items of data in the table below has been incorrectly typed. The following checks may be used on data:
   • range check   • character type check   • check digit.

Copy and complete the table, placing a tick if the error can be detected using the above checks and also stating which validation check is the most appropriate for the data.

Type of data	Item	Tick if error would be detected	Validation check
(a) Name	John Brwn		
(b) Sex (M or F)	N		
(c) Date of Birth (day/month/year)	310994		
(d) Examination subjects	English Physics		
(e) Exam fee paid	£2350		

INVESTIGATIONS

You work part-time in a video rental shop which is part of a large chain of 100 shops scattered throughout the country. Each member is given a six figure membership number when they first join. The number needs to be this large because it is possible for a member to hire videos from any of the branches. The shops are having problems with members of staff keying in wrong membership numbers when hiring out videos. This has several consequences. When a membership number has been incorrectly keyed:

1 the shops have an incorrect record of who has hired the video
2 if that video is returned late, then letters are sent to the wrong member.
3 if the video is not returned at all, then the wrong member is invoiced for it.

All of this wastes time and loses customers.

The staff aren't all to blame because some customers forget their membership card when renting but just quote their membership number instead. Occasionally they may accidentally (or deliberately) quote the wrong number.

1 Figure 7.7 shows what the video membership card looks like. Would changing the design of the card help? If so, design a card using appropriate software and say why your design is better.

2 What procedures could be adopted by staff when videos are being hired out to reduce the problems mentioned above? You need to consider both verification and validation. It is best to consider various options to start with and then to choose a combination of the best ones.

Visions Video Club

Member's name	Stephen Doyle
Membership no	632158
Date	15/10/98

Figure 7.7 *Visions video membership card*

8 *How Data is Stored*
Databases

A database is an organised collection of information or data. Putting information into a computer database gives you far more flexibility in organising, displaying and printing that information.

The parts of a database

Files
Think of a box of filing cards like those sometimes used in libraries. A computer's equivalent of the complete box is a file. The computer's file is usually stored on a disk, which may be optical or magnetic.

Records
Within the library card box are the individual cards, each of which contains information about one book. In a computer database, the cards are known as records and most databases will display one record on the screen at a time, just as if you were browsing through the cards in a card box.

Fields
On each card will be a number of different items of information: a library card might list the title, author, publisher and ISBN (a unique number for a particular book).

Each item of information on the computer record is known as a field, and it consists of two parts: the field name and the field data. The field names are the words 'Title', 'Author' or 'Publisher'. They are the same on each record and indicate what the field data represents. Figure 8.1 shows the relationship between fields, records and files.

A card box filing system

On a card in a card box you can squeeze extra information in by writing smaller, or by writing on the back of the card. This is not possible with the computer equivalent. With a database, one of the first things you have to do is to specify the size and design of the record screen. You need to consider how you want the information to be arranged on the record and how long the data for each field will be. It is no good specifying an author field to allow up to 10 characters when you have several books by an author with a surname such as Forbes-Hamilton in the library.

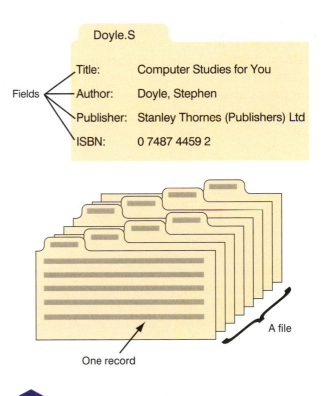

Figure 8.1 *The relationship between fields, records and files*

You could of course go to the other extreme and specify a field length of 30 characters for names of authors. The problem here is that larger fields will take up more space on your floppy or hard disk. Another problem is that longer files take longer to process. If you have 2000 members or customers in your database, with a maximum surname length of 16 characters, then the surnames alone will take up 32 000 bytes on your disk. If you have allowed 30 characters for each surname, though, you have probably reserved 60 000 bytes, wasting 28 000 bytes in blank space!

As with most things, the best answer is a compromise. You should try to design your fields to cope with the largest entry you can imagine making, without reserving unnecessary disk space by over-specifying. You may find it worthwhile abbreviating the longest entries, if the overwhelming majority are shorter.

Record design

Modern databases give you freedom to design your own records. They give you an empty screen on which you can add the field names, fields and other background text such as the title. On some databases you can even put boxes around headings and even change the colour of the text.

Num	Field name	Field type	Width	Dec	Index
1	ADD-PROP	Character	50		N
2	AREA				
3	TOWN				
4	POSTCODE				
5	TYPE				
6	NO-BEDS				
7	RECEIPT				
8	GARDEN				
9	GARAGE				
10	FREEHOLD				
11	PRICE				
12	DOM				
13	PROP-AGE				
14	OWNER				
15	TELEPHONE				

Figure 8.2 *Template for the design of the structure. Only the first line has been filled in*

Some databases require you to create a different type of field for different information. You usually have to specify the type of data to go into the field. This can be:

1 numeric, which means it contains only numbers. Make sure that a number does not have any starting zeros or dashes (e.g. a telephone number 0181-888-3456)
2 character text, which means that numbers, letters and other symbols can be entered.
3 date, which means that the date is entered like this: 09/10/96.
4 logical, which allows Y/N (for yes/no) or T/F (for true/false).

As well as selecting the field names and the type of data to be entered some of the more sophisticated databases allow you to specify some validation checks to the field.

Figure 8.2 shows the template for the design of the database structure. The information for the first field has been filled in.

QUESTIONS

Figure 8.2 shows a database structure for a database to be used by an estate agency. A database package is to be used to store the details of all the properties that the agency has on offer. Copy out the table and fill it in with appropriate field types and widths. The column headed 'Dec' is used to specify how many decimal places there are in the numeric field so you need to fill this in only if the field type is numeric. In the Index column you can just put N for no for all the fields.

Key fields

A key field is a field that may be used to search a file. It is always useful to have one field which is unique to a particular record. For example, each pupil starting at a school will be given an admission number. This is a number that no-one else will have and so it is unique to a particular pupil.

With the library system, the key field would be a number given to the book when it is bought by the library. The International Standard Book Number would distinguish between different books but it could not be used to distinguish between copies of the same book and therefore would not be unique.

QUESTIONS

Databases can use any field in order to perform a search.

(a) Why should we not to use the pupil's surname as the key field?

(b) The school secretary says that there are only 1000 pupils in the school so we do not need an admission number of more than four characters. Do you agree? Explain your answer.

(c) A letter needs to be sent to a pupil who has an unreported absence from school of over a week. The teacher knows the name of the pupil but not the admission number. What other fields could be used to perform this search?

Personnel file

Employee Number:	1473
Surname:	Doyle
Christian:	Jane
Date of birth:	15/01/54
Job title:	Systems analyst

Payroll file

Employee Number:	1473
Surname:	Doyle
Christian:	Jane
Date of birth:	15/01/54
Salary:	£22 000

Department file

Employee Number:	1473
Surname:	Doyle
Christian:	Jane
Experience:	15 years

Figure 8.3 *Data duplication with manual systems*

Manual filing systems

Figure 8.3 shows three records from three different files kept by departments in a company. As you can see, some of the data is the same on each file. This is called data duplication and is one of the main problems with manual filing systems. Data duplication means that more space is taken up by the files and more work is needed to retrieve the information.

The main problems arise in the following situations:

1 We may need to obtain information that is held on several files. Suppose we wanted to find out the names of systems analysts, with fewer than 16 years experience and who earn over £20 000 per year. We would need to use all three files, which are held by three different departments.

2 Also, because the data is not shared, a change in information, such as a change in surname because Jane got married, would cause three files to need updating.

3 If two people need to look at information on the same file at the same time then it is necessary to photocopy the information, which is time consuming and wasteful.

4 If a file is put back in the wrong place finding it again can prove an awesome task (Figure 8.4).

Figure 8.4 *The file for Adams was in the Ws!*

Computerised databases

Advantages

The main advantages of a computerised database are as follows:

1 It is usually necessary to store the information only once, since most database software allows you to access information from several files.
2 Files can be linked together, which means that if you update one of the files, all the other files that depend on the same information will automatically be updated. Not all databases are able to do this but those that can are called relational databases.
3 If you find that the record structure needs changing after you have put a great deal of data into a database, this is easily done. To do this manually would be impossible.
4 Access to the information is rapid and there is less likelihood of the data becoming lost.
5 Validation checks may be made on the data as it is being entered into the database which means that there will be fewer errors in the data.

Disadvantages

The main disadvantages of a computerised database are as follows:

1 If the computer breaks down, you are not able to access the details.
2 It is easy to copy computer files, so sensitive data should be protected by passwords.
3 Training is needed to use the system and this takes time and costs money.

Database management system (DBMS)

A database management system (DBMS) is a set of programs that allows the creation of datafiles, the alteration of the data in these files and the extraction of data from the files. The idea with a DBMS is that all the data is kept centrally and only authorised users can access data via the DBMS.

All database management systems allow the following:

1 the data files to be set up by creating tables (or datafiles) which may be linked together
2 the users to ask questions (known as queries) of the data (i.e. they allow the user to search for data meeting certain criteria)
3 the addition of more data (appending), the deletion and editing of existing data
4 alteration to the structure of the datafiles or tables
5 some security, by allowing only certain people access to each of the datafiles or tables
6 the user to import data into the database from other packages and data to be transferred to another package (exporting).

File organisation

There are several methods you can use to organise files.

Serial files

With a serial file, the records do not follow each other in any particular order, so if another record needs to be added it can just be added to the end of the file.

Sequential files

Sequential files are like serial files except that the records are held in a certain sequence. For instance, you might decide to order the pupil file in admission number sequence.

Random files

Random files have to be stored on disk and, as the name suggests, they are not stored in any order on the disk surface. The disk operating system (the programs that control the storage on the disk) keeps a map of the disk surface and using this map the read/write heads can go straight to the data. In this way the data is found without the whole disk having to be read. Random access allows data stored on disk to be found extremely quickly.

Methods of accessing files

Serial access
To read a serial file, a computer has to read each record until it reaches the one required.

Sequential access
With sequential access the records are in order, so if just one record is required then the method is slow but if all the records are required then it is very fast.

Direct access (random access)
With direct access files it is possible to go directly to a record without having to look at any other records first. You can access both sequential and random access files directly.

Types of files

There are various types of files.

Master files
A master file is the most important file since it is the most complete and up-to-date version of a file. If a master file is lost or damaged and it is the only copy, the whole system will break down.

Transaction files
Transaction files are used to hold temporary data which is used to update the master file. A transaction is a piece of business, hence the name transaction file. Transactions can occur in any order, so it is necessary to sort a transaction file into the same order as the master file before it is used to update the master file.

Backup or security files
Backup copies of files are kept in case the original is damaged or lost and cannot be used. Because of the importance of the master file, backup copies of it should be taken at regular intervals in case it is stolen, lost, damaged or corrupted. Looking after your disks is not enough; you should always keep backup copies of all your important data, especially project work such as IT tasks and system tasks.

Transaction log files
Transactions are bits of business such as placing an order, updating the stock, making a payment, etc. If these transactions are performed in real time, the data input will overwrite the previous data. This makes it impossible to check past transactions and so would make it easy for people to commit fraud.

A record of the transactions is kept (the transaction log file) which shows all the transactions made over a certain period. Using the log you can see what the data was before changes were made and also what the changes were and who made them. Transaction log files therefore maintain security and can also be used to recover transactions lost due to hardware failure.

The grandfather–father–son principle
There is always a slight chance that the data contained on a master file may be destroyed. It could be destroyed by an inexperienced user, a power failure, fire or even theft. For a large company, the loss of vital data could prove disastrous. But using the grandfather–father–son principle it is possible to recreate the master file if it is lost.

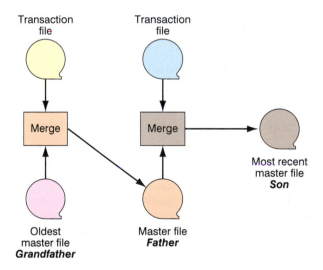

All these files are kept so that if one or more of the files are lost they can be recreated

Figure 8.5 *The grandfather–father–son principle, often used for file security*

The principle works like this. Basically, three generations of files are kept. The oldest master file is called the **grandfather** file and it is kept with its transaction file. These two files are used to produce a new master file called the **father** file which, with its transaction file, is used to create the most up-to-date file, called the **son** file. The process is repeated and the son becomes the father and the father becomes the grandfather and so on. Only three generations are needed and the other files may be re-used. This system (sometimes called the ancestral file system) is usually used for tapes, although it could also be used for disks. Figure 8.5 summarises the principle.

QUESTIONS

Backup copies should always be taken at regular intervals.

(a) What is meant by a backup copy?
(b) Some programs such as databases and word-processors automatically take backup copies. Your friend says 'my wordprocessor takes backup copies so I don't need to worry'. Explain what is wrong with her argument.
(c) John has a disk box in which he keeps all his disks. The box is labelled with his name, form, address and phone number. He realises that data can be lost so in his disk box he also keeps his backup copies. Is he doing all he can to keep his data safe? Explain.

Fixed and variable length fields

A fixed length field is one where the length of the field has been decided in advance. If we decide that the field for surnames is to be 30 characters long, then even if the surname is only five characters long (like Jones) then the field still takes up 30 characters. We specify how long each field is going to be when we set up the structure of a database. Some fields, such as date or logical fields, have a length already set by the database. If all the fields in a record are of a fixed length, then the size of the record itself will be a fixed length. For instance, if the record has the structure shown in Figure 8.6, we can calculate the length of the record as follows.

If the admission number is always five digits long, then the surname will start six

characters from the start of the record and this is extremely useful when a computer is processing a file.

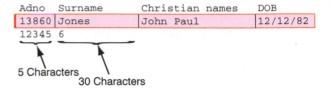

Figure 8.6 *Finding the start of a field with fixed length fields is easy*

Variable length fields take up only as much space as the data requires. So, if a person's surname is Jones this takes up the space occupied by five characters. Hence, with this method there is no wasted space. With variable length records there is a special character used to separate the fields and to find a particular record the computer has to read through all the characters, counting the separators until it reaches the required record.

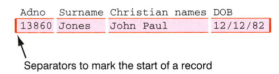

Figure 8.7 *Variable length fields do not waste as much space but it is harder to find the fields*

Common file processes

The beauty of any computerised filing system is the ease with which sorts, searches, merges and updates may be performed. With manual filing systems these tasks are performed only with great difficulty.

File updating

File updating involves bringing a file up-to-date with any changes that have occurred since it was last updated. There are various processes that can take place during updating.

Insertions

Suppose we had a file containing the details of pupils in a school. A new pupil may have joined the school and so that pupil's details will need to be added to the file.

Deletions

A pupil could have moved to a new school so that pupil's details will need to be removed (deleted) from the file.

Amendments

A pupil has moved house so the address field needs changing. This is called amending the details.

File manipulation

The common file manipulations are sorting and merging.

Sorting

Often a field needs to be sorted into a particular order. For instance we may need a list of all the pupils in the school arranged in alphabetical order. It is also possible to sort according to several fields. So we could produce a list of all the pupils arranged in year order, with the list for each year arranged in alphabetical order.

Merging

Sometimes we want to combine the contents of two files to form a single file. The process of combining the files is called merging. If the two files to be merged are on magnetic tape, then we must sort the tapes into order before merging them. The new tape file produced will also be in order.

Merging is very useful if we want to divide the work. For instance, if a school wanted to convert its manual files for 1500 pupils, then to do this quickly, it may decide to split the work of inputting the details into the database. In effect two separate databases would be created with the same structure. These could then be merged to produce the complete database. In this way one person might type half the data and someone else could type the other half.

File interrogation

Interrogation involves getting information from a file. Fields are selected and the computer then searches through the records, finding all the records which match the field or fields being used for the search. A report (printout) is then produced which has either all the records found or only certain fields of those records.

Data analysis

Some databases allow the data to be analysed in some way once it has been entered. For instance, you can produce bar charts, pie charts and line graphs using selected fields from the database. Tables can also be produced using fields from several different files.

Geographical information systems

Many computer databases contain information about geographical areas. For example, your school or college will keep a record about you which includes your address. They may want to find out in which areas most of the pupils live so that a new bus route to the school can be planned. How might this be done? They could get a large map and insert map pins (ones with coloured heads) where each pupil lives. This would take a long time and the map would need to be updated regularly as pupils leave or join the school or change address. Instead a geographical information system (GIS) could be used, which is like a map and database combined. Information from the database can be displayed on the map. The roads where most pupils live could then be identified from the map and a suitable bus route chosen. If any of the data in the database changes, the map will always be produced from the latest data available.

Geographical information systems are systems which organise data according to location, based on a map. They are powerful tools and need a powerful computer to cope with the processing needed.

Geographical information systems are used by many organisations. They allow data which is difficult to understand to be displayed on a map. Here is a list of some of the many uses to which GIS has been put:

1 Providing marketing information for stores. They can display customer density in the surrounding areas as different colours on a map.
2 They can be used by the utility companies (gas, electricity and water) to show where pipes, wires, substations, etc. are located.
3 They are used by BT when deciding where to position new telephone boxes or where to site new transmitters for their mobile telephone network.

4 Local authorities use them to keep data on pavements, lamp posts, road signs, etc. They also use them for planning routes for the emptying of bins and street cleaning.
5 Emergency services (police, ambulance and fire brigade) use them to route vehicles to emergencies via the fastest route.

TEST YOURSELF

Using the words in the list below, copy out and complete sentences A to J, underlining the words you have inserted. The words may be used more than once.

master   records   database   duplication

security   grandfather   files   fields   structure

transaction   son

A An organised collection of data is called a
_____.

B A database usually consists of many _____ which may be linked together.

C Files consist of a series of _____, each one about a certain company, person or item.

D Within each record we have _____ such as name, address, date of birth, etc.

E When designing a database on a computer you have to specify the _____ of a record by telling the program what fields are needed, the type of each field and the length of each field.

F There are many problems with manual filing systems. Data _____ means that the same data is stored several times on different files.

G A _____ file is the complete, up-to-date version of a file on a certain subject.

H Master files are kept up to date with changes using a _____ file.

I Backup files are always kept for _____ reasons.

J So that a master file can be recreated if it is destroyed, the _____–father–_____ principle is used.

Things to do

1 You are responsible for updating a file which contains details of all the members of a sports club. Copy out and label the following changes to be made at the end of one month as I, D or A according to whether they are insertions, deletions or amendments.

Change	Type of update
(a) Change of address	
(b) Resigned from the club	
(c) New member	
(d) Member changed her name through marriage	
(e) Changed from annual member to life member	
(f) Member died suddenly	
(g) Previous member has re-joined	
(h) Member resigned through ill health	
(i) Member's telephone number has changed	
(j) Member has emigrated to Australia	

2 A school keeps information on each of its pupils and part of the information contained on the computer file is shown below.

Admission number	Surname	Christian name	Date of birth	Tutor initials
2312	Doyle	Stephen	19/12/84	KF
2344	Kendrick	Graham	23/06/85	PK
2367	Smith	Julie	12/09/87	HT
2380	Jones	Susan	09/01/86	BG
2381	Jackson	Joan	01/01/86	JS

(a) How many records are shown?

(b) How many fields does each record have?

(c) In all computer database systems there is a unique field.
   (i)   Which is the unique field in this section of the file?
   (ii) Why is it important to have a unique field?

(d) Only part of the complete file is shown. Name two other fields that could be added to this file and give reasons for their inclusion.

IT TASKS

Task 1

Sid's Motors is a used car dealer which keeps a stock of around 300 used cars. Sid, the garage's proprietor, has decided to computerise the records held about each car.

1 Look at the adverts in your local papers or a specialist publication such as 'Autotrader' for adverts for used cars. These adverts will give you ideas about what people look for when they are buying a used car. Here are a few to start you off.

   Make: Ford
   Model: Probe
   Engine Size: 2.5 litres
   Mileage: 13 000
   etc.

   Write a list of the details you need to record for each car. Put them into a suitable order, with what you consider are the most important features of the car at the top of the list.

2 Now design a form which can be filled in each time a car is added to the stock. Compare it with a friend's form to see if you have missed anything important. It is important to make sure that enough space is left for the details to be inserted.

3 Sid is pleased with your effort and has asked you if the details on the form could be put into a database.
   (a) What advantages does a database have over the cards arranged in a filing cabinet?
   (b) Sid often receives telephone calls asking whether he has a particular make of car. How could the database be used to help him?

IT TASKS

Task 2

Develop a suite of letters and standard paragraphs that your form teacher could use to send to parents, to inform them, for example, about school trips, parents' evenings, sports events, etc. Ask your form teacher what kind of details should be included. Your form teacher is fairly new to computers and so will need some documentation as to how to use the system you have developed.

You frequently need to merge (i.e. combine) the contents of two files. Type in the following letter and then save it using the name SMO1.

Grange Hill Comprehensive School
Shawfield Road
Grange Hill
London
NW10 4AA
Telephone: 0181-220-2300
Today's date

Dear Parent,

I regret to inform you that your daughter has been found smoking in school and I am concerned that you should know. Apart from the bad example that this is giving to the other children, she is unwise to risk attachment to a habit which is widely regarded as both anti social and damaging to health.

Yours sincerely

Mrs A Johnston (Headteacher)

The following paragraph is often incorporated into other letters when pupils have been found swearing, smoking, fighting, etc. This paragraph is referred to as DET1. Type this paragraph into your wordprocessor and save it with the filename DET1.

I should be grateful for your support in discouraging such behaviour by reinforcing the school's punishment of a school detention on Wednesday until 5 p.m.

Julie Hill has been found smoking so the standard smoking letter is to be sent to her mother Mrs A Hill. Load in the letter SMO1 and insert the variable details such as her mother's name and Julie's as well as today's date. The headteacher decides to place Julie on school detention, so she has asked you to incorporate (i.e. merge) the detention paragraph DET1 into SMO1. You should perform this task whilst in the SMO1 letter by inserting a file and not by retyping.

Skills Building

Types of Computer Operation

Life in the fast lane

John is a high-flying marketing executive for a leading brand of soft drink. He works hard and has trouble fitting his schedule into 24 hours. John has to travel urgently to Frankfurt to solve a problem that the company is having with a new rival brand of cola. He needs to book on the earliest flight he can get to Frankfurt. First he tries to ring British Airways direct, but the number is engaged. He tries the German airline, Lufthansa but Lufthansa is also engaged. He thinks and then decides to drive to his local travel agent. After waiting in a queue for 20 minutes (it is January and the shop is packed with people booking their summer holidays) he gets to talk to one of the assistants.

The travel agency uses an on-line enquiry and booking service, where a terminal is connected to the main processor via a telecommunications link. A terminal is simply a VDU and keyboard or a VDU, keyboard and a processor with some backing store. The former is called a dumb terminal because it relies for its intelligence on the main processor and the latter is called a smart terminal because it has its own processor. The telecommunications link could be a telephone line, a microwave link or a radio link.

The assistant uses a terminal which has an opening screen similar to that shown in Figure 9.1. to dial automatically the number of the British Airways computer. The screen changes and the terminal asks her for the travel agent's ABTA number and a password, which she types in. It then asks for the code of the outward airport and that of the arrival airport. She supplies this information. This type of system, where the computer constantly asks for information which the user supplies, is called an interactive system. It is like the computer is conducting a conversation with the

QUESTIONS

1 Years ago the travel agent's assistant would have had to ring each airline in the same way as John and would encounter the same problems of the phone being engaged.
   (a) What advantage is there in using a terminal rather than the phone?
   (b) Explain the meaning of the term on-line.

2 As well as being able to get details on flights and holidays the travel agent can also access the Prestel system (the viewdata system provided by BT).
   (a) Explain what the main differences are between the Prestel system and the teletext system most people have on their televisions.
   (b) Explain how the Prestel system might be useful to the travel agent.

user. The travel agent then accesses the information on seats available on today's flights from Manchester to Frankfurt. She tells John that there is one seat available and asks if he wants it. He says yes. The assistant takes his

```
        Database Directory

  DIR    Name                Tel No
   1     Cosmos Holidays      639485
   2     Thomson Holidays     719385
   3     Airtours             691879
   4     British Airways      398272
   5     Kuoni Travel         818552
   6     Fastrak              112111

  Press 1 to 6 or #
  for manual dialling

  DISCONNECTED
```

Figure 9.1 *The travel agent can dial the database by typing a number from 1 to 6 on the keyboard*

credit card details and hands him booking confirmation which means he only has to pick up the ticket at the office in the airport. Airline and many other booking systems, use such real-time processing.

Real-time processing

With real-time processing, the system is automatically updated when a change is made due to a transaction occurring. So, if I book the only available seat on a plane from Manchester to Frankfurt at a travel agent's office, then if you went to another travel agent and tried to book the same seat the computer would tell you that the plane is full. In the fast world we now live in, it is important that data is kept bang up-to-date so real-time systems have to be used.

Since in a real-time system the terminals must be connected to the computer, you can see that a real-time system must also be an on-line system.

The advantage with real-time systems is that the current situation is always being shown. At a travel agency we can find out which flights or holidays are actually available. Many shop systems use real-time processing: as soon as an item is sold the system automatically deducts that item from stock so the stock file always shows the true stock position.

Real-time processing is essential for computer control. Examples of computer control include traffic lights, robots, process control (e.g. steel works and chemical processes) and flight simulators.

Doing all the processing in one go: batch processing

Problem

An electricity board wants to send out over three million electricity bills, all within a few days of each other.

Looking at the system in its simplest form gives the following outline:

1   When a person moves to a new house they have to go to the electricity company's office to fill in a form for the supply of electricity.
2   The details contained on the form are input via a terminal to the main computer. These details are recorded on a main file called the customer master file.
3   Every three months, the computer produces a list of customers, arranged in order of houses in a certain street for the meter reader to visit. The meter reader is given a sheet like the one shown in Figure 9.2, which is used to record the meter readings.

Figure 9.2 *A meter reading sheet with mark sense boxes. Information is coded by shading in the boxes*

4 After they have been recorded, the meter readings are then sent to the computer centre for processing.

5 First of all, the meter reading sheets are read by an optical mark reader and the details placed on magnetic tape in what is called a transaction file.

6 This magnetic tape is then sorted into the same order as the master file to produce a new tape called the sorted transaction file. You cannot sort a tape and put it back on the same tape again, although you could do this if a disk system were used.

7 This transaction file is then processed with the master file, which is also held on tape. A new updated master file is produced along with the electricity bills to be sent out to the customers.

The production of electricity bills in this way is an example of batch processing. This is a system of collecting all the inputs together and putting them into the computer in one go or 'batch'.

Batch processing is used when a particular job needs to be done in one go rather than in a number of parts. All the relevant data is collected and processed together. The main advantage with batch processing is that the computer operator can load the data in only one operation, no matter how many meter reading sheets there are in a batch. The programs in the computer go through the various processes and the final result is a pile of bills to be sent out to customers and an updated master file with the latest information added.

Batch processing has other uses. Preparing a company's payroll is a suitable application. Here, all the relevant information, such as hours worked, pay per hour, tax and national insurance contributions, is collected for each employee and put into the computer. Batch processing is suitable because payroll processing is usually carried out once a week or once a month.

Multitasking and multiprogramming

Any processing unit works relatively quickly, so if it is working on just one task then most of its time is spent waiting for the slow peripheral devices to catch up. Rather than

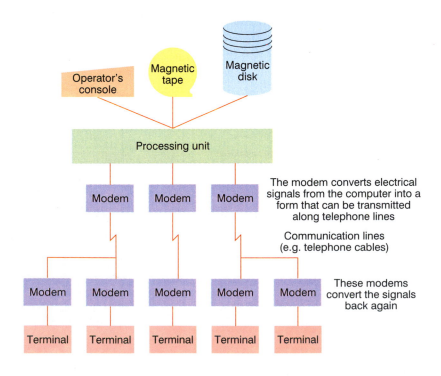

Figure 9.3 *How a multi-access system can be used by many people at different locations*

waste this valuable processing time, the processing unit can be made to process the data from several programs at once. The speed of the computer makes it appear as though it is doing two jobs at the same time, although what is happening is that the computer works on one task for a short period and then on the next. Such a system is called a multiprogramming or multitasking system.

Using Windows software you can print out a job at the same time as working on a different task using other software.

Transaction processing

Transaction processing takes place when needed, rather than at set intervals like batch processing. Rather than wait for the data to accumulate, demand processing is usually performed on individual items of data. Suppose a monthly-paid employee leaves halfway through the month. Instead of waiting for the payroll to be done at the end of the month as a batch process, the data could be input to a disk-based system and the pay worked out for the one employee.

Multi-access and timesharing

With timesharing many users can have access to the same data apparently at the

same time. For instance, in the airline booking example, other travel agents could be using the same airline database at the same time. Multi-access systems give the user the impression that she is the only one using the computer. In fact the computer serves other people during the time she takes to press the keys (see Figures 9.3 and 9.4).

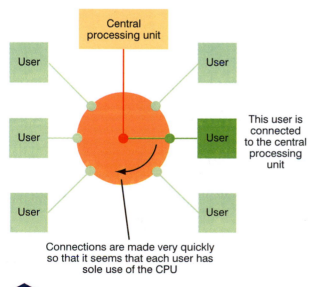

Figure 9.4 *A multi-access system with users at a single location*

Central processing unit

User

User

User

User

This user is connected to the central processing unit

User

User

Connections are made very quickly so that it seems that each user has sole use of the CPU

TEST YOURSELF

Using the words in the list below, copy out and complete sentences A to H, underlining the words you have inserted. The words may be used more than once.

timesharing   multi-access   on

interactive   control   real-time   batch

multiprogramming

A If a device is _____-line it means that it is under the control of the central processing unit.

B The type of system where the computer conducts a 'conversation' with the user, is called an _____ system.

C The type of processing where changes are immediately acted upon and any files are immediately updated, is called a _____-_____ system.

D _____ systems must always be real-time systems.

E _____ processing is used where a job is all done at one time rather than in parts .

F _____ allows the computer to work on several programs apparently at the same time.

G A _____ system allows many terminals to access the CPU.

H Each terminal has a certain amount of time allocated to it. This is called _____.

Things to do

1 Real-time processing is being used increasingly because the information is always up-to-date. Batch processing still has advantages for doing certain types of jobs.
(a) What types of jobs are these?
(b) What advantages does batch processing have over real-time processing?
(c) What is meant by the term up-to-date?

2 You go to a travel agency to book a holiday in Spain, travelling by air. The travel agent makes an initial enquiry for you, using the interactive computerised enquiry system.
(a) What input device would you expect to see on his desk?
(b) What is meant by the term 'interactive'.
(c) Why is an interactive system necessary for enquiries?

You decide to make the booking.

(d) Give seven items of data that the airline booking clerk will need before a flight can be booked for you.
(e) The clerk gives you a booking immediately. How can he be certain that the seats will not be double booked?

The booking will be recorded on the airline's backing store.

(f) What type of access is necessary for booking information?
(g) What backing storage would be most appropriate?
(h) Give three reasons why the computerised booking system is more efficient than the previous manual one.

3 For each of the applications given below, state whether the method of processing would be real-time or batch. In each case give one reason for your choice.
(a) A bank cash dispenser which can also give a report of the current balance in a customer's account.
(b) An examination board system for collecting marks from examiners using mark sense forms.
(c) A flood warning system which uses sensors to continually monitor the water level in a river.
(d) The production of bank statements to be sent out to bank customers at the end of the month.
(e) A supermarket POS (point-of-sale) terminal where, when an item is sold, it is automatically deducted from stock.
(f) A central heating control system where each room can be kept at a different constant temperature.
(g) A fast moving arcade type computer game.

10 Data Transfer

It is common in computing to have to transfer data between different software packages and even between different computers. Some years ago you would have had great difficulty in doing this but today it is not too much of a problem.

File conversion

File conversion is an important part of computing. Suppose you are using an existing database system and your files, which have been set up over a period of 10 years, contain several thousand records. To type these in again to a new system might take several months of full-time work. If it is decided that the system needs upgrading then you need to be sure that the new database software will read the files from the old database. This is usually possible if the software is a newer version of the same software. The problem gets more difficult if the original software developer is no longer in business or if you have changed to a different database package. However, all is not lost. Most database, spreadsheet and wordprocessing files can be read by other packages, but it is always important to make sure that any new software you buy can read your old files.

ASCII files

ASCII stands for American Standard Code for Information Interchange and is a code for representing characters (letters, numbers, etc.) as binary codes. All computers can store data as ASCII code and a file used to hold ASCII code is called an ASCII file.

The 8-bit binary codes used to hold the letters of the alphabet are shown in Figure 10.1

Character	ASCII code	Character	ASCII code
A	0100 0001	N	0100 1110
B	0100 0010	O	0100 1111
C	0100 0011	P	0101 0000
D	0100 0100	Q	0101 0001
E	0100 0101	R	0101 0010
F	0100 0110	S	0101 0011
G	0100 0111	T	0101 0100
H	0100 1000	U	0101 0101
I	0100 1001	V	0101 0110
J	0100 1010	W	0101 0111
K	0100 1011	X	0101 1000
L	0100 1100	Y	0101 1001
M	0100 1101	Z	0101 1010

Figure 10.1 *The ASCII codes for the letters of the alphabet*

Other ASCII codes are used for the digits 1, 2, 3, etc. and also for commas and the arithmetical signs (+, –, =, etc.). Even a space has its own ASCII code 0010 0000. Thus to store the word HELLO!, the computer uses an 8-bit binary code for each character. Here is the way the word would be held in the computer's memory.

```
0100 1000  H
0100 0101  E
0100 1100  L
0100 1100  L
0100 1111  O
0010 0001  !
```

QUESTIONS

Show how your full name would be stored using ASCII code. Don't forget to include the ASCII code for the space between your names.

Transferring files between wordprocessors

The most common type of file transfer is between different wordprocessors. Even within large organisations people often use different wordprocessors or different versions of the same wordprocessor so it is essential that they can read each other's files. You may for instance want to send someone some notes through the post. If you send them a disk of wordprocessing files, you could save on postage costs and it will also allow the other person to edit the files. Most wordprocessors, but not all, have a file transfer facility so that, for instance, a Word file could be read by a WordPerfect wordprocessor. The only sure way to transfer text between different wordprocessors is to store everything as ASCII files. When you transfer files of ASCII code the formatting commands (margins, tabs, etc.) and features such as underlining, bold and different fonts are all lost but the body of the text will still be there.

Comma separated variables

One common file format is 'comma separated variables' or CSV for short. The CSV file format is useful because of the ease with which it is possible to transfer files. Files in this format can be read by most spreadsheets and databases.

File handling packages

Backing storage devices such as disk drives are able to store files outside the central processing unit. These files could be program files which hold the series of instructions that enable a computer to perform a useful task or they could be, for example, a file used to hold a drawing you have drawn using a paint package. Most computers now come with very large hard disk drives capable of holding perhaps 10 GB of data. This is a very large amount of data.

Frequently we need to perform file processes such as deleting, copying or merging files. We can do this using operating system commands. Using either of these can be tiresome if we want to, say, delete or copy a large number of files. It is for this reason that special software called file handling packages have been developed. These packages display the file names and enable you to mark the files you want copied or deleted. Because they can save so much time, they are very popular packages. Modern operating systems are excellent at file handling.

Evaluate the process of transferring a piece of text between two different wordprocessing packages. You will have to create a text file using one wordprocessing package and then transfer it to a different one. When you have done this, see if you can transfer a piece of text from one package to the other using ASCII files.

In your evaluation you should mention:
- whether the package was able to read the files directly. If it did not then explain what you had to do to make it read the files
- whether any strange characters appeared in your document and if they did, how you removed them
- whether the text kept the same margins as before and whether each line was joined up to the next
- all the problems and how you overcame them; include a conclusion.

You will need to do the above twice: once for transferring the files from the format of the first wordprocessor to the second and again for transferring from one wordprocessor to the other using ASCII code.

Skills Building

Data/file compression

Suppose you wanted to use a colour scanner to scan a photograph of yourself into your computer. Unless you are lucky enough to have plenty of spare space on your hard disk or one of the newer high capacity disks, which have a huge capacity, then you could run out of storage space when trying to save the photograph. One way around the problem is to use compression software to reduce the size of the picture file. Special software is able to reduce the size of files to about one quarter of their original size.

You may have heard of a zip file. Zip files are often used by magazine publishers when they include a free disk with their magazines. A zip file is one that has been compressed before being put on the disk. One disk is therefore able to hold a much greater number of files, but you need to unzip or decompress the files before they are used.

Program and data files are often compressed before they are sent over the Internet. This cuts down the time taken to transfer a file which also cuts the length of the phone call and hence the cost.

Digital and analogue computers

Data can either be analogue or digital. Digital quantities have values which jump from one to the next without any 'in between' value. An on/off switch on a radio is a device that could be thought of as digital because there is no state between 'on' and 'off'. Some quantities can vary over a whole range of values. Temperature is an example, since it can be 10, 10.1, 10.01, 10.001°C, and so on. In fact, temperatures can be an infinite number of values. Quantities which have an infinite number of values are called analogue quantities. For analogue quantities to be processed by a digital computer they need first to be converted into digital quantities using an analogue to digital converter.

There are two types of computers: digital computers and analogue computers. Most people use digital computers; in fact analogue computers are quite rare. Analogue computers are used mainly for the control of processes in factories and for some forms of modelling.

Digital computers like to be given their information in the form of numbers (i.e. in the form of binary digits). All information eventually has to be turned into groups of binary digits (0s and 1s).

Digital data	Analogue data
The number of cars in a car park	Temperature recorded using a mercury thermometer
Traffic light sequences	Position on a compass dial
Digital watch	Old fashioned watch with hands
Barcode	Room light dimmer switch
Data stored on a magnetic disk	Time read from a sun dial

QUESTIONS

1 Say whether the following devices would be analogue or digital:
   (a) a mercury-in-glass thermometer
   (b) the floor indicator on a lift
   (c) a radio tuning dial
   (d) the display showing the track that is being played on your CD player
   (e) a speedometer on a car.

2 More and more devices which previously had analogue displays, now have digital displays. Why do you think this is?

Figure 10.2 *Sampling a waveform*

Sound sampling

Provided you have a multimedia computer system running the operating systems Windows 95 or 98 and have a microphone, then you can play a recording or a live sound into the sound card of your computer. The sound card listens to the sound and takes a measurement of the height of the signal many times a second. The measurement is called the sound sample.

Sound is an analogue waveform and for a computer to be able to process, store and play it back, it has to be turned into a digital signal. Figure 10.2 shows the waveform of the analogue sound signal being sampled at times t_1, t_2, t_3, etc. At time t_1 the signal lies between 3 and 4, although it is nearer to 4 so it is given the value 4. At time t_2 the signal's sampling level is 3.

The sampling rate is the number of times the sample is measured per second and it is measured in kilohertz (kHz). The higher the sampling rate, the better the sound reproduction. There are implications in having perfect sound: the higher the quality of the sound, the larger the file will be. For a three minute high quality recording the file can be as large as 30 MB.

Analogue to digital conversion (ADC) and vice versa

In chemical factories, the processes used to make chemicals are usually controlled with the help of computers. Often, a batch of chemicals must be kept at a precise temperature. The signal from a temperature sensor is usually a continually changing analogue signal and this must be converted into digital form before it can be processed by a computer. This conversion is done with an analogue–digital converter (ADC). The computer may then control the process by outputting a digital signal, through a digital–analogue converter (DAC) to an electric motor which can open or close a valve.

Modems are used to enable data to be passed from one place to another using communication links (telephone wires, optical cables, radio links, etc.).

A modem (modulator–demodulator) is used to convert the binary digits from a digital computer into an analogue signal that may be passed along ordinary telephone wires. The modem at the other end of the wire converts the analogue signal back into a digital one that the computer is able to understand.

Things to do

1 (a) Briefly describe the difference between analogue and digital data.
   (b) A car fuel injection system counts revolutions to measure the engine speed and uses an electronic sensor to measure the engine temperature.
      (i)   Indicate why the engine speed is the digital signal.
      (ii) What extra piece of equipment does the analogue temperature signal need and what does it do?

2 (a) John is writing a novel and the publisher would like to receive the final copy on disk rather than as hard copy. John already uses a wordprocessor, so this is no problem.
      (i)   What are the advantages to the publisher of receiving his work on disk?
      (ii)   What are the advantages to John of sending his work in on disk?
      (iii) What are the advantages in attaching the file to an e-mail?
   (b) Before the disk is sent, the publisher asks John which wordprocessor he uses. Why is this important to them?

IT TASKS

Task 1

You are working with a friend on a joint project at school and have agreed to split the work between you. You will type half the work and your friend will type the other half. Since you are using the same word-processor, joining the files will not be a problem. Find out and then write instructions so that a complete novice could join the two files together.

IT TASKS

Task 2

Using the *Encarta* Multimedia Encyclopaedia or another similar encyclopaedia you can copy and save tables in text format. For instance there is a table of chemical elements.

Design a system where you can take these tables from an encyclopaedia held on CD-ROM and put them into either a spreadsheet or database. Write a user guide so that a person who knows very little about computing could understand what to do. Let someone else try to copy the tables using your instructions. Can they do it? What improvements do they suggest? Incorporate the improvements into your system.

Ways of Presenting Your Data

There are various ways that we can present computer output. We can present the data:

- as a screen display
- as hard copy, i.e. as printouts on paper (text, pictures, graphs, charts)
- with multimedia presentations (sound, text, pictures, graphs and charts)
- using virtual reality
- using sound.

Hard copy

Printed information is still the main form of computer output. It is used because everybody is a 'subscriber' to the system. We all have letter boxes and know the various processes involved in sending mail. Paper's universal use and acceptability makes it a very difficult system to replace. Nevertheless, there are some disadvantages with paper. With electronic mail, messages can be created, sent and read completely on computers without ever being printed on paper. Many people think that the mail service will never be replaced, but others think that electronic mail will soon replace it. What do you think?

Hard copy (printouts on paper) may gradually be replaced and the reasons for this are:

1 paper is expensive to buy and to store
2 the use of paper encourages people to photocopy it so that they don't lose it
3 many bills, invoices, etc. are preprinted and this is expensive
4 the use of paper is not environmentally friendly
5 moving paper around an organisation takes time.

There are, however, some advantages:

1 with legal documents, it is hard to prove that an electronic letter has been received and seen

2 everyone is able to use a paper based system
3 paper is easier to read than a computer screen
4 it is easier to flick back and forth in a paper document
5 paper can be read on the move and in circumstances where a computer might not be available.

Presentation graphics

Graphics consist of a combination of diagrams, text and charts which are used to make a visual impact when people see them. Graphics may be presented as slides, transparencies to be used with overhead projectors, paper or even as computer displays. Salespersons frequently use screens to display their products or services to potential customers. Some of them now use multimedia.

Multimedia

'Multimedia' is the mixture of text and graphics with motion and sound, including video, audio, animation and photographs. Multimedia is interactive which means that the user can decide on different routes through the software. The images may be controlled either using a mouse or a keyboard. Multimedia is ideal for learning new things because you can control the program to work as slowly or as quickly as you like and it will not tell you off if you get things wrong. In a way, multimedia software can be an ideal teacher. Learning boring topics can be made fun using multimedia. For instance you can learn about decimal points via an adventure called 'Who stole the decimal point?'

A multimedia system consists of an ordinary PC which has several additional devices attached to it. These extra devices typically include a CD-ROM drive or DVD drive, a sound board and speakers. Figure 11.1 shows the arrangement.

Computer aided learning (CAL)

Computers can interact with pupils to enhance the learning process. The development of multimedia has led to a huge growth in the use of computers as an educational tool in the classroom. Computer aided learning can be used to instruct pupils and then test them on what they have learnt.

Speakers   Sound card   CD-ROM (can be internal)

Figure 11.1 *The components of a multimedia system*

Producing multimedia software

You will have seen the wonderful displays, video clips and sounds provided by multimedia software, but how are these packages written? As you can imagine, a lot of equipment is needed to produce really good software. You can prepare your own multimedia software if you have a multimedia authoring package.

Using an encyclopaedia on CD-ROM

The beauty of encyclopaedias on CD-ROM is the small amount of space that they take up. For instance the paper based Grolier Encyclopaedia consists of 21 volumes. The multimedia version occupies a single CD-ROM. It is very quick to search for references, as well. For example, to search for information on 'computers' you simply type in the word and lists of articles that mention computers are displayed on the screen. You can then use your mouse to highlight each article you want to read. If you want a printout of the article then this is easily done.

You are not just restricted to text either. You can look at video clips, with speech, of historic moments such as man's landing on the moon. You can also see animations showing how things work, such as the human heart or the internal combustion engine. Pictures are also included which may be printed out and used to illustrate your project work.

CD-ROM

Without the technology of CD-ROM, multimedia would be impossible because of the large storage capacity needed for photographs, animation and video clips. There are many useful features of CD-ROMs:

1 they are easy to handle and more durable
2 they can be used for multimedia presentations
3 a single CD-ROM can hold around 650 MB of data; hundreds of floppy disks would be needed to store the same amount of data
4 they are environmentally friendly; Friends of the Earth estimate that a single CD-ROM full of text can save up to 15 trees worth of paper
5 they can store text, sound, graphics and video.

Sound

One feature of a multimedia system is the use of speakers. A special sound card contains chips and other circuitry that enable a computer to produce high quality sound. You can then feed the sound through speakers or headphones so that you can play games, look at and hear a variety of information on CD-ROM or just listen to your favourite music on an ordinary CD. Figure 11.1 shows the components of a multimedia system.

MIDI

MIDI stands for musical instrument digital interface. Software and hardware that are designed to MIDI standards are able to send electronic messages to MIDI devices such as keyboards, musical synthesisers and drum machines. You can also use MIDI systems to control specialised devices such as theatrical lighting. An organised series of MIDI commands is called a sequence.

Suppose we connect a keyboard to a computer using a special MIDI interface. The frequency, pitch and other musical information is converted to digital information which can be read by the computer. Music played on the keyboard can therefore be stored on the computer, and because the computer is able to produce digital signals it can send signals back to the keyboard.

Virtual reality

You may have seen pictures of children wearing headsets and gloves wired up to a computer and wondered what they are. This is the world of virtual reality.

A lot of research in virtual reality is directed towards military uses. Virtual reality can be used to recreate a terrain where fighting is likely to take place. To a soldier wearing a headset and gloves the battle situation can be as near to the real thing as possible.

Many other uses for virtual reality systems are being developed. One example is possible use for simulating traffic accidents for use in court. If a witness says that they saw an accident then the court can be shown exactly what the witness would have seen from a particular position on the road.

Figure 11.2 shows the headset and gloves in a virtual reality system.

Figure 11.2 *Part of a virtual reality system*

TEST YOURSELF

Using the words in the list below, copy out and complete sentences A to F, underlining the words you have inserted. The words may be used more than once.

hard copy   electronic mail   multimedia

transparency   sound card   posted

A Output from a computer on paper is often referred to as _____ ____.

B Printouts have the advantage that they can be _____.

C The service that involves passing electronic messages from one computer to another is called _____ _____.

D Graphics may be produced using a computer and then printed out on a _____ to be viewed using an overhead projector.

E A mixture of text and graphics with motion and sound is an example of _____.

F To use multimedia on a PC you need to insert a special circuit board called a _____ _____ in order to produce sound.

Things to do

1 Friends of your family have young children and already have a computer with a large amount of memory and a large hard disk drive.

The friends have heard about multimedia and think that it may be able to help their children with their schooling. In particular they would like to use a couple of encyclopaedias to help the children do project work.
  (a) What additional equipment would they need to add to their computer to make it able to be used for multimedia?
  (b) They do not know much about multimedia. Write a short paragraph explaining briefly what its capabilities are.
  (c) Give three features of an encyclopaedia held on CD-ROM that would help the children with their project work.
  (d) Recommend a couple of titles of encyclopaedias that might be of use to the family.

2 Presentations are often used in businesses to sell companies' products.
  (a) Explain what a presentation is.
  (b) What equipment could be used in such a presentation?
  (c) Presentation packages are available that produce slides and overhead projector transparencies. Give the name of a package that you could use for a presentation and give some idea of the features it has.

3 Output from computers can be presented in many different ways.
  (a) Software to log data in a science laboratory can present data on a screen or as hard copy. State one advantage and one disadvantage of these two methods.
  (b) In publishing systems, it is necessary to combine text and various forms of graphics.
    (i) Why is it often necessary to import graphics files into a DTP package?
    (ii) Why is it becoming increasingly easy to do this?

(NEAB/WJEC Option Q)

IT TASKS

Task 1

You have been asked by the teacher responsible for health education, to produce a group presentation for first and second year senior school pupils on current health issues. Since you are working with a group you will need to select a group coordinator who will divide the various tasks up between the group members. You can use any computer equipment at your disposal.

Some of the issues you could look at are:

- drugs
- personal hygiene
- alcohol abuse
- sex.

After the presentation, you should jointly produce a report on the way you used IT to help with this task and the reasons for your choice of the software used.

How to Describe an Information System

Describing systems

A system is a group of connected operations or things. We can describe systems in various ways. Often we can describe them in terms of inputs, processes and outputs (see Chapter 1). Figure 12.1 shows the simplest system.

Figure 12.1 *The three steps involved in the processing of data*

A diagram like this doesn't really tell us too much, so we could draw a diagram like that in Figure 12.2, which tells us a little more. Don't be afraid of drawing your own diagrams like this to describe your systems. These diagrams do their job well because everyone understands them and they help you to think about the problem as you are drawing the diagram. Don't try drawing a diagram in one go: instead try to concentrate on one aspect or part of the system. You can always draw several diagrams and then join them together to obtain an overall picture.

Structure diagrams

Structure diagrams can be used to describe information systems. An overall task is broken down into smaller more manageable tasks. These may then be broken down further into smaller tasks. This way of describing tasks is described as the 'top down' approach.

The top down approach

Let's take a look at drawing a structure diagram for a task we are probably all familiar with: doing the weekly shopping.

Figure 12.2 *A video library system*

First we place the overall task at the top and we write a brief description of the overall task in the box (i.e. doing the weekly shopping) (Figure 12.3).

Figure 12.3

This task is then divided up into a series of tasks required to do the main task. For instance, to do the shopping we may have to:

- prepare a shopping list
- do the shopping
- put the shopping away.

So we now have the structure shown in Figure 12.4.

Figure 12.4

Again this second set of tasks may be split up as shown in Figure 12.5.

| Check cupboards | Look in fridge | Write down items needed | Drive to shops | Select items | Pay for items | Unpack shopping | Put some food in fridge | Put some food in cupboard |

We write these in the order in which they are performed ⟶

▲
Figure 12.5

We can now put all the stages together to produce the final structure chart as shown in Figure 12.6. When drawing structure diagrams, don't worry that yours looks different from other people's. They are rarely the same.

As you can see, the purpose of a structure diagram is to show the tasks in more detail as you move down. The top box is the overall view (doing the weekly shopping), and hence the term 'top down approach'. You could carry on breaking each task down, but there comes a point where you have broken the tasks down into enough detail.

We write these in the order in which they are performed ⟶

▲
Figure 12.6 *A structure diagram for doing the weekly shopping.*

QUESTIONS

1 Pick one of the following tasks (preferably the one you are most familiar with) and draw a structure diagram for it:
 (a) renting a video from a video shop
 (b) borrowing a book from your local library
 (c) programming your video recorder to record a programme
 (d) getting ready to go for a night out
 (e) washing the dishes.

2 Draw a structure diagram for making a roast dinner with turkey, roast potatoes, carrots, sprouts and gravy. Figure 12.7 shows the top part of the diagram to start you off.

▲
Figure 12.7 *The start of a structure diagram to make a roast dinner*

Data flow diagrams

Data flow diagrams are used to consider the data without bothering about the equipment used to store it and are used as a first step in describing a system. Four symbols are used in these diagrams and these are described overleaf.

The box

The box is either a source of data, such as an order form from a customer, or a part of the system which uses or consumes the data, called a sink. We are not concerned with what happens to the data before it reaches the box if it is a source, or what happens to it after it goes past a sink.

The sausage

The sausage shape is sometimes replaced by a circle on some data flow diagrams and is used to denote a process performed on the data. A process is something which is done to the data like a calculation. The process might be sorting the data or combining it with some other data. A brief description of the process should be placed inside the box.

The open rectangle

The open rectangle represents a data store. This is where the data is held. It could represent the data being held manually or on a computer. Basically, a data store is a logical collection of data. A description of the store can be placed inside the box.

The arrows

The arrows are used to show how the other symbols are connected.

Let's now draw a series of data flow diagrams for a system for a video library. The first diagram follows the data flow that takes place when a new member joins the library. To join the library it is necessary to fill in an application form and to show certain documents to provide proof of identity. If the potential member does not have this documentation, then the library manager will refuse membership. After the membership details have been checked (or validated) a membership card is produced and given to the new member and the member's details are recorded. If the member borrows a video or if the manager wants to know whether a particular person is a member, then the details can be found. Figure 12.8 shows the data flow diagram for this part of the system.

Now we can look at the data flow diagram for a video being added to the library. This is a simple system, with the details of the video,

Figure 12.8 *A data flow diagram for a video library*

such as name, price, etc. being recorded and then stored. Figure 12.9 shows this part of the system.

Figure 12.10 shows the data flow diagram for the process of borrowing a video. Notice that the member data and video data are needed because the loans store of data will only contain the video number and the membership number. This is done to save space. By storing the video and member number together it is possible to find out a member's details and the video details if they are needed.

We could, if we wanted to get an overall view of the system, join these diagrams together but it is much easier to draw them for each part of the system and then to draw a diagram with them all joined.

Figure 12.9 *The data flow diagram for adding a new video to the library*

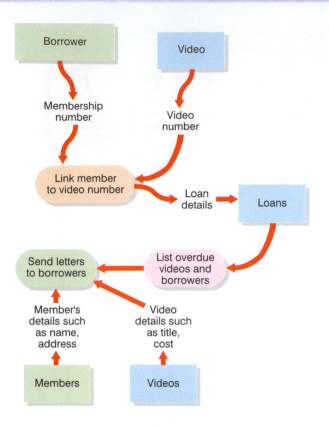

Figure 12.10 *The data flow diagram for borrowing a video*

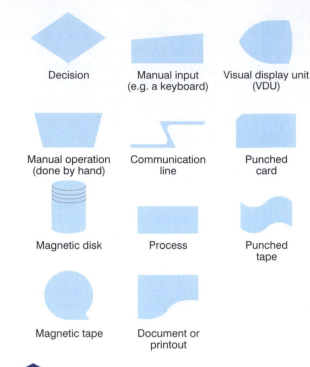

Figure 12.11 *Symbols used in systems flowcharts*

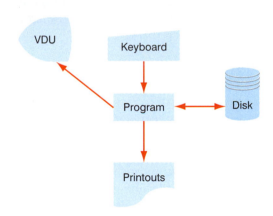

Figure 12.12 *Systems flowchart for a simple database system*

QUESTIONS

Your form teacher marks the register twice a day. Find out what happens to these attendance marks and draw a data flow diagram for the system.

Systems flowcharts

A systems flowchart is a diagram which gives an overall view of a system. It shows the tasks that are performed on the data, such as sorting or updating and also shows the type of media (magnetic disk, tape, etc.) used to hold the data. Figure 12.11 shows some of the usual symbols. The flow is always indicated by arrows. A tape will always have an arrow going into it or coming out of it, but a disk may have one in either direction or both.

For a small database system using a single computer, the systems flowchart shown in Figure 12.12 is very simple.

Notice the following:

- There is a double arrow going between the disk drive. This shows that data can be read into the computer and written to the disk drive.
- There are two ways of outputting the information, either on a VDU or as a printout (often called hard copy).

Systems flowchart for producing gas/electricity bills

The production of gas/electricity bills is an example of batch processing. Look back at Chapter 9 to see the steps involved in producing an electricity bill. Electricity companies each have millions of customers, so they use large mainframe computers. These usually consist of a separate processor or processors, backing storage devices such as tape or disk drives and terminals.

Figure 12.13 shows the stages involved in producing the bills. The diagram itself is fairly easy to understand. Because every customer gets a bill and there are so many customers, batch processing is used, with magnetic tape as the storage medium. The transaction file

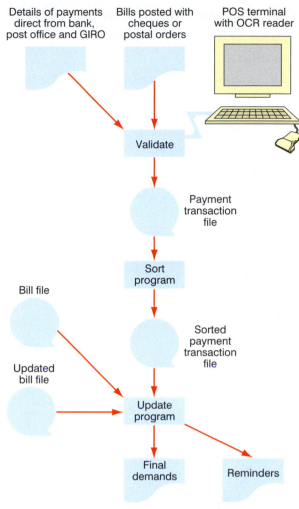

Figure 12.14 *Systems flowchart for processing the bills file*

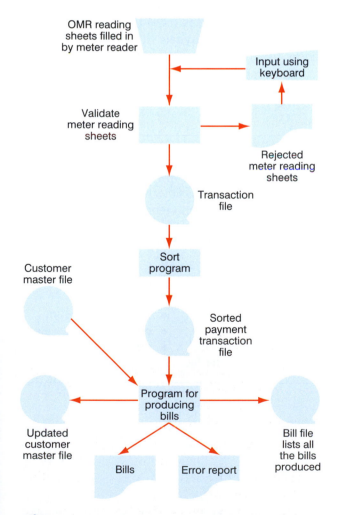

Figure 12.13 *Systems flowchart for producing gas/electricity bills*

containing all the meter readings has to be sorted into the same order as the customer master file, otherwise the processing would be very slow, because tapes would need to be wound backwards and forwards until the records matched. The bills file, also on magnetic tape, contains details of the amounts owed by the customers and this will need updating as the customers pay their bills. Figure 12.14 shows the systems flowchart for processing the bills file. Notice that there are several ways of making the payments and the payments must be validated before being recorded on the transaction file. The update program is used to produce reminders and final demands to the people who haven't yet paid their bills.

Systems flowchart for a payroll system which uses batch processing

The following system is used to produce the weekly wages for a large number of staff who work in a factory.

Each employee is given a clock card at the start of each week which contains the employee's name and works number. This card is placed into a special clock which records their arrival and departure time, and the date. For a complete five day week, there will be 20 times recorded onto the card. The process of recording the times is called clocking in and clocking out.

The machine punches holes into the card to record each time and these cards can be placed directly into a machine which is able to read this coded data. The data is transferred directly to a transaction file, which may be on either magnetic tape or disk. The transaction file is validated and then sorted into employee works number order. Details of incomplete clock cards (e.g. from someone who has forgotten to clock out) will be output as a list called an error report. These clock cards will need to be dealt with by a separate system. A disk file is used to hold details regarding an employee's hourly rate, tax code, taxable pay to date, etc.

The systems flowchart used to represent the above system is shown in Figure 12.15.

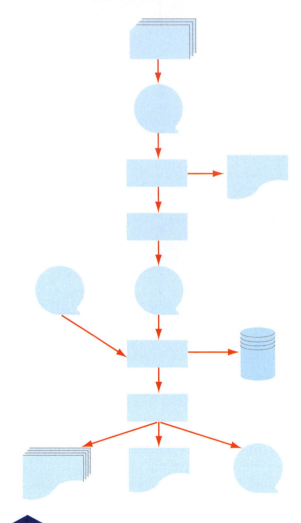

Figure 12.15 *A systems flowchart for a payroll system that uses batch processing*

1 The following system is used to update the files for payments received from customers by a small firm. Customers send their payments to the firm's offices, where the details are entered into the computer using key-to-disk. These entries form the payments transaction file. After validation, the records are output to a second disk file. Any errors are corrected and re-input. The valid fields are then sorted and used with the customer master file to produce an updated file and a list of people who still owe money.

(a) Insert the letter for the correct expression into each space in the systems flowchart in Figure 12.16.

A   sort payments records into customer account number order
B   old customer file
C   updated customer file
D   error report
E   error report
F   validated payments transaction file
G   payments transaction file
H   payment records
I   corrected payments records
J   correct errors
K   update
L   sorted valid payments transaction file
M   list of people who owe money
N   validation

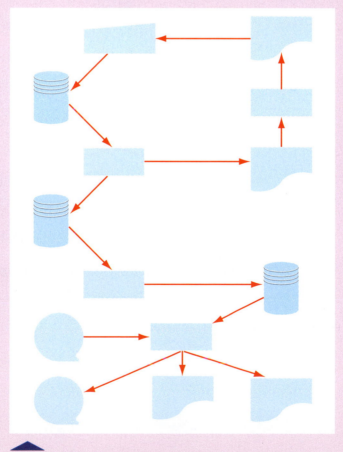

Figure 12.16 *Systems flowchart for payments update*

(b) Why is the payment transaction file sorted to customer account number order?

(c) If the customers do not send part of the bill back when they are paying, which one piece of information is needed before the payment may be processed?

(d) What name is given to the field that contains that piece of information?

(e) Three days after paying her bill, a customer received a request for payment. Why has this happened?

(f) The flowchart shows three disk files and two magnetic tape files in use. Which file will become the new son file?

(g) Which file will be the new father file?

(h) After which two stages are errors found?

(i) Name the three files which must be kept for security reasons.

2 The systems flowchart shown in Figure 12.17 shows the process of updating the master file at the DVLA (Driver and Vehicle Licensing Authority) using a transaction file.

(a) Explain why it is necessary to sort the transaction file.

(b) There are three different types of processes which are undertaken during an update. Name these three processes.

(c) Give two examples of errors that could occur during updating and which might be included in the error report.

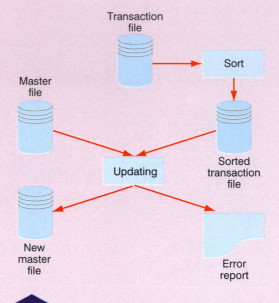

Figure 12.17 *Updating a master file at the DVLA*

Systems Analysis
Sounds Hard: What is it?

In this chapter we are going to find out what systems analysis is by looking at how we would perform one for a company called Harlequin Aquatics. The initial background to the company is given below.

Harlequin Aquatics

Harlequin Aquatics is a company involved in the selling of fish-keeping equipment to the public. Most of the company's business comes from a catalogue which is distributed with the monthly fish keeping magazines. The customers select the items from the catalogue and either fill in the order form (Figure 13.1) at the back of the catalogue or, if they need the equipment very quickly (which is often the case), they ring up quoting their credit card number and the goods they require. The goods can be selected from the warehouse and dispatched to the customer. As well as the mail order business situated at the head office in Liverpool there are five smaller shops situated in Chester, Manchester, York, Leeds and Birmingham. These shops do not get involved in the mail order side of the business, except when they have goods which are out of stock in the main warehouse. At present all the tasks in the company are being performed manually and, although the company is very profitable, the directors realise that it has become very inefficient.

As a first step the directors wish to streamline the most profitable part of the company situated at the head office and main distribution centre in Liverpool. At the moment there are five telesales staff who take the orders over the phone and deal with occasional fax orders. There are also three other staff who deal with the orders through the post.

As soon as an order is received it is typed on a form which contains an order number. This form is in three parts: one to be sent to the warehouse, one to the accounts office and one to be sent to the customer with the goods.

The company bases its success on the fact that orders can be dealt with promptly (within 24 hours if the customer is prepared to pay for express delivery) but lately, with the volume of orders, this has become increasingly difficult to achieve. Increased competition has meant that a price war has started, with each company promising to beat each other's prices. This has meant that Harlequin Aquatics needs to be more efficient. The increase in orders has prompted the directors to look at the possibility of employing more staff, but they have now decided that they will try to deal with the greater volume of orders with the same number of staff as before. They are now looking to computerise the business and have recruited you as an outside consultant to investigate the possibilities for their business.

At present the head office of the company is located in an old converted church (used as the shop and the warehouse for the distribution of the mail order goods) with a small new office block of three storeys at the back.

Figure 13.1 *An order form for Harlequin Aquatics*

In this chapter we will look at the steps involved in systems analysis. Harlequin Aquatics has not used a computer system before so the company can start a new system from scratch. The steps involved in systems analysis are:

- fact finding
- a feasibility study
- an analysis phase
- system design
- implementation
- testing
- documentation
- evaluation.

We will look at what each of the above entails.

Fact finding

Fact finding is concerned with finding about the existing system. It may be that computers are already used but not to their full extent or it may be that a manual system exists which needs computerising. In either case, we need to find out how things are done at the moment, before we can suggest any improvements.

There are four main ways of finding out about existing systems, these are:

1 asking questions (interviewing people)
2 getting people to fill in carefully designed questionnaires
3 sitting with various people to observe how the job is done at the moment
4 inspecting any bits of paper, screen displays and files which are used in the present system.

The final step in fact finding is to produce a report which describes the existing system and its shortcomings, together with some description of the output needed from the new system.

Feasibility study

The feasibility study looks at the chances of being able to solve a particular problem at a reasonable cost. The feasibility report is the

QUESTIONS

1 Have another read of the scenario on Harlequin Aquatics. You are going to carry out a systems analysis on this company.

Imagine you have just received instructions to go and investigate their present system. You have no other background information apart from the scenario.

(a) Prepare a questionnaire which you could get the company to fill in before you arrange an interview. Your questionnaire should be general to start with but then go on to ask more details later. Prepare this using suitable software.

(b) After receiving back the questionnaire you decide to arrange a visit. Write a list of questions you would ask in the light of the results of your questionnaire. Try to not ask too many questions that are simply answered yes or no but ask open ended questions such as 'can you tell me what problems you have had with the existing system?'

2 One part of the fact finding process is to collect the various pieces of paper used in the business and then examine them. Read the scenario again and decide which pieces of paper you would like to examine.

document produced at the end of the study and will give an idea of the time the project is likely to take, along with some estimate of cost. The aim of the feasibility study is to see whether it is possible to devise a system that can be implemented and will work at reasonable cost.

The feasibility study ends when a decision has been reached whether or not to proceed with the project.

The following are usually included in a feasibility study:

1 a description of what the system is required to do (called the objectives of the system); Figure 13.2 shows some of the objectives for the Harlequin Aquatics' system
2 some preliminary design so that the costs may be estimated

3 some alternative designs so that the most suitable one can be chosen

4 a cost/benefit analysis; this looks at the benefits and makes sure that they outweigh the costs. The costs of a system are not just the costs of the hardware and the software needed. Figure 13.3 shows some of the costs you might not have thought of

5 the conclusion, which states whether it is worth going ahead with the project and which design has been chosen.

5 the human, technical and economic factors:
   - do the staff have the expertise to cope with the new system?
   - is the technology available, i.e. can it be done?
   - is there enough money to go ahead?

6 a plan for the implementation

7 a proposed course of action (i.e. what the consultant/systems analyst suggests the company should do next).

Figure 13.2 *Some of the objectives of a system for Harlequin Aquatics*

The feasibility report

The feasibility report is a written report given to the directors of Harlequin Aquatics and is really a summary of the results of the feasibility study. Usually the report is written but it can also be given in the form of a spoken presentation.

The feasibility report should include the following:

1 a brief description of the business and any problems with the existing system

2 details of what part of the business is being looked at; for instance with Harlequin we are looking at the processing of orders

3 the objectives of the proposed system

4 a list of some of the alternative solutions considered and why these alternatives were rejected

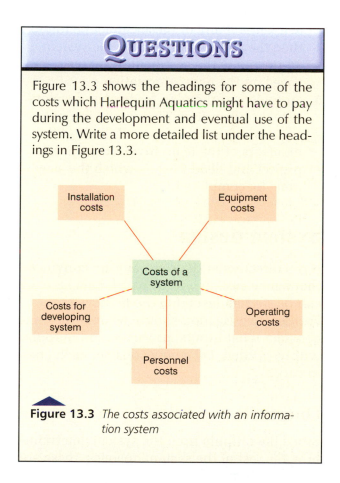

QUESTIONS

Figure 13.3 shows the headings for some of the costs which Harlequin Aquatics might have to pay during the development and eventual use of the system. Write a more detailed list under the headings in Figure 13.3.

Figure 13.3 *The costs associated with an information system*

Analysis phase

The feasibility study outlines what is required from the system and in the analysis phase this study is used to design the new system. To perform the analysis, the systems analyst will need to look at the system in greater detail than for the feasibility study. When the present system is investigated, the systems analyst will find more weaknesses in it.

In the analysis phase, the charts (systems flowcharts and data flow diagrams) should be drawn as an aid to understanding the present system.

Included in the analysis phase are:

1 detailed objectives of the proposed system
2 facts about the parts of the old system being replaced by the new system
3 any constraints on the system: these are limitations on the solution to the problem. Many problems can be solved if the money, technical expertise and time are available. If any of these cannot be found, then they are constraints on the system
4 an update of the cost/benefit analysis based on the new information
5 an update of the plan for further development of the system. This would include such things as the responsibilities of the members of the team involved with the project and deadlines by which the stages must be completed.

System design

If the directors of the company are convinced that a new system will be worth having, work can be started designing the new system. Further investigation should be undertaken to consider what inputs, processes and outputs will be needed. Let's now consider each one in turn:

Outputs

Since the outputs from the system determine how the rest of the system operates, these are looked at first.

We need to look at each of the following areas.

1 What output is needed? For instance, we may decide that for our system we need the following:
   - an invoice (bill) which is sent out to each customer
   - a copy of the invoice to be sent to the accounts office
   - a dispatch note to be sent with the goods
   - a picking list for the storekeeper
   - a screen display so that we can find out if a particular item is in stock.
2 We must then look at what needs to be on these documents and screens. We may be able to use the same document for different processes. In this way we could make several copies of the invoice using multi-part stationery and give one each to the customer, warehouse and accounts office.
3 How frequently do these documents need producing? For instance we may need a list of all the stock at the end of each day or a list of all the past customers just once a year when there is a sale on.
4 What is the volume of output? How many orders are dealt with each day? How many items are on each order? All of these determine the type of system we need to use and the input method chosen. If lots of orders are dealt with, methods other than keying need to be looked at.

Inputs

Questions the systems analyst will need to answer are as follows:

1 Where does the data come from? In our company the orders come in a variety of ways. They are placed on an order form and posted, or they may be telephoned or faxed.
2 What data needs to be input into the system? This would include catalogue numbers, descriptions, prices, quantities, etc.
3 How much data needs to be entered and how often it needs entering? For our company, it would be useful to determine how many orders were received in a day, what was the number of items on each order and so on. To determine the sizes of files we need to find out how many customers the company has and how many items there are in the catalogue.
4 Which input device should be chosen? This really depends on the volume of data and whether any of the data can be captured using OMR, OCR, barcoding, etc.

The systems analyst will also need to look at the design of the input screen, which should preferably match the design of the order forms.

Data preparation

Data preparation involves getting the raw data into a form that can be processed by the computer. Verification and validation are included in data preparation. Verification makes sure that, if a keyboard is being used, no typing mistakes have been made. Various validation methods can be used to trap some of the errors. Remember that validation is performed by a computer program.

Code design

We can use codes to save time typing and also save storage space. Codes need to be carefully designed if they are to be useful.

File design

We need to decide how many files are needed and then to design the structure of each of the files. To understand how this is done look at Chapter 8 on databases. When designing files we should make sure that we do not duplicate any of the information.

Hardware configuration

If more than one computer is used, it makes sense to network them. Harlequin Aquatics needs a network, since paper would then not need to be transferred between the sales office and the other areas such as accounts and the warehouse. Hardware configuration also includes deciding on the type of computer, and on peripheral devices such as disk drives, printers, etc.

Software used

We first need to decide what software to use. We could hire someone to write it specially which is very expensive. Alternatively, we could use a software package. For Harlequin we would use a database package. There are many database packages available and each would need to be evaluated. Once the application package has been chosen we then need to look at the operating system it requires.

Testing the system

Before it is introduced the new system must be thoroughly tested. The testing of a system may be broken down into five stages.

1 The system is tested with data that contains no errors to see if it produces the correct results.
2 Known errors are now introduced into the data to see how the computer will process it. Ideally all the errors will be picked up by any validation procedures but we must remember that it is impossible for the computer to detect all types of error.
3 We now start trying to process very large amounts of data to see how the system copes with this. This is really to see how the system copes with extra work that might be necessary in the future.
4 Some processing is only done now and again. For instance, we might need a stock report at the end of a month so this will need to be fully tested.
5 Extreme data should be entered to make sure that the range checks included in the validation program will work.

If all goes well, we move onto the next stage which is the implementation of the system.

Implementing (or introducing) the new system

How you implement a new system really depends on its size. Solutions range from a microcomputer or two, to a system that uses a number of networked PCs or even a system based on larger computers.

Systems may be introduced into an organisation in three ways and we will look at each of these in turn.

Direct implementation

With direct implementation the users decide to start using the system on a given date. In practice, this method is only used for small computer systems since in larger ones problems reveal themselves during the first month and the result can be havoc. Usually the number of computing staff is quite small compared with the administrative staff, so if too many problems occur then they will be unable to cope.

Phased implementation

With phased implementation, each job is introduced separately rather than all jobs being introduced in one go, as with the previous method. For instance we may decide to look at the order processing first and get this running before we deal with other areas of the business. One snag with this method is that it takes much longer and the benefits of the new system are delayed.

Parallel running

With parallel running, the new system is run alongside the existing system. If the new system fails, then because we still have the old system, we can use that until the problems are sorted out. Parallel running provides an ideal opportunity to compare the results from the new system with those of the old system, since both systems will be in operation at the same time. However, it does have the serious disadvantage that since each job is done twice, there is much more work for users while the two systems are running in parallel. (Figure 13.4.)

Documentation

Documentation is of two types: user and technical.

User documentation (or user guide)

A user guide or manual is documentation that the user can turn to for learning a new procedure or for dealing with a problem that has arisen. The guide should cover such things as how to load the software, how to perform certain functions, how to save and how to print. It is a good idea to include examples and exercises to help the user understand the system. Since users are usually non-technical, any specialist, technical language should be avoided.

The guide should detail what to do in exceptional circumstances. For instance if the system fails to read a disk or data is sent to the printer without it being switched on and the machine is locked, a user will need to know what they have to do.

As always, users have the best view of a system and so should be asked to evaluate any proposed user guide. Their comments should be incorporated into the guide. You have probably tried to find things in manuals so you will realise just how important they are.

Figure 13.4 *Parallel running*

Technical documentation

Technical documentation is used to explain a system to a specialist, either a programmer or a systems analyst. Since these people understand computer jargon this guide does not need to be as simple as the user guide. This documentation is extremely important since it might be used by someone new to the project and there may be no one around who was involved with the original project.

Changes always need to be made to a system at a later date so this documentation will be needed when the system is improved or upgraded.

System evaluation

After a project has been implemented it should be reviewed periodically to make sure that it is still meeting its objectives.

A good way of evaluating a solution is to ask the users of the system. They will be able to tell you if a system does what they originally wanted or if there are any improvements needed.

There are always constraints placed on the system and these might include time, money and the lack of qualified staff involved in the project. Hence the solution has some limitations placed on it. Perhaps with Harlequin Aquatics a wide area network could be used to link all the shops to the head office but the cost or lack of technically qualified people to look after it would prevent its use. Such a system could be considered in the future if Harlequin Aquatics has more money and when the staff are more familiar with computers.

TEST YOURSELF

Using the words in the list below, copy out and complete sentences A to K, underlining the words you have inserted. The words may be used more than once.

output   fact find   systems analyst   parallel

documentation   analysis   feasibility study

trained   evaluated   design   feasibility report

A A _____ _____ is the person who looks at the manual system to see which parts to computerise.

B She looks at the manual system in terms of three stages: input, process and _____.

C To begin with, she will perform a ____ _____ in order to find out a variety of facts about the business.

D Going on from this, she will then perform a _____ _____ which will then look at whether an alternative system would be feasible.

E When she has completed this, she will submit a _____ _____ to the directors of the company.

F If the directors are happy with the report, they will give the go-ahead for the system and the analyst can start to _____ the system.

G Detailed systems _____ then follows where outputs, inputs, files, software, etc. are all decided.

H The personnel involved with the new system will need to be _____.

I Also, _____ will need to be written.

J There are three ways that a system can be implemented: _____ running, phased implementation and direct implementation.

K After a system has been in use for some time, it needs to be _____ to make sure that the objectives of the system are still being satisfied.

1 John, the head of mathematics at a large comprehensive school, decided to take early retirement and start up a tutorial agency matching tutors to students. He advertises nationally for both tutors and students. He does the marketing and advertising while his wife deals with all the paperwork. The business has been a huge success but the amount of paperwork now generated is getting them both down. They are using a manual system at present but would like a new computerised system.

 (a) The head of information technology at his old school suggests that they need to perform a feasibility study which will cover hardware, software, staffing and operating costs. Explain why such a study will help John and his wife select the best system.

 (b) Explain the steps involved in a feasibility study.

 (c) John and his wife have now performed a feasibility study and have decided to buy a Pentium computer with a 1000 MB hard disk and a tape streamer. They have also chosen a laser printer. Explain how they might go about choosing the correct supplier for this equipment.

 (d) Once they have decided on a system, how should they go about getting their new system up and running?

2 A rail company uses an on-line system for reserving train seats. Documentation has been written for various users of the system. For each of the users below, explain what should be in the documentation.

 (a) A reservations clerk.

 (b) A senior supervisor.

 (c) A systems analyst, who has to maintain the system.

(SEG IT IS)

3 One stage in systems analysis is called fact finding, where the person performing the task, usually a systems analyst, will need to determine answers to a wide range of questions.

 You have been asked to find out about an estate agent's system. The estate agent operates 20 agencies in a particular city and its surrounding suburbs. One of the larger shops acts as the head office.

 (a) Write down at least 30 facts that you would need to find out about the estate agent's business in order to be able to advise the company on a suitable system.

 (b) You are worried that you might encounter some opposition to the introduction of a new system. What can be done to ensure full co-operation from all staff?

IT TASKS

Task 1

You have been asked by the owner of a video library to investigate its present manual system because they are thinking of computerising it. The video library has only one shop and about 1800 customers and 2000 videos. Prepare a list of questions in order to perform an initial fact find before a feasibility study.

IT TASKS

Task 2

Harlequin Aquatics has decided to place stock details on the computer. A section of the catalogue is shown below.

(a) Look at the section of the catalogue, which is only approximately one hundredth of the whole catalogue. Think carefully about the uses to which the stock file will be put and decide what fields are needed. You will also need to decide on the type of field (numeric, character, date, logical, etc.). Now design the database structure for creating a stock file.

(b) A customer rings up and says 'can you let me know what internal filters you have in stock and what prices they are?' Could you answer this, bearing in mind that internal filters are just a small section in the total stock. If you can't, you will need to make some alterations in your stock file design. You could use a coding system to distinguish between the different sections.

(c) When you are happy with your structure, you can start putting the data into your database using the data in the above list and some data which you will need to supply yourself.

(d) Obtain a copy of a fish-keeping magazine and have a look at some of the advertisements. Using the information from these advertisements, fill in your stock file until it contains 30 records.

(e) Give examples of reports (lists and results of searches and sorts) that you can get from your stock file.

(f) Finally evaluate your system. Does it do what you intended and what shortcomings does it have?

Internal Filters

Catalogue number	Description of item	Price
52773	Rena Filty Internal Filter	£11.99
52774	Rena 225 Internal Filter	£15.25
52775	Rena 245 Internal Filter	£22.75
52776	Rena 245S Internal Filter	£22.75
52777	Rena 325 Internal Filter	£25.99
52778	Eheim 2252-200 L.P.H.	£64.99
52779	Eheim 2248-600 L.P.H.	£45.95
52780	Eheim 2209-80 L.P.H. inc media	£26.95
52781	Eheim 2207-180 L.P.H.	£16.25
52782	Fluval 1 180 L.P.H.	£ 8.99
52783	Fluval 2 360 L.P.H.	£10.99
52784	Fluval 3 540 L.P.H.	£14.99
52785	Fluval 4 900 L.P.H.	£19.99
52786	Visijet IF 100-400 L.P.H.	£22.99
52787	Visijet IF 200-600 L.P.H.	£27.99

Part of the Harlequin Aquatics stock list

IT TASKS

Task 3

You have been asked to build an information system for your school library from scratch. This is a substantial task and to perform it you will need to go through the various steps involved in systems analysis.

Some of the tasks you will need to perform include the following.

(a) You need to carry out a fact find of the manual system, which should include use of questionnaires and involve an interview with the library staff. Any forms, file cards and other documentation should be included in your initial report on the existing system.
   You need to get an overall view of the existing library system in terms of the number of books, the number of borrowers, the number of loans per day/week, the average number of books per borrower, etc. You will need to find out how books are catalogued according to subject or author and how the reminder system for overdue books works. At the end of this analysis you should be able to identify the strengths and weaknesses of the existing system.

(b) You will need to design a system. To do this you will need to look at the objectives of the system. You will then need to look at which software, hardware and peripherals should be used. In addition you will need to design input and output screens, database structures and any printouts needed.

(c) A pilot implementation should be done to check whether the system is likely to work. Any likely training implications should be identified and finally an evaluation of the pilot should be undertaken.

(d) Some idea of the cost of the full implementation and the timescale should be given.

(e) A full-scale library system should be investigated like the one used by your local library and it should be compared and contrasted with the suggested system for your school library.

Weather Forecasting
An Application of Data Logging

Weather reporting: the old way

Figure 14.1 shows a typical school weather station. It consists of a slatted box, called a Stevenson's screen, in which are held certain instruments such as thermometer, maximum and minimum thermometer, and wet and dry bulb thermometer (used to measure the amount of humidity). Outside the box are a rainfall meter, used to measure in millimetres the amount of rainfall, and an anemometer which is used to measure the wind speed. A sunshine recorder reports on the number of hours of sunshine in the day.

Collecting the data

The readings are taken by the pupils in the morning immediately before school starts. Two pupils take the readings and they fill in a form with the relevant data.

QUESTIONS

Design a form that could be used to obtain the weather data over a week. This form will eventually be used by the pupils in maths and geography lessons.

Before you design the form think about what the requirements of the form should be. It would be better if all the data for one month could be placed on a single piece of A4 paper. Are there any other requirements?

The geography teacher decides that she would like more frequent readings made. Julie and John who have to take the readings are not very keen on this idea. Although they find collecting the data interesting they don't find it that interesting!

Another problem is that readings are unavailable over the weekend and if both pupils are away from school on the same day, then no readings are taken for that day. Also, the equipment is not read over the summer holidays. Overall, the weather data collected is incomplete.

Problem

Ideally, the geography teacher would like the following:

1. complete records of weather data over 365 days of the year (even Christmas day!)
2. more frequent measurements (say four times a day)

3 greater accuracy of readings (sometimes the instruments are read incorrectly).

The maths teacher who has been illustrating the use of statistics with the data would like:

1 computer printouts of weather patterns over various periods of time
2 to be able to use a computer package to draw the various graphs.

The solution

Some way is needed of recording the data at set intervals, automatically. This will solve the problems outlined above. If the equipment could transfer the data directly to a computer without necessarily being connected to the computer all of the time, this would be another advantage. A data logging system would be an ideal choice for this system.

Data logging

A data logging system automatically collects data over a certain period of time. As well as being able to alter this time, you can alter the frequency with which the measurements are made. Since there is no human error, the measurements will be more accurate than before.

Weather reporting

Weather reporting is an application of data logging. Data logging involves recording quantities automatically over a set period of time. For weather reporting, these quantities are illustrated in Figure 14.2.

Most data loggers do not need to be connected to a computer all the time. Instead they store the data in the logger for a period (50 hours for one particular package). It is also possible to display the data continuously, but this ties up a computer and prevents it being used for other things. Figure 14.3 shows an automatic data logging weather station with its various sensors.

Figure 14.2 *For weather reporting, information about all of these needs to be recorded*

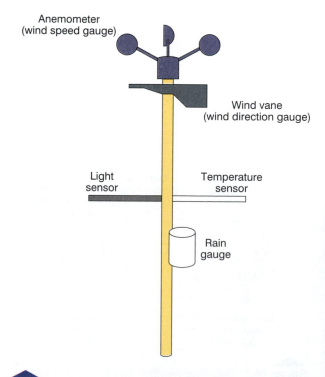

Figure 14.3 *An automatic data logging weather station*

The sensors

Sensors act as the input devices into the computer. Figure 14.4 shows the detailed arrangement of the components of the Weather Reporter, a fully automatic data-logging weather station (see page 342). The sensors measure the following:

Temperature

The temperature sensor gives an analogue temperature signal which is converted via an analogue-to-digital converter to a digital signal, which is then stored by the microprocessor.

Wind speed

An anemometer measures wind speed by using an optical sensor to generate a binary signal each time it rotates. The wind speed is recorded in kilometres per hour.

Figure 14.4 *Arrangement of the components in the 'Weather Reporter'*

Wind direction

The wind direction is detected on a grey code disk. As the wind vane rotates, three optical sensors read the disk and generate a three bit binary pattern. Each pattern represents one of the eight wind directions. For instance the pattern 010 might represent north-west.

Rainfall

Rainfall is measured using a tilting bucket. As the bucket fills with water, it starts to tilt. When it is full the bucket tips the water out and brings another bucket into position ready to collect more water. An optical sensor detects the number of tips and this digital signal is passed to the microprocessor.

Daylight and sunshine hours

Sunshine is detected by a special diode. The signal from this is then passed to the microprocessor after it is converted from an analogue signal to a digital one. The digital signal is then used by the microprocessor to determine sunrise and sunset time and also to measure sunshine hours.

Additional sensors

Additional sensors that measure atmospheric pressure and relative humidity (a measure of the amount of moisture in the air) may also be connected to the system.

Analogue-to-digital conversion

All the quantities measured by the Weather Reporter are analogue quantities, because they are continuously variable and do not jump in steps from value to value. For instance, temperatures don't jump from one degree straight to the next; there are many values in between. Quantities which have continuous values are called analogue quantities and those that jump from one value to the next are called digital quantities.

A rainfall meter measures rainfall which in this system is an analogue quantity but the sensor itself counts the number of buckets that are filled. This is only ever 1, 2, 3, etc., so it is therefore a digital value. Digital values can be fed directly into the microprocessor or computer but analogue values need to be converted to digital values using an analogue-to-digital-converter since most (but not all) computers process only digital values.

QUESTIONS

Fill in the table shown below saying whether each physical quantity is either analogue or digital.

Physical quantity	Digital or analogue
Wind speed	
Wind direction	
Temperature	
Rainfall	

Now look at the section on the sensors used to detect these quantities and fill in the following table.

Sensor	Digital or analogue
Wind speed (optical sensor)	
Wind direction (optical sensor)	
Temperature (integrated circuit sensor)	
Rainfall (optical sensor)	

Advantages of data logging

Data logging is performed automatically without the need for a human to make the measurement. Also, because of this, the data can be collected more frequently than would be possible doing it manually. The frequency with which the data is logged may also be varied. The electronic signals from the sensors can be relayed through communication lines (by radio or through phone wires) so the sensors can be situated anywhere in the world. Figure 14.4 shows a remote weather station as used by the Meteorological Office. Figure 14.5 shows how the weather data is presented on the screen using equipment and software such as the 'Weather Reporter'.

Figure 14.5 *Information that can be shown on the computer screen of a fully automatic data logging weather station*

Transferring weather data to another package

It is possible to transfer weather data obtained from the 'Weather Reporter' to another package. To do this the weather data is converted to a special format which can be loaded into a spreadsheet package such as Excel or a database package. Transferring data out of one package is called exporting. Transferring the data into another package is called importing.

Weather satellites

By using 'Weather Reporter' and images from a satellite orbiting the Earth, a more complete picture of the likely weather can be obtained. Figure 14.6 shows an image from a weather satellite.

Satellites can be placed in geostationary orbits 36 000 km above the surface of the Earth. At this height the time that a satellite takes to orbit the Earth is the same as the time that the Earth takes to complete one rotation: one day. Therefore the satellite stays at the same point above the surface of the Earth.

Other weather satellites, such as METEO-STAT, move between the poles in complex orbits and a computer package calculates their position over the Earth.

How weather satellites produce pictures

Weather satellites transmit pictures as coded radio signals. The coded signal is picked up with a satellite dish on the Earth and decoded before being displayed on a screen. The coding ensures that only people who have paid to receive the service can use it.

Uses of satellite images

From the satellite images, we can determine the amount of cloud cover and, if we know from which direction the wind is likely to come, we can predict the weather. If infra-red (heat) images are obtained then we can see the relative temperatures of land and sea.

Still pictures can be taken over a period of time and stored, then played back together. (This is just like animating a cartoon by joining the individual pictures up.) The changing weather pattern can now be observed and one can see the way storms and hurricanes develop and move. Colours can be added to the image by the computer so that certain features stand out.

Figure 14.6 *An enhanced image from a weather satellite*

1 When the weather station is used on its own (i.e. not connected to the computer), the data from the sensors is stored in non-volatile RAM.
(a) What does the abbreviation RAM stand for?
(b) Why is it important that the RAM is non-volatile?

2 When the data is sent from the sensors to the microprocessor, the time must be sent as well. Why is this?

3 The program that controls the microprocessor is stored in ROM.
(a) What does the abbreviation ROM stand for?
(b) Why is it necessary to store the program in ROM rather than in RAM?

4 Compare and contrast the collection of weather data manually using a Stevenson's screen etc. and by using an automatic data logging system such as the 'Weather Reporter'.

5 Manor Top is a secondary school which teaches a full range of subjects. Wherever possible the teachers at Manor Top encourage the pupils to use computers as part of their studies. Manor Top has 20 computers that the pupils can use but there are over 600 pupils. Mrs Logit, the teacher responsible for information technology, is anxious that the pupils should experience computers being used for data logging and control.

A group of senior pupils and Mrs Logit design and construct an automatic weather station. The weather station consists of such devices as a rainfall meter, a sunshine recorder, and an anemometer. Each device has to be connected directly to one of the school's computers. As it is important that the weather data is collected on a regular basis, Mrs Logit and her pupils have to write some computer programs that will run all the time.

Pupils and teachers who are involved in science, geography, the environment and statistics soon become very interested in the data that the weather station is collecting. Hence Mrs Logit is finding that she is under pressure to provide more and different data.

The computer connected to the weather station stores, in a computer file, the amount of sunshine detected each day.
(a) Name the software package that could be used to store the sunshine data.
(b) A software package is used to produce the output shown in Figure 14.7.
   (i) Name the software package.
   (ii) The chart shows two things that cannot be true. State what they are.
   (iii) Explain why, in this case, the result of the average sunshine per day must be wrong.
(c) Each day, the computer connected to the weather station stores the date and the rainfall in centimetres for that date. A database package is used to analyse the file of rainfall data. Describe what information would be given by the following database instruction:

IF RAIN IS MORE THAN 5 THEN OUTPUT DATE

(d) Tilda Shower is a geography teacher.
   Tilda wants the rainfall data to be recorded every day for a whole year. She wants the results to be printed out in the form of a booklet.

Figure 14.7

Average sunshine per day = 6.3 hours

Day of the month

(i) Describe how this amount of data could have been collected without the aid of a computer.

(ii) Explain why, in a school, it would not have been practical to collect this amount of data without a computer.

(iii) State one advantage to Tilda's pupils of having this amount of data.

(e) The instructions below are part of a computer program which, every 30 minutes, stores the temperature that the weather station detects.

    WAIT 30
    DETECT TEMP
    STORE TEMP

Tilda now wants the temperature to be stored every 15 minutes.

(f) Show how one of the instructions will have to be changed.

(g) (i) Explain why these three instructions by themselves would not keep on storing the temperature.

    (ii) Show the extra instructions that would be needed so that the computer will store the temperature 'forever'. (You may invent your own instructions.)

(h) 50°C is very very hot; −50°C is very very cold. Sometimes the weather station does not work properly so silly temperature values are stored. Explain how the program could be improved to prevent the computer storing silly values for temperature.

IT TASKS

Task 1

1 Use a satellite-receiving system capable of receiving pictures from the weather satellites NOAA and METEOSTAT. The computer could be used to add false colours to these images. As evidence you could either produce screen dumps to a printer or take actual photographs of the screen (ask your physics teacher how to do this).

2 Use the satellite system to produce an animated (moving) picture of
   (a) cloud movements over a period of time, or
   (b) temperature variation over a period of time.

   Also, you could monitor the passage of a weather system over a set period.

3 Use electronic mail to transfer your data along the telephone lines to other schools and colleges in Britain. Use appropriate software to see the way the weather changes from one part of the country to another.

4 Use a weather recording system to obtain regular readings of wind speed, temperature, hours of daylight, pressure, wind direction, hours of sunshine, rainfall and humidity. Collect the data either manually, or by using data logging equipment and transfer it to a computer for processing. Display the readings in a suitable way on the computer. Can you predict the weather tomorrow from your data? Produce a 'school weather forecast' and print it out. How accurate were you?

5 Consider 4 in conjunction with 1 and see if this would make your weather predictions more accurate.

IT TASKS

Task 2

Design a complete weather forecasting system over a period of several weeks or months. Collect your readings either manually or by using a data logging system and transfer these to the computer for processing. Processing could include producing graphs.

15 Transferring Data Around

A Company with a Communication Problem

Binscope is a retail organisation that is in business to sell high quality optical equipment: terrestrial telescopes, astronomical telescopes, binoculars and microscopes. In addition to the above the company also sells books on astronomy, bird watching, etc., as well as many accessories such as eyepieces, camera attachments, tripods, cases, etc. It also has a small workshop where optical equipment is repaired.

At present Binscope has seven shops: in Liverpool, Birmingham, London, Manchester, Leeds, Glasgow and Chester. The whole Binscope operation is controlled from the head office and warehouse next to the Liverpool shop. Figure 15.1 shows the Binscope 'empire'.

Figure 15.1 *The Binscope empire*

Much of the equipment comes from abroad and it all arrives at the Liverpool warehouse where it is checked before being dispatched via carrier to the various shops.

John Bird and his wife Anne opened their first shop in Liverpool in 1989. Both of them had been teachers. The rapid expansion of the business to seven sites along with the employment of a large number of staff has caused many problems.

Many of the problems stem from the fact that the shops are scattered throughout Britain. Transfer of information between the shops and the head office causes problems and some of these are outlined here.

Problems with the existing system

1 Lists of stock are prepared by head office and sent to each branch by fax before the shops open in the morning. The shops have to send the head office a list of what they have in stock just before they close in the evening. Since stock is continually changing throughout the day, no one really knows what the actual stock situation is.

2 To compensate for point **1**, staff have to ring around the other branches to find an item that a customer wants, if it is out of stock in their own branch. This takes time and ties up sales staff. Customers frequently get annoyed waiting while this is done and inevitably sales are lost. In addition the phone bills have been excessively large.

3 New price lists, product literature and maintenance schedules are sent by post and this takes too long.

4 Sales figures have to be telephoned to the head office at the end of each day. This is tedious, since all the shops tend to try to phone at the same time and it can take a long time to get through.

5 Orders from the manufacturers are dealt with by the head office and this makes it difficult to inform a customer in one of the branches when a particular product will be delivered without phoning the head office first.

6 The company likes to keep in touch with its customers, so it sends them a list of new products and special sales from time to time. Since each branch keeps its own database, one customer who had shopped at three of the branches, receives three copies of these lists.

113

7 Because of the problem with stock, there are frequent delays in ordering goods from suppliers. The company runs out of goods which are in high demand and sales are lost because customers go elsewhere.

8 Fax is used to send orders to suppliers but suppliers would like to receive payment electronically. Much of the optical equipment comes from Japan or Germany, two technically advanced countries. Companies in these countries have suggested that Binscope uses EDI but the directors of Binscope don't even know what it is.

9 John and Anne Bird frequently need information from the shops in order to manage the business effectively. This information takes time to get and this is very frustrating for them.

Binscope realises there is a problem so the directors hire a computer consultant for some advice. The consultant, who is a qualified systems analyst, will look at the present system in detail, and will identify their needs and come up with some solutions.

After looking at the business and having talks with the various staff, the consultant suggests that they need the following:

1 a stock file that is accessible to everyone
2 a faster way of sending mail and pictures (for advertising) between the head office and the shops
3 a faster ordering system between Binscope and its suppliers
4 a central file of customers that is accessible to everyone
5 a way of paying the suppliers directly using some form of fund transfer from the bank
6 as each sale is made at the various shops, the details of the transaction (piece of business) need to be sent automatically to the head office where the stock file and the customer file can be automatically updated. Since this happens in real time it means that the stock file is continually updated and reflects the true stock position of Binscope.

QUESTIONS

1 At the moment faxes are used to transfer some important information between sites. Explain what is meant by faxes and how they are used. Use the glossary at the back of the book to find what a fax is if you don't already know.

2 Anne Bird has suggested that the sales figures for each shop should be transferred to a 3.5 inch floppy disk which is sent by a carrier to arrive before the start of business the next day. The stock details for the whole company can then be faxed back to the shops at around 10 a.m.
   (a) The head office has a couple of stand-alone PCs. Explain what the term 'stand-alone' means.
   (b) Why is it useful for the head office to receive the stock details on a floppy disk rather than by fax?
   (c) Why do you think that the stock position is not given back to the shops on a floppy disk?

3 Put yourself in the position of one of Binscope's customers. Write a list of the problems and frustrations you might have in dealing with this company.

4 Put yourself in the position of a manufacturer of telescopes. What problems might you have in dealing with Binscope?

The solution to Binscope's problem

The consultant decides that the company needs a communications system. She suggests that all the computers should be networked so that data is easily transferred between the sites. She decides that a local area network (LAN) is used in the head office, with a wide area network (WAN) between the sites. Also, the company needs to consider the possibility of using electronic mail. This all sounds very complicated to Anne and John, so the consultant has made some notes to explain how the system works. Here they are.

Networks

A network is a series of computer systems that are linked together so that they are able to share computing power or storage facilities. The link may be between computers in the same building or between computers in different parts of the country or even in different parts of the world.

Binscope needs to make sure that when a network is chosen, room is left for future expansion. Who knows, in five years' time the number of shops may have doubled. For this reason the systems analyst has suggested that a dedicated file server is used. This is generally a much higher specification than the other computers, with a very large hard disk drive. All the common data such as the stock file will be held on the file server's hard disk. A dedicated file server monitors and controls the network and while it is performing this important task, it is not available to be used as a normal workstation.

Local area networks

Local area networks (LANs) are confined to a small area. Usually this small area is within a single building although it need not be confined to just a single office. Sometimes LANs spread through several buildings on the same site. Messages can be sent between the terminals and this is very useful for sending memos between offices. Figure 15.2 shows the local area network proposed for the Binscope office.

Wide area networks

Wide area networks (WANs) cover a wide geographical area. For instance, banks and building societies have their main computers situated in one place with connections made by telephone wires to all the various branches. Using WANs, computers may be linked together in different countries using satellites, microwaves or telecommunication links.

In practice, LANs are often connected to WANs via a special gateway. Using a gateway any computer system can be accessed

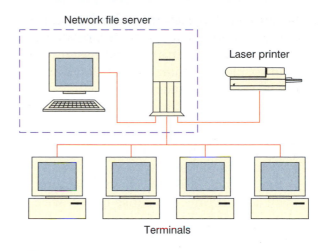

Figure 15.2 *The local area network in Binscope's head office*

provided that it is connected to one of the many communication systems in use.

Advantages and disadvantages of networking

Advantages

1 Expensive peripheral devices such as laser printers and scanners can be shared between users.
2 Messages can be sent between users on the same site with LANs or anywhere in the world with WANs.

Figure 15.3 *Sending messages across a local area network can be useful*

3 All users can access the same files so this avoids having to duplicate information.

4 Network software can be purchased which is often cheaper than buying an individual package for each machine.

Disadvantages

1 If a WAN is used, sophisticated equipment is needed and the rental of telecommunication links makes it very expensive.

2 A loss in the ability to transmit data for even a short time can cause havoc, with tasks having to be performed manually.

3 File security is more important with networks, especially if they are connected to the public telephone system. For instance, if a virus were to get onto a network then it could affect all the networked terminals.

4 Wiring can be expensive both to buy and to install. Wiring has to be sunk to avoid it trailing across a floor where it would be dangerous.

Network topologies

There are many different devices that may be connected to a network such as CPUs, disk drives, printers, point-of-sale terminals, etc. All of these need to be brought together in some way. Most often, cables will be used to connect the terminal and other equipment together although radio communication links can be used.

When a diagram of a network is drawn, lines are used to show the communication links between devices. Devices in a network, called **nodes**, can be connected in a variety of different ways or **topologies**.

There are four common network topologies called **ring**, **line (bus)**, **star** and **hierarchical**.

Ring topology

In the ring topology the terminals or other equipment are connected together in a circle (see Figure 15.4a). None of the computers in the network is any more important than any of the others. One of the main disadvantages in the ring topology is that if there is a break in any part of the communication line, then

A schematic diagram of the ring network

Figure 15.4a *Ring topology*

all of the devices on the network will be affected.

Line (or bus) topology

In line or bus network, the data is sent to all the devices on the network at the same time (see Figure 15.4b). This means that if a terminal is not working properly others are not affected. Like the ring topology, there is no central computer used to control the network so each of the terminals has equal status. The main advantages of the line or bus network is that it is cheap and reliable.

Star topology

In the star topology, there is a computer at the centre that is used to control the whole of the network (see Figure 15.4c). If this

Figure 15.4b *Line or bus topology*

machine breaks down, then the whole network breaks down. Star topologies use more cabling and are therefore more expensive than other topologies. However, since there is a path from each terminal to the central computer, this type of topology is very fast.

Hierarchical networks

Hierarchical networks are those networks where one or more computers are more powerful than the rest. Hierarchical networks are often called client–server networks because a more powerful computer called the server is used to look after printing, file maintenance and other peripherals. Less powerful computers (sometimes without any processing power or disk drives of their own) called clients are connected to the network. These client computers are able to make use of the services provided by the server.

There are two types of server; the print server and the file server.

A file server is a computer used for managing the files on a network. Some file servers are dedicated file servers, which means that they spend all their time managing the network. These file servers are not available for use as terminals. The file server is used to store both programs and data and is generally a much more powerful computer than the others to which it is connected. In some ways a file server can be considered a giant hard drive to which all the other computers on the network have access.

A print server is the name given to a computer in a network which has a printer connected. This server manages all the print

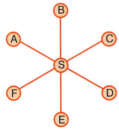

A schematic diagram of the above star network
(notice the central controller node, S)

Figure 15.4c *Star topology*

requests from users on the network. The advantage in using a print server is that the individual computers are no longer tied up managing their printers.

Modems

For Binscope's computers in the shops to communicate with the head office system, each computer in the shops will need to have a modem.

A modem (short for **mo**dulator–**dem**odulator) allows data to be passed along telephone lines from one computer to another. This device converts the digital signals produced by the computer into analogue signals. These analogue signals are sent along a telephone line to another modem, where they are converted back into digital signals for the receiving computer. (Figure 15.5.)

The speed at which data is transferred is measured in bits per second (bit/s for short). The faster the modem, the quicker the data can be transferred and it is possible to get up to speeds of around 56 500 bits per second. Speed is important in terms of the cost of transmission: the time spent connected to the phone line is directly related to the cost. If the time can be decreased, then the cost of transmission will be reduced. Some modems are able to compress the data before sending it and this also reduces the transmission time and cost.

The bits which make up a network

Networking is not simply connecting up a few computers with cables. Here are some parts that can be found in a typical network.

Software
Network software may be part of the operating system (such as Windows 98 or Windows NT) or it can be special software for managing a network.

Figure 15.5 *Using modems to transmit signals down telephone lines*

Cables

Connecting cables are usually used to connect devices on a network, although some networks make use of radio or microwaves to provide the link. Cables vary in both performance and cost.

Connectors

Connectors are used to connect network cables to terminals or other devices.

Network cards

To use a personal computer as a terminal on a network it is necessary to include a device called a network card inside the computer. The network card looks like a small circuit board and slots into one of the connectors on the main circuit board inside the computer (called the mother board). Network cards have connectors on them for network cables.

ISDN (Integrated Services Digital Network)

ISDN is a service provided by the telecommunications companies such as BT that enables ordinary telephone lines, like the one you probably have in your house, to carry digital communications. You do not need a modem but instead need a device called an ISDN terminal adapter. It uses a technique whereby several digital signals can be sent along the same wire, which means that you do not need separate lines for voice (ordinary telephone calls), video and data transmission. A home user then can surf the net and receive telephone calls or fax messages using the one line.

Using ISDN, faster data transmission speeds (typically 128 000 bits per second) are possible; this compares with a typical data transmission speed using a modem of 33 600 bits per second. It is also possible to compress the data before sending it and with this compression, ISDN speeds increase to 512 000 bits per second. One main advantage of ISDN is that it is now possible for a user with relatively inexpensive equipment to conduct meetings using videoconferencing. Such a user could transfer files to another person whilst at the same time holding a telephone conversation with them.

Telecommunications

Telecommunications has been a big growth area over the last few years. More and more people are involved in working from home, using computers and telecommunications to transmit their work to an office or to other workers in the electronic chain.

Telecommunications can be used to link up to many on-line databases.

Internet Service Provider (ISP)

Unless you are from a large company or organisation which can have a file server permanently connected to the Internet, you will have to use the services of an Internet Service Provider (ISP). The ISP provides a permanent connection to the Internet. When you log on, your modem dials the number of the ISP and when your password has been validated you are allowed access to their file server. As well as providing a connection to the Internet,

Reproduced with the kind permission of AOL

Figure 15.6 *Opening screen from the Internet Service Provider AOL*

ISPs provide a lot of content of their own. Figure 15.7 shows just some of the things a typical ISP provides.

Examples of Internet Service Providers are AOL (America On Line), Demon, Tesco, BT and CompuServe. In some cases the ISP will have a set monthly fee no matter how much you use the service, sometimes there is a charge based on the usage. There are even some free ISPs, with the charges being paid for by the constant stream of adverts you have to sit through.

The Internet

The Internet can be described as a network of networks. Almost any type of information or person can be found on this network. You can access anything from a database on space science held by NASA to the touring arrangements of your favourite group. You access the Internet through Internet Service Providers such as Demon or AOL.

Using the Internet, data can be rapidly transferred around the world. This can cause problems. If an untrue story about a well known person was placed on the Internet, then it is difficult or even impossible to determine who put it on. Once on the Internet many people all over the world can read it and believe that it is true.

The global nature of the Internet means that information about atrocities, human rights violations (people locked up by governments for no justifiable reason), etc. can be passed around the world quickly. It is much harder for oppressive regimes to keep secrets. Actions by groups of countries (such as the United Nations) can then be taken to bring pressure on these countries.

World Wide Web (WWW)

The World Wide Web (WWW) is a part of the Internet where graphics, sound, video and animation are used, as well as text. The word used for this mix of media is 'hypertext'.

Figure 15.7 *Some of the services that Internet Service Providers can offer*

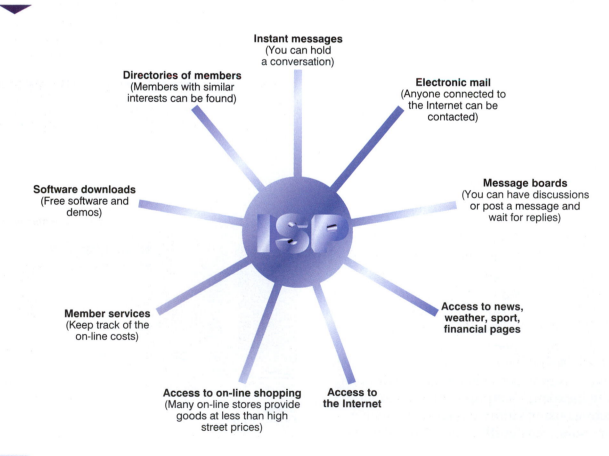

Special hypertext links are built into the World Wide Web that allow the user to move around by clicking with a mouse on words or graphics on the screen. Special software, called browser software, is needed to take full advantage of the World Wide Web. The most popular WWW software browsers are Netscape, Internet Explorer and Mosaic.

Websites

All organisations, including schools and colleges, are reaping the benefits of having their own websites. Basically, a website allows communication between the organisation and the outside world. For commercial organisations, it allows potential customers to learn about the organisation, its products or services. Some websites allow the user to place electronic orders. The cost of conducting business on the web is low compared with other more traditional methods.

Websites can be written using Hypertext Markup Language (HTML) which is easy to use and you can get instructions on how to create a website on-line from your Internet Service Provider. Most websites include a counter to count the number of visitors to the site. This is a measure of how useful other people have found the site. When you make up your own website, it is stored on space allocated to you by your ISP (e.g. AOL, Demon, CompuServe, BT, etc.).

Website hosts

When you connect up your home computer to the Internet you need two things: firstly a modem and secondly you need to connect to an Internet Service Provider (ISP). This ISP

has a computer permanently connected to the Internet so when you log on with them, they provide the mechanism for getting you on the Internet.

Many large companies who are not Internet Service Providers also need a computer permanently connected to the web so that they can send e-mail and files etc. to other sites. They may also use the computer as a website host so that they can provide details of their goods and services to anyone interested. Additionally these people may decide to place on-line orders.

Avon Cosmetics: business over the Internet

Avon Cosmetics is a name most people are familiar with. Catalogues used to be issued at three-weekly intervals and were delivered to the customers' doors by an 'Avon lady' (although they now have many men working for them). The catalogues include a variety of products, such as skincare, makeup, perfume and other non-cosmetic items such as ornaments and toys. The customers fill in an order form and give it with their money to the representative who then sends the order to the head office. The goods ordered are

Reproduced with the kind permission of Avon Cosmetics

Figure 15.8 *Screen shot showing the Avon site*

picked at the warehouse and then packaged and sent to the representative by a carrier. The representative finally delivers the order to the customer's home. This offers a very personal service which is one of the benefits of the existing system.

This is now set to change with the setting up by Avon of an Internet shopping site. The site will allow on-line ordering of products from an on-line catalogue. These on-line catalogues are updated as frequently as the traditional catalogues. The on-line ordering system has been integrated with all the existing systems and this has meant that orders can be sent electronically to the warehouse for picking.

Avon say that this system is set to enhance the door-to-door service especially for those people working long hours who are unlikely to come into contact with one of the representatives. Customers ordering using the site have to pay for the goods by credit card and these details are encrypted (coded) so that they cannot be intercepted as they pass along the communication lines.

If you are interested in looking at the Avon site, it can be found on www.uk.avon.com

Electronic mail

Electronic mail (e-mail) is a method of sending messages from one terminal to another via a communications link. There are various providers of electronic mail, including Internet information service providers. Many people are confused about how electronic mail works. To communicate using electronic mail, you first have to have an e-mail address of your own and you must, of course, also know the e-mail address of the person to whom you wish to send a message. You can then write your message using e-mail software. Next you need to use your communications software and modem to connect to a service provider's file server. Once you are connected you can transmit your message.

The message is then placed in a mail box on a main computer. As soon as the person to whom you have sent the message logs

onto the system they can access their mailbox and read any letters that have been sent. One of the advantages of electronic mail is that the same message can be sent to many different people at the same time simply by referring to their e-mail addresses.

Obviously you cannot send mail in this way to a person who is not a subscriber to one of the electronic mail systems.

QUESTIONS

1 A lot of people think that when you send a message by electronic mail it automatically pops up on the screen. In fact it is stored in a mailbox on a file server.
   (a) Why can't you simply send the message to the other person's computer where it could be stored on their disk drive?
   (b) Many people get fed up with all the junk mail that they get in their mailboxes when they subscribe to electronic mail services.
      (i) What is meant by 'junk mail'?
      (ii) What feature of electronic mail makes it easier for suppliers to advertise their products and services?

2 Someone says that eventually electronic mail will replace the postal service. Do you think this is likely? Write a paragraph to support your opinion.

Message sending

Sending data down a communications line is not just a question of sending the streams of bits that represent each character. The problem is that each computer manufacturer has its own standards for encoding data. However, there is a standard for the connection of PCs which enables communication between all the components. This is called Open Systems Interconnection (OSI).

Protocols and handshakes

When human beings communicate with each other, we have a set of rules that we use. Although we do not think about them when we are holding a conversation, they still exist. For instance, we wait until the other person has finished talking before we say something and usually acknowledge that we have understood what has been said by nodding occasionally. In other words there is a protocol between the individuals.

We also have protocols in telecommunications. Protocols ensure that each computer behaves predictably and provides information in an understandable way.

We have already come across a gateway. A gateway translates the protocols between computers so that different computers are able to communicate with each other.

Before sending data a computer performs what is called a handshake. The handshake is an exchange of signals which establishes the communication between the devices.

File compression

File compression is the process of condensing repetitive information. It is used when sending data through a telecommunications link, since the smaller the file, the cheaper the file transfer will be. File compression may be performed by software before the data is sent or by the modem itself as the data is being sent.

Speed of access

The speed with which you can surf the web or view data over a wide area network depends on a couple of factors. The speed of your modem will determine how fast the pulses are sent and the speed of the receiver's modem will determine the speed with which they can arrive. The speed of the slowest modem will determine the speed of the overall link.

Different types of cabling also influence the speed, with fibre optic cables being much faster than metal wire cables.

Together these factors determine the bandwidth that limits the quantity of data that can be passed along the link in a certain time period.

Bandwidth

When you are using the Internet you may have wondered why on certain days it seems to take forever to load the website you require. The reason for this is to do with something called bandwidth. Bandwidth determines how fast the connection will be. A smaller bandwidth means data will arrive more slowly. Sending data along a communication line (like a telephone line) is like trying to get water through a pipe. The narrower the pipe, the slower the water comes out.

Bandwidth is determined by the medium through which the data is transmitted. Ordinary wire cable like that used with telephone lines has a lower bandwidth than fibre optic cable.

Figure 15.9 *The bigger the bandwidth, the greater the speed of flow of data.*

Cost of installation

The costs involved in the installation of a network are as follows:

- terminal costs
- server costs
- cabling costs (wire is the cheapest and fibre optic cable is the most expensive)
- network cards (each terminal usually has its own network card)
- software
- backup devices (tape streamers, Zip drives, Jaz drives, etc.)

- the cost of the modem or ISDN adapter if a LAN has to be connected to a WAN/Internet
- Internet Service Provider (ISP) costs, if access to the web is needed
- telephone or other communications charges
- connectors.

Electronic Data Interchange (EDI)

Many companies are using a system called electronic data exchange, which links them to their banks so that they can make immediate payments to their suppliers electronically. The old method of paying by cheques involves more expense, such as the time spent by well-paid executives to scrutinise and sign the cheques placed in front of them. However, there is one advantage of the older method – the delay in payment is often useful if there are cash flow problems and the excuse can always be made that the 'cheque is in the post'.

EDI works as follows. Companies receive invoices electronically from their suppliers asking for payment. These are checked by computer against the purchase ledger to make sure that they are correct. The computer then sends details to the bank's computer to make the payment electronically to the supplier. This would be ideal for Binscope since many of the company's suppliers are in other countries: EDI would cut down on the paperwork and problems with late payment due to the post.

Benefits to the person sending money

The person sending money benefits because:

1 no paper is needed to pay the accounts since everything is done electronically
2 the relationship with the supplier is improved, since all the invoices are paid promptly without reminders
3 future cash flow can be predicted with a greater degree of accuracy
4 bank charges are reduced.

Benefits to the person receiving money

The person receiving money benefits because:

1 they can be sure of receiving the funds and there is no waiting for a cheque to be cleared
2 the sales ledgers may be updated immediately without the use of paper
3 errors in data entry are eliminated since the data is captured electronically
4 bank charges are reduced.

TEST YOURSELF

Using the words in the list below, copy out and complete sentences A to H, underlining the words you have inserted. The words may be used more than once.

gateway   protocol   LANs   WANs   network

modems   electronic   analogue

A A group of computers linked together in order to share facilities is called a _____.

B Networks confined to a single site are called _____.

C Networks that use communication lines and are separated by a distance, are called _____.

D Computers connected together using a communications line need two _____, one at each end of the line.

E Modems convert the digital signals from a computer into _____ signals which may be passed along the telephone line.

F _____ mail allows messages to be sent from one terminal to another which may be in another part of the country or even the world.

G For computers to communicate with each other they must share the same _____.

H Different types of computers may communicate with each other provided that a _____ is used.

Things to do

Read the paragraph below, and then answer the questions.

In a busy local office of a large motoring insurance company there are about 10 computerised workstations, linked to each other by a LAN. The system is controlled by a powerful file server with a 20 GB hard disk, which is accessible by all workstations. The file server also has a tapestreamer attached to it. Each workstation can access any one of the 20 black and white laser printers connected to the network. There are also two colour laser printers attached, that all workstations can access.

There is also a gateway that enables access to the Internet.

(a) What does LAN stand for?

(b) Briefly explain what the purpose of a file server is?

(c) Why would it not be worth the company having a laser printer attached to each of the workstations?

(d) Give three advantages of using a local area network rather than use individual, stand alone computers.

(e) State three advantages to the company in being connected to the Internet.

(f) Explain the purpose of a tapestreamer.

Skills Building

Binscope would like you to design an advert for the company to be placed in a specialised magazine called *Bird Watching*. The advert is for the mail order part of the business, so only the Liverpool Head Office's address, phone and fax number need be quoted. It is February, typically a quiet month for Binscope, so they have decided to stimulate sales by offering 10% off all prices until the end of the month. The prices quoted in the advert will still be the original prices though.

Here are some of the things you will need to include in the advert. They are not in any particular order so you will have to decide the order for yourself. You can also include your own information. Remember that the purpose of the advert is to sell Binscope's equipment.

- Binscope
  67 Crosby Road East
  Crosby
  Liverpool
  L23 6TY
- Phone: 0151-211-9000 Fax: 0151-234-8976
- February Special Offer: 10% Off Everything!
- You can use your ACCESS or VISA card to order by telephone.
- Goods dispatched promptly.
- Mail order: insurance, packing and postage are free.
- Mail order service available Monday to Saturday 9 a.m. until 5 p.m.
- The friendly experts professionals recommend!

Include as many special effects, fonts and typefaces as your software allows.

Try to incorporate some diagrams or clip art into your advert. There are some diagrams on the next page that you may be able to scan in if you have access to a scanner. If not, have a look through any clip art with your graphics package and see if there are any suitable pictures. If not, don't worry. The magazine will probably charge more if there is artwork anyway. If you feel adventurous, you could try your hand at drawing some pictures yourself.

Produce a couple of drafts. Make sure that there are no spelling mistakes and show them to someone else, maybe your art teacher, for their comments.

Here are details of the equipment Binscope wants placing in the advert.

Kowa telescopes

TSN 1	£349.00
TSN 2	£349.00
611	£316.00
612	£296.00
TSN 3	£649.00
TSN 4	£649.00

Kowa eyepieces

20 × Wide Angle	£ 74.00
25 ×/40 ×	£ 63.00
20-60 ZEP	£127.00
27 × Wide Angle	£109.00

Leica binoculars

8 × 32 BA	£649.00
7 × 42 BA	£698.00
8 × 42 BA	£718.00

Nikon binoculars

Compact 8 × 23	£ 99.00
Compact 9 × 25	£109.00
Sportstar 8 × 20	£119.00
Sportstar 8 × 30	£299.00

Nikon telescopes

Fieldscope 2	£379.00
Fieldscope245	£399.00

Figure 15.10 *Some optical equipment which you could scan for your Binscope advertisement*

IT TASKS

Task 1

Use the Internet or any other electronic mail system to contact pupils or students in a school in another country. If you have any pen friends you could try contacting them or perhaps your town is twinned with another that you could contact.

Try to co-ordinate this task with your language or geography teacher. For instance, you could wordprocess a document to be sent to a French school and for them to reply to you in English.

Remember that this task needs to be looked at from an information technology point of view and when writing it up for your IT task you should consider the following:
- a description of what you are trying to achieve
- which software you used and why it was chosen against other types of software
- the hardware needed for the system and why it was needed
- what you actually did to perform the task and your reasons for doing it in this way
- the advantages of electronic mail over telephone, letters, fax, etc.
- evidence of the results you have obtained such as printouts of the electronic mail messages (both those sent and those received).

IT TASKS

Task 2

John and Anne Bird frequently like to attend sales exhibitions of optical equipment and any other opportunity for them to show their equipment. The problem is knowing where and when there are country fairs, shows, etc. What they need is to know which on-line communication systems are available and whether they would be of any use to them. You have been asked to investigate.

IT TASKS

Task 3

John and Anne Bird frequently have to travel to various cities and towns by train. You are employed at Binscope and have been asked how to find out travel information from any railway databases available using the Internet. In your documentation compare the way the computer system works with finding out the information using timetables and fare details available from the main stations.

System Security

Computer security

Computer security is concerned with taking care of hardware, software and most importantly, data. The cost of creating data again from scratch can far outweigh the cost of any hardware or programs lost. Loss of data can have various consequences, some of which are shown in Figure 16.1.

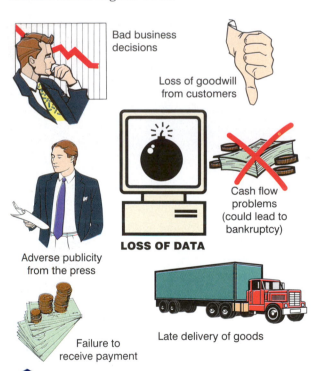

Bad business decisions

Loss of goodwill from customers

Cash flow problems (could lead to bankruptcy)

LOSS OF DATA

Adverse publicity from the press

Late delivery of goods

Failure to receive payment

Figure 16.1 *Some of the consequences of data loss*

Physical security

Computer equipment and its data need to be protected from physical harm. Hazards could include natural ones such as fire, lightning, water damage, etc., and can also include deliberate damage or theft.

Computer theft

Although there are many ways of making sure that unauthorised people are denied access to a system through the use of keyboard locks, passwords, etc., it is more difficult to prevent a thief from picking up a system and stealing it. Locks, bolts, clamps, alarmed circuits and tags are all methods of hardware protection. Although not many people would consider leaving a bicycle without a lock, people do often leave thousands of pounds worth of computer equipment unlocked and unattended.

Sometimes it is easier to improve the security around a computer system. Usually, if a building is secure, the computer system will be secure.

Having fewer entrances to buildings, using alarms on emergency exits, using security badges and having keypad locks on all rooms will all help.

Preventing computer theft

1. A note should be made of all the serial numbers of computers and peripherals, since this may be the only way that the police can identify stolen equipment.
2. It is possible with some computers to lock the case of the computer, which prevents the computer from being turned on. This should always be done when the computer is not in use and the key should be safely stored in a secret place and not in the top drawer of the desk that the computer stands on.
3. Data should be backed up regularly and stored securely away from the computer. If the computer system is stolen then at least the data, which would be a lot more expensive to recreate, is safe.
4. All staff should be made aware of security and encouraged to question suspicious behaviour.
5. If an ID badge system is used (where staff and visitors have to wear a security badge which contains their photograph, name,

etc.) then everyone from the chairman to the cleaners must wear them since this indicates to outsiders that the firm is security conscious.

Protection from fires

Fires which start in computer rooms are rare. Usually they are the result of faulty wiring or overloaded sockets. It is more likely that a fire will start in adjacent offices or in storage areas. Fireproof doors help contain fires. Smoke detectors should be used to detect fires at an early stage. Gas flooding systems are used in large computer installations and are preferred to water ones because the damage done by water is often greater than that by the fire.

Protection from dust and extremes of temperature

Air conditioning is more important for larger mainframe systems where the temperature and the humidity (amount of water in the air) must be controlled. The air must also be pure and is therefore filtered before it enters the room.

Software security

Viruses

Viruses are mischievous programs the purpose of which is to disrupt the sensible use of computers. Many viruses do little more than display a message (usually insulting!) on the screen, but some are designed to act after a certain period of time and do such things as make the letters start to drop off the screen or even erase the entire contents of your hard disk. As their name suggests, viruses are able to spread by 'infecting' other disks and they do this by copying themselves onto other disks which are being used by the computer. Although there are many viruses (over 2000 to date), the main problems are caused by a handful of very familiar ones with names such as: Cascade, Form, Jerusalem and Stoned.

Since these viruses have been around for some time, they are well understood and easy to remove from computers by anti-virus software. Viruses are quite common, especially in situations where there is a large number of users such as in a school or college.

Antivirus software

Antivirus software can be used to scan a computer's memory and disks to detect viruses. Any viruses detected are then removed using the software (disinfecting a disk, as it is often called). When choosing antivirus software, speed of checking is important.

Figure 16.2

Avoiding viruses

1 Don't buy secondhand software unless you can scan it first.
2 Check your computer for viruses if it has been recently repaired.
3 Do not download software from bulletin boards, since this is the easiest way for the people who produce viruses to distribute their handiwork.
4 Be suspicious of all software distributed freely, such as shareware and software which comes free with magazines as these have sometimes had viruses on them.

5 Try not to use too many different computers, since this will increase the risk of passing on a virus.

6 On your own machine, install anti-virus software which checks for viruses on the hard disks every time the system is booted up and checks all floppy disks before data is taken from them.

Backing up data

Backing up data means taking a copy of the data and keeping it away from the computer in a secure place. Obviously it is no good keeping a backup copy on the same disk.

The most common way to lose a file is through user error, where a person makes a mistake with one of the commands and deletes a file or a whole series of files which they did not intend to delete. Although there are software packages available to recover such data these should not be relied upon and there is no substitute for having a backup copy of the data in a secure place.

Rules for backing up

1 Never keep backup disks near the computer. If the computer is stolen the thieves may take the disks as well. Never keep the disks in the drawer of a desk since this is the first place thieves will look.

Figure 16.3

2 If you hold a lot of data which would be very expensive to recreate, then you should invest in a fire-proof safe to protect your backups against theft and fire.

3 Keep at least one set of backup disks in a different place (i.e. at a different site).

Archiving

Archiving means placing important computer files in a safe place so that they can be found easily if needed.

Disk failure

It is important to bear in mind that all microcomputers will suffer at least one serious fault during their lifetimes. A typical hard disk unit has a mean time between failures of between 20 000 to 200 000 hours. This means that if a computer was used for 12 hours per day, 5 days per week and 52 weeks a year then you could expect its hard disk to break down once in about six years. If the computer is being used as a file server (i.e. used to control a network) it could be switched on 24 hours per day 365 days per year, so the hard disk would fail on average every 27 months. Couple this with the chance of other components failing and you have a complete computer which is likely to break down every 14 months.

Backup copies of the programs and data on a hard disk should be taken at regular intervals. A tape streamer is usually used. This looks a little like an ordinary tape recorder. Transfer from the hard disk to the tape takes place quickly and you don't have to supervise the computer while backup is taking place. Should the hard disk become damaged, then it is easy to restore files.

Figure 16.4 shows some of the security features of a 3.5 inch floppy disk.

Some systems use two hard disks in parallel with each other, which means that whatever is stored on one disk will be stored automatically on the other.

Protecting your files

Software can be written which does not allow access to a computer unless a password is keyed in. The password, which is never shown on the screen, should be changed regularly and should never be written down. Obvious names, such as the surname of the person using the machine, should be avoided, along with other obvious passwords such as 'access'.

Always write where the disk should be returned if lost (e.g. name and address of home or school or a phone number)

My Name   Class

Write protect tab

Front of disk

If you can see through the write protect hole then you will only be able to read the data and not alter it. If the hole is closed by moving the tab down you will now be able to read and write data.

Figure 16.4 *Some of the security features on a 3.5 in disk*

Many large systems use software to limit each user's access to only those files that are needed for the performance of their particular job. So, for instance, an accounts clerk could have a password that allows access to files needed for checking invoices, whereas the accountant would have access to all the accounts files.

It is also important to try to restrict access to a computer's operating system particularly for inexperienced users. A simple command at the operating systems prompt can erase an entire hard disk. Restricted access can also be used to prevent people from copying data from the hard disk to a floppy disk.

Encryption

Sometimes files which contain sensitive data are encrypted (i.e. coded). If a tape or disk containing sensitive files is stolen it would then be impossible to read the data without the decoder.

Encryption is often used when important data is transmitted from one place to another.

The data is coded before being sent and then decoded at the other end. Both processes are performed automatically by computers. Should the data be intercepted, then it will be impossible to understand or alter. When people are making payments for goods bought over the Internet using a credit or debit card the details are always encrypted.

Project advice

Always keep backup copies of your work and don't keep your backups in the same disk box as your original disks.

If a disk becomes corrupted for whatever reason and you haven't taken a backup don't immediately throw the disk away. There are various programs that are able to recover data from corrupted disks. Norton Utilities is one such package. If you do have a corrupted disk ask your teacher to use one of these packages to look at the disk and if it is possible to recover any of the data.

If you have accidentally deleted a file that you wanted to keep, tell your teacher. Again, using special software it is possible to get the file back.

The difference between security and integrity

Data integrity

Data integrity is concerned with the 'correctness' of the data. Errors may be introduced into data in a variety of ways. They can be introduced when the person typing in the data misreads it off a source document or if a program or machine errors corrupt the data. Some types of corruption can be caused by simple typing errors. Validation and verification checks are performed on data to ensure its integrity and further information about this can be found in Chapter 7.

Data security

Data security is concerned with keeping the data safe from the various hazards that could destroy it.

TEST YOURSELF

Using the words in the list below, copy out and complete sentences A to J. Underline the words you have inserted. The words may be used once, more than once or not at all.

> water data physical encrypted backup
>
> gas smoke viruses antivirus tape
>
> keypads passwords

A Computer security is concerned with protecting the hardware, software and _____.

B _____ security is used to protect against theft, fire, etc.

C As computers become smaller, they become more portable. To protect against theft _____ may be used on doors to prevent unauthorised access.

D Copies of data or programs kept for security purposes are called _____ copies.

E _____ copies should always be kept away from the computer since if the computer is stolen then the thieves will probably take the disks as well.

F To provide early warnings of a fire, _____ detectors are used and _____ flooding systems are used to extinguish the fire.

G Programs that are written to disrupt serious computer use mischievously are called _____.

H _____ software is used to detect viruses and to remove them.

I To copy the entire contents of a hard disk quickly a _____ streamer is used.

J Data is often _____ to prevent tampering before it is sent along communication lines.

Things to do

1 It is Friday the 13th and yet another story is on the news about a computer virus which lies dormant until, on this date, it springs into life and destroys all the files.

(a) Your father doesn't understand what a virus is and how it is caught by a computer. Write a short paragraph to explain viruses.

(b) Your father uses a personal computer at work. After your comments in part (a) he starts to look worried.
What can he do to:
(i) determine whether there are already viruses lurking on his computer, and
(ii) make sure that no viruses enter his system?

2 Michelle is an accounts executive for a large advertising agency. She uses a personal computer at work for storing the artwork for all the agency's major customers. No backup copies are kept, since to backup a 10 GB disk full of files takes a long time and 'in any case the computer has been very reliable so far'. Michelle often brings the machine home at weekends, partly to do some extra work but mainly for the use of her son who likes to play computer games. He has just received a copy of a disk from a friend of a friend and is looking forward to playing the game that is on it.

Michelle needs to be made more aware about security.

(a) Explain what a backup copy is and why it is made.
(b) Why should Michelle not rely on her machine's reliability?
(c) What security risks are introduced by bringing home the computer in her car and letting her son play games on it?

(d) Suggest a list of guidelines that Michelle should adopt regarding the security of her data.

3   Your teacher/lecturer is fed up with people not looking after their disks. Disks with no names on them are constantly being left in machines after the lessons. Some pupils are losing the data because disks have been mishandled. Pupils have not been taking backup copies on a regular basis. Your teacher has asked you to use a graphics package to design a poster that could be placed on the computer room wall. Using appropriate software, design and produce a suitable poster. (You may find it easier to work on paper to start with and then to do the final design using the computer.)

Look through some computer suppliers' catalogues at the security devices available for micro-computers. Write a brief report, using wordprocessing software, explaining how these gadgets work and how much they cost.

INVESTIGATIONS

In this project you will be given various situations which have actually arisen. You need to read about them carefully and then suggest improvements that would prevent each situation from occurring again.

1. Virus attack

A firm of typesetters used computers for desktop publishing. Their software package became infected with a virus called the 'Lazy Harry', which distorts the text on the screen and also causes the system to crash now and again. The company at first suspected that it was a hardware fault and its overall effect was to slow the company down and cause missed publication dates. This in turn caused financial problems. Eventually the firm discovered that the problem was a virus that had been brought into the company by the senior partner's son who had been playing games on the office PC. The work dropped by 25% and some customers were not sent invoices, which cost the company £20 000.

What strict guidelines would you lay down to make sure that this did not happen again?

2. Power failure

A minicomputer was installed in the offices of a food processing plant high up in the Pennines and in an area where lightning frequently occurred. As the lightning struck, the power supply would go off for one or two seconds, which was sufficient time for the computer system to fail. Backup copies had to be used to restore the data and sometimes this would need to be done four or five times a day.

What could be done to help this company?

3. Theft

A health authority had eight microcomputers in a busy department. The public had access to the department and the computers were visible from the street. One evening all the computers and associated equipment were stolen. The thieves gained access through the front door which had only a single Chubb lock. The theft occurred at nine o'clock at night and was witnessed by several people who thought that the department was moving to another office.

What possible security measure could this authority have taken?

4. System failure

A young inexperienced computer operator was working in a computer room with a minicomputer. He switched it on early in the morning and a grating sound was heard coming from the disk drive when he loaded the operating system. He took the disk out and placed the backup copy in the drive and tried to reload the operating system. He heard the same grating sound as before. He turned to the other drive and placed each disk in turn into it and again heard the grating sound. An engineer was called and he told the operator that both disks and drives were ruined. The problem appeared to be caused by dust on the disk.

What could the company do to prevent this happening again?

INVESTIGATIONS

You have been asked to review the security of your school's or college's computer operations. Write down a list of the questions you would ask the person in charge of the computers.

Here are a few questions to start you off.

1 How often are the passwords changed?

2 Does each person using the system have the same password or are the passwords used by a group of people?

3 Does a screen turn off if a user hasn't used a terminal for a while?

4 Can a user get into the operating system?

From the answers to your questions, write down, with reasons, whether you think the security could be improved. Then make suggestions of what could be done to improve security.

17 Data and You
The Data Protection Act

Computers and privacy

The rapid explosion in the use of computers in the last 15 years has benefitted us in many ways. Many things that we now take for granted, such as the use of credit cards and cash dispensers would have been impossible without them. However, there are problems. As more computers are used, more and more information about each of us is stored on computers. By linking the information gained from several computers together it is possible to build up a complete picture of a person's life. Figure 17.1 shows just some of the organisations that hold personal information about us.

Suppose that Richard goes abroad for a fortnight. Let's see how much we could find out about what he did on the holiday, if we had access to computers that stored information about him.

By linking in to travel companies' computers we could find out where he went on holiday, whether he went on his own, how long for and the dates. From the bank's computer we could find out how much money he took with him. We could find out from the travel insurance company's computer whether he had any existing illnesses before he went. If he paid by travellers' cheques or credit cards we could find out what he bought while on holiday. If he was a member of a library we could even find out which books he took with him!

A more sinister example

The example above is a fairly trivial one. Let's now look at another example; this time it is a more sinister one.

Suppose we live in an undemocratic country, where there are no elections and the president is only there because he has the army to back him and people are too frightened to resist. He wants to keep control of the country, which he can do by fear. The church in the country provides the only opposition. All opponents are arrested and thrown in jail and the president would like to round up all the major members of the church.

Just think how useful computers could be to him. He could find out from libraries who has borrowed religious books. He could get lists of the clergy from computers. Computers can store a person's photograph. Then when an unknown person is photographed, perhaps leaving a church, the computer can identify the person. This all sounds very far-fetched but the technology exists and there are many countries ruled through force.

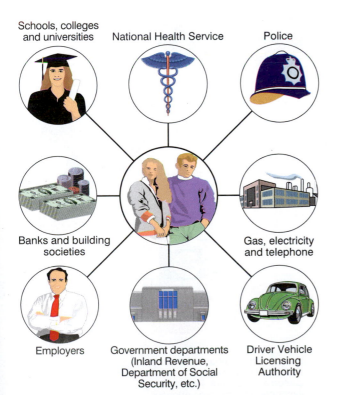

Figure 17.1 *Some of the organisations that hold personal information about us*

- Schools, colleges and universities
- National Health Service
- Police
- Banks and building societies
- Gas, electricity and telephone
- Employers
- Government departments (Inland Revenue, Department of Social Security, etc.)
- Driver Vehicle Licensing Authority

When mobile phones are switched on, their whereabouts can be located fairly accurately

Cameras at ports record the registration numbers of vehicles entering or leaving the country

Loyalty cards and credit cards link you to the purchases you make

ATMs (cash dispensers) record transaction details (date, time, location, amount withdrawn, etc). Some will secretly take your photograph

Internet 'cookies', without you knowing, record details of the web sites you have visited

Figure 17.2 *Your private life is becoming less and less private*

- When making their purchase either by cash, debit card or credit card, the loyalty card links the customers to their purchases.
- The card adds a certain number of points, based on their bill and the items bought, to the total.

As well as making the customer loyal to a particular store chain, the scheme can be used to provide useful marketing information about each customer and the items they have purchased. Before loyalty cards, if you paid cash, then the store did not know who you were. They had no way of linking you to the purchases you had made. Now they can find lots of information about you and what you like to buy.

The customer fills in an application form

The card that the customer is given when her account is opened has a magnetic stripe, so that her account number can be read each time she buys goods

Based on the amount of money spent, points are added to the customer's account. Points can be exchanged for reward vouchers

Figure 17.3 *How loyalty cards work*

Loyalty cards

Most large store chains now have what is called a loyalty card scheme. Each time the customer uses the card, points are added. When the number of points earned reaches a certain value customers are given vouchers that can be used in the store instead of cash. The scheme works like this (see Figure 17.3):

- The customer fills in an application form to join the scheme.
- The customer is given a reward/loyalty card that contains a magnetic stripe.
- Each time the customer goes to the shop they take the card with them.

Figure 17.4 *What the items in your shopping basket may reveal about you*

Here are some of the things store chains could find out about you:

- what newspapers, magazines and paper-back books you read
- what drinks you like (alcoholic or otherwise)
- the method you use to pay for your purchases
- whether you have a petrol or diesel car
- if some or all of the members of the household are vegetarian
- what pets you have
- whether there are any young children in the family
- whether you or any member of the family is on a diet
- whether you or any member of your family smokes.

QUESTIONS

The above list shows just some of the many interesting facts about a person's lifestyle that can be found from the things they buy from a supermarket.
(a) List five additional things your shopping could reveal about you.
(b) Some people are concerned that the use of loyalty cards invades a person's privacy. Why might some of these concerns be founded? Explain briefly.
(c) Loyalty card schemes can cost the stores a lot of money to set up. Give two reasons why it is important for the stores to know as much about their customers as possible.

Why electronically stored information is easier to misuse than information kept in conventional form

1 Cross referencing
It is easy using a computer to link the data from different systems.

2 Danger of hacking
If the system uses communication links then there is a risk of people gaining unauthorised access (called hacking) and looking at, or changing confidential information.

3 Making alterations
If alterations have been made to data on paper then these can usually be seen. With a computer, there is no such evidence.

4 Faster access to data
It is much quicker to gain access to electronically held data and copy or print it out than it is to search through and photocopy manually held files.

The reasons behind the Data Protection Act

As more and more information came to be stored on computers, much of it personal data about individuals, there became the need for some sort of control over the way that it was collected and the way it could be used.

There was an earlier Data Protection Act in 1984 which set out to address some of these problems. There is now a new act, called the Data Protection Act 1998.

The 1998 Data Protection Act

The Data Protection Act 1998 replaces the earlier Data Protection Act 1984. The purpose of the new Act is to deal with some of the things that weren't around when the older Act was introduced. These new things include the Internet, loyalty cards and the use of huge customer databases for marketing purposes. The new Act also covers manually held data not covered by the earlier Act.

The Data Protection Act 1998 covers the processing of data, either manually or by a computer.

The Act places obligations on those people who record and process personal data; these people are called the data controllers in the Act. Data controllers must be open about their use of the data by telling the Data Protection Commissioner (the person who enforces the act) that they are collecting personal data and how they intend to use it. They must also follow a set of eight principles, called the Data Protection Principles.

The Data Protection Principles

The principles state that:

1 The personal data shall be processed fairly and lawfully and, in particular, shall not be processed unless at least one of the following conditions are met:
   Processing conditions:
   - The data subject has given their permission for the processing.
   - The processing is necessary for the performance of a contract which involves the data subject.
   - The data controller has a legal obligation to process the data.
   - The processing is necessary to protect the vital interests of the data subject (e.g. the disclosure of a data subject's medical history to a casualty department after the data subject has had an accident).
   - The processing is necessary for the administration of justice or for a government department.

2 Personal data shall be obtained only for one or more specified and lawful purposes, and shall not be further processed in any manner incompatible with that purpose or those purposes.

3 Personal data shall be adequate, relevant and not excessive in relation to the purpose or purposes for which they are processed.

4 Personal data shall be adequate and, where necessary, kept up to date.

5 Personal data processed for any purpose or purposes shall not be kept for longer than is necessary for that purpose or those purposes.

6 Personal data shall be processed in accordance with the rights of data subjects under this Act.

7 Appropriate technical and organisational measures shall be taken against unauthorised or unlawful processing of personal data and against accidental loss or destruction of, or damage to, personal data.

8 Personal data shall not be transferred to a country or territory outside the European Economic Area, unless that country or territory ensures an adequate level of protection for the rights and freedoms of data subjects in relation to the processing of personal data.

Sensitive Personal Data

The Act mentions data called sensitive personal data, which may not be disclosed and this includes information about:
- the racial or ethnic origin of the data subject
- their political opinions
- their religious beliefs
- whether or not they are a member of a trade union
- their physical or mental health or condition
- the commission or alleged commission by them of any offence or
- any proceedings for any offence committed or alleged to have been committed by them and if they are convicted, the sentence they were given.

QUESTIONS

1 The Data Protection Principles outlined above are very wordy and need to be translated into everyday language. Use a dictionary if you need to. Explain what the following words mean:

   lawfully   specified   purposes   disclosed   incompatible   adequate   relevant   undue   excessive   appropriate   unauthorised

2 Now write a set of summarised data protection principles, in your own words and without using any of the words in the list above.

A data controller means a person (by themselves or with other people) who determines the purpose for which, and the manner in which, any personal data is processed. The data controller is therefore the person who decides what to do with the data once it has been entered onto the system.

Notifying the commissioner

The Data Protection Commissioner, the person who enforces the Data Protection Act, must be notified by the data controller if they hold data not falling into one of the categories covered by the exemptions. The data controller must give certain particulars including:

- their own name and address
- a description of the personal data which is being processed
- a description of the purpose for the processing of the data
- a description of the recipient to whom the data controller intends to disclose the data.

When the data controller notifies the Commissioner, the data controller must say what security provisions there are to protect the personal data. There is a fee which needs to be paid with the notification.

What happens if an organisation doesn't register?

If an organisation does not register its use of personal data or it provides false information to the registrar, then the organisation may be fined up to £5000 in the magistrates' court or an unlimited fine in the High Court.

Is compensation payable?

If a person suffers damage or damage and distress because of things the data controller does which contravene the Act, then they may be able to claim compensation.

Data subjects and data controllers

Everyone, whether we like it or not is a 'data subject', because organisations and companies, called 'data users', hold personal details

about us on their computer systems. The worrying thing about this is that, because of the power of and the ease of communication between computers, this data can be transferred from one computer to another at the press of a button. This means that data collected by one computer user can be transferred to other users, who can use the information for completely different purposes.

There are many examples where data collected for one purpose is used for another and some of these are shown in Figure 17.5. For example, if you rent a television, then your details will be automatically passed to the TV licence centre. The Driver and Vehicle Licensing Authority is linked to the Police National Computer. Banks and building societies automatically notify the Inland Revenue if a person receives over a certain amount of interest in a year.

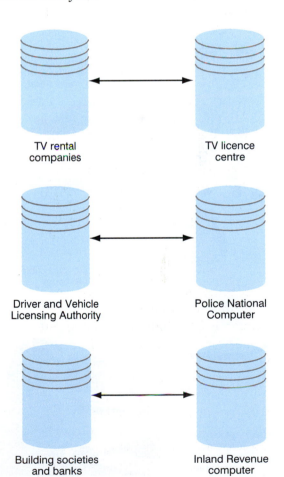

TV rental companies   TV licence centre

Driver and Vehicle Licensing Authority   Police National Computer

Building societies and banks   Inland Revenue computer

Figure 17.5 *How data collected for one purpose can be used for another*

The transfer of personal data between computers does have some advantages. For example, without the rapid transfer of records the capture and conviction of criminals would be made more difficult.

However, there are dangers. Suppose your record gets mixed up with someone else's record or that incorrect data is entered into your record? This could have various results: you could be refused credit or benefits or even a job. In certain cases it could result in you being arrested. Figures 17.6 and 17.7 tell you more about who has computer records about you and the possible consequences of the information being incorrect.

The Data Protection Act gives us the right to see our personal data kept on computer and to get it corrected if it is wrong. It also gives us the right to complain to the Data Protection Registrar if we don't like the way the data is collected or the way that it is used.

I was arrested driving my own car – the police reckoned it was stolen

According to my building society I died three years ago

I've been refused a loan. According to the computer I'm a bad credit risk

Figure 17.6 *Serious problems can be caused when records become mixed up*

The Inland Revenue holds information about incomes on computer. If this is incorrect you could pay too much tax

Mail order companies obtain names and addresses from many different sources. What do they know about you?

Employers can have a lot of information about you. Who else might they give this information to?

Banks not only know how much money you have in your account, they also know your income and where you spend your money. How might they use this information?

Figure 17.7 *Who knows all about you?*

Do all the uses of personal data have to be notified?

Not everyone has to register their use of personal data, so, if you hold your address book or your Christmas card list on your home computer, you can sleep at night.

The following use of personal data is exempt. In other words, you do not need to register your use of personal data if your use falls into any of the following categories:

1 when the data held is being used only in connection with personal, family or household affairs, or for recreational use
2 where the data is being used only for preparing the text of documents
3 where the data is being used only for the calculation of wages and pensions or for the production of accounts
4 where the data is used for the distribution of articles or information (e.g. unsolicited mail, that is mail that advertises goods or services that you have not asked for))
5 where the data is held by a sports club or a recreational club which is not a limited company.

Your rights as a data subject

You have the right to see any personal details about you held on computer or held manually. You also have the right to a description of the data being processed. This means if you do not understand what the data means, then you can have it explained. You are also entitled to know the logic behind any decisions made when the decision is made automatically. To see the details it is necessary to send a letter or e-mail to the organisation concerned.

> The Date
>
> Dear Sir,
>
> I wish to make an application under the Data Protection Act 1998. Please supply me with any information which you hold about me to which I am entitled or confirm that none is held.
>
> If you require further information from me or a fee, please let me know as soon as possible.
>
> If you do not normally handle these requests for your organisation, please pass this letter to your Data Protection Officer or other appropriate official.
>
> Yours faithfully,

Figure 17.8 *A formal letter asking about personal details held on computer*

The organisation may ask for a small fee to cover the expense in providing the information. They have 40 days to respond to your request.

You do not, however, have the right to see all the information held about you. You may be denied the information if it is being used for any of the following purposes:

- the prevention or detection of crime
- catching or prosecuting offenders
- collecting taxes or duty (e.g. VAT)
- medical or social workers' reports in some instances.

Personal data which consists of a confidential reference (for a course or for employment) is exempt from subject access. This means you cannot apply to see your personal reference.

Examination scripts and examination marks are also exempt from subject access. So you can't demand your exam scripts back or see your exam results before they are formally published.

Things to do

1 Banks use information technology to handle information about customers and their accounts.
   (a) List four items of information about customers and their accounts.
   It is possible for a bank to use this personal information for purposes of which the customer would not approve.
   (b) Describe such a potential use of the customer's personal data.
   (c) Explain why this is easier when the data is stored electronically than when it is just stored on paper.
   (d) Describe the possible effects of inaccuracies in the customer's data.

   (RSA IT Short Course Sample Question)

2 When a baby is born, its record is immediately put on to the hospital's computer. After a week or so, the birth will be registered on the Register of Births, Marriages & Deaths. This data will then be passed to the Office of Populations Census & Surveys (an extra person has been added to the population). The baby's details are also sent to the Department of Health and Social Security. As the baby grows up, more and more organisations store information on computer about it.
   (a) Write down the names of four organisations which hold personal information about a 16 year old.
   (b) Write down the names of five organisations which could hold information about you when you reach the age of 18 that they are unlikely to hold at 16.

3 Computerised information about individual people is held in separate databases by a wide range of organisations.
   (a) Name two organisations that might hold computer records about a teenager who has just applied for a job.
   (b) Many people are worried about the misuse of computer data. Outline four principles that you would lay down to reassure people that there would be no misuse of the information held about them.

4 (a) Mary has been feeling ill so she goes along to her doctor who examines her and says there is nothing wrong with her. She thinks the doctor is hiding something so she asks to see her medical records held on computer. Is it likely that she will be allowed access?
   (b) John has committed a robbery. Later he is arrested by the police and released without charge. As time goes by he thinks he may have got away with it. He applies to see the records held about him on the Police National Computer. Will his request be granted?

5 A doctor is thinking of storing her patients' records on a computer system. She is however very worried about the confidentiality of the information and the problem of unauthorised access. Explain the various methods that could be used to ensure that the data remains confidential.

6 Part of the application form to be filled in by all potential XYZ Ltd employees is shown in Figure 17.9. If an applicant is successful then the information on the form is transferred to a database held on a personal computer in the personnel office.

Application Form for XYZ Ltd

Name_____ Height _____ Weight _____

Address _____

_____

Tel No: _____

Date of birth _____

National Insurance Number

Married (Y/N) _____ If so, how long for?_____

Religion _____

No of chidren _____

If applicable, ages of children _____

Bank Account Number _____

Are you a union member? _____

If answer to above is Y, give name of union _____

Outstanding value of mortgage and other loans _____

Do you travel to work by public transport? _____

Have you visited your doctor in the last 12 months? ____

If so, what for? _____

Have you ever been refused credit? _____

Figure 17.9 *Application form for XYZ Ltd*

   (a) Write down a list of any of the questions in the application form on the previous page which you feel infringe on your privacy. Explain why you would not like the company to know these details.

(b) Choose three of the more personal questions in the application form and for each one explain what use the answer would be to the company.

7 The following situations concern the security of files held on computer. For each one of the following situations write a short paragraph explaining what could have been done to prevent the breach of security.

You may need to look back at the previous chapter on security.

(a) Mrs Jones, a cleaner, is cleaning the personnel office and notices that her best friend's personnel record is displayed on a screen. There is no-one around, so she presses the printscreen button and obtains a printout which she then takes.

(b) Sid the sneak thief goes into his doctor's surgery to order a prescription. He notices a personal computer on the desk and since there is no-one around, he unplugs it, picks it up and carries it to his car.

(c) Dianne wishes to gain access to her manager's computer. She is leaving the company soon and since she is going to work for a competitor it would be useful to obtain a list of the names, addresses and value of the orders for all the customers. She switches on his computer and it springs into life. However, a message is displayed asking for a password to be entered. Not one to be put off, Dianne looks around and finds a piece of paper attached to the back of the monitor with a single word written on it. She tries it and it works. She now gains access.

(d) John would like a reference for a job. John applied for a job a couple of months ago which he did not get. He suspects he may have got a bad reference from his boss. He would like to see the reference which he knows is on his manager's personal computer. John goes into his manager's office and turns the power on and nothing happens. He notices that a key is needed. He tries the top drawer of the desk and finds the key. He starts up the computer and has a look at his reference.

INVESTIGATIONS

For this project you will need to obtain detailed information on the Data Protection Act 1998. You can get this information from the Data Protection Registrar in the form of a student pack. This is free from:

The Data Protection Registrar
Wycliffe House
Water Lane
Wilmslow
Cheshire
SK9 5AF

Tel (01625) 535777   Fax (01625) 524510

The information contained in the chapter is not sufficient to enable you to perform the following task to a high standard. It is therefore necessary for you to do a certain amount of research before you start this project.

Perfect Partner Dating Agency

You have just been appointed as the computer manager for the Perfect Partner Dating Agency which has been formed by the merger of three smaller agencies. You are in complete charge of the computer facilities and it will be up to you to run your department as you see fit.

Nearly all the clients (the people who are looking for partners) were enrolled with the smaller agencies before the merger. These clients had their details recorded on cards held in filing cabinets. At present there are approximately 6000 clients on the books but with a recently planned advertising campaign in most of the daily newspapers, the new agency hopes to double this number in about six months.

About 40% of business comes from adverts in magazines, where people fill in and send to the agency forms with their names and addresses. As soon as the agency receives the forms it intends to key people's names and addresses into a database. This enables the agency to send letters using the mail merge facilities of a wordprocessor. In doing this, the agency hopes to convert a greater number of enquiries into sales.

Each potential client is given a detailed application form which they are expected to fill in 'truthfully'. This form covers their own likes, dislikes and physical attributes, along with the qualities they would like to see in their 'perfect partner'. When the forms are sent back, the details are then typed into a database. For each client, this database uses a program which searches for clients of the opposite sex with as many of the desired qualities as possible who preferably live in the client's area.

As well as being used for the above task, the computer will also be used for working out the staff wages each month. At present there are 47 staff employed in the head office, but, in addition to these, there are various agents who advertise in local papers, take the enquiries by telephone and then inform head office about potential new clients. These agents are paid by the numbers of enquiries they obtain, with a bonus for each person that signs up with the agency. There are 80 local agents and their pay is processed by the computer.

In addition, the company intends to keep records of the personnel files of all its staff on the computer.

Read over the scenario several times before looking at what you have to do. All your solutions to the following tasks need to apply to this scenario.

1 The directors of the company, who have had little exposure to computers apart from having to type a few private letters now and again on the wordprocessor, have just heard about the Data Protection Act. They have asked you to produce a brief report outlining what the main purposes of the Act are, why it was introduced, and how it could apply to the type of business they are running.

2 The directors would now like to know if any of the following files stored on the computer would be exempt from the Data Protection Act:
   • the client database (it contains all the clients' information)
   • the name and address enquiry database (for sending mailshots)
   • the payroll file for staff and agents
   • the personnel file for staff and agents.

   Write a memo (a brief note) to your managing director explaining which of the above files are exempt and why they are exempt.

3 Realising that it is necessary for the company to register its various uses, the directors have decided that you, as the computer manager, should be responsible for this process. Explain what steps need to be taken in order to register.

4 One of the directors is very sceptical about all this. She feels that this is just another example of government interference in the running of businesses. She has asked you what you think. You are in favour of the Act.

   Produce a brief written argument in favour of the Act giving examples of how the Act can help ordinary individuals in their lives.

5 The same director is still sceptical and wants to know, 'What if we don't register?' Write down the various possibilities.

6 The seventh data protection principle states 'personal data should be surrounded by proper security'. With reference to your company outline the various security techniques that could be used to prevent data from falling into the wrong hands.

INVESTIGATIONS

Read the following passage on the lifestyle database.

The lifestyle database

You have just been out to buy a copy of your favourite monthly magazine. When you get it home a small booklet drops out which promises a free entry to a prize draw for £5000 if you take the time to fill in a questionnaire and send it off. There are questions such as how much you earn, how often you go on holiday, whether you donate to charity, how often you order goods through the post, down to which particular make of soap you use. There are six pages covering about 100 questions which you start to fill in. In filling in the questionnaire, you are giving the company a complete profile of your lifestyle. So who wants to know this information? Well, almost any company involved in selling goods or services. For instance, suppose a particular charity is launching a postal appeal, it can send out letters to people who said in the survey that they donate to charities and who hold a credit card. In doing this they are targeting a group of people who are more likely to respond. This is only one of the many ways that such a database could be used.

Task 1

You have decided to make your own 'lifestyle database'. Your first task is to make up a series of questions to find out when people are likely to buy goods or services. Design an attractive questionnaire using suitable software (you could use wordprocessing, DTP, graphics or even spreadsheet software).

Task 2

Get all the members of your class to fill in a questionnaire. Look at the answers they have given to your questions and then decide how this information might be used to market goods and services. Write a short description on how the information could be used to market goods and services.

18 Computers and the Law

Computer crime

With the growth of information systems there has been an increase in computer crime. There has been a move away from cash transactions, so much less cash is held by companies than it used to be. Many more employees are now paid by cheque or by direct payment into their bank accounts. The opportunity for the criminal to steal cash is limited. However, the ease with which transactions now take place has opened a whole new area of credit card fraud.

Credit card use

There are many types of card in use: credit, debit and cash cards. Debit cards are used as an alternative to cheques. When goods are bought using a debit card, the money is immediately transferred from the shopper's account to the store's account. Cash cards are used to obtain cash from a cash dispenser.

Credit cards, as the name suggests, enable people to obtain instant credit either against goods bought or for cash from a cash dispenser. Obtaining credit for goods involves the retailer filling in a docket either manually or by using the till and then asking the customer to sign the docket. If the card signature and the signature on the docket are the same then the customer is given the goods and the retailer sends the docket to the credit card company, where the transaction is recorded and the retailer paid. The cardholder receives a statement at the end of each month which outlines:

- the balance at the start of the month
- the interest payable on this outstanding balance
- the amounts and details of any transactions that have taken place during the month
- the balance owing at the end of the month.

The cardholder is then able to make the decision on how much of the balance he wishes

Figure 18.1 *Using a credit card*

to pay off provided that it is greater than the minimum payment specified by the credit card company. The whole of this process is summarised in Figure 18.1.

It is now very common for there to be no documentation at the time of purchase, since so many goods and services are bought by phone with credit cards or debit cards.

Automated teller machines (ATMs)

Cash machines are sometimes called automated teller machines (ATMs). The system for obtaining cash from a cash dispenser using a credit card is more secure, since a number called the PIN (personal identification number) has to be keyed before access to the machine is allowed. The PIN is known only to the cardholder, so the card on its own cannot be used to obtain cash from a dispenser. When the PIN is entered at the keypad, the dispenser compares the PIN entered with the number contained in the magnetic stripe on the back of the card. This method provides a higher level of security than when a credit card is used to buy goods, since signatures are so easily forged.

Figure 18.2 shows the reverse of a cash card and the magnetic stripe where the PIN is stored.

Magnetic stripe

Figure 18.2 *The PIN number is stored in the magnetic stripe*

More and more payments are being made with payment cards. They are rather like cheques in the sense that the money comes directly

from the holder's account, but payment cards have the advantage that they are quicker to use, since EFTPOS (electronic fund transfer at point of sale) terminals write slips out for users to sign. When a cardholder's signature is confirmed, the money for the goods is immediately transferred from the cardholder's bank account to the retailer's bank account. Again, because signature verification is used, the system is open to abuse if a card is stolen. A Switch card is one example of a payment card. Payment cards are also called debit cards.

Credit card fraud

Credit card fraud costs the credit card companies hundreds of millions of pounds each year. It is not surprising that ways of reducing this fraud have been looked into.

One way around the problem is to authorise each transaction as it occurs by checking via the phone or a special terminal whether the card has been stolen. Another way is to make people key in their PIN at the checkout when making purchases using credit or payment cards.

Biometric testing can also be performed, whereby the user places an index finger into a machine which compares the fingerprint with one previously recorded. Another method looks at the way a person writes a signature by concentrating on the timing, the rhythm and the invisible pen movements. Figure 18.3 shows a fingerprint being checked. There are also systems which use the pattern on the retina of a person's eye.

Figure 18.3 *Biometric testing is an important weapon to protect against credit card fraud*

Electronic fraud

Electronic fraud is the use of computers or communication systems to commit fraud for financial gain. The main problem with this crime compared with traditional crimes is that the criminals tend to be quite intelligent and technically competent and therefore make considerable efforts to prevent discovery. They frequently see weaknesses in systems and set out to exploit them.

Electronic fraud often involves setting up false suppliers, who send invoices to a real company for payment. When payments are made to these fictitious suppliers the money is stolen. Great efforts are then taken to make sure that the real company's accounting system will still balance. Firms try to get around this type of fraud by making sure that several people are responsible for dealing with invoices so that to commit a fraud would need the co-operation of several members of staff.

Careful recruitment of staff and making sure that no single member of staff carries out the whole process can help reduce fraud. Some companies keep swapping staff around different departments to avoid these problems.

Phantom withdrawals

There has been a lot of discussion in the press regarding 'phantom withdrawals'. This is money which has been debited (taken out) mysteriously using an ATM without the person who owns the card, using it. This withdrawal of money usually only reveals itself when the customer checks their monthly statement. Although the courts have taken phantom withdrawals seriously, allowing groups of individuals jointly to take action for the return of their money, the banks have remained adamant that this cannot happen. In many cases, the banks say, the money has been removed by someone in the user's household who has borrowed a user's card and found the PIN number. The banks further support their case by saying that nearly all 'phantom withdrawals' take place near to the card holder's home.

Figure 18.4 *'Phantom withdrawals' are on the increase*

Barclays Bank has introduced a pilot scheme where a pinhole camera secretly concealed near the screen of the cash dispenser, takes a picture of the person withdrawing the cash. This picture is digitally compressed and stored on disk along with the details of the withdrawal, such as date, time, branch and account details. These cameras may further be used to photograph vandals who try to vandalise machines, when sensors inside the machine are activated.

Smart cards

A smart card is a plastic card which contains its own built-in microchip, which performs two security functions. First it carries the holder's identification data and secondly it verifies this data against the PIN code that the cardholder enters at a card-reading terminal. In addition to this, the smart card can also hold details of the holder's credit limit and carry a record of the transactions made within this limit.

The main objection to the use of the smart card has been one of cost, since many ATMs and POS terminals would need converting to be able to read smart cards. Also, it has been found that smart cards used to decode the TV signals transmitted by BSkyB have been successfully counterfeited. Nevertheless, smart cards are used extensively in banking systems in many European countries.

Software piracy

Software piracy involves the illegal copying of computer software. It is estimated to cost the software developers around £3000 million per year. In 1992 it was estimated that about 66% of the software used in Europe was illegal.

If a company has developed its own software rather than used off-the-shelf software it will have spent a lot of time and money on development. Large programs are usually written by a team, with each person writing a particular section or module. The number of man hours taken to write the programs can be large. Suppose five programmers are working on a project and it takes each programmer 200 hours, then the total number of man hours worked on the project is $5 \times 200 = 1000$ man hours. The programs for the Police National Computer have been estimated to have taken around 2000 man years to write and test.

The Copyright, Designs and Patents Act 1989

The Copyright, Designs and Patents Act makes it a criminal offence to copy or steal software.

Under the act it is an offence to copy or distribute software or any manuals which come with it, without permission or a licence from the copyright owner, who is normally the software developer.

It is also an offence to run purchased software covered by copyright on two or more machines at the same time, unless the licence specifically allows it.

The act makes it illegal for an organisation to encourage, allow, compel or pressure its employees to make or distribute copies of illegal software for use by the organisation.

The Computer Misuse Act 1990

With the widespread use of computer and communication systems, problems started to arise about the misuse of systems. The problems centred on a variety of uses that were not covered by existing laws. Several cases went to court but the courts were unable to convict because older laws did not cover these misuses. One particular case involved a schoolboy using his computer at home with a modem to hack into the Duke of Edinburgh's electronic mailbox and read his correspondence. Other schoolboy hackers were able to get through to stockbrokers, hospitals, oil companies and even the Atomic Energy Authority's computer systems.

The courts were reluctant to use the theft laws, which weren't intended to cover these situations, and advised Parliament that it would need to make specific new laws. This gave rise to the Computer Misuse Act 1990.

Figure 18.5 *Hacking is illegal*

The Computer Misuse Act 1990 covers a variety of misuses which were not covered by existing laws. It deals with the following:

- deliberately planting viruses into a computer system to cause damage to program files and data
- using computer time to carry out unauthorised work, such as using a firm's computer to run a friend's payroll
- copying computer programs illegally (i.e. software piracy)

- hacking into someone's system with a view to seeing the information or altering it
- using a computer for various frauds; people have been known to put fictitious employees on a payroll program and use false bank accounts opened in the name of these employees to steal money.

TEST YOURSELF

Using the words in the list below, copy out and complete sentences A to H, underlining the words you have inserted. The words may be used once, more than once or not at all.

> credit card   hack   hacking   piracy   theft
> PIN   phantom   misuse   patents   smart

A The largest growth area of computer crime is that of _____ _____ fraud.

B Mysterious withdrawal of money from a person's account is often referred to as a _____ withdrawal.

C Cards which look a bit like a cash or credit card but which contain a microchip, are called ——- cards.

D The number coded in the magnetic stripe on the back of a credit or cash card is called a _____.

E Illegal copying of software is called software _____.

F Copying of software is an offence under the Copyright, Designs and _____ Act of 1989.

G The Computer _____ Act of 1990 makes it an offence to _____ into a computer system.

H _____ means gaining access to private data using communication systems.

Things to do

1 You are in charge of a small computer network with six terminals located in different offices, but in the same building. You have been worried about the threat from viruses and some of your staff have been putting their own programs onto the computers (particularly games which they play when you are out of the office!). You have decided to put up a notice which is to be placed near to each terminal listing a set of rules that must be obeyed when using the company computers.

Using suitable software of your choice (e.g. graphics, wordprocessing, DTP) design a suitable, hardhitting notice to discourage such practices.

2 It is often said that, if software piracy could be eliminated, then so could most of the problems with viruses.

Using what you have learnt about software piracy and viruses, explain the above statement.

3 (a) Mary buys a copy of a popular wordprocessing package called WordPerfect which she intends to use on her computer at work and on her home computer. She copies it onto each hard disk. Is she breaking the law?

▶▶

(b) John buys a copy of a graphics package called Microsoft Powerpoint which he copies onto the hard disk of his computer. He puts away the program on the floppy disks in a safe place. Is he breaking the law?

(c) Paul has bought a new computer game which he shows to his friend. His friend asks him to 'make him a copy'. Is he allowed by law to do this?

(d) Sophie is approached by her boss who tells her that she will have to learn a new desktop publishing package in order to produce new company price lists. Her boss says that she needs to install the package on the computer and to photocopy the manual because her friend wants it back. Should Sophie do this? Write a short but polite memo explaining to her boss why she will not do it.

The Social Effects of Information Systems

Social and economic effects of IT

Before the industrial revolution nearly everyone worked in agriculture. Communication was by word of mouth or paper. When the industrial revolution came, life became more complicated. People started to work in factories and the factories needed offices to deal with administration. The amount of paperwork needed for trade started to increase. As time went on, technology was used to develop machines such as the typewriter, telephone and telex machines and eventually, the computer (Figure 19.1).

We are now in an 'information age' and our society is very dependent on information storage and communication. Many people are now using some form of information technology to help them.

Figure 19.1

Is information technology a good thing?

Some arguments for and against IT are given below. You may agree or disagree with these. Where you disagree, explain you arguments.

Arguments in favour

1   The jobs replaced by computers are the rather mundane ones. People are free to do more interesting tasks.
2   Higher productivity enables people to work fewer hours and yet have the same standard of living. A greater amount of leisure time will improve people's quality of life.
3   Other countries make use of IT. If we did not, our goods and services would become uncompetitive and there would be even more unemployment.
4   There are many things that would be impossible without the use of IT. Air-traffic control, credit cards, and space travel are just some examples.
5   New jobs are being created by the introduction of information technology, e.g. programming, network managing, etc.

Arguments against

1   Life without IT is slower and less stressful.
2   Computers are cheaper than people so if a job can be done by a computer then it will be, leading to even higher unemployment.
3   The new jobs being created by the use of IT are only for highly skilled and qualified people.
4   The people who did the boring repetitive jobs now done by computers no longer have jobs.
5   The storage of personal data held on computer has eroded people's privacy.

6 The gap will be widened between those countries able to afford the new technologies and those that can't.

Changing employment patterns

With the introduction of computer controlled technology employment patterns have changed considerably. Changes include the following:

1 Many of the manual tasks such as assembly work and paintspraying in factories are now being performed by robots.

2 Many industrial processes operate 24 hours a day and are continually being monitored and controlled by computers.

3 There are fewer paper-based systems in offices. Some jobs such as filing clerks no longer exist. New jobs involving computers have been created.

4 More and more people work from home, with the advantage of no travelling and the freedom of being able to live in any part of the country (or the world for that matter).

5 Computers are sometimes used to monitor the performance of their users. For instance, in supermarkets they can tell the management about the number of customers dealt with per hour or how many items are passed through the scanner in a day. Order entry clerks and airline booking clerks can have their work similarly monitored.

6 There is a continual need to retrain people, who no longer spend year after year doing the same job.

Reduced number of manual jobs

The opportunity of working from home

De-skilling or even elimination of some office jobs

THE EFFECT ON THE INDIVIDUAL

Increased unemployment

The creation of new and interesting jobs

The opportunity to work for yourself

The need to continually update skills

Figure 19.2 *The effect of IT on the individual*

Identity cards move a step closer

Driving licences are now to be in credit card format and have a photograph of the driver on them like the one shown in Figure 19.3. Eventually the government would like to add a microchip to these cards, thus making the card into a 'smart card'. Stored on the chip will be details of any endorsements for motoring offences, whether the driver is willing to donate organs and health details such as allergies. These cards might also store National Insurance details, which would enable health details to be located.

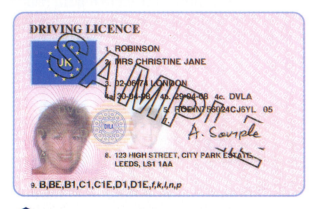

Figure 19.3 *The 'smart' driving licence*

Figure 19.4

Many people are worried about this card, since they see it as an identity card disguised as a driving licence. Some people argue that an identity card would help fight crime and Britain is the only European country not to have one.

Big Brother is watching you

There is a new, revolutionary system making use of cameras and computers to recognise criminals and to alert the police. Although many people see it as another important weapon in the fight against crime, civil liberty groups are alarmed that states could misuse the system and adopt a 'Big Brother' attitude.

The idea is to have cameras constantly scanning railway stations, shopping centres, car parks, etc. The cameras pick out people as they pass and the image is then compared with a database of known criminals stored on the main computer. The scheme is to be operated by local councils and if the system recognises someone wanted by the police, a council officer is alerted and a code given relating to the suspect. The officer then contacts the police who will know from the code who the person is.

If the person tries to disguise him or herself by wearing a wig, a beard, or sunglasses, the system may still be able to recognise them. The system gives a percentage, which represents how near the image from the camera resembles the photograph stored in the database.

QUESTIONS

The new development outlined above could make life more difficult for the mugger, the robber and the yob. One paper said of the new system that 'the overwhelming majority of law-abiding citizens would be only too happy to be watched over by a camera with a memory for criminal faces'.

What do you think? Write a short paragraph explaining why you agree or disagree with the statement.

Computer game addiction

Some children are addicted to computer games, sometimes playing them for more than 30 hours per week. Many experts are worried that this solitary activity is affecting the social and educational development of such children. Many computer games do not mimic reality and often involve simulated violence. Other people are worried that many children are becoming 'couch potatoes', are not involved in any physical activity and do not interact very well with adults or people their own age.

The shape of things to come

The merger of three technologies: the silicon chip, fibre optics and satellite communication (Figure 19.5) has led to the concept of the information superhighway. This is a global network of computers capable of moving huge amounts of information via satellite and cable. This digital revolution is likely to change all our lives considerably. By pressing a key at any time of the day you will be able to get information in a suitable form on demand anywhere in the world. The information is not restricted to business: community information and learning data will be provided.

Environmental, ethical, moral and social issues raised by information technology

Environmental issues

Reduced energy consumption

Computers now control many of the heating systems in offices and factories so it is possible for only the rooms that are being used to be heated. This can save huge amounts of energy.

Reduced wastage in industrial processes

There are many process control systems used in our factories and because these are more accurate, there is less wastage, thus saving valuable resources. For example, Chapter 24 describes how H P Bulmer, the cider maker, uses computers to control the fermentation process. Ruined batches of cider caused by human error are now a thing of the past.

Saving trees

The use of the electronic office and EDI has led to paper being almost eliminated in many offices and this means that fewer trees need to be felled, so not only are the trees saved but the energy that went into the making of the paper is also saved.

Reducing car pollution

Teleworking (working at home using information technology) means that some people no longer have to travel to the office to work. This reduces petrol consumption and car pollution.

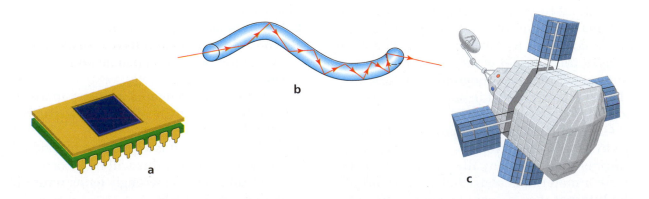

Figure 19.5 *The three main technologies of the information superhighway are:*
a silicon chips b fibre optic cables c satellites

Ethical, moral and social issues
Software theft
It could be said that the use of personal computers has made many users into thieves. How many people could honestly say that all the software on their hard disks has been purchased by them? As you can see from the Copyright, Designs and Patents Act 1989, it is a criminal offence to copy or steal software.

Hacking
Hacking means gaining illegal access to someone else's computer system. Many people see this type of thing as a challenge and not as an illegal activity.

Privacy
As more and more information is held there is more chance of some of it being incorrect. Your private life is becoming less and less private.

Job losses
Is it right to develop new systems in the knowledge that staff will inevitably be made redundant? Should we put shareholders' dividends and profits before people? These are difficult questions and ones which need to be addressed Everyone has their own opinion on this. What is yours?

Social and ethical considerations for the Internet
The Internet provides access to a variety of information on every topic and this information comes from many different countries throughout the world. One problem with the Internet is that all the information is freely available once a user is connected. There are areas of the Internet which contain large amounts of illegal pornographic material. Material that is illegal in some countries may be perfectly legal in others.

Governments have the problem of finding a way of allowing users to gain access to the Internet but not to any illegal areas. If access to such material is restricted on one part of the Internet then a user can simply move to another area to find a way to access the material.

There is a problem in restricting access. The Internet is a global system and it is difficult for single countries to make laws to control it. Another problem with restriction is that it could lead governments to begin attempts to censor, legislate and regulate the Internet for political, cultural and religious reasons. Civil liberty groups are naturally concerned about this aspect of control.

Social considerations for a cashless society
A future without any form of cash is unlikely but over the last ten years the use of cash for making payments has reduced considerably. We will now look at the advantages and disadvantage of a cashless society.

Advantages
1 It is far more convenient not to have to use cash. Mortgage and loan repayments, gas, electricity and phone bills are paid automatically so you don't need to remember to pay them.
2 You no longer need to take large sums of money out of the building society or bank to pay for expensive items: the risk of being robbed is reduced.
3 You don't have to queue at the bank, building society or cash machine to get the money out.
4 Credit cards allow people to buy goods and then decide whether to pay for them at the end of the month or obtain them on credit, paying a proportion each month.

Disadvantages
1 Credit is normally given only to people who are working and have a steady source of income, so certain people aren't able to get it.
2 It is possible for people to spend more than they can really afford and so easily get into debt.
3 More information is kept about individuals. Inevitably some of this will be incorrect and lead to people wrongly being refused cash or credit cards.
4 It is harder for people to keep track of how much they have spent, since statements

are usually sent only once a month, although statements can usually be obtained more frequently if they are requested.

Crime prevention and detection

Crime prevention

IT can be used to help prevent crime and the systems employed include the following:

1   Speed camera systems and camera systems which detect cars jumping red lights deter people from offending.
2   Computer controlled camera systems deter violent crime in many city centres.
3   Tagging of offenders means that they are less likely to commit crimes whilst on bail.
4   Tagging systems on bikes, cars and other property reduces the chances of them being stolen.
5   Computer controlled house security systems deter some burglars.

Crime detection

IT can be used to catch criminals and some of the ways it can do this are as follows:

1   The Police National Computer (PNC) is used to hold details of all crimes committed and of criminals.
2   The National Criminal Intelligence System is a computer system used to piece together information about individual criminals and their illegal activities. The computer can interact with data supplied by Interpol, the PNC, Customs and Excise, the Inland Revenue, and the bank and building society computers. This system is used to gather material on organised crimes such as drug smuggling.
3   DNA profiling and fingerprinting systems enable valuable, and often conclusive, evidence to be collected.
4   Police headquarters computers for each police force are used in the day-to-day administration of all the usual police work.

e-mail

Viruses

Working from home (Telecommuting)

Chat: you can make friends with people around the world. Learn about different cultures.

Censorship of certain material

Books and newspapers waste paper

You can work from anywhere

Surfing the net can waste time

Information is more likely to be up-to-date

Sites set up by criminals part people from their money

Hacking

Vast amounts of information can be accessed from anywhere in the world

Figure 19.6 *Global network issues*

Problems with the Police National Computer (PNC)

1 There is a risk that illegal access to the PNC could allow people outside the police force to gain information.

2 There are worries that the running of the PNC will be passed over to a private company. The PNC contains criminal records, details of wanted or dangerous people, disqualified drivers, stolen cars and guns and also the records of 30 million motorists. Some files indicate that a person is HIV positive. In addition to all this there are details of 70 000 people of 'long-term interest' held. The concern is that a private company running the PNC would not be trusted as much as the police and people could be reluctant to pass information to the PNC.

3 Information on the PNC might be incorrect and this could stop someone getting a job or could even result in a person being wrongly arrested for a crime.

Things to do

1 It has been suggested that motorists might be charged for their use of roads by having a system which identifies each car. When a car passes over a sensor in the road a central computer will record that car's entry into a charge zone. One of the side-effects of this is that a record could be kept of every car's movements. Discuss some of the social implications of such a system, giving reasons why certain groups of people may be for or against the system.

(SEG NT HT Spec)

2 It was mentioned in this chapter that many people would like to see the introduction of an identity card which everyone would be required to carry. Write a short paragraph explaining, and giving your reasons, whether or not you are in favour of the introduction of this card.

3 Information technology has replaced or changed many jobs.
   (a) Give the names of **two** types of job that have been replaced by IT.
   (b) Some jobs have changed their nature due to the introduction of IT. Name **two** jobs where this has happened.
   (c) With the creation of the information superhighway some jobs are in danger of being lost. Name **two** of these jobs.

4 The advertisement in Figure 19.7 appeared in newspapers during the early days of computing when many businesses were being computerised for the first time. Naturally, many people felt that their jobs could be in jeopardy and the aim of this advertisement was to explain how, in the long term, the use of computers would benefit mankind.
   (a) The list below shows some negative aspects of computerisation. For each item in the list try to present a positive aspect. For instance, someone may say that the use of a wordprocessor de-skills the job of a typist. The positive aspect to this might be that, because the wordprocessor is easy to use, everyone can produce high quality, accurately typed documents.
      (i) Computers lead to unemployment and are therefore a bad thing.
      (ii) Some computers are able to report on the number of keystrokes made per hour (particularly in supermarket point-of-sale terminals), so computers can make the employees slaves to their machines.
      (iii) People need to be retrained, sometimes against their will.
      (iv) There might be a reduction in the amount of overtime available.
      (v) All the information held about people invades privacy.
      (vi) Computers can be very impersonal.
   (b) Write a report outlining some of the advantages of the use of information technology. Try to contrast the way jobs were done before the introduction of the new technology with the way they are done now.

Figure 19.7

20 Controlling Things

When people think of computers they usually think of them being used in offices for administrative purposes. There are other things that computers can do: they can be used to control things. In this chapter we will look at how computers can be used to control devices.

Robots

We have all seen robots in science fiction films. The robots can usually talk, walk, reason with humans and occasionally go berserk. The robots in these films are far removed from the robots actually being used in factories.

Robots are used in factories because they can reduce labour costs and improve the quality of the finished products. A robot may be defined in the following way:

> An industrial robot is a reprogrammable, multi-functional manipulator designed to move material, parts, tools or specialised devices through various programmed motions for the performance of a variety of tasks.

This explains why an industrial robot being used in a factory to make motor cars can be called a robot, whereas a washing machine would not be regarded as one. An industrial robot can be used in different ways: it could be used to spray paint or for welding body panels. Although it has different programs, a washing machine is restricted to washing clothes.

An industrial robot may be considered to consist of three parts.

1 The **manipulator** – This is the moving part which in Figure 20.2 resembles a moving arm on a stand. Various tools can be placed in the 'hand' of the arm.
2 The **power supply** – For robots that need a lot of strength this will be a compressor which will work the hydraulic system. For lightweight robots which use stepper motors (motors which can be turned through a set angle) the power supply would be the electrical supply.
3 The **controlling computer** – A computer is a very low current device, so it needs something called an interface in order to

Figure 20.1

protect it from the much higher currents needed for motors and solenoids when they are connected to it. These interfaces also allow analogue to digital, and digital to analogue conversion.

Figure 20.2 *A robot arm being controlled by a micro-computer*

Robots on the move

When robots start to move from place to place there are several problems to solve.

1 How are robots able to navigate themselves?
2 How do robots avoid colliding with each other and with other objects?
3 How is the power provided?

How to solve these problems

To allow robots to navigate themselves, tracks are provided which are set into the floor and the robots follow these. This type of system is used in factories, where movable robots are used to move materials around the production line and also in warehouses where robotic fork lift trucks move goods. The robots also keep a record of the distance they have travelled and the angles they have turned through so that they always know their exact position.

What would happen if a person stood in the way of one of these moving robots or another robot dropped something in its way?

Figure 20.3 *When developing robots, some practical difficulties have to be solved*

On each robot there is an ultrasonic detector which emits a beam of infrared radiation. If anything gets in the way of the beam, the robot just stops.

Power is usually provided by batteries. When the batteries need recharging, the robot automatically goes to a place where the batteries can be recharged.

Computers in control

Using sensors

Sensors are used to detect various physical quantities, such as temperature, pressure, sound, light, etc. The sensors are connected to a computer through an interface and with special software the physical quantities can be displayed in a variety of ways on a computer screen.

Figure 20.5 shows a selection of sensors. Let's now look at each one together with examples of how they can be used.

Mercury tilt switch

If a device is tilted or moved then a blob of mercury in the switch touches the contacts and completes a circuit. Such a switch can be used in a pinball machine to detect whether someone is tilting the machine. It could also be used to trigger an alarm in a vending machine.

Figure 20.4

Mercury tilt switch

Light sensor

Push switch

Temperature sensor

Sound sensor

Proximity sensor

Position sensor (senses the angle of a spindle)

Figure 20.5 *Input sensors*

Light sensor

A light sensor has many uses. For instance it can be used to detect low light levels so that street lighting is turned on. It could also be used to detect the light reflected from a barcode.

Push switch

You might find a push switch being used to turn on the interior light inside a car when the door is opened. You could also use one for detecting when a fridge door is opened, so that the light is then switched on.

Temperature sensor

One of the most common sensors is a temperature sensor. These are used, for example, in central heating systems to keep the temperature of a house constant.

Sound sensor

Environmental health officers could use sound sensors to record the level of sound coming from shops, clubs, houses, etc. where loud music is being played.

Proximity sensor

A proximity sensor is made in two halves. If the halves are moved away from each other then a signal is activated. You often see these sensors on windows, so that if the window is opened the two halves of the sensor are separated and an alarm is activated.

Position sensor

A position sensor detects the angle of a spindle. It could be used to feed back the position of a robot arm.

pH sensor

A pH sensor is used to find out how basic or acidic a solution is.

Humidity sensor

A humidity sensor is used to determine the amount of moisture present (in the air or perhaps in soil).

Figure 20.6 *The interface connects the sensors to the computer*

QUESTIONS

Give the name, with reasons, of the sensor you would use to:

(a) detect the temperature of the air inside a greenhouse
(b) find out whether a pinball machine has been tilted by a player
(c) detect whether a refrigerator door has been opened
(d) measure the loudness of the music coming from a boutique
(e) determine if a cup of tea has cooled sufficiently to enable a person to drink it
(f) determine whether a solution is acidic or basic
(g) measure the water content of the air in an art gallery
(h) determine whether a pot plant needs watering
(i) find out if a box on a conveyor belt has passed a certain point
(j) determine whether the street lights should be switched on.

Interfaces: what are they and why are they needed?

An interface is the name given to the hardware and associated software needed to compensate for the difference in operating characteristics (e.g. speeds, codes, etc.) of the peripheral units and the computer. Figure 20.6 shows an interface used to connect sensors to the computer. Sensors (a maximum of four) can be linked to the interface box which is then connected to the computer. The software is then loaded and the computer knows to which sensors it is connected.

Buffers

The speed of data transfer of a device connected to a computer may be different to that of the computer. Usually a special store area, called a buffer, is used to hold data temporarily to compensate for any difference in speeds.

Actuators

Actuators are hardware devices, such as motors, which react according to signals given to them by computers. An actuator motor would, for example, be used to open a window in a greenhouse when it gets too hot.

Stepper motor

A stepper motor, as the name suggests, is a motor which turns in a series of small steps. Stepper motors generally look fatter than ordinary motors and have several wires coming out of them.

Figure 20.7 shows the positions of a typical stepper motor. The rotor can be turned through a certain angle from, say, position 1,1

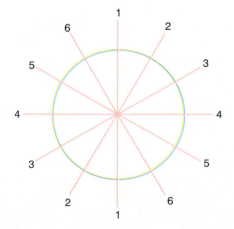

Figure 20.7 *Positions of a stepper motor*

to 2,2 and so on. Pulses sent from the computer instruct the motor to turn through the required angle. Stepper motors can also be sped up or slowed down and can also be operated in forward or reverse direction. To connect a stepper motor to a computer, we use a buffer. Stepper motors are used in robot arms.

Using sensors in hospitals

The medical condition of a patient in an intensive care unit can be continually monitored using sensors connected to the patient. Respiration, blood pressure, temperature and electrical activity of the heart and pulse can all be measured by the sensors. A computer is used to continually monitor the results from the sensors and if the patient's condition changes suddenly or values exceed given thresholds then an alarm sounds to alert medical staff.

QUESTIONS

1 What advantages are there in using computers to monitor the condition of seriously ill patients?

2 Are there any disadvantages?

Open-loop control

Suppose we want to move the arm of a robot through a certain angle. To do this we need to supply a set number of pulses to a stepper motor to tell it to move through a certain angle. With open-loop control, the computer assumes that once the command has been given the arm will move to the new position. If, for instance, there is something blocking the path of the arm then the computer will assume that it has reached its required position and carry on as normal. Some sensors are needed that are able to detect the actual position of the robot and feed this information back to the computer. With open-loop control, the output does not affect the input.

Closed-loop control and feedback

In closed-loop control, sensors are used to continually monitor the actual position of the arm and to relay the position back to the computer. If the robot arm is found not to be in its correct position, then remedial action is taken until it is in the correct position. Here, the output from the system directly affects the input. Such a system is said to employ 'feedback'.

Computer disk drives make use of feedback. For instance, if you tell a computer to look for a file on a floppy disk and there is no disk in the drive then a sensor will detect this and send a signal back to the computer. The computer then displays an appropriate message on the screen. Because this happens instantly, we can say that this is real-time control.

Process control

Computers are used throughout manufacturing industry for the control of many industrial processes. They are able to monitor and control a process automatically. Like robots, they also make use of feedback.

Process control is used in nuclear power stations, oil refineries and in the chemical industry. Various sensors are used to relay electronic signals back to computers. Such sensors include devices that measure temperatures, pressures, liquid flow rates, etc. Because these systems operate in real time they are able to respond instantly to variations in these quantities and make slight adjustments to the controls.

The advantages of computer control include the following:

1 Computers are able to respond instantly to changes in conditions.
2 Fewer staff are needed, so costs are reduced, making the final product cheaper.
3 The system can keep working 24 hours per day, 365 days a year.
4 Some processes are dangerous. Keeping people away from these processes can help prevent accidents.

5 It is easy for a manufacturer to change a product by reprogramming a computer.

The disadvantages of computer control are as follows:

1 Fewer people are needed to do a job, so this leads to unemployment.
2 Computers tend to be expensive to introduce initially.

Pseudo-code

Pseudo-code is useful for writing instructions in ordinary English before these are translated into a language that the computer can understand. With pseudo-code you can express the logical flow of a program in ordinary words. Many control languages use a language similar to pseudo-code.

Using pseudo-code you start at the highest level by writing a list of the tasks that the program must perform. You can then refine the program by making it more structured. Let's now look at a task you should be familiar with: washing the dishes.

The first level could be a simple description of the task such as:

wash the dishes

This could then be broken down into the sub-tasks like this:

collect dishes
take to the sink
fill sink
add small amount of washing-up liquid
wash dishes
put on drainer to dry
dry hands
dry dishes with a cloth
put dishes away

Each of these sub-tasks could be broken down even further. For instance, 'fill sink' could be broken down in the following way:

put in plug
turn on hot tap
turn off hot tap
if water too hot
turn on cold tap
turn off cold tap

If you look at the above list carefully you will see that it probably doesn't represent the way you would actually fill the sink. For example, there is nothing that tells you when you should turn off the hot or cold taps. Also it does not cover the situation where the sink is about to overflow. We need to refine this program to take into account these situations. Here is the final attempt:

IF water in sink
pull out plug
wait for water to drain away
ENDIF
put in plug
turn hot tap half on
turn cold tap half on
DO UNTIL water is deep enough
IF water too hot
turn down hot tap
turn up cold tap
ENDIF
IF water too cold
turn down cold tap
turn up hot tap
ENDIF
ENDO

Even the above could be broken down further, but it is in sufficient detail as a general program. However, if a robot were to be washing the dishes it would need to have a lot more information. For instance the part of the above program for turning on the hot tap could be broken down into the following:

move arm to position above hot tap
lower hand until it touches tap
get hold of tap
turn tap anti-clockwise
rotate tap for half a turn
release tap
move arm away from tap

Breaking down a large complex task into its smaller more manageable parts is called the top-down approach. We used the same approach when we drew structure diagrams in Chapter 12.

Computers in greenhouses

For successful growing of plants it is necessary to give them the correct environment and to keep this environment constant. In particular, the temperature and humidity (the amount of moisture) in the air must be kept constant. Sensors are used to record the humidity; signals from these sensors are sent to a computer. If the humidity falls then the computer will operate a motor to close any open windows and then switch on a pump for a certain period, which will spray water as a fine mist inside the greenhouse. An increase in humidity (i.e. too much moisture in the air) will cause the windows to open to assist in ventilation and drying out the air.

The temperature may be controlled in the following way. If the greenhouse gets too hot, the windows are opened. If it gets too cold, then the windows are closed and a heater is switched on. Plants grow much faster with such careful control of conditions.

The inputs and outputs of the system are as follows:

Inputs
humidity – analogue signal
temperature – analogue signal.

Outputs
windows – digital signal (either open or closed)
heater – digital signal (either on or off)
pump for water spray – digital signal (either on or off).

In practice, the control could be much more complicated than this. For example, we could have windows which opened by small amounts depending on the temperature and the humidity.

Computers and safety of cars

Many new cars are fitted with a braking system called ABS (antilock brake system). ABS uses sensors to detect the rotational speed of each wheel when the brakes are applied. The speed of each wheel is relayed to the computer. If the wheels start to lock, the computer sends a signal which eases the pressure on the brakes at each wheel. This prevents the wheels from locking and sliding out of control. Using ABS, a driver is able to control the car more safely during braking.

QUESTIONS

The greenhouse in Figure 20.8 is used to grow delicate plants and must be kept at a constant temperature of 24–28°C throughout the year. If it gets too hot, the glass panel is opened by a motor. If it gets too cold, the glass panel is closed.

You now have to write some pseudo-code which will do the following:

- start with the window closed

- wait for the temperature to rise above 28°C

- produce a sound (e.g. a buzz) and then open the window to allow the cooler air in

- wait for the temperature to fall below 24°C

- produce a sound (e.g. a buzz) and close the window.

It is decided that this system would be incapable of maintaining the temperature in the winter, so a heater needs to be included. Decide on the series of steps that the system would take and write a new piece of pseudo-code for the control program.

Figure 20.8

Data logging

Data is often collected automatically over a period of time and then processed at a later date. You may have seen pressure sensors which look like thick wires placed across the road to record the volume of traffic passing.

If you follow these sensors they lead to a black box which is usually padlocked to a lamppost to prevent it from being stolen. This box, called a data logger, records data about the volume of traffic passing. The alternative way of recording this data would be to use humans to do it manually. This is clearly expensive and not the most exciting of jobs.

There are two main types of data loggers: those which need to be connected to the computer all the time and those which don't.

Data loggers with permanent computer connections

These data loggers take readings and then send them to the computer via a wire or an electronic signal. The computer can either process the readings at once to produce a graph or store them on disk for processing at a later date. These data loggers are ideal for experiments in the laboratory but suitable ones for use in the field are too expensive for schools to use.

Data loggers with temporary computer connections

These data loggers are ideal for monitoring environmental conditions over a period of time in the field. As with all data loggers, the time intervals (the time between each reading) and the period over which the logging takes place can be varied.

The readings are stored by the data logger then at a later date loaded into the computer

where they can be processed and displayed. Because they are used in remote places, these data loggers need their own power supply.

Data logging has many advantages:

1 it can be performed 24 hours per day, 365 days per year if necessary
2 it is possible for processing to be carried out immediately if the data logger can send the data in the form of a radio signal to the main computer.

QUESTIONS

You have been concerned about the road where you live being used by lorries, vans and cars as a short-cut to avoid a busy junction. You have persuaded local residents to sign a petition which has been sent to your local council.

The council has said that it will monitor the situation and place a data logger on the road for two weeks.

(a) Explain what a data logger is.
(b) To monitor the flow of traffic you got together with the other residents to stand at the side of the road and to count the number of certain types of vehicles travelling along the road between 10 and 11 in the morning.
   (i) What advantages does the data logger have over your manual method?
   (ii) What methods of display could be used to present the data from the data logger?

Things to do

1 (a) A computer program is used to control a robot, which is moving and stacking boxes in a warehouse. The program uses commands to control its movements
FORWARD steps
BACK steps
RIGHT angle
LEFT angle
UP steps
DOWN steps

Figure 20.9

For example,

FORWARD 50   moves the robot forward
50 steps in a straight line.

RIGHT 45   turns the robot 45° to the right.

UP 2   raises the forks 2 steps.

The robot is found to be dropping the boxes in the wrong place.

Give two different mistakes in the program that could be causing this.

(b) Following a nasty accident, the robot has to be adapted to stop if it meets an unexpected obstacle in its path. What changes would need to be made to the robot design?

(NEAB/WJEC)

2 In Figure 20.10 the heating of water in a tank is under the control of a microprocessor. Cold water enters the tank via valve 1. It is heated to a set temperature and leaves the tank via valve 2.

(a) Describe how feedback could be used in the system.

(b) (i) Where should an analogue-to-digital converter be placed in the system? Draw your answer on the diagram.

(ii) Why is an analogue-to-digital converter necessary?   (MEG)

Figure 20.10

3 (a) A washing machine is designed to wash, rinse and spin for predetermined times regardless of whether the washing is clean or not. Is this an open-loop or closed-loop control system?

(b) A central heating system is continually monitoring the temperature of a room. If it is too cold, the heating is switched on. When the room gets too hot the system switches the heater off. Is this open-loop or closed-loop control?

(c) Traffic lights may either use closed-loop or open-loop control. Using traffic lights as an example, explain the difference between open-loop and closed-loop control.

4 Computer systems are now being used in hospitals as part of life-support systems.

(a) Blood pressure is a human physical response suitable for monitoring by computer. Suggest two others.

(b) Give three reasons why computers are used in life-support systems.

(c) Give three tasks for which human medical staff are more suitable than computers.

5 A car park entrance (shown in Figure 20.11) is controlled by a microprocessor.

When a car approaches the barrier a ticket is produced, which the driver takes. The barrier then opens, and the light changes from red to green. When the car has passed, the light changes to red and the barrier comes down.
(a) Describe a suitable sensor for detecting the approaching car.   (2 marks)
(b) List the steps involved in carrying out this process, using suitable instructions.   (4 marks)
(c) What information needs to be on the ticket?   (2 marks)
(d) Give two ways in which this can be encoded in machine readable form.   (2 marks)

(SEG NC IT Spec)

Figure 20.11

6 The table below shows a number of different situations. Fill in the boxes to show the time intervals between logging and the overall period of logging.   (NEAB/WJEC Option Q)

Situation	Sensor	Time interval	Period of logging
Collecting data on seasonal temperature variations for weather records	Heat		
Collecting data about the temperature change which takes place when ice is added to a beaker of water	Heat		

7 The greenhouse shown in Figure 20.12 must be kept at a temperature between 24°C and 28°C throughout the year. It has been decided to use a computer controlled system. Produce an outline design for the system which is required.

(NEAB/WJEC Spec Option R)

Figure 20.12

8 A diagram of a refrigerator is shown in Figure 20.13.
  (a) What quantity does the sensor measure?
  (b) A refrigerator makes use of feedback. Explain what feedback means and say why it is necessary to have it in the refrigerator.
  (c) A control program is stored on the chip. Write down a series of instructions which will help keep the refrigerator at a constant temperature.
  (d) When the door of the refrigerator is opened a light comes on. Examine your fridge at home and see if you can find out how this sensor works.
  (e) Insurance companies pay out large sums of money each year to people who have ruined food by leaving the door slightly open. Design a system which could help prevent this problem.

Figure 20.13 *Refrigerator*

21 Computers and your Health

The problems

There are many health problems that can occur when you are working with computers for long periods. Repetitive strain injury (RSI), backache, eyestrain, headaches and skin rashes are conditions which can occur. By using various devices, correct posture and good working practices, these conditions can be prevented. Figure 21.1 shows some things you ought to pay attention to when working with VDUs.

Figure 21.1 *What you need to work efficiently at a computer*

Repetitive strain injury (RSI)

RSI is caused by the joints in the fingers constantly being pounded by typing at high speed. RSI causes pain in the joints and can cause long term disability. Good keyboard design, a well positioned keyboard, a good typing technique and frequent breaks can help prevent RSI from occurring. You can also buy wrist guards which ease fatigue when you are using keyboards for long periods.

Eyestrain

In a study of VDU operators, it was found that nearly 70% suffered some form of eye problem such as eyestrain, irritated eyes or blurred vision. However, eyestrain is fairly common in other types of close work. One way of avoiding eyestrain is to look at a distant object now and again (ask your physics or biology teacher to explain why this helps). Regular computer users should have regular eye checks.

Reproductive hazards

There have been some stories in the newspapers regarding abnormal births in pregnant women who have been using VDUs for long periods. VDUs, like a lot of other electrical appliances, give out radiation when they are working. Most of this radiation is given out from the back and the sides of the VDUs. A large amount of research has been done on this and at the moment there is little evidence that VDUs do any damage.

Figure 21.2 *There are lots of scare stories concerning radiation from VDUs. There is no real evidence though, so you needn't worry*

Figure 21.3

Protecting the workforce

Because of the various health problems that can occur with incorrect computer use there is now a law which requires employers to provide the following:

- **Inspections** – Desks, chairs, computers, etc. should be inspected to make sure that they reach the required standard.
- **Training** – Employees should have training on health and safety matters.
- **Job design** – The job should be designed so that the worker has periodic breaks or changes of activity when using computers.
- **Eye tests** – For computer users there should be regular free eye tests, with glasses provided if necessary, at the employer's expense.

The law also lays down some minimum requirements for computer systems and furniture. All new furniture and equipment bought must meet these standards:

- **Display screens** – These must have a stable picture with no flicker. Brightness, contrast, tilt and swivel must be easily adjustable. There must be no reflection off the screen.

- **Keyboard** – This must be separate from the screen and tiltable. Keyboards should be easy to use and the surface should be matt to avoid glare. There must be sufficient space for people to change position.
- **Desks** – Desks must be large enough to accommodate the computer and any paperwork and must not reflect too much light. An adjustable document holder should be provided so as to avoid uncomfortable head movements.
- **Chair** – This must be adjustable and comfortable, and allow easy freedom of movement. A foot rest must be available on request.
- **Lights** – There must be no glare or reflections on the computer screen. Windows must have adjustable coverings.
- **Noise** – This should not be loud enough to distract attention and disturb speech.
- **Software** – This must be easy to use and appropriate to the user's needs and experience.
- **Other matters** – Heat, humidity and radiation emissions must be kept at adequate levels.

Things to consider when designing an office

1 Single pendant lamps (like the ones you have in your house) should be avoided since they produce glare on the screen. Instead, fluorescent tubes with diffusers (plastic covers) which spread out the light, should be used.
2 Carpets made of man-made fibre should be avoided. These cause static electricity which can destroy data stored on magnetic disks.
3 Windows should have adjustable blinds on them to avoid sunlight producing glare on the screen.
4 Cables should not be left trailing across the floor.
5 Ample sockets should be fitted so that it is not necessary to use multiple sockets, which could be dangerous.

Things to do

Figure 21.4

1 The cartoon in Figure 21.4 shows all sorts of poor working practices and bad equipment. How many can you spot? Write a list and say what needs to be done to put them right.

2 There are various products for sale in computer catalogues which are aimed at the 'computer safety market'. Look at these catalogues and write a brief report stating what devices are available and how much they cost.

3 You have been asked to look at the equipment and the working conditions in your school or college's computer rooms. Some of the things you should look at are:

- whether sockets have too many plugs in them
- whether carpets are made of man-made fibre
- whether document holders are provided
- whether there are adjustable blinds on the windows
- whether wires trail across the floor.
  - (a) Your task is to complete this list of things to look for. After you have completed your list design a suitable document which can be filled in when you look around the room. This document should be wordprocessed.
  - (b) Look around the computer room and fill in the document.
  - (c) Prepare a report which gives a summary of what you have found, making any recommendations where necessary.

The paper chase

Processing insurance claims

Claims occur when, for instance, a car is crashed and the money is claimed for its repair. Here are the steps that used to be taken by an insurance company when it was processing claims:

1 The post was opened.
2 The appropriate file was found in the series of filing cabinets.
3 The files were taken to the person who was handling the case.
4 The person who was handling the case wrote letters concerning the case.
5 Letters were sent to the typist for typing.
6 Typed letters were received back by the person handling the case.
7 Letters were signed and posted, and copies of the letters were placed back in the file.
8 The files were sent back to the filing clerk for filing.

The above system of 'paper chasing' took several days and another problem arose: if a customer rang, it was difficult to locate a file. This all resulted in slower claims and high administration costs. These costs meant that the company had to charge more for its insurance and this caused loss of business to other insurance companies, who were more efficient and therefore cheaper.

The company therefore decided to try to remove paper from the office and to do as many tasks as possible electronically. In other words the company decided to convert to an electronic office.

When the electronic office was introduced, everything was stored on the system. All correspondence, including diagrams of scenes of accidents and photographs could be scanned into the system. Paper correspondence and photographs are destroyed quickly

(usually after about seven days). When claims staff arrive at work they now log into the system and it gives them a list of jobs which need action. The system provides a complete history of the claim, including brief details of any telephone calls made.

Advantages of the new system

1 The clerks do not need to leave their desks, since all the information relating to a particular claim is available from the computers on their desks.
2 Claims are handled much more efficiently, which in turn means more satisfied customers.
3 Paper costs have been cut and photocopying costs are much lower, since it is no longer necessary to keep a copy of every letter sent out.
4 The costs of phone calls have decreased: it is no longer necessary to call people back because files needed to be 'hunted down'.

Figure 22.1 *Electronic office in a school*

Equipment and facilities in an electronic office

Fax

A fax machine is rather like a long distance photocopier, where you put the document into the fax machine at one end and a copy comes out of a fax machine at the other end. The original is first scanned with a beam of light and then converted into electronic signals that can be passed along the telephone lines. The copy is printed out at the other end on the recipient's machine.

Faxes are particularly useful, since drawings can be transferred. Also, because a fax is really a picture of the document, letters or contracts which include a signature may be sent and this is useful to lawyers. If you have a fax/modem then you can send faxes from your computer without the need to print out and then scan them.

Electronic mail (e-mail)

With electronic mail (e-mail), data or messages can be sent electronically via the telephone network or other data networks and via a central computer. Electronic mail has advantages of speed and economy (there is no need for stamps, envelopes, etc.). With electronic mail both sender and recipient can store the letters or documents on disk for future reference.

Electronic mail is used extensively by companies that have networks for their internal mail. The wider use of electronic mail is hindered because not everyone has the facilities.

Figure 22.2

Electronic data interchange (EDI)

EDI is the method by which different companies' computers automatically exchange data. Large food retailers such as Tesco use this method. When Tesco stores are running low on a certain item such as baked beans, an order is automatically issued and sent electronically to the supplier's computer where it is dealt with. Payment for the goods is made electronically from the retailer to the supplier via their bank accounts. This all happens without any paperwork.

Things to do

1   Draw a diagram of a paper-based office and include on your diagram the usual areas such as:
    - photocopier and print room (containing a photocopier and a duplicating machine)
    - filing room (containing filing cabinets and a microfilm reader)
    - typing area (containing manual typewriters)
    - accounts area (containing typewriters and calculators)
    - post room (containing addressing machines, postage meter, sorting racks for incoming mail, telex and telephone switchboard).

2   Now draw a diagram of the office after it has been converted into an electronic office.

3   With the introduction of electronic offices, some people's jobs will change, while others may even disappear. With reference to the following list, say how each job might change and state which, if any, of the jobs will remain the same.
    - filing clerk
    - copy typist
    - shorthand typist
    - secretary
    - post-room clerk
    - manager
    - accounts clerk.

4   An ordinary telephone which has no special features can be used only to dial numbers and receive incoming calls. Investigate the latest phones and explain the features that are now available.

5   There has been a great increase in the use of systems involving communication between computers.

    Describe a system which makes use of a communication network.

    (NEAB/WJEC Spec Option Q)

23 Simulations

Almost as Good as the Real Thing

Figure 23.1 *Computer modelling*

We can create on the computer a 'pretend' economy and then take certain courses of action and see what the results are. Doing this, we can see the effect of any disastrous decisions on our artificial economy rather than have to suffer the consequences on the real economy.

This all sounds simple. If it works, why do we have such high unemployment? Well, we could produce a model of the economy in many different ways. Different models use different equations. For instance the model used by the UK Treasury has about 1300 equations. As you can see, there is plenty of room for error here.

In this example we have used the words model and simulation. There is a difference in the meanings of these words. A model consists of a set of equations which describes the behaviour of a process or object. In a computer model we use the computer to

Modelling

Suppose for a moment you are the Chancellor of the Exchequer (Figure 23.2). Your job will be to control the economy as best you can. You will have to make decisions about what to do. For instance, you can alter the amount of taxes people pay, how much the government spends on education, benefits, the NHS, etc. Changes in any of these will affect the economy. One false move could plunge the country into a recession and make life miserable for millions of people.

Before making any decisions, the chancellor needs to ask 'what would happen if I did this?' For instance, if a minimum national wage were to be enforced (i.e. no one could be paid below a certain amount) what would the result be? Would it reduce poverty or would it lead to mass unemployment?

A computer simulation can be used to provide an answer to these sorts of questions.

Figure 23.2

Expert systems

Expert systems are programs that mimic the intelligence of a human expert in a specific field of knowledge. For instance an expert system could be set up to give medical advice. The computer is given a base of knowledge from the expert and then given the rules for processing the information. The idea is that the computer asks questions similar to those the expert would ask and then comes to a similar conclusion.

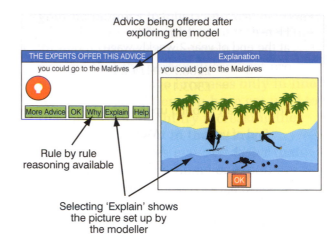

Figure 23.5 *You can add diagrams using Expert Builder*

Figure 23.4 *Model to provide advice about holiday destinations*

Expert Builder

Expert Builder is another package that enables you to construct logical diagrams of your knowledge. This software helps you to understand a problem more clearly and consolidate this knowledge. Figure 23.4 shows a screen from Expert Builder. Here, the model is being used to provide help about holiday destinations. As with Model Builder, you can add diagrams like the one shown in Figure 23.5 to provide explanations.

Energy Expert

Energy Expert is a software package consisting of four modules, covering advice, heating, forecast and comfort.

- The 'advice' module investigates how to save energy by using insulation, etc. A screen is shown in Figure 23.6.

Figure 23.6 *Advice on how to save energy*

- The 'heating' module is used to explore the heat losses in a typical house and how these can be reduced using certain features when the house is built. Heat losses and gains can be calculated using a spreadsheet and these can then be displayed graphically. Figure 23.7 shows the model.
- The 'forecast' model is used to compare the links between outside temperature and domestic demand for heating. Figure 23.8 shows a typical screen.
- The 'comfort' model looks at the way the human body regulates its temperature. It looks at biological concepts such as cell respiration, human temperature regulation and homeostasis (Figure 23.9).

Figure 23.7 *Heat losses in a typical house*

Figure 23.8 *Using a spreadsheet to compare the links between outside temperature and domestic demand for heating*

Figure 23.9 *Looking at why one person can feel hot while another can feel cold, even in the same room*

Simulations

When most people think of simulators they think of flight simulators, but there are other types of simulation. Simulations are useful, for example, in experiments that would be too difficult, too dangerous or too costly to carry out.

Examples of simulations include:

- experiments in chemistry
- nuclear physics experiments
- airline training
- queues at petrol filling stations
- traffic light systems
- queues at supermarket checkouts.

When new bridges or buildings are being designed by engineers, they can simulate the construction by using the computer to calculate the stresses at various points and discover the safest construction without having to build it first. Simulations are usually performed to avoid the expense or danger of making mistakes.

Flight simulators

Airlines find it very expensive to tie up aircraft for the training of pilots, so they use simulators instead. In addition, all manner of dangerous flying conditions, some of which the pilot would never be likely to experience, can be simulated. A landing simulation with ice on the runway, thick fog and only one of the four engines working would really test the pilot's ability.

Flight simulators like the one shown in Figure 23.10 enable pilots to experience turbulence, snowstorms, thunderstorms, fog and airpockets as well as landing at different airports throughout the world, without leaving the ground.

If you look at Figure 23.11 you can see that a flight simulator is a windowless capsule that looks like a spacecraft. The hydraulically controlled struts (i.e. the legs) can propel the machine in six directions, simulating the pitch and roll of a real plane. In helicopter simulators a vibrating pilot's seat is used to add reality; and in fighter plane simulators the seat has air pumped into

Figure 23.10 *Inside a flight simulator*

Figure 23.11 *Flight simulator viewed from the outside*

it to simulate the 'g' forces when the pilot performs tight turns.

The scene out of the 'windows' is as realistic as the behaviour of the plane. When a particular airport is chosen the scene looks identical to the surroundings of that particular airport.

An example IT task
A predator/prey model

Suppose that we wanted to protect the vegetables in a greenhouse against attack by greenfly. We could either use pesticides, or use a 'natural' method by introducing a predator of the greenfly, namely the ladybird. To find out the optimum number of ladybirds to introduce, we have to understand something about how the predator (the ladybird) and the prey (the greenfly) reproduce. With no control over their numbers, the greenfly would multiply at an alarming rate and eventually destroy all of the crop. On the other hand, it is hard to eliminate all the greenfly and, if we did this, the ladybirds would all starve to death. The optimum state is when the population of the greenfly has reached equilibrium, where the numbers of greenfly are constant. When this occurs the ladybirds will have enough to eat and the damage to the crop will be minimal.

When setting up this model you need to decide on the inputs to the system.

What are the inputs?
We can divide the inputs into two:

- inputs for the predators (i.e. the ladybirds)
- inputs for the prey (i.e. the greenfly)

The inputs for the predators will be:

- the number of ladybirds at the start of the year
- the breeding rate (factor by which they increase each month)
- the number of greenfly each ladybird eats each month.

The inputs for the prey will be:

- the number of greenfly at the start of the year
- the breeding rate (factor by which they increase each month).

We now need to design a spreadsheet model. We will use three columns:

Start of Month	Number of ladybirds	Number of greenfly

Let us first look at the situation for the first month, January. The situation will be as follows:

Start of Month	Number of ladybirds	Number of greenfly
Jan	10	100

At the start of February the following will happen. The number of ladybirds will increase by a factor of 1.5, so there will now be 15 of them. The greenfly will breed, increasing their population by a factor of 4, making their number 400. However, during January some of them will be eaten. If we assume that the 10 ladybirds at the start eat 30 greenfly in the month, then 300 greenfly would be eaten making a total of 100. So, at the start of February, we will have 15 ladybirds and 100 greenfly, as shown in the table:

Start of Month	Number of ladybirds	Number of greenfly
Jan	10	100
Feb	15	100

Problems with the model

The above model is too simple. It does not take account of the following areas.

1 The breeding rates of the ladybirds and the greenfly won't stay the same throughout the year. The rates will probably increase in the warmer months. We really need to alter the breeding rates for the summer months and make them different from the winter months.

2 If there is not enough food for the ladybirds to eat, they will die.

3 We also need to incorporate a death rate for the ladybirds into our model. To make it simpler, you could assume that the greenfly will remain alive provided that they do not get eaten by the ladybirds.

QUESTIONS

1 Produce a revised model taking the above into account.

2 You have been asked to extend this model for the whole of the 12 months. Do this using a spreadsheet and make sure that you link the cells using formulae.

Things to do

1 Write down one reason why computerised simulation is better than using a manual simulation for each of the following situations:
   (a) a simulation to find out how many checkouts will be needed at a new supermarket
   (b) an experiment to find out the best temperature for carrying out a chemical process.

2 You can use spreadsheet software to make a computer model.
   (a) Give an example of an investigation for which you would use a spreadsheet package to make a computer model.
   (b) Describe how you would set up the model on the spreadsheet.
   (c) Explain why you would use the computer model instead of creating the real thing.
   (MEG)

3 (a) Give one advantage of using a computer model to study the relationship between hunting animals and their prey.
   (b) Give two reasons why your teacher may prefer to use a simulation rather than a school trip to an African jungle.
   (c) What software package would you use to display the data collected.
   (MEG)

4 Flight simulators are used to train airline pilots.
(a) Describe what a flight simulator is.
(b) What advantages are there in using such a flight simulator rather than using a real aircraft?

5 A local council wants to know if it should re-design a road junction. It has three options – leave it as it is, put in a set of traffic lights, or construct a roundabout.
(a) Explain how a computer model could be useful to the council.   (3 marks)
(b) What data would be required for the model?   (3 marks)
(c) For each item of data above, describe how the council could collect the data. (3 marks)
(d) What other variables might be used in the model?   (2 marks)

(SEG q4 HT Spec Question)

1 A certain type of bacterium increases its numbers at the rate of 20% per hour. If there are 100 bacteria at the start of the day produce a model showing how the population will have grown over each hour in the day.

2 This task is suitable only for students taking level R mathematics at GCSE.

The iterative formula for finding the cube root of a number n is given by

$$a_{n+1} = 1/3 \, (2a_n + N/an^2)$$

Produce a spreadsheet where you can put in a number n, and the computer simulates the iterative process and comes up with the answer correct to five decimal places. Test your model using the following numbers: 27, 50, 1480 and 3600.

Some ideas for models and simulations

1 Explain the effect of pollution on a river system.

2 Collect data from a science experiment and then use the data from the results to find the relationship between the variables.

3 Look at the heat supply and the heat loss from a house.

Skills Building

IT TASKS

Task 1

The depreciation of cars

You have been asked by a car dealer to produce a model of the depreciation of cars. You will need to consider the following when building or refining your model.

- Is the depreciation the same for each year or do cars depreciate more in the early years?
- Do some cars depreciate more than others? How can this be built into the model?
- You could try comparing the values in your model with values obtained from a car price guide which you can obtain from any newsagents.
- You could produce a series of graphs showing how the price varies over a number of years.

Finally, produce a report on your model/simulation.

IT TASKS

Task 2

Dangerous situations

Simulations are often performed using computers where the real situation would be too costly or dangerous to perform any other way. Investigate such situations and produce a brief report outlining your findings.

HP Bulmer Ltd (cider makers)

HP Bulmer is a medium sized British company based in Hereford and has been involved in the making of cider for over 100 years. Cider is an alcoholic drink made by fermenting apples and it has enjoyed an upturn in popularity over recent years. The company produces the brands Woodpecker, Strongbow and Scrumpy Jack, amongst others (Figure 24.1). There are around 1000 employees and approximately 500 of these use computers. About 400 use personal computers (PCs) in the course of their work.

Figure 24.1 *Three of the top ciders in Britain's bars – Strongbow, Scrumpy Jack and Woodpecker*

Bulmer's information systems

As with a lot of companies, it is common to see old information systems being replaced by modern systems.

The older computers are being rapidly replaced by Unix equipment. Unix is an operating system used primarily in multi-user computing where a lot of terminals are needed. The advantage of Unix over other operating systems is that it can be used with a variety of different computer hardware. In the past, if you bought one make of computer hardware then you generally had to stick with the same company when upgrading the system. This tended to make systems expensive both to buy and to maintain. There is a very large number of application programs available to Unix users and this is another of its advantages.

One problem with the old system was that there was more than one customer file used by different departments. This meant that analysing sales was difficult because the results were different depending on which version of the customer file was used.

The new system

The largest system used by Bulmer is the Distribution Management System. This organises the distribution of the bottles, cans and kegs (the aluminium barrels) to the customer, telesales and credit control (making sure the company is paid for the cider).

There are other systems. For instance, there is a system that deals with giving important financial information and is able to track the bartop equipment which is installed in many pubs up and down the country. Other systems are involved in pricing, and customer and product information.

The keg information system

Bulmer sells draught cider in tens of thousands of pubs, wine bars and restaurants throughout the UK. The keg technicians are responsible for installing and repairing the equipment needed to dispense the draught cider at the bar. This equipment includes the pump you see on the top of the bar, the cooler unit and all the pipework which goes to the keg.

When something goes wrong with the equipment or a new customer needs equipment installing, a telephone call is made to the head office where the scheduling is organised. The schedules for each of the 30 technicians scattered throughout the UK are transferred overnight via telephone lines to each technician's hand-held terminal.

During the day, the technicians record the jobs they have done using their hand-held terminals and this information is relayed back over the telephone lines to Bulmer's head office where the central computer files are updated. Using this system, the technicians are able to deal with more calls in a day and the people involved in co-ordinating this activity can be engaged in other tasks. A future development might be that technicians will be given portable modems in their cars so that the files can be updated in real time. If any problems crop up in the course of the day, then the technicians can be alerted. If a particular technician is near where the problem is, then that technician may be able to squeeze in an extra visit.

Personal computers

All the company's PCs are networked in a local area network (LAN). Each terminal can therefore be used for sending electronic mail. Electronic mail is also used to send mail to a subsidiary company in Australia and is now being used with some of the company's major customers.

Electronic data interchange

Many of Bulmer's larger customers operate electronic data interchange (EDI), where orders and invoices are sent and received electronically, thus eliminating the need for paperwork.

EDI works by connecting personal computers via a modem to a carrier called Tradanet. In this way Bulmer can deal electronically with all its main suppliers such as the bottle manufacturers and its main customers such as Tesco .

Process control by computers

The way in which cider is made at Bulmer's world-famous Hereford cider mill has almost jumped a century. The traditional methods of the nineteenth century, which had changed little since Percy Bulmer founded the business in 1887, have been replaced by the latest computer-controlled technology. Cider maker Jonathan Blair now has a computer screen to assist in the art of cider making (see Figure 24.2).

In 1994 the company invested £20 million in a brand new cider-making plant, giving it the most modern cider-making plant in the world. All the processes such as fermentation, microfiltration (to remove the yeast and make the cider clear) and the movement of the cider around the plant, are controlled by computer. Figure 24.3 shows a cider production worker checking the flow of cider on the computer. Figures 24.4 and 24.5 show the inside of the fermentation hall and the view of the 50 feet high fermentation vessels from the outside. Overlooking the hall is a control room where a single person can run several processes using computers.

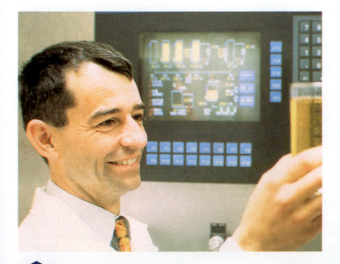

Figure 24.2 *Cider maker Jonathan Blair now has a computer screen to assist the art of cider making*

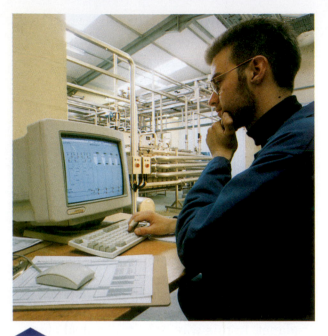

Figure 24.3 *A cider production worker checking the flow of cider on the computer*

Figure 24.4 *Inside the fermentation hall*

So that the changeover to the new equipment went as smoothly as possible, the staff took part in 'hands on' simulation courses. Here they could use computers to simulate control of the new system. Any mistakes did not matter, whereas if they happened with the actual equipment mistakes could ruin a 50 000 gallon batch of cider.

The use of this equipment allows Bulmer to produce a consistent high quality product at a lower cost.

Computers in the laboratory

To make sure that the cider is of the highest quality, frequent tests are performed on it. The laboratory systems record the results of the tests and action can be taken if necessary. Although it is possible for the computer-controlled equipment to measure the alcohol quantity (Figure 24.6) etc. the real flavour of the cider can only be appreciated by a human taster (Figure 24.7). For this reason Bulmer

Figure 24.5 *A view of the 50 feet high fermentation vessels from the outside*

Figure 24.6 *Computer control enables the strength of the cider to be continually monitored*

to the company's own staff. Because of the costs involved in sending presentation material to outside agencies the company is now able to produce the material itself.

Bulmer has a graphics presentation unit with scanning equipment, a special printer capable of printing acetate slides in colour and a large 37 inch VDU to display the work.

A graphics analyst is employed, whose job it is to run the unit. This person checks the work that comes in from other departments to make sure that it is of a high standard before it is printed. The cost of sending the material to an outside agency was around £200 000 per year; doing the task within the company has reduced the cost to about £70 000 per year.

still uses a panel of tasters whose job it is to taste the cider (and spit it out, unfortunately). As you can imagine, this is a difficult job but someone's got to do it!

Using computers to help with presentations

At Bulmer, presentations have to be given regularly to the city, potential customers and

Possible new developments

One new development that is currently being pursued is to equip the sales staff who visit new customers with portable PCs so that they are able perform account planning using spreadsheets and so that they can record details of contacts and arrangements for follow-up calls. Already, they are using multimedia packages for customer presentations.

Figure 24.7 *Some jobs, such as cider tasting, are best left to humans*

Things to do

1 (a) Bulmer uses an operating system called Unix.
   (i) Name two other operating systems.
   (ii) Give three functions of an operating system.
  (b) Large companies frequently upgrade their systems. Explain what this means.

2 PCs are connected together to form a local area network (LAN).

  Give three advantages of using a network rather than using stand-alone machines.

3 Bulmer uses EDI (electronic data interchange).

  Explain what advantages there are to:
  (a) Bulmer
  (b) the company's customers in using this system.

4 As well as using computers for administrative tasks, Bulmer also uses computers for controlling the processes involved in the making of cider.
  (a) Explain what advantages there are in using computerised process control rather than doing the tasks manually.
  (b) Before the new process control equipment was introduced, staff were sent on a course which involved computer simulation.
   (i) Explain what simulation is.
   (ii) What is the advantage of using simulation rather than actual equipment?

5 Bulmer is now giving presentations using multimedia and uses portable PCs for graphics presentations.
  (a) What is multimedia and how does it differ from a presentation on an ordinary computer system?
  (b) In what ways do you think multimedia would be useful in promoting the company's products or image.

6 Bulmer can be considered an environmentally friendly company. After reading this chapter, what evidence is there to suggest this?

7 What do you think are the benefits and drawbacks of the new system? How has the nature of the work changed over the years?

1 The data below shows the volume share of the premium cider market. Premium cider is the more expensive, higher strength bottled cider. The percentages shown below refer to the years 1992 and 1993.

Name of brand	Year	
	1992	1993
Merrydown	38.0%	28.8%
Diamond White	29.7%	22.8%
Scrumpy Jack	6.8%	9.5%
K	6.2%	8.3%
Strongbow Super	3.6%	6.8%
Red Rock	5.0%	4.5%
Electric White	0.8%	3.7%
Blackthorn Super	2.2%	2.4%
1727	0.1%	2.1%
Others	7.6%	11.1%

(a) Using spreadsheet or graphics software, produce a side-by-side bar chart so that the market information in the above table can be compared.

(b) From the bar chart you have produced, write a brief report on the brands that have done well and those that have suffered.

2 To produce new brands that will appeal to the new drinker, Bulmer has to do market research. The company has to find out what characteristics a typical cider drinker has. The table below shows a profile of today's cider drinker.

	All adults	Strongbow drinkers	Regular lager drinkers
Regularly read: The Times/FT/ Guardian/Independent	9%	13%	9%
Agree that:			
"I like to try new drinks"	27%	44%	39%
"I like to stand out in a crowd"	12%	19%	15%
Drink:			
Brandy	29%	36%	32%
Port	22%	32%	24%
Malt whisky	21%	30%	27%

Also important is a profile of the type of outlet (e.g. pub, wine bar, etc.). You have been asked to prepare a questionnaire that the Bulmer representatives or technicians can fill in when they visit a new establishment. They need to find out if it is a typical old fashioned 'boozer' full of older men drinking pints of bitter or mild, or a new trendy place for younger people drinking newer bottled premium beers and cider. You should include boxes to be shaded in so that the forms can be read using an optical mark reader.

3 When people buy cider from retailers such as Tesco, Asda, Sainsbury, etc., they are able to buy it in a variety of different sizes and packaging. For instance they can buy cans and bottles of different sizes. To see which are the most popular packages and volumes bought, the following data has been collected.

	1989	1992	1993
Cans	5.9%	12.0%	15.6%
1/1.5 litre	30.4%	23.6%	20.8%
2.0 litre	47.4%	43.5%	41.5%
3.0 litre	5.3%	9.9%	11.1%
Other	11.1%	11.1%	11.1%

Using graphics or spreadsheet software, produce a pie chart for each year to show the above data.

By looking at each one, say what trends you can spot. Produce a brief report using wordprocessing software and, if you can, try to incorporate the charts you have created into your wordprocessed document.

4 The following recipe is for Cider Mulled Punch.

Ingredients
2 small eating apples
6 cloves
10 cm (4 in) cinnamon stick
10 ml (2 level teaspoons) ground ginger
50 g (2 oz) soft brown sugar
1 small orange
1 bottle Strongbow cider

Method
(a) Remove the cores from the apples and 2.5 cm (1 in) width of skin from around the tops.
(b) Stick two cloves into the sides of each apple and then bake in a moderate oven at 180°C (350°F) gas mark 4 for 20 minutes.
(c) Meanwhile, put the other two cloves, the cinnamon stick (broken into four pieces), ginger, sugar and water into a medium sized pan.
(d) Heat the pan slowly until the sugar dissolves, bring the mixture to the boil and simmer it for five minutes.
(e) Cut the orange into thin slices. Remove the pan from the heat, immediately add the orange and leave it to stand.
(f) When the apples are cooked, transfer them to a punch bowl and break up the flesh without removing it from the skin.
(g) Strain the spiced water into the punch bowl. Pour in hot (but not boiling) cider and serve at once.

This recipe looks rather dull the way it is presented here. Try to make it more appealing by using DTP, graphics or wordprocessing software. Can you incorporate any graphics or clip art to brighten it up? See what you can do.

5 Figure 24.8 shows a table which has been drawn and then typed. Your task is to produce a copy on your wordprocessor. Not all wordprocessors have the facility to produce tables so you will need to check with your teacher. If your wordprocessor is unable to do tables then see if you can do it using spreadsheet software.

Skills Building

STRONGBOW   COMMENTS

Appearance: Clear, straw-coloured, lightly sparkling.
Aroma: Slightly fruity with a bittersweet apple char-
                   acter.
Flavour: A medium dry, fruity, full-bodied cider with a
                   clean slightly astringent aftertaste.

WOODPECKER

Appearance: Clear, amber-coloured, lightly sparkling.
Aroma: Sweet and fruity with a slight toffee-apple
                   note.
Flavour: Clean and sweet with a fruity cider apple char-
                   acter.

ORIGINAL

Appearance: Clear, pale amber, lightly sparkling.
Aroma: Fruity dessert apples.
Flavour: Sweet, dessert apple cider.

SPECIAL RESERVE

Appearance: Clear, amber, lightly sparkling.
Aroma: Alcoholic, fruity dessert apples.
Flavour: Clean, slightly sweet and alcoholic with a
                   full body and slightly sharp culinary apple
                   character.

Figure 24.8

Skills Building

Information technology: helping to solve crime

Crime has become very sophisticated and, as a result, harder to detect. To handle this, the police have very sophisticated methods of crime detection at their disposal. Information is the key word in crime detection and this information must be accurate and obtained quickly.

The Police National Computer (PNC)

The Police National Computer (PNC) now provides rapid access, day and night, to information of national as well as local significance, to all the police forces in England, Scotland and Wales. The large mainframe computer is linked to terminals in police stations throughout the country. Since there are a large number of terminals linked to the main computer there is a complex switching mechanism and this allows each terminal to obtain information from the main computer in as short a time as possible. Some police vehicles are equipped with terminals which are used to access the PNC directly.

The information held on the PNC is separated into indexes, each index dealing with a particular subject. Some of these indexes are cross-referenced. Here are some further details on each of the main indexes.

Stolen and suspect vehicle index

Every day hundreds of vehicles are stolen. Some are taken only for joy rides and recovered by the police fairly quickly, while others are stolen permanently and are re-sold or stripped down for their parts. Many stolen cars are used in other crimes or are involved in accidents.

As soon as an owner reports that a car is missing, information such as the registration number, make, model and colour are keyed into the PNC at one of the many terminals. Once this information has been obtained, it is transmitted via radio to policemen in patrol cars, who are then on the lookout for the vehicle.

As well as holding the obvious details about the car, the index also holds chassis and engine numbers, since many cars will have their identities concealed by the use of false plates or by being sprayed a different colour.

There is a partial registration number facility, so if only part of the registration is known, then a list of cars can be produced fitting the bill. This is very useful if the car is used for a robbery or if it has been involved in a hit and run accident and witnesses can only partially remember the number or type of vehicle.

Vehicle owner index

The information for this index comes from the DVLA (Driver Vehicle and Licensing Authority) at Swansea. The index contains all the names and addresses of the registered keepers of vehicles, together with descriptions of the vehicles.

If the registration number is known, then the owner can be contacted if the car is stolen and he/she is not aware of the theft. Again, if the number is only partially known, the vehicle can still be traced.

It is possible for the stolen and suspect vehicles index and the vehicle owner index to be searched together, using the registration number as the search key.

Names indexes

The police have records in these indexes of people who fall into any of the following categories:

1 persons convicted of serious offences
2 persons wanted or sought by the police for various reasons

3 persons missing or found
4 disqualified drivers.

As soon as the police receive details about any person who falls into one or more of the above categories, they can obtain information from the PNC.

The computer can assist the police by informing them if a suspected person is likely to be armed or dangerous. It is also possible for the computer to search all the files simultaneously to find out everything known about a particular person.

Computerised fingerprint index

Fingerprinting is the science of using the patterns of ridges on our fingertips for identification purposes and it was one of the earliest forms of scientific evidence accepted by courts of law.

Fingerprints obtained from objects at the scene of a crime are taken and then compared with the suspect's fingerprints. Although fingerprints cannot always prove that a suspect committed a crime they do prove that they were at the scene of the crime at some time. Fingerprints used to be compared manually but now many police forces use a computerised system designed to store and match the prints.

Broadcast system

Other than indexes, the PNC is also used to help the police in other ways. The broadcast system allows one police force to send urgent information to other police forces. If a car is stolen and used in a serious crime, then all the police forces along, say, a certain stretch of motorway can be alerted. Ports and airports can also be alerted using this system, to stop criminals escaping to another country.

Other computers used by the police

As well as being able to access the Police National Computer, all police forces have their own computer systems situated at their headquarters for help with administration and also to help in solving major crimes. One system called MIRIAM (Major Incident Room Index and Action Management) is used to

store information from enquiries about serious crimes so that senior officers can decide how to go about their investigation. Figure 25.1 shows how MIRIAM co-ordinates all the information.

Figure 25.1 *How MIRIAM sorts out all the information from a large scale enquiry, so the senior officers can make decisions about how to solve the crime*

Using 3-D modelling to help to solve crimes

In many murder cases the body is found months or even years after the crime was committed. Frequently there is only a skeleton left, so identification of the victim is made very difficult. It is often necessary to produce a picture of what the person might have looked like using the skull as a frame. In the past this was done by an artist working with a Plasticene model. Now, detailed measurements of the skull are input to a computer and the computer comes up with a three-dimensional model of the likely face belonging to the skull. The advantage of the new system is that the face can be modelled quickly and costs are reduced.

Electronic security cameras

Electronic security cameras have helped cut down violent crime and robberies in many of our city centres. Sometimes these cameras are visible and act as a deterrent, whereas others are hidden and are used during police surveillance. Although most people feel safer in city centres with the use of these cameras, some people feel that they are an infringement of privacy. Cameras are also used for traffic control at busy junctions and on motorways.

Figure 25.2 *The police often use hidden cameras*

Information technology in the supermarket
Tesco: a case study

Tesco is the largest food retailer in Britain. Tesco used to have many small shops on every high street, but the company has been concentrating on the development of the huge units we see today called superstores. Each superstore stocks over 14 000 food lines alone and has a sales area of over 25 000 square feet.

The laser scanning system (barcode reading system)

Tesco was one of the first high street companies to use the barcode reader which is now called a laser scanner.

The objectives of the scanning system are to improve the service to customers and to increase company productivity and profits. Figure 25.3 shows the scanning system used to scan in a barcode.

The scanning system uses a laser beam to read the barcode on the goods. The bars contain the same information as the numeric code at the bottom of the barcode without the likely inaccuracies of typing the number in. As the barcode is passed across the scanner this number is read and the price and description of the goods are obtained from the computer, the sale registered and an itemised receipt produced.

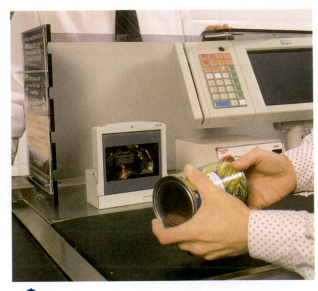

Figure 25.3 *Using a barcode reader in the desk of a point of sale terminal*

Benefits of the system to the customers

There are numerous benefits to customers and these include the following.

1 With the old system, prices were entered into the cash register manually. With the scanning system this is done automatically, which eliminates typing errors, so accurate pricing is assured.
2 The scanning till is estimated to be 15% more efficient, so customers will spend less time waiting to be served.
3 Produce such as loose tomatoes are weighed at the checkout so customers no longer have to queue twice; once at the pricing point and again at the checkout.
4 Customers can have their cheques and credit card vouchers automatically printed.

5 Customers using a debit card such as Switch can withdraw up to £50 in cash from any checkout.

6 More promotions may be offered, such as 'buy two and get one free' (multisaver).

7 An itemised receipt is produced. This receipt will often include detailed information about what has been bought.

Benefits of the system to the company

Some benefits are easily quantified but others are more difficult.

1 Checkout accuracy is improved. There are no longer any operator errors and fraud is limited, since in the past it was possible to key in a lower price and pocket the money.

2 Throughput is faster and more efficient. There is, on average, a 15% saving in time to register the goods in a shopping trolley.

3 Customer service can be improved. New services such as Clubcard, multisavers, etc., ensure customer loyalty.

4 Productivity is increased. There is no need to price each individual article, as in the past. Prices are included on the edges of the shelves next to the articles. Weighing and pricing at the checkouts eliminates the need for separate pricing points.

5 Sales information from the checkout is used to create the orders for stock replacement.

6 Stock levels can be reduced. More efficient stock control means less money tied up in stock and less likelihood of running out of certain items on the sales floor.

7 Wastage is also reduced. Perishable goods such as fresh meat and salads can be ordered accurately using the sales information obtained from the checkout.

8 Promotional analysis and sales analysis are improved. Scanning data can be used to assess the effectiveness of special promotions and can provide important information about the sales of certain goods.

The barcoding system

Figure 25.4 below shows a barcode from a tin of Heinz baked beans. The number at the bottom is called the European Article Number (EAN); a number is allocated to all product manufacturers by the Article Number Association. The system works as follows:

- the first two digits represent the country where the goods are produced
- the next five digits identify the manufacturer of the goods
- the following five numbers identify the product
- the final number is a check digit and is used to check that the other 12 numbers have been entered correctly.

EFTPOS and the use of debit cards

EFTPOS stands for electronic funds transfer at point of sale and is the method used by Tesco to transfer money from customers' credit card companies or debit cards directly

Figure 25.4 *How a computer uses a barcode*

to the Tesco bank account. A debit card is rather like a cheque, since the money comes straight out of the bank account. However, there is no limit to the amount you can spend using one of these cards, provided that you have the money in your account. This is in contrast to cheques where there is a limit (usually £50 or £100) to the value of the cheque that is covered by the guarantee card.

Using checkout information for planning bakery production

Sales information from checkouts is used by in-store bakeries to plan the production for the same day for the next week. This reduces wastage and means stores are less likely to run out of bread.

Sales-based ordering

Sales-based ordering is the automatic re-ordering of goods from the warehouse using the sales information from the checkouts. If, for example, 200 tins of baked beans are sold from a certain store in one day, then 200 tins will be automatically re-ordered and delivered to the store the following day from one of the Tesco distribution centres.

The large articulated vehicles you see are specially constructed: they have compartments which can be kept at different temperatures, so, for instance, chilled food, frozen food and other types of food which do not need cooling may be carried in the same vehicle.

Stock control

All ordering is performed by computer. There are fast electronic communication lines between the shops, the distribution centres and the head office. There are also direct links to the major suppliers, which means that orders can go straight through to production lines. One advantage of this is that stock arrives just in time before sale so it is always fresh. Another advantage of this system is that money does not need to be tied up in stock and can be used for more productive purposes.

Electronic shelf labelling

Tesco is developing a system with liquid crystal shelf labels containing the price, description and ordering information about goods. The label is operated from the computer using radio signals and this avoids human error, where a price change on the computer is not transferred to the shelf. This means that changing a price on the computer database and shelf can be done at the same time so the price stored and that on the shelf will always be the same.

Electronic data interchange (EDI)

Electronic data interchange is a method of speeding up the transfer of orders to suppliers. Using EDI eliminates the need for paperwork, since the ordering is done by data being transferred between the supplier's computer and Tesco's computer. This system is less expensive and faster than sending the orders by phone, post or fax and cuts out errors, such as lost or wrongly printed orders. Tesco can send information to suppliers regarding sales forecasts and information about stock levels so that they may plan their production appropriately.

Once an electronic order has been placed, the electronic invoice is generated automatically by the supplier's computer. This is sent back and checked by the Tesco computer before payment is made.

Tesco: the hardware

We have looked at the systems in use by Tesco. As you can imagine, the computers to run these types of operations are some of the most sophisticated and powerful computers in the world.

The mainframe computers are situated in two computer centres and each is capable of running the company's systems on its own. The computers are capable of delivering 216 MIPS (million instructions per second) and are the fastest commercial computers in the world.

Since computers are so vital to Tesco's operations, there are backup procedures in place so that even if one of the computer centres were completely destroyed, the other would be able to re-establish the vital systems within 48 hours. The backup procedures are tested each year so that staff know exactly what to do if a disaster were to occur.

Designing store layouts using CAD

It is no longer necessary to use drawing boards for planning new stores and re-designing existing ones. Instead, computer aided design (CAD) is used and this has reduced the time taken to plan new stores. A databank holds designs and plans from many stores and these may be adapted for new stores. CAD is also able to show three-dimensional views of the stores; colours, lighting and different finishes of material can be altered simply with a mouse.

When a new store is to be placed in an existing high street, photographs of the existing shops in the street can be used in conjunction with CAD to see what the street will look like with the Tesco front in place.

CAD is also used to design warehouse layouts, the roads and the surrounding areas around the distribution centres. This is important since the company needs to make sure that there is ample room for the large articulated vehicles to turn round.

Warehouse systems

Computers are used in the warehouse to monitor complex stock control procedures and make the best use of space, time and labour. Like all areas of retailing, better operating methods need to be found to ensure Tesco's continued success. As with all the other systems, paperwork has been eliminated wherever possible, so the thick binders containing stock items are replaced by computer terminals. In fact, these terminals can be found mounted on fork lift trucks; they give the operators information regarding the movement of the pallets so that they may be moved quickly and efficiently. If some stock goes out of the warehouse then a slot is available for the new stock arriving and notification of this is obtained from the terminal. Efficient use of the available space means that the trucks have to travel shorter distances and the whole process is therefore faster.

The computer system also monitors where each fork lift truck is situated in the warehouse so that a particular job can be given to the fork lift truck best able to complete it in the least amount of time.

Electronic mail

Tesco, like a lot of forward looking companies, has realised the benefits of using electronic mail. With conventional methods of communication there many problems, such as lost post, unanswered telephones, engaged fax machines, people not at their desks, etc. To try to contact someone urgently during office hours can be more difficult than you think. Electronic mail eliminates many of these problems.

The store system used by Tesco uses a series of standard forms, so memos, letters, reports, etc. all have a set format. Advantages to Tesco in using electronic mail include:

1 The recipient does not need to be there when the message is sent; he or she can receive mail at any terminal connected to the system. Compare this with a telephone call where someone needs to be available to answer the call.
2 People can be sure that the messages are received.
3 It is possible to send mail to a department or a group of people. Anyone in the company can send mail to a whole department without knowing anyone in the department by name.
4 The electronic mail system is used as a company information and notice board. Members of staff can find out about the latest job vacancies and appointments, and look at the latest share price.
5 Electronic mail can be sent to the major suppliers, thus speeding up orders, etc.

Information technology in the music industry

Sound recording

Sound recording involves detecting sound and then storing it somehow in analogue or digital code on either tape or disk so that it can be played back at a later date. During playback, the coded data on the storage medium is recovered, amplified and fed to loudspeakers to create a copy of the original sound.

Synthesisers

In a modern recording studio, the sound waves are picked up by microphones which convert the sound signals into electrical signals. The signals from each microphone may be combined together using a device called a mixer to give the final recording.

In many pop recordings, the electrical signals which correspond to the desired sounds or notes are generated directly using a device called a synthesiser. These signals can be combined with signals produced from conventional instruments and recorded.

Recording studios

Many rock groups do not just turn up and play a piece of music for it to be recorded. Instead they like to experiment with the music and try many different approaches. Often the vocals or rhythm patterns are on the first track of a 24-track tape. Different instruments, such as drums, pianos, guitars and keyboard synthesisers are added one at a time to the other tracks. Certain qualities of the music from each track can be altered separately, such as volume, echo and reverberation. Then all the tracks can be mixed together. Because the music is recorded onto tape, this process can take a long time.

The use of computers in recording studios has considerably speeded up the recording process. Modern studios use tapeless recording, with the music initially stored digitally in the random access memory (RAM) of the computer. For permanent storage, the music can be stored on the computer's hard disk. Because the music is initially stored in RAM there is immediate access should it need to be altered. Sounds can be added or removed very easily.

Sound sampling

Sound sampling is performed when a sound is taken into a computer system. For instance, a microphone can be used to take 'a sample' of a certain sound such as the bark of a dog. The computer stores the sampled sound as a digitally coded signal which can be altered if necessary and replayed when needed.

IT and the TV/video industry

Computer generated graphics

Computer generated graphics are images designed by graphic artists that are used for logos, commercials and news inserts during television or video transmissions. The artists use systems similar to a painting package produced for microcomputers. Some of the more sophisticated graphics systems allow artists to produce three-dimensional images.

Special effects

Sometimes when watching the television you see images manipulated in some way to produce special effects. These may be produced with digital video signals, since each pixel (dot of light) on the screen can be moved individually. Using a computer with special software it is possible to change the shape of a picture to, say, a circle or hexagon. You can also zoom into the image, rotate it and even manipulate several different images on the screen at the same time.

Animation

In the past, to produce animation, it was necessary to draw a series of images, each one differing slightly as the movement proceeds. A picture was taken of each diagram (frame) and then the series of frames played back. This process is tediously slow and requires whole teams of artists, so the final piece of animation or cartoon is very expensive.

Individual frames can be created using graphics software. A start frame and an end frame are produced. The software then produces the animation between these two frames automatically. The computer has to be told about the rate at which the intermediate images are to be produced. Because the number of frames is often quite large, powerful computers with large hard disk capacities are used for this type of work.

Information technology and medicine

All hospitals make use of information technology and, because of the diverse nature of the work that hospitals do, the computer has many quite different uses.

Organ transplants

Computers are very good for looking at and comparing lists. When a person dies and their organs are donated, the computer can be used to match and identify a patient to receive them. This needs to be done extremely quickly and this is why computers are essential (Figure 25.5).

Figure 25.6 *Computer diagnosis!*

Figure 25.5

Computers are used to diagnose many illnesses (Figure 25.6). Often the information is fed directly into the computer from machines attached to the patient, such as electrocardiographs, which measure the heartbeat, and body scanners.

Computers can be used to locate tumours at an early stage when, by other means, they cannot be easily and surely detected. Body scanners send rays into the body (Figure 25.7) and these are picked up by a detector. Signals from the detector are analysed by

the computer and converted to a digital form which can then be displayed as a picture on a television screen (Figure 25.8). On screen the tumour appears as a dark patch.

Figure 25.7 *Using a body scanner with computer diagnosis*

Intensive care

In intensive care units, computers are used to monitor instruments which record important data about the patient. If the data moves outside certain limits, an alarm is sounded, so that immediate medical help can be brought.

The measurements constantly taken by the computer might include blood pressure, pulse rate, heart waveshape from an ECG, respiration rate and volume, and electrical signals from the brain. Previously, these measurements needed to be taken so regularly that a nurse was needed for each patient. Now, many more patients can be looked after by one nurse.

Computers are also used to monitor vital data during surgery in the operating theatre.

Keeping patients' records

Computers can be used to provide a complete, accurate, up-to-date and readily available source of information about patients' health. Records of patients are usually kept for the duration of their lives so, in the past, a large amount of space was taken up by paperwork. There were also problems in locating a particular patient's file – especially if, say, the patient moved about the country a great deal.

Most hospitals now store patients' records on magnetic tapes or disks. The information can be found immediately by the computer. There are terminals at certain places in the hospital where doctors or nurses can find details of a particular patient very quickly.

Inpatients' records are probably best kept on magnetic disk. This method allows quicker access because it is a random access storage medium. These records will be needed much more often than the outpatient records. Outpatient records contain a large quantity of information that may only be used, say, a couple of times in a patient's lifetime. So these records can be stored on magnetic tape which has a slower access time.

New data can be added to the patient's records by keying this into the computer via a terminal. Thus the patient's record can be kept up-to-date with the latest information about his or her condition or circumstances.

Figure 25.8 *Information from the body scanner is used, here, to build up a picture of the human brain, in sections. Any tumours can thus be precisely located*

Doctors and nurses used to spend about 30 per cent of their time processing information in files, but now this has been vastly reduced because of the introduction of computers.

One problem with using a computer in this way is that very confidential information is kept about the patient. Obviously, many patients would not like this information to be seen by just anyone. One way round this problem is to introduce a code or password which the user needs to type into the computer before he or she can gain access to the patients' files. Another way, used in some of the extremely complicated systems, is to allow the terminals only a certain amount of necessary information for different users. So, a nurse could obtain some information, and a doctor would be able to get further details.

Information technology and banking

Banks were one of the first business organisations to use computers and this experience has meant that they have always been at the forefront of any new technology. Banks make use of a variety of systems and many of these have already been encountered. If you need any information on the following aspects of banking, then you should refer to the index. To help you locate this information, here is a list of topics that have been covered elsewhere in the book.

    MICR (magnetic ink character recognition)
    EFTPOS (electronic funds transfer at point of sale)
    EDI (electronic data interchange)
    Credit card use
    EFT (electronic fund transfer)
    Credit card fraud
    Smart cards

Some aspects of banking which have not been covered elsewhere are detailed below.

Cheque clearing

Suppose Jane wants to buy a portable colour television from Comet Electrics and pay by cheque. Jane banks with Lloyds and Comet Electrics banks with Barclays. The Figures here and on the next page show what happens to the cheque, from when it is given to

1   Jane writes out a cheque for £240.00 made payable to Comet Electrics.

2   Comet Electrics pay the cheque into their Barclays branch.

3   Barclays Bank types in the amount of the cheque in magnetic ink characters so that it can be read at the clearing house using MICR.

4   All cheques, including this one, are sent to a bank in London called a clearing house. Here, all the cheques are sorted into bank sorting code numbers.

5   The details of all the transactions (items of business) are sent on magnetic disk to the Bank of England from the clearing house. The Bank of England transfers the £240 from Lloyds Bank to Barclays Bank.

6   The cheque is sent from the clearing house to Jane's branch of Lloyds Bank, identified by a sorting code number, where the amount is deducted from her account.

7 Barclays Bank receives notification that the cheque has been cleared and credits Comet Electrics' account with £240.

8 The whole process of cheque clearing takes a minimum of three days.

Never mind about clearing me to bank, I needed clearing to land!

Figure 25.9

Comet Electrics to when the money is subtracted (debited) from Jane's account and added (credited) to Comet Electrics' account. This process is called **cheque clearing** and, because of the huge number of cheques cleared each day, computers are used for nearly all of the process.

Bankers' Automated Clearing Services (BACS)

Bankers' Automated Clearing Services Ltd was set up by the larger banks to deal with standing orders and direct debit payments. It is situated in Edgware, north-west of London, on the spot where the old De Havilland aircraft factory stood and where Amy Johnson's famous aeroplane was built in the late 1920s.

As well as processing transactions that take place in this country, BACS also houses the Swift computer for the UK which deals with international payments.

The BACS service is used to pay two-thirds of all monthly salaries directly into employees' accounts. It is also used to pay regular bills and payments such as pensions, council tax, mortgages, loan repayments, etc.

The BACS computers keep a diary of all the payments to be made. These payments are made and are transferred between the banks on magnetic tape. The fact that not many people have heard of BACS shows the system's reliability and success.

ATM (automated teller machines)

ATMs are the 'hole in the wall' cash dispensers which many people use when the bank is not open or when they do not want to queue inside.

Here are some of the things you can do using an ATM:

- get cash out
- find out the balance in your account
- change your PIN (personal identification number)
- make deposits (i.e. put cash, cheques or both into your account)

- obtain a mini statement listing your recent transactions (i.e. money in and out of your account).

How the system works

1 The customer is given step by step instructions on how to operate the cash dispensing machine.
2 The keyboard (input device). The customer types information in here, including the customer's secret number (PIN).
3 a This is where the customer inserts the plastic card. The card must be inserted the right way round.
  b From here, the amount of money the customer has keyed in is released.
  c This is the VDU screen where messages appear, such as 'Enter personal number'. The screen gives instructions to the customer.

Figure 25.10 *Using an ATM*

Benefits to the banks in using ATMs

There are some benefits to the banks in the use of ATMs and these include:

- Staff are freed from performing routine transactions so that more profitable sales-orientated work can be done.
- Fewer staff are needed since the computer does much of the routine work.
- A 24 hour per day service is provided to satisfy their customers' demands.
- The system makes it impossible for a customer to withdraw funds from their account unless they have the money in their account.

Benefits to the customer in using ATMs
- Some customers prefer the anonymous nature of the machine since it cannot think you have stolen the cheque book or that you are spending too much.
- It is possible to use the service 24 hours

per day; ideal for those people who work irregular hours.
- It is possible to park near the dispenser in the evening, so getting cash is a lot quicker.
- There are fewer queues since the transactions performed by the ATM are a lot faster.

Traffic control systems

Computerised traffic control systems are a feature of all large towns and cities. Their purpose is to keep the traffic moving particularly during the morning and evening rush hours.

The main aims of a traffic control system are:

- to improve traffic flow
- to reduce accidents caused by driver frustration (e.g. changing lanes frequently)
- to make sure that delays in a journey are kept to a minimum
- to reduce the pollution caused by the exhaust fumes from stationary or slow moving traffic
- to reduce the amount of fuel used by drivers (cars use fuel inefficiently when crawling along).

Traffic lights need to be set to a sequence that can be varied throughout the day. During the morning rush hour the lights can be set on green longer for those main routes into the town and in the evening the lights are on green longer for the routes out of town.

One system called SCOOT does not work with a set sequence for the lights. Instead the traffic lights are sequenced to try to keep the number of lights on red to a minimum. Sensors in the roads are used to detect the frequency of the vehicles on either side of a junction and these are used as the inputs to the computer system. The data from these sensors are sent to the computer using either wire-based or fibre-optic cables. The computer then analyses the data and sends signals back to the lights that amend the traffic signal timings and the offset between the sets of lights.

In an emergency, the system is able to give emergency vehicles an uninterrupted path through a system of linked traffic lights. It does this by giving a green signal to the emergency vehicle as it reaches each set of lights along the route.

Car park management systems

Car park management systems are computer-controlled systems that direct vehicles round town centres to car parks with available space. The special signs tell motorists how many spaces are available in each car park by working out how many vehicles have arrived and how many have left. These signs, which operate in real time, reduce congestion by getting the cars into the nearest available car park without them having to drive around from one car park to another.

Vehicle speeding systems and red light cameras

Vehicle speeding systems consist of sensors to detect the vehicle speed and a camera that takes a picture of the speeding vehicle with the speed superimposed on the photograph. Using the registration number, the Police National Computer (PNC) is used to obtain the name and address of the registered keeper of the vehicle so that appropriate action can be taken.

Red light cameras detect and photograph those vehicles that have jumped traffic lights.

Figure 25.11 shows a truck passing through a red light detected using a red light system.

Weather forecasting

The Traffic Control Centre also has several remote weather stations which collect data about the weather and relay the data back to the centre using modems and telephone lines. The physical quantities measured by the system include the following:

- wind speed
- humidity
- air temperature
- ground temperature.

Although the data from the weather station is also passed to the Meteorological Office (weather centre) for the production of weather forecasts, the data can also be used

Source: Tracon Systems Ltd

Figure 25.11 *Jumping the lights*

to predict the likelihood of black ice on the road surface. When the weather system shows that there could be black ice forming overnight, an ice alert goes out which means that the gritting teams who put salt and grit on the road can be sent out.

There is another important type of sensor that is able to detect the amount of salt on the road surface. For instance, if a road has been gritted the previous night, and it has not rained or snowed, there may well be enough salt left on the road to avoid the need for further gritting. The whole system saves both overtime money paid to the gritting teams and the cost of the grit used.

Pollution monitoring

Local authorities often have to monitor air pollution in their areas. Most of them do this remotely and they have sensors which monitor the main polluting gases (nitrous oxides and sulphur dioxide) situated at the busiest junctions. The data from these is used to monitor the air quality and it is also used by the Meteorological Office to record air quality information for the region as a whole. Again modems and telephone cables are used to transfer the data to the authority's technical department where the traffic control system centre is situated.

Advice on Coursework

Coursework is the main element in GCSE Information Technology and can be worth up to 60% of the total marks. Your teacher will tell you about the problems you have to solve using IT. Problem solving skills are important in doing this coursework. This means that the examiners want to make sure that you have approached a problem correctly. Therefore, as well as solving a problem, you have to provide evidence that you have gone about the task in the right way. You need also to test your solution to make sure that it works. You must fully document your solution, which means that you have to write about it and provide evidence along the way. 'Evidence all the way' should be your motto when doing coursework. Unless you have written about it or produced other evidence such as printouts or even photographs, then the examiner will not know that you have done the work.

Figure 26.1 *Evidence all the way*

What software can I use?

The minimum list of software you should have experience of is:

- wordprocessor
- database
- spreadsheet
- desktop publishing
- data logging or control software
- simple modelling/simulation software.

You may also need to know about the following:

- hypermedia software (another name for multimedia software)
- graphics
- statistical software
- drawing and painting software
- web authoring software.

You can use other software in addition to the types above but always make sure that the software you are using is the most suitable software for performing the task.

Hints and tips

1 Plan your work beforehand and make sure that you have or can obtain the software and hardware necessary for the task.
2 Choose your coursework carefully (if you have a choice) and don't be too ambitious. Discuss it with your teacher to make sure that it is not too difficult.
3 Wordprocess or desktop publish your work. Since you are following an IT course, you should make use of all the latest technology.
4 To save time, type your work directly into the wordprocessor without writing it out first. If you need to make changes, such as insert text, delete text or shuffle material around, then this is easily done.
5 Always include all your work, even the parts that didn't work. The work provides evidence of your solution and must be included to maximise your marks. Remember that a good solution to a problem is a good solution partly because of all the bad solutions that have been rejected.

6 Make the front cover look attractive but do not spend too much time on it.

7 Include diagrams wherever possible. They brighten up the page and by using them you can cut down on the number of words used. Diagrams you should use, if appropriate, include systems flowcharts, structure diagrams, etc.

8 Always keep backup copies of your work on disk and do not keep the backup copy with the original. It is a good idea to get a photocopy of any text.

How much do I write?

Remember that it is quality, not quantity, that the examiners are looking for. Some examination boards stipulate a maximum number of pages for each piece of coursework and you should check with your teacher whether your exam board is one of them. Usually the number of pages excludes computer output. Do not think that because a friend's project is much thicker than yours, that it will be better.

Use diagrams wherever you can to help describe the project and do not include anything that is not relevant.

Can my teacher help me?

Your teacher might be able to give you some ideas for projects. In fact some of the boards have projects set by the teachers themselves. He or she will know your abilities and will give you advice on the suitability of your project choices.

No one other than your teacher should help you. You will be asked to sign a form to say that the work is your own.

Note – Your teacher/lecturer will be keeping an eye on your coursework as it progresses and will know the level of your abilities. If someone helps you, this will be cheating and your teacher will be able to tell.

Do you get marks for your English?

All GCSE subjects, and IT is no exception, have a small percentage of the marks allocated for grammar, spelling and punctuation.

When you are doing the coursework you can use the facilities offered by most word-processors and some DTP and graphics packages to check the spelling. Some advanced wordprocessors will even check your grammar for you.

Don't forget that if you use these tools, they are not substitutes for careful proof reading. It is a good idea to get someone else to proof read your work for any obvious mistakes.

What is entailed in the coursework?

The coursework really depends on the examination board and the syllabus you are following. It is always a good idea to get a copy of the syllabus so that you know exactly what you have to do. Your teacher may be able to supply you with a syllabus or you can buy one by asking for a price list of syllabuses and past papers from the examination boards, whose addresses are at the back of this book.

Learning about software

Suppose you want to learn about how to use a particular package, what is the best way?

There are many different ways in which you can build up your expertise and skills in using software and these include:

Using computer magazines
Computer Active is a cheap computer magazine published every fortnight and contains step-by-step workshops which show you how to do things using popular software.

Get your parents, relatives or friends to show you
Many of them will have used the packages and will probably be only too glad to help you. By sitting down with an experienced user for an hour or two you can learn very quickly.

Use a computer manual
Sometimes these come with the package but many rely on on-line help to give advice. Libraries and bookshops are sources of a

wide range of guides to suit all levels of expertise.

Use the on-line help facility

Most packages come with excellent on-line help. Many people forget that this help is available and are quite amazed at what they can find out using it once they are shown. Sometimes in the on-line help there is a complete tutorial which guides you through using the package. Try to get used to using this facility and it will really help you improve your skills in using the package and also improve the mark you will get for the coursework and in the examination.

Figure 26.2 shows how you search for help on a certain topic in Microsoft Word.

Figure 26.2 *Searching for help in Microsoft Word*

Figure 26.3 is an example of the on-line help provided with Microsoft Word 97. The user wants to know how to put a box around text that has been typed on the screen. In this case they have typed in what they want to do (i.e. putting boxes around text). The help routine finds the topics nearest to what you want. You can then look at these.

Figure 26.3 *On-line help in Microsoft Word 97*

Using the previous screen, the user has chosen to find out about the difference between a text box and a frame. Next the help screen in Figure 26.4 appears.

Figure 26.4 *The difference between a text box and a frame*

Coursework for your examination board

Because the type of coursework you have to do differs so much from one examination board to another, it is impossible to look in detail at the requirements for each one. Your teacher/lecturer will give you details about what is expected from you. In the next section we will look at a brief summary for the main examination boards.

SEG Full course

You will be required to submit reports on two coursework tasks, one from each of the following themes:

- communicating and handling information
- controlling, measuring and modelling.
- Both of the coursework tasks will carry the same number of possible marks and each of them should take between 15 and 20 hours to complete.
- A report of approximately five sides of A4 should be produced for each coursework

task along with any other evidence such as printouts, graphs and photographs.

- Both reports should be wordprocessed.

The marking scheme is arranged in the following way and you should format your report so that you have material falling under most of these headings:

- choice of problem
- description of problem
- investigation and analysis of problem and specification of solution
- design of solution
- implementation of solution
  - resources
  - data collection, data capture and input
- data verification and validation
- data and program structures
- output format
- testing of solution
- documentation of solution
- evaluation of solution.

Communicating and handling information

Your coursework task covering this theme needs to be on an application where IT is used to process and present information. Any of the following software could be successfully used to produce a piece of coursework covering this theme. You could base your project on just one of these packages or a number of them:

- wordprocessing
- graphics
- desktop publishing (DTP)
- computer aided design (CAD)
- database
- spreadsheet
- presentation graphics packages such as Microsoft Powerpoint
- development of a website.

Controlling, measuring and modelling

Your courseware task covering this theme will need to focus on applications where IT is used to model a real life situation, or to investigate 'what if problems' and to measure and process physical data.

Any of the following software could be successfully used to produce a piece of coursework covering this theme:

- spreadsheets
- specialist modelling and simulation software
- expert systems
- programming languages.

SEG Short course

For the short course in IT you are required to submit a report on one coursework task from either of the following themes:

- communicating and handling information
- controlling, measuring and modelling.

Guidance is given on how long you should take over the task and how much you need to write:

- The single coursework task should take between 15 and 20 hours to complete.
- The report on the coursework task should consist of approximately five sides of A4 along with any other evidence such as printouts, graphs and photographs.
- The report should be wordprocessed.

The single report should cover the same headings as in the full course outlined above.

London Full course

Coursework contributes 60% to the final mark. For this exam board and syllabus, you will be required to solve a total of FOUR distinct problems.

For each of the four problems you have solved, you will need to keep notes to provide evidence for your solution. These notes should be structured under the following headings:

- identify
- analyse
- design
- use and/or implement
- evaluate.

You may not be able to put notes for your solution under all of these headings since the headings may not be suitable for certain solutions.

There must be four distinct problem types and two of them must be:

- file creation and interrogation
- creation and manipulation of spread-sheets.

The remaining two must be chosen from the following:

- data logging and control
- wordprocessing
- desktop publishing
- free choice 1
- free choice 2.

London Short course

Coursework contributes 60% to the final mark. For the coursework, you will be required to solve a total of TWO distinct problems. For each of the two problems solved, you will need to keep notes to provide evidence for your solution. These notes should be structured under the following headings:

- identify
- analyse
- design
- use and/or implement
- evaluate.

You may not be able to put your notes for your solution under each of these headings since the headings may not be suitable for certain solutions.

Two distinct problem types must be addressed, chosen from the following list:

Either (i) Type (a) or Type (b)
OR (ii) Type (a) and ONE of (c), (d) or (e)
OR (iii) Type (b) and ONE of (c), (d) or (e)

(a) File creation and interrogation
(b) Creation and manipulation of spread-sheets
(c) Data logging and control
(d) Wordprocessing
(e) Desktop publishing

Northern Ireland GCSE Information Systems Full course

Coursework will account for 30% of the total marks for the course. For this board you will be required to produce a single piece of coursework which solves a particular problem. The coursework will be marked under the following headings:

- analysis
- design
- implementation (communication of solution and testing strategy)
- user documentation
- review
- presentation and coherence.

The coursework should take the form of a written report which should:

- include a table of contents which makes reference to numbered pages
- be presented under the headings outlined above
- not exceed 20 A4 pages, excluding print-outs
- be wordprocessed where appropriate.

OCR Full course

Coursework accounts for 60% of the total marks for the course. The coursework for this course consists of a 'compulsory practical coursework task' and either the board sets an 'associated task' or a 'centre set task.' The centre set task is a task which your school or college set you and which has been approved by the examination board. In addition to this, you must complete a case study of an IT application.

OCR Short course

Coursework accounts for 60% of the total marks for the course. You must submit coursework that covers any two of the following:

- communicating
- handling
- measuring
- control
- modelling.

To cover any of two of the above you can use either one or two pieces of coursework. Your teacher/lecturer will give you either tasks made up themselves or ones obtained from the examination board. If you wish to, you can re-submit the coursework for the full course at a later date.

WJEC Full course

For the final asssessment, 60% of the marks are based on coursework. The coursework consists of a portfolio and a project (30% for each). The portfolio of work is assessed and in it you will have shown your capabilities in information technology. In your portfolio you have to demonstrate your best achievement in at least one of the following :

- communicating
- handling information
- controlling and measuring
- modelling.

For the project, you will have to submit a report on the solution to a problem which you use to demonstrate your information systems capabilities. You can draw the subject matter for your project from any suitable area. You must also make sure that your project is based on two of the elements not covered by the portfolio.

There are four sections you have to include in your project and these are:

- statement of the problem and its analysis
- design of the solution
- development of the solution, implementation and testing
- evaluation.

WJEC Short course

For the final assessment, 60% of the marks are based on coursework. The coursework consists of a portfolio of your work which demonstrates your best achievement in two of the following:

- communicating information
- handling information
- controlling and measuring
- modelling.

As part of the documentation for the coursework, you have to provide information under the following headings:

- analysis
- design
- implementation and testing.

NEAB Full course

Coursework contributes 60% to the final assessment and consists of an examination board-set assignment and a project.

The board-set assignment (25%) consists of a description of a situation where the appropriate use of IT will solve some given problems. For this you have to produce a report where you will demonstrate your ability to analyse a problem in order to identify what the requirements are and to make use of IT to provide solutions which you will then design, implement, test and evaluate.

For the project (35%), you have to submit a report on the solution to a problem which demonstrates your IT capability. You can choose the area from which the project has been chosen.

NEAB Short course

Coursework contributes 55% to the final assessment and consists of an examination board-set assignment. You will be given this assignment to do by your teacher. The assignment will consist of a description of a situation where the use of IT will solve some given problem. You will be asked to produce a report which demonstrates your ability to analyse a problem, identify the requirements and make use of appropriate IT in providing a solution. You will then design, implement, test and evaluate this solution.

IT TASKS

Task 1

Example projects

Carry out a survey of shops and/or amenities in your local area. Collect suitable data and produce information for use by the following groups of people:

(a) residents of the area
(b) tourists visiting the area
(c) the manager of the shop/amenity listed
(d) the local council.

One or two samples of work suitable for each group of people are required. The samples should cover a wide variety of output.

Asthma, a disease which makes it difficult to breathe, is on the increase. A simple survey of the people in your class will reveal just how many people suffer from it. There are many different drugs on the market to help the sufferer, and the doctor has the difficult choice of deciding which one would be best for the patient. One way of deciding this is to use a device called a peak flow meter.

A peak flow meter is used to find out how good someone's breathing is. The patient blows into the mouthpiece, a marker moves along the barrel and a reading is obtained. The higher the reading, then the better the person's breathing. Usually three readings are taken and the highest reading is the one that is recorded.

Readings are taken using the meter twice per day, once before the patient gets up and once before they go to bed. The doctor gives the patient medicines to take and, using the peak flow meter, the doctor can see which one works best. The best medicine will give the highest peak flow readings.

Readings from a peak flow meter

Date	a.m. reading	p.m. reading
22/6	390	560
23/6	260	560
24/6	380	520
25/6	250	550
26/6	270	550
27/6	400	580
28/6	320	560
29/6	410	550
30/6	300	350
1/7	300	400
2/7	400	570
3/7	430	550
4/7	440	570
5/7	480	580
6/7	480	560
7/7	450	540
8/7	460	550
9/7	470	560
10/7	460	570
11/7	450	560
12/7	450	570

(a) Design a form to be used by a patient to record the peak flow readings over a 21 day period. The readings are taken twice a day (three readings each time) and the highest of the three readings is the one that is recorded.

(b) A patient has been using a peak flow meter and has obtained the readings on the previous page. Using graph/spreadsheet software, plot this graph. Write a suitable title for the graph and label both the x and y axes.

You should be able to spot the following from your graph:

- when the patient had a very bad cold
- when the patient was transferred to the new medicine which improved her condition.

(c) The company that makes the peak flow meter has heard of data logging and would like to investigate a system whereby the meter could log the data over a 14 day period, store it and then be able to feed it into the doctor's personal computer so that the graph is obtained automatically.

Investigate this idea. Some of the things you should look at include:

- what sensors to use
- what additional equipment might be needed
- whether it would be too expensive.

Produce a feasibility report with your findings.

IT TASKS

Task 2

You are to produce two reports on the connection between the number of doctors in various parts of the world and the deaths of young babies. One is for a popular newspaper, and the other is for a serious environmental magazine.

Use the World Development Database to find out which countries have high and low numbers of people per doctor, and which have high and low proportions of infant deaths. Use graphs to provide further evidence for a connection between the number of doctors and the deaths of babies.

Use suitable software to produce the draft of a newspaper article, which will not contain any graphs. Write 100 words, making your findings as dramatic as you can.

Choose software which can combine your lists and graphs with the article. Adapt your article to suit the more serious magazine style, extend it to 300 words and incorporate appropriate lists and graphs to illustrate your points.

(RSA NC IT)

Wordprocessing and Wordprocessing Exercises

Wordprocessing packages are the most popular type of computer software. For many people a wordprocessing package is the only software they use. It is hard to think of a single job where some use for wordprocessing could not be found.

Many people now type their own documents directly into a computer rather than give them to a typist. This saves time, if people can type quickly. Because the text is stored in memory once it is typed, people can alter their text before finally saving and printing (Figure 27.1).

Now, even printing letters is becoming out-of-date because electronic mail is often used to send wordprocessed documents in electronic form from one place to another. There is no need for an envelope or a stamp and the recipient may store the letter on disk for future reference, thus saving valuable storage space.

Hardware and software for wordprocessing

The most common hardware arrangement is:
- a microcomputer
- a high quality printer (a laser or ink-jet printer)
- a mouse (necessary if the wordprocessor uses Windows or the Macintosh operating system)
- a keyboard.

Apart from the operating system, the only software needed is a wordprocessing package. This can be a separate package which just does wordprocessing or part of an integrated package, where wordprocessing is only one part of the complete package.

You can also use special voice recognition software to dictate straight into a wordprocessor.

Notes prepared beforehand — Thoughts, ideas keyed directly in

Figure 27.1 *Typing your thoughts directly into the wordprocessor saves time, but it's not quite as easy as working from notes*

The advantages of wordprocessing

Wordprocessing has several advantages compared with typing.

1 Much more professional results can be obtained by everyone and not just those who are experienced typists, because typing mistakes are easily altered on the screen before printing out.

VDU — Laser printer — Microcomputer — Mouse — Keyboard

Figure 27.2 *A typical wordprocessing system*

Figure 27.3 *Some of the things you might find in a typical wordprocessing package*

2 Fewer resources are used, provided that material is carefully proofread on the screen before finally printing. Since we can edit and correct mistakes before printing, this reduces the amount of paper used. Most large companies now send all their internal letters and memos using electronic mail. The widespread use of electronic mail will help to conserve valuable resources.

3 More people are able to produce their own documents rather than pass them to someone else to type. This can save both time and money.

4 More wordprocessors are becoming like simple desktop publishing packages. These extra facilities enable people to produce notices, posters, tickets, etc. with very little training.

What can you do with wordprocessing software?

Wordprocessing software is software that is able to store, edit and manipulate text. All wordprocessing software allows you to enter text then edit and rearrange it before storing it and printing it out. Some wordprocessors are 'WYSIWYG' ('what you see is what you get'). This means that you are able to see on the screen exactly what the page will look like when it is printed out.

Most wordprocessors allow you to change the fonts (type styles and sizes). Figure 27.3 shows some of the things you might find in a typical wordprocessing package.

Spell checkers
Nearly all wordprocessors have a dictionary against which the words in a document can be compared to check their spelling. Most allow you to add words to the dictionary which is useful if you use special terms in subjects such as law or medicine. It is important to

note that spell checking a document will not remove all the errors. For instance, if you intended to type 'the' and typed 'he' instead, then the spell checker will not detect this since 'he' as a word is spelt correctly. After using a spell checker it is still necessary to proof read a document.

Thesaurus

A thesaurus is useful for creative writing (perhaps for English GCSE coursework). It allows you to highlight a word in a document and the computer lists words with similar meanings (called synonyms) (Figure 27.4).

Figure 27.4

Mail merge

Mail merging involves combining a list of, say, names and addresses, with a typed letter, so that a series of similar letters is produced, each addressed to a different person. The list is either created using the wordprocessor or by importing data from a database of names and addresses. The letter is typed, using the wordprocessor, with blanks where the data from the list is to be inserted.

Indexing

Indexing allows you to highlight words that you would like to use in an index. The

wordprocessor keeps a record of the words, and creates an index when instructed to.

Macros

Macros allow you automatically to produce a sequence of keystrokes so that, for example, you can just press one key or a combination of keys and have your name and address printed at the top of the page. You can also insert dates just by pressing a couple of keys. Macros are very useful for things that need to be done repetitively.

Grammar checkers

Some of the more sophisticated wordprocessors have a feature called a grammar checker. This is useful if your English is not so good. If the wordprocessor you use does not have this facility, then you can buy a separate grammar checking package to use with it. Figure 27.5 shows a grammar checker being used. Because of the complexities of the English language, grammar checkers do have their limitations. As yet they find only a few faults and do tend to provide an incorrect analysis of the grammar of writing. You need to exercise care when using them.

Figure 27.5 *The text above contains a grammatical error. The grammar checker on this wordprocessor is able to find it and suggest how it could be corrected*

TEST YOURSELF

Using the words in the list below, copy out and complete sentences A to F, underlining the words you have inserted. The words may be used more than once.

wordprocessor DTP high electronic mail grammar spellchecker

A The most commonly used piece of software is the _____.

B With a wordprocessor, you can type in a letter and then send it directly to another part of the country or even the world, using _____ _____.

C One of the main advantages of wordprocessing is that an inexperienced typist is able to produce _____ quality documents.

D Many wordprocessors now contain features you would normally find only in ___ packages.

E The most useful advanced feature on the wordprocessor is the _____, which is used to check the spelling of an entire document after it has been typed.

F The more advanced wordprocessors have _____ checkers where you can check that the structure of the English is correct.

1 (a) What does a wordprocessor consist of?
(b) As a document is being typed, where is it stored?
(c) Why is it always advisable to save your document before printing it and not the other way round?
(d) The minutes of a meeting have been typed on a wordprocessor and stored on a disk. The draft copy shows one mistake. In the middle of a long paragraph, the word 'the' has been typed in twice. Describe briefly how the operator would correct the minutes.

2 A friend of yours has never used a wordprocessor before. Explain to her what advantages wordprocessors have over conventional typewriters. Give at least four advantages.

3 You have just loaded the 'Quickword' wordprocessor and the menu shown in Figure 27.6 appears on the screen. You want to retrieve a previously saved document, make a couple of alterations and finally produce a printout. Write down the order in which the commands should be used.

Quickword
Choose an option by typing the number
1. Edit document
2. Load document
3. Print document
4. Save document

Figure 27.8

Things to do

Task 1

Load your wordprocessing software and type in the following text making sure that you do not press the return or enter key at the end of a line unless you want to leave blank lines between paragraphs.

When you first start to use the wordprocessor you may find it hard to think up what you are going to say and have to write it down first. This does destroy the point of the wordprocessor (i.e. it is supposed to save time). Try to type your work directly in and remember that the beauty of the wordprocessor is its ability to let you change things around.

Also, beginners often correct their mistakes as they go along whereas high speed typists will probably not know they have made the mistake until they carefully read through their document (proof read) afterwards.

(a) Proof read the above document and correct any errors that you spot.
(b) Save your document.
(c) Print the document.

Task 2

Here is a Christmas menu. As it is presented it does not look very interesting. You have been asked to improve the presentation but not the content using your wordprocessor. You could try centring each line and use different sized text and fonts for the headings. Do you have any Christmas clip art that you could include?

Christmas Fayre
MENU
Freshly Made Soup of the Day
or
Egg Mayonnaise with Tuna
or
Prawn Cocktail (£1 Extra)
Roasted Lincolnshire Turkey with chestnut stuffing, cranberry sauce, chipolata sausage and bacon, three fresh vegetables, roast potatoes and gravy.
Christmas Pudding
or
Sweets from our trolley
Freshly Percolated Coffee with mint wafers
£9.95
(Available All Through December)

Task 3

Type the following letter into your wordprocessor.

Dear Mrs Hanley

This is just the chance you have been waiting for. You have been specially selected to enter our prize draw. Just imagine the difference our £100 000 first prize would make to your lifestyle. Or if you don't win the first prize, imagine the envy of your neighbours when a brand new Nissan 200 SX sports car appears on the Hanley drive.

All you have to do Mrs Hanley, to enter our new competition is to purchase a copy of 'Your rights as a consumer'. This useful book looks at all matters related to consumer problems and deals with such things as your rights when taking goods back, problems with credit, how do deal with shoddy home repairs. In fact nearly every problem you could encounter is mentioned in this invaluable book.

All you have to do Mrs Hanley is return the enclosed entry form. You do not need to send any money. The book will be sent to you together with the invoice for £19.95. If you do not wish to purchase the book, simply return the postage paid package within 14 days and you will still be entered for our prize draw. If you reply within 7 days then you could win a cash bonus of £10 000. Can you afford not to reply, Mrs Hanley?

1 Proof read the document by carefully comparing it with the original. If there are any errors, correct them.
2 Save, and then print a copy of the document.
3 Highlight 'Your rights as a consumer' using bold print.
4 Underline 'You do not need to send any money'.
5 Search for and then replace all occurrences of 'Mrs Hanley' by 'Mrs Ho' (n.b. you must use the wordprocessor's search and replace facility to do this).
6 Search for and then replace all occurrences of £100 000 with £50 000.
7 Start a new paragraph for the sentence starting 'If you reply within 7 days …' by leaving a blank line.
8 Save the revised document.
9 Print the final document.

Task 4

You have been asked to produce a slip to explain a special deal that a company which manufactures calculators has given your school. The slip is to be photocopied and one is to be given to each pupil in the school (there are 1600 pupils in the school). Because the school wants to save paper and photocopying charges, it would like to copy this document three times, if possible, onto an A4 page.

Type in the following text:

S P E C I A L   O F F E R

Here is a very special offer to all our pupils. We have managed to negotiate a special price on a CASIO 6543 scientific calculator which we recommend to all our pupils. This calculator is the cheapest on the market at only £9.99 and has all the features of calculators costing twice as much.

It is easy to get a calculator. Just fill in the form and return it with payment (cash or cheque payable to Green Hill PTA) to the school secretary, who will supply your son/daughter with the calculator.

Name ....   Form ....

Number of calculators you wish to buy ....

Signature of parent/guardian ....

(a) Try to make this advert as appealing as you can by the use of bold type, italics, underlining and different fonts.

(b) Copy this document to see if it will fit on an A4 page, three times.

(c) When you are happy with it, save and print the page.

Task 5

Load your wordprocessor and type in the following document.

Curriculum vitae

A curriculum vitae is used to tell people about yourself and what you have done with your life so far. By reading it, another person is able to get an impression of you by the personal details and experience you have put down. CVs are normally attached to a letter of application for a job. A CV should include what your achievements have been to date and an outline of your qualifications (or exams taken if you are still awaiting the results). A CV is very important so you need to take time to produce a good one.

It is best to produce a list of the things you need to include and then produce a first draft. Ask another person to read through it. Your English teacher may check it for spelling mistakes and grammatical errors. You should then produce the final version.

Make sure that you leave plenty of space between the various items and that it is no longer than about two sides of A4 size paper.

Make sure that you include such things as qualifications, what interested you at school, any work experience, any positions of authority you have held, details of hobbies and sports played. Remember, the purpose of the CV is to sell yourself.

(a) Type in the above document exactly as it appears above.

(b) Proof read the document by looking at it carefully on the screen and checking that it compares exactly with what was written above.

(c) Save your file using a suitable name.

(d) Print out a copy of the file.

Task 6

In task 5 you typed in a passage about CVs. Now you are going to design one of your own. Imagine that you are applying for a college place or a job and have been asked to supply a CV. Produce your CV using wordprocessing software.

Task 7

Your maths teacher would like you to investigate how to type equations into the wordprocessor. He would like to be able to use the wordprocessor to produce a worksheet on Pythagoras' theorem. As well as the equations, he would like you to investigate the possibility of including labelled diagrams of triangles in the worksheet. He has handed you the following hand written sample of part of the worksheet.

▶▶

Using Pythagoras' theorem

$AC^2 = AB^2 + BC^2$

$AC^2 = 4^2 + 3^2$

$AC^2 = 16 + 9$

$AC^2 = 25$

$AC^2 = 25$

$AC = \sqrt{25}$

$= 5\ cm$

Figure 27.8

Design and produce a worksheet which could be used by the mathematics teacher to teach Pythagoras' theorem. Your worksheet should look appealing and not too cluttered. Try to import labelled diagrams of the triangles into the document.

The mathematics teacher shows your efforts to the chemistry teacher, who is very impressed. She would now like you to find out about doing similar worksheets containing chemical equations. Although she is familiar with the simple functions of the wordprocessor, she has no idea how to import diagrams or how to produce the equations. She has asked you to produce a guide for her, along with a couple of examples of what can be done.

The chemistry teacher supplies you with the following equation as an example of a typical chemical equation.

$$H_2SO4 + 2NaOH = Na_2SO4 + 2H_2O$$

Task 8

Using the tabular features of your wordprocessor, produce a copy of your school or college timetable.

Task 9

Investigate the mail merge facility on your wordprocessor.

Spreadsheets and Spreadsheet Exercises

What is a spreadsheet?

Spreadsheets are much easier to use than to explain. A spreadsheet consists of a grid of cells into which may be placed text, numbers or formulae. Spreadsheets are useful for 'what if' calculations. If you change the contents of one cell, then all those cells whose contents depend on it will change as well.

Rows, columns and cells

Figure 28.1 shows a spreadsheet grid with its horizontal rows and vertical columns.

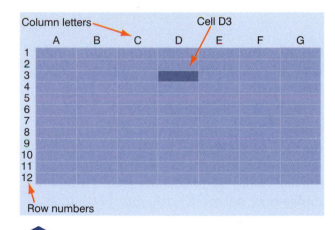

Figure 28.1 *Spreadsheet grid*

This small figure can show only part of a spreadsheet. Spreadsheets are frequently very large and only a small part of the sheet can be viewed on the screen at any one time. It is rather like looking at the sheet through a movable window as in Figure 28.2.

Spreadsheets are made up of cells, each of which has its own address. For instance, the intersection of column D with row 3 will give a cell with the address D3.

All spreadsheets can total columns or rows of numbers. To do this, you type a formula into the cell where you want the total to be displayed. This formula must state which

is the first cell in the series that is to be added up and which is the last.

CASH FLOW ANALYSIS FOR J HUGHES MARKET GARDENER											
APR	MAY	JUN	JUL	AUG	SEP	OCT	NOV	DEC	JAN	FEB	MAR
245.31	303.58	458.31	683.92	647.84	609.72	648.67	560.98	758.42	858.90	680.40	416.84
120.00	120.00	120.00	120.00	120.00	120.00	120.00	120.00	120.00	120.00	120.00	120.00
115.00	115.00	115.00	115.00	115.00	115.00	115.00	115.00	115.00	115.00	115.00	115.00
480.31	538.58	693.31	918.92	882.84	844.72	883.67	795.98	993.42	1093.90	915.40	651.84
80.00	80.00	80.0	918.92	882.84	844.72	883.67			85.00	85.00	85.00
40.00	12.00	0.							48.28	84.30	126.00
240.00	0.00	0.	80.00	80.00	80.00	85.00	85.00		12.00	25.62	12.80
8.62	4.84	3.	0.00	0.00	0.00	0.00	0.00		25.60	17.23	14.00
12.00	13.00	10	0.00	0.00	0.00	0.00	0.00		14.85	13.23	12.56
54.84	54.84	54	0.00	0.00	0.00	286.30	15.00		54.84	54.84	54.84
40.00	15.00	2	3.22	3.41	4.84	5.26	6.00		1.85	0.00	0.00
32.00	10.80	0	10.54	8.21	7.54	14.80	28.50		2.64	15.70	0.00
85.00	0.00	0	54.84	54.84	54.84	54.84	54.84		18.50	20.00	45.00
18.00	18.00	18	2.50	1.80	0.00	0.00	12.00		18.00	18.00	18.00
12.00	125.00	0.	.00	0.00	0.00	0.00	0.0		0.00	0.00	0.00
14.00	5.00	0							0.00	0.00	0.00
25.00	0.00	0.00							27.00	0.00	1.80
120.00	120.00	120.00	120.00	120.00	120.00	120.00	120.00	120.00	120.00	120.00	120.00
781.46	45848	289.10	286.26	285.22	584.20	339.34	300.38	411.44	428.56	453.92	490.00
-301.15	80.10	404.21	632.66	597.62	260.552	544.33	495.60	581.98	665.34	461.48	161.84
0.00	-221.05	484.31	1036.87	1230.28	858.14	804.85	1039.93	1077.58	1247.32	1126.82	623.32

Figure 28.2 *Looking at a spreadsheet through a 'window'*

What can you put into a cell?

You can put in:

1 words (titles, row headings, column headings, etc.)
2 numbers (ordinary numbers, currency, dates, etc.)
3 formulae (used to perform calculations with the numbers).

Figure 28.3 shows an Excel worksheet.

Entering data correctly

There are two common mistakes that people make when using spreadsheets.

1 Entering numbers as text

When people first start using spreadsheets, they like to be able to centre the data when they type it in. They soon find that they can do this by pressing the space bar several times before they type in the data. If a number is typed in after the space bar has been

Figure 28.3 *The opening screen of Microsoft Excel 5*

pressed then the number will be treated like text and it will be impossible to use this number in calculations. Most spreadsheets have a function which will move the cell contents to the right, left or centre. It is best to get all the data typed in and then change the position of the data in the cells.

2 Referring a formula to its own cell

Suppose we wanted to add up the data in the cells C1 to C7 and put the total in C8. If we typed in =sum(C1:C8) then we are using the cell where the formula is, which is not allowed. Instead we need to type:

= sum(C1:C7)

Here is a sample spreadsheet:

	A	B	C	D	E
1	Expenses				
2	Phone	152·80			
3	Electricity	262·40			
4	Gas	189·00			
5	Stationery	76·00			
6	Postage	101·00			
7	Car expenses	896·00			
8	Total				

To calculate the total and put it into cell B8 we could move the cursor to this cell and then type in a formula like this:

+B2+B3+B4+B5+B6+B7

This is tedious, especially if we had to find the total of 100 cells, and there is a quicker command =sum(B2:B7) which adds up all the cells from B2 to B7 inclusive. These formulae may not work with your particular spreadsheet. Unfortunately not all spreadsheets are the same so you will need to ask your teacher how to enter formulae if the above does not work.

If we change the electricity cost from £262·40 to £362·40, then as soon as we enter it, the spreadsheet automatically recalculates the new total (see Figure 28.4).

Let the spreadsheet do the work for you

When using spreadsheets for the first time many people reach for the calculator to do the calculations or even do them in their heads. This defeats the object of the spreadsheet. It means that if you change one of the

	A	B	C	D	E
1	**Expenses**	**£**			
2	Phone	152.80			
3	Electricity	262.40			
4	Gas	189.00			
5	Stationery	76.00			
6	Postage	101.00			
7	Car expenses	896.00			
8	Total	sum(b2:b7)			
9					

Figure 28.4 *Adding up data in Microsoft Excel*

cells, then you will possibly have to re-calculate many other cells. If there had been a formula, then the spreadsheet would have done all this work for you.

Also, the spreadsheet will always arrive at the correct answer, provided that you have given it the correct formula of course.

Cell referencing

There are two ways of making a reference to another cell in a spreadsheet: using relative referencing or using absolute referencing. This is particularly important when you copy or move cells. An absolute reference always refers to the same cell on the spreadsheet. A relative reference, however, always refers to a cell which is a certain number of columns and rows away from the current cell. This means that when the current cell is moved or copied to a new position, the cell to which the reference is made, will also change position.

This is best seen by referring to Figures 28.5 and 28.6.

You do not need to do anything to change cell references into relative cell references since they are this by default. Relative cell references are useful because the spreadsheet can adjust the formulae automatically when the formulae are copied to other cells. If you need to refer to a particular value in a certain cell (such as an interest rate, VAT rate, etc.) then you need to make any references to it

absolute and this is done by putting a dollar sign in front of the column and row number. For example, the relative cell reference C4 could be converted to an absolute cell reference by inserting the dollar sign as follows: C4.

Cell B5 contains a relative reference to cell A2.
If the contents of cell B5 are copied to E8
then cell E8 will refer to cell D5.

Figure 28.5 *Relative references in a spreadsheet*

If cell B5 had an absolute reference to cell A2,
then if the contents of cell B5 are copied to E8,
cell E8 will still refer to cell A2.

Figure 28.6 *Absolute references in a spreadsheet*

Some of the many features of spreadsheets

Spreadsheets can do many things besides just perform simple arithmetic such as adding up columns of numbers. In this chapter we look at some of the more advanced and more powerful features of spreadsheets. Here are just some of the many more powerful features you will find as part of a typical spreadsheet package:

- **Borders** – you can add borders around the whole of your spreadsheet or just around certain parts.

3 To work out the VAT at 17.5%, we can use a formula in cell C3. To calculate 17.5% of the net price we can use the formula VAT = net price × 17.5/100. To enter the formula into the spreadsheet at cell C3 we have to adapt the formula to read: +B3*17.5/100. When the formula is entered, the VAT is put automatically into the cell. The next formula is placed in cell C4 and would be =B4*17.5/100. In fact it would be very tedious to do this all the way down the column, so there is a way of copying the original formula, taking into account the slight change in cell positions. This is called replicating (or copying) a formula relatively. Find out how to do this for your spreadsheet package and complete the column.

4 We now need to add the VAT to the net price to give the total price. The formula =B3+C3 is placed in cell D3. This formula is then copied relatively down the column.

5 To work out the total amount, we multiply the total price by the number of items sold. Do this by placing the correct formula in cell F3 and copy this formula relatively down the column.

6 Save your spreadsheet, calling it MSALES.

7 Print your spreadsheet, trying to get all of it on a single page if you can.

Task 2

Last year Jordan Kung kept a record of his finances using a spreadsheet package. Figure 28.20 shows what his spreadsheet looked like at the end of the year.

	A	B	C	D	E	F	G	H	I	J
1	Month	Wage	Rent	Elect	Gas	Phone	Food	Car	Clothes	Hols
2	Jan	850	120	134.76			129.34	138.12	86.21	30
3	Feb	850	120			45.23	135.98	125.34	23.78	30
4	March	856	120		189.23		78.21	128	12.98	25
5	Apr	857	120				200.76	134	48.99	45
6	May	912	120	287.02			100.23	187.98	201.99	70
7	June	908	120			23.39	78.34	143.98	100.23	100
8	July	945	120		103.67		176.19	125.9	10.99	100
9	Aug	965	120				123.53	145.65	34.99	80
10	Sept	965	120	120.98			123.76	154.65	76.45	30
11	Oct	1000	120			56.99	109.01	200.07	230.12	10
12	Nov	987	120		100.05		165.45	167.95	201.76	10
13	Dec	1200	120				250.45	140.98	300.34	10

Figure 28.20

1 Start off with the heading 'Jordan Kung's income and expenses for the last year'. Type in the data exactly as it appears in Figure 28.20.

2 In the next empty column, insert the heading 'Expenses'. Expenses are the total amount of money that Jordan is spending each month. In this column total the January expenses on the January row.

3 Replicate this formula relatively, down the column for February to December.

4 Using a formula, deduct the expenses for January from the wages for January and put this in the next empty column, under the column heading 'Balance'. This is the amount of money he had left.

5 Replicate this formula down the column for February to December.

6 Calculate the total income, expenditure and balance for the whole year. Put these in a suitable position on the spreadsheet.

7 Save your spreadsheet using a suitable filename.

8 Print your spreadsheet.

Task 3

The table shown in Figure 28.21 shows the number of calories you burn up when you do certain activities.

Activity	Men	Women
Moderate cycling	256	192
Hard cycling	660	507
Domestic work	200	153
Ironing	160	120
Rowing	800	600
Moderate running	592	444
Hard running	900	692
Squash	600	461
Moderate swimming	300	200
Hard swimming	640	480
Tennis	448	336
Moderate walking	224	168

Figure 28.21 *Number of calories burnt when you do certain activities*

1 Enter this table into a spreadsheet (you will need to widen some of the columns).

2 Design a form to give to your friends to record the time spent doing the various activities during the day.

3 Design a method by which the spreadsheet could be used to work out the calories burnt per day by each of your friends.

4 Explain carefully, using printouts where appropriate, how you solved this problem. Mention any things you tried before you arrived at the final solution and explain why you discounted them.

Skills Building

Desktop Publishing

With the aid of desktop publishing software, people can produce high quality documents without having to go to a typesetter. This can save time and money.

Desktop publishing (DTP) can be used to produce pages that combine text and graphics (photographs and line drawings) for books, magazines, posters and leaflets. Different typefaces (fonts) can be used to add interest, and diagrams can be added, with the text flowing around them. Photographs can be scanned in and their size adjusted so that they fit in a particular position on a page. The only real limit is your own imagination.

Figure 29.1 shows examples of a poster and a brochure that have been produced using DTP. Figure 29.2 shows the types of document you can use desktop publishing for.

Figure 29.1 *Just two examples of DTP documents*

Equipment needed

The computer

To work effectively with DTP packages you need a computer with a high specification, ideally with the largest amount of RAM (random access memory) and the highest capacity hard disk that can be afforded. DTP files consisting of text and pictures take up a lot of disk space. Ideally, either a PC or an Apple Macintosh computer is used.

A mouse

The mouse is one of the most important tools in desktop publishing. The mouse is moved around on the desk and transmits the movement of your hand and fingers to the computer. Buttons on the mouse are pressed in order to make selections.

Desktop publishing software

There is a variety of software available. If you require only simple features, then you may

Figure 29.2 *Some of the documents you can produce using DTP*

be able to buy a wordprocessing package which contains them. The more features you require, the more likely you are to need to buy specialist desktop publishing software.

The visual display unit

The monitor should be the largest that you can afford (usually a 17, 19 or 21 inch screen) in order to avoid eyestrain. You often have to work with two pages on the screen at once, so the text can be quite small and difficult to read.

The printer

Either an ink-jet printer (cheaper) or a laser printer could be used to output DTP documents. For really high quality a colour laser printer can be used.

The scanner

If you want to incorporate your own photographs or hand drawings into your documents, then you will need to use a scanner to scan them in. Flat-bed scanners are the most popular type of scanner and most are able to capture colour images. The quality of the scanned image depends on the resolution (in dots per inch) of the scan.

Figure 29.3 *A flat-bed scanner*

Digital cameras

Digital cameras are able to take photographs and store the image on a disk in the camera. You do not need a film and there are no developing costs. Instead the image can be directly transferred to the computer. It can then be altered, sized and incorporated into a DTP prepared document.

Some features of desktop publishing

Figure 29.4 shows some of the features of DTP.

Figure 29.4 *Some of the features of DTP*

Columns

In wordprocessors you work in pages, but in DTP you will need to be able to work in both pages and columns. A look at a newspaper or magazine will show you how common the column format is.

Frame layout

Many DTP packages use a frame-based system of layout. Here, text and graphics are placed in boxes called frames, which can be moved and repositioned around the pages. Some software, including one of the most popular packages, PageMaker, is, however, not frame-based.

Embedded graphics

It is possible to place drawings and pictures in position and then to flow the text around them, as shown in Figure 29.5.

Figure 29.5 *Notice how the text flows around the photograph on this page*

Templates

Templates are used to record certain properties of a document such as its page size, margins, headers (the space at the top) and footers (the space at the bottom). Templates usually also include styles and any standard text that will be included in all documents to be based on them.

Style sheets

Style sheets are used to help make the main text, headings and subheadings consistent. When you are choosing the fonts and type sizes for a DTP document, you can highlight each paragraph or heading in turn and select the typeface and size. However, if a document is to be consistent it is better and faster to set up style sheets and then apply styles to the text.

Scaleable fonts

There are many fonts available in DTP packages and sometimes it is difficult to choose which one to use. It really depends on the type of document you are designing. Some fonts would not be used for business type

documents but could be ideal for invitations to an 18th birthday party. A huge range of sizes is usually available for each font, varying from the very small to the very large. Font sizes are measured in points. One point is 1/72 of an inch.

Advantages of desktop publishing

Here are just a few of the advantages of DTP, for preparing books, magazines, posters and leaflets, compared with wordprocessing alone.

1 You have much more control over the way the text is laid out compared with an ordinary wordprocessor especially over the formatting and arrangement of text.
2 DTP can be used to bring lots of different files together on the same document.
3 DTP may be used to produce the output in a certain way so that the material can be professionally printed, if required. This is usually done if you want to print a large number of copies of your document. If your work is going to be output professionally, then you will need to make sure that you use one of the major DTP packages such as QuarkXPress, PageMaker or Publisher.

When to use a DTP package

Modern packages are so full of features that it is difficult to choose software. Wordprocessors have some DTP facilities, and some graphics packages can be used to produce simple posters and leaflets. For a simple poster, like the one shown in Figure 29.6, you will probably find that a graphics package is the easiest one to use.

As far as your coursework is concerned, you need to decide which type of package to use. You have to give reasons why you choose a type of software for a particular job (e.g. why you might choose a DTP rather than a wordprocessing or graphics package). The reason could simply be that the task couldn't be performed with the other two or it could be that you found the DTP package was better suited to the job.

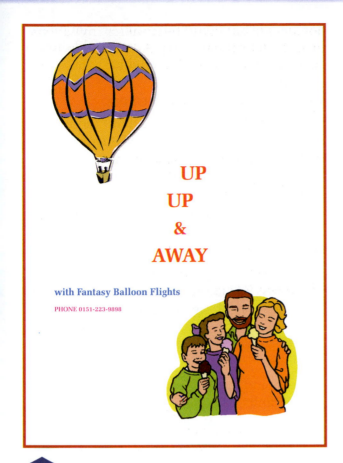

Figure 29.6 *Poster designed using a graphics package*

Figure 29.7 *DTP acts as an integrator, bringing lots of different files together*

DTP acts as an integrator because with this software you can bring many different files together into the same document. You can bring in text from a wordprocessor, graphics from a painting or drawing package, images from a scanner, frames from a video grabber and stills from a camera. Figure 29.7 illustrates this.

Basic techniques used in DTP

Here is a list of some of the basic techniques used in desktop publishing.

Page set up

The first step in preparing a DTP document is often to specify the size of the pages and whether they are to be in portrait or landscape format (see Figure 29.8). The second step in setting up the page is to decide on the number of columns.

Figure 29.8 *Pages arranged in landscape and portrait formats*

The column guides make the text word-wrap to the columns automatically. It is rather like wordprocessing in a single column. Figure 29.9 shows snaking, where, once one column is filled, the text automatically flows to the top of the next column.

Typing text

Most DTP packages allow you to type text directly into them, but you may find it easier to use a wordprocessor to do your typing and then import the files into the DTP package.

Figure 29.9 *Snaking using three newspaper-style columns*

Wordprocessors tend to have more facilities such as spellcheckers and thesauruses and they are often quicker to type into.

Placing text

When you import text you can decide in which of the columns the text should be placed.

Placing graphics

When you import graphics you need to decide on the graphics you will be using and their position on the page. It is possible to place a blank area around a graphic so that the text cannot flow too close to the drawing or photograph.

Sizing and cropping graphics

Cropping means removing part of a picture by cutting off and discarding the part that is not needed. For instance, in a photograph of a group of people scanned in with a scanner, you might want to include only one of the people. You could crop the picture and leave just the required part. This part could then be resized to fit the space available.

Drawing lines and boxes

You can make your text stand out more by placing it in a box. Sometimes it is possible to choose different designs for the box and to have, for instance, shading around the box.

Summary of the main features of a DTP package

The size of the font can be altered to make parts of, say, an advert stand out.

The **font** *style* **can** be *varied* to add more interest

You can add some appropriate clip art or photographs to make it more attractive.

You can use frames to vary the layout.

- You can add bullets
- to list your points.

You can add a border to make your design stand out:

You can add **colour** to produce an eye-catching look.

You can use a pre-stored design and just alter it slightly. This way you will have a professional design.

You can use a spellchecker to check that your advert contains no embarrassing spelling errors.

Your DTP package might also have a grammar checker to ensure there are no grammatical errors

Glossary of terms used in desktop publishing

Bold text Text in heavy type.

Bullet A symbol placed before a paragraph in a list to make the paragraph stand out.

Clip art A library of artwork from which you can choose to put into your documents.

Clipboard A temporary storage place for text, frames or pictures which have been cut or copied.

Crop Select part of the image and discard the rest.

Cut Remove an area containing text or a picture and place it on the clipboard.

Font A complete set of characters of the same design/style; it will be available in a range of sizes.

Frame A rectangular box in which you can place text, pictures or graphics.

Header The line of text included at the top of every page.

Import To load text or pictures created by a different package.

Italics Text that slants to the right; the characters are a different shape.

Justified Text that is aligned with the right and left margins.

Kerning The process of adjusting the spacing between the characters.

Leader This is usually a row of dots to guide the reader across the page in, for example, a table of contents.

Paste The process of inserting the contents of the clipboard into a document.

Template The master page and paragraph styles for a given document.

TIFF A special file format used for images.

WYSIWYG Stands for 'what you see is what you get'. You see on the screen exactly what will be printed out.

Things to do

1 (a) With DTP packages, text can be imported from a wordprocessing package.
   (i) What does the abbreviation DTP stand for?
   (ii) Explain, in simple terms, what the above sentence means.
  (b) Pupils in your school are going to produce a school newsletter which will be produced using desktop publishing.
   (i) Give three items of hardware which they might use apart from the computer (i.e. apart from the CPU, keyboard, VDU and mouse).
   (ii) Give reasons for your choices in (b)(i).

2 Why is it important to use a large VDU if you are working on DTP packages all the time?

3 Describe fully the features which would be desirable in a desktop publishing package for it to be used to prepare a high quality school prospectus. State clearly why each of the features is necessary.

(NEAB/WJEC Spec Option R)

4 In order to advertise the Xmas fayre, the secretary created the poster in Figure 29.10 using her wordprocessor:

XMAS FAYRE

Come and
visit
Santa

At
Middlebrige School

Sat. December 4th 1999
2.00 p.m. start

XMAS FAYRE

Come and
visit
Santa!

At
Middlebrige School
Sat. December 4th 1999
2.00 p.m. start

Figure 29.10

Figure 29.11

To improve the appearance of this poster, it was decided to use a desktop publishing package and the resulting poster is shown in Figure 29.11.
(a) Describe the changes to the poster which have been made by using the desktop publishing package.
(b) Explain how you could have created such a poster using your desktop publishing package.

(NEAB/WJEC Spec Option Q)

Importing text into a DTP package

Here is a piece of text which you should type in to your wordprocessor exactly as it appears here.

Basically a DTP package in its simplest form, allows you to deal with graphics and text at the same time. Usually, a DTP package has some wordprocessing and graphics facilities but they are never as comprehensive as the facilities in the separate packages. Some DTP packages may contain a spellchecker. This is very useful to make sure that you don't produce posters with spelling mistakes that everyone else spots except you.

A feature of a DTP package is its ability to import text from a wordprocessing package. Using your DTP package import the text you have just typed into your wordprocessor.

Choosing the right font

Selecting the right font is very important in DTP work. For each of the following, choose a suitable font and then use your DTP package to type the relevant sentence in the font you have chosen:

Skills Building

Skills for Coursework

- an invitation to a party
- a poster for a disco to be held in your school hall
- an advertisement for a new restaurant or pub
- a menu for a wedding
- an advertisement for a new car
- an invitation to a mediaeval night at a local castle.

DTP skills

Here is a series of tasks you could have to carry out when doing project work in IT or other subjects:

- select pictures or photographs from a CD-ROM and place them in separate files
- type in the text to go with the artwork on your wordprocessor
- load the pictures into your DTP package and adjust them if necessary
- load the text from the wordprocessor and make it flow around the artwork.

Try to do the above tasks using the software and hardware you have available.

IT TASKS

Task 1

Take a look at a leaflet or poster. Look at it from the DTP point of view (choose one that is not too complicated).
- How many different fonts have been used and why have they been selected?
- How many sizes of type have been used?
- Does the text flow around any diagrams or photographs?
- Has any clip art been used?

IT TASKS

Task 2

Your company is a rapidly expanding mail order company that sells aquarium equipment from adverts placed in specialist fish-keeping magazines. You have been asked to investigate desktop publishing for your company and produce a report on its value.

In your report you should include the following along with any other material you think is important:
- what DTP is (is it hardware or software or a combination of the two)
- the minimum equipment for running DTP
- any additional equipment which might be useful, e.g. scanners
- how DTP is different from a sophisticated wordprocessing package such as Word
- what an average DTP package can do
- what packages are available, how much do they cost, which one you think is the best and why.

IT TASKS

Task 3

Your local police station wishes to crack down on crime. It wishes to draw people's attention to crime prevention. The police have asked you to produce some fact sheets and posters with hard-hitting messages on crime prevention. To help you with this you could try to get hold of crime statistics and incorporate these into your material.

IT TASKS

Task 4

The information technology co-ordinator in your school has been asked by the headteacher to run an 'introduction to computers' course on a Tuesday evening. The course is to start on Tuesday 12th September between 6 p.m. and 9 p.m. and will run for 30 weeks. The cost of the course is £75.

The course is practically based and covers:
- wordprocessing
- databases
- spreadsheets
- graphics
- desktop publishing.

You have been asked to produce a desktop-published leaflet that can be placed in local libraries, supermarkets, etc. advertising the course.

All the essential course information needs to be included and it is decided that a map showing where the school is should also be included.

Database Coursework

Before looking at this coursework chapter it would be a good idea to refresh your memory on the contents of Chapter 8 'How Data Is Stored'. In this chapter some of the database concepts and terms are explained. In particular you should understand the terms *file*, *record* and *field* and you should be able to design a record.

Creating a database

Before creating a database, you first have to give some thought to its structure. To help you, here is a list of steps which should be taken.

1 Decide on which fields you need and write them down as a list. Then put your list into order of importance, with the most important field at the top (the most important field is usually the key field).

2 Give each field a suitable fieldname. The fieldnames do not have to be the same as in step 1 and you will probably want to abbreviate the longer ones. Make sure that, when you are describing your system, you mention what the various abbreviations mean. Also, try not to make the field-names too long, since they may have to be typed in when you are performing searches.

3 Decide on the field types. This is whether they are numeric, character, date or logical fields.

4 Decide on the field lengths. A sample of the data you are going to put into the database will reveal how many characters long each field needs to be.

Sometimes you will need several databases. For instance, for a system to be used in a video library, there would be three:

- a member database to hold all the members' details such as name, address, etc.

- a video database, to hold details of the videos kept by the library, such as title, price, etc.

- a rental database to hold the details of the rentals, such as the video number, member's number and date borrowed.

We will now look at a problem and see how we can design a database to provide a solution to the problem.

The problem

Widgets Ltd is a small manufacturing company employing around 40 staff. The company has its head office in Chester and this is where most of the administration work is done. At the head office there is a personnel department which keeps information on all the staff. At the moment, although other departments make use of computers, the personnel department still keeps manual records of all staff in a series of filing cabinets.

There are various problems with the manual system and these are:

- files can take a long time to find, especially if someone has put them back in the wrong place

- to answer questions such as 'How many women do we employ under 20 years old?' would involve looking at every file and then calculating everyone's age from their date of birth; doing this could take a long time

- files need to be kept about ex-employees in case they want a reference in the future. The filing cabinets are taking up more and more space.

Research

A questionnaire has been sent to all the members of the personnel department asking them about the sort of information that they frequently need to know about the employees.

Interviews with the staff who will be using the system and the results of a questionnaire filled in by staff revealed that the following information was necessary for each member of staff:

- surname
- forename
- title
- first line of address
- second line of address
- third line of address
- postcode
- home phone number
- date of birth
- date the member of staff started with the company
- job department the staff member is in (i.e. production, sales, accounts, etc.)
- job grade (each job is given a grade from 1 to 5: grade 1 is the highest level of responsibility)
- job salary (how much each staff member earns per year before deductions)
- job hours (how many hours per week each staff member is contracted to work)
- days off work sick so far this year
- National Insurance number
- holidays total (the number of days holiday entitled to)
- holidays taken (number of days taken this year).

We now need to decide on the field names that we are going to use for the above and the type of data that will be in each field, i.e. numeric, character (sometimes called text), etc., and also the number of characters or numbers in each field.

QUESTIONS

What would be the best way of determining the width of the fields for the above data?

After careful examination of the manual records to make sure that the field lengths are adequate and the type of field is correct, the following structure was developed.

Num	Field Name	Field Type	Width	Dec
1	EMPLOYEE_NO	Character	4	0
2	SURNAME	Character	30	
3	FORENAME	Character	20	
4	TITLE	Character	4	
5	ADD1	Character	30	
6	ADD2	Character	30	
7	ADD3	Character	30	
8	PCODE	Character	9	
9	HPHONE	Character	13	
10	DOB	Date	6	
11	START_DATE	Date	6	
12	JOB_DEPT	Character	10	
13	JOB_GRADE	Numeric	10	
14	JOB_SALARY	Numeric	8	2
15	JOB_HOURS	Numeric	2	0
16	DAYS_SICK	Numeric	3	1
17	NAT_INS_NO	Character	1	5
18	HOLS_TOTAL	Numeric	2	1
19	HOLS_TAKEN	Numeric	2	1

Figure 30.1 *Database structure*

At this stage it is not too important to get the structure exactly right since, in our example, a database program is being used where it is possible to go back and change the structure even after data has been entered. Ask your teacher if you can do this with the database software you are using.

IT TASKS

Task 1
1 Load your database program.
2 Create a new database, calling it Person.
3 Set up the structure set out in the table in Figure 30.1.
4 Save your structure.
5 Print a copy of your structure.

Putting data into the database

Once the structure has been set up, the data may be put into the database. This usually involves typing the data in using the keyboard but this isn't the only method. If the equipment is available, you could scan data in.

Widget Ltd has decided to type the data in. Figure 30.2 is a list of some of the employees.

N.B. You need to decide on the format of the data you are going to type in. It is probably best to use capital letters for the start of a word and then small letters for the rest of the word.

IT TASKS

Task 2

Produce a list of all the records in the database and verify them by checking that they are identical to the list in Figure 30.2. Make the corrections if necessary.

EMPLOYEE_NO	0001	0002	0003
SURNAME	Gregson	Dawkins	Prescott
FORENAME	Margaret	Steven	Simon
TITLE	Miss	Mr	Dr
ADD1	12 Wood Lane	3 River Road	The Verlands
ADD2	West Derby	Aintree	Warren Road
ADD3	Liverpool	Liverpool	Liverpool
PCODE	L13 8BQ	L9 4HG	L23 3ED
HPHONE	0151-252-3542	0151-525-0999	0151-924-0008
DOB	12/12/41	01/03/46	01/07/54
START_DATE	01/03/71	03/09/93	05/05/88
JOB_DEPT	Production	Sales	Production
JOB_GRADE	2	3	1
JOB_SALARY	14800	12300	28500
JOB_HOURS	35	35	35
DAYS_SICK	0	03	07
NAT_INS_NO	YY432512D	YY346523E	FX208974R
HOLS_TOTAL	28	28	30
HOLS_TAKEN	09	07	21

EMPLOYEE_NO	0004	0005	0006
SURNAME	McGinley	Ahmed	Johnston
FORENAME	Stuart	John	Mark
TITLE	Mr	Mr	Mr
ADD1	3 Robin Close	12 Moor Lane	5 Forrest Court
ADD2	West Derby	Waterloo	Crosby
ADD3	Liverpool	Liverpool	Liverpool
PCODE	L13 9MM	L22 6RT	L23 5RR
HPHONE	0151-252-6875	0151-928-8732	0151-924-7865
DOB	12/04/65	12/05/70	01/02/69
START_DATE	07/01/86	12/11/98	10/12/78
JOB_DEPT	Production	Sales	Accounts
JOB_GRADE	5	3	4
JOB_SALARY	4800	6700	7100
JOB_HOURS	40	40	40
DAYS_SICK	14	21	05
NAT_INS_NO	SD453623G	GH346512Y	HJ901834K
HOLS_TOTAL	28	28	28
HOLS_TAKEN	05	10	26

EMPLOYEE_NO	0007	0008	0009
SURNAME	Hughes	Sumner	George
FORENAME	Julie	Suzanne	Julie
TITLE	Mrs	Miss	Mrs
ADD1	5 Orchard Hey	2 Ocean View	The Coach Hse
ADD2	Maghull	Blundellsands	Hesketh Bank
ADD3	Liverpool	Liverpool	Southport
PCODE	L31 8AF	L23 8TT	PR8 9YT
HPHONE	0151-520-8100	0151-931-6534	01704-12776
DOB	03/07/60	26/10/69	07/01/65
START_DATE	09/10/86	03/06/92	02/08/85
JOB_DEPT	Admin	Admin	Accounts
JOB_GRADE	2	5	1
JOB_SALARY	14500	6300	20500
JOB_HOURS	35	40	35
DAYS_SICK	01	0	08
NAT_INS_NO	YY872322P	TT765323U	FF983203P
HOLS_TOTAL	35	28	35
HOLS_TAKEN	20	06	23

EMPLOYEE_NO	0010	0011	0012
SURNAME	Murphy	Davies	Jones
FORENAME	Sean	Paul	Samantha
TITLE	Mr	Mr	Miss
ADD1	12 Bewley Road	12 King Street	54 Moor Drive
ADD2	Kirkby	Wavertree	Hesketh Bank
ADD3	Liverpool	Liverpool	Southport
PCODE	L13 7YY	L17 8UU	PR5 9YU
HPHONE	0151-531-9089	0151-342-7765	01704-34223
DOB	01/02/55	30/12/53	25/02/40
START_DATE	09/03/92	23/11/75	23/05/66
JOB_DEPT	Sales	Production	Sales
JOB_GRADE	3	4	1
JOB_SALARY	12300	18000	28900
JOB_HOURS	30	35	35
DAYS_SICK	12	09	0
NAT_INS_NO	WW769000T	RR600004T	YY454672K
HOLS_TOTAL	28	35	35
HOLS_TAKEN	10	21	24

EMPLOYEE_NO	0013	0014	0015
SURNAME	Flynn	Jones	Jones
FORENAME	James	Debbie	Julie
TITLE	Mr	Ms	Miss
ADD1	2 Copy Lane	5 Bellair Ave	5 Bellair Ave
ADD2	Maghull	Aintree	Aintree
ADD3	Liverpool	Liverpool	Liverpool
PCODE	L31 9KJ	L9 7HH	L9 7HH
HPHONE	0151-531-0009	0151-534-4566	0151-534-4566
DOB	12/11/50	27/09/70	30/01/73
START_DATE	09/12/76	12/12/97	03/04/94
JOB_DEPT	Production	Marketing	Admin
JOB_GRADE	2	2	3
JOB_SALARY	19000	21000	14500
JOB_HOURS	40	35	35
DAYS_SICK	12	03	08
NAT_INS_NO	TT231276F	RT900078Y	RO679797G
HOLS_TOTAL	28	35	28
HOLS_TAKEN	13	28	14

Figure 30.2 *Part A*

EMPLOYEE_NO	0016	0017	0018	EMPLOYEE_NO	0025	0026	0027
SURNAME	Dewer	Stephenson	Ho	SURNAME	Sinnot	Jones	Rowlands
FORENAME	Alison	Carl	Michael	FORENAME	Jackie	Gareth	Julie
TITLE	Miss	Mr	Mr	TITLE	Mrs	Mr	Miss
ADD1	5 Cobley Court	4 Moor Drive	6 Pit Street	ADD1	23 Osbert Road	2 Firs Close	3 Blandford Rd
ADD2	Wavertree	Crosby	Everton	ADD2	Blundellsands	Formby	Ainsdale
ADD3	Liverpool	Liverpool	Liverpool	ADD3	Liverpool	Liverpool	Southport
PCODE	L24 6FT	L23 6HH	L12 6TT	PCODE	L23 8GY	L34 5TR	PR4 5DS
HPHONE	0151-675-8900	0151-924-5565	0151-253-9000	HPHONE	0151-924-7322	01704-98899	01704-11223
DOB	03/11/67	01/08/70	30/09/48	DOB	01/11/47	27/08/58	30/09/59
START_DATE	01/05/81	04/09/95	23/08/76	START_DATE	12/02/79	12/12/91	12/12/91
JOB_DEPT	Sales	Admin	Accounts	JOB_DEPT	Production	Sales	Admin
JOB_GRADE	5	4	5	JOB_GRADE	2	4	2
JOB_SALARY	3400	5200	2800	JOB_SALARY	4700	14500	17000
JOB_HOURS	25	25	15	JOB_HOURS	15	40	35
DAYS_SICK	02	02	03	DAYS_SICK	0	07	10
NAT_INS_NO	YY909076G	HH897678R	GG878789U	NAT_INS_NO	TH435200T	YY767678R	FT090976R
HOLS_TOTAL	20	20	15	HOLS_TOTAL	12	35	35
HOLS_TAKEN	17	08	07	HOLS_TAKEN	03	12	10

EMPLOYEE_NO	0019	0020	0021	EMPLOYEE_NO	0028	0029	0030
SURNAME	Johnston	Stuart	John	SURNAME	Doyle	Doyle	Smith
FORENAME	Mark	South	Jones	FORENAME	Norma	Ruth	Tony
TITLE	Mr	Mr	Mr	TITLE	Mrs	Miss	Mr
ADD1	5 Hart Street	5 Fir Crescent	4 South Road	ADD1	5 Trevor Drive	5 Trevor Drive	4 Bridge Road
ADD2	Formby	Southport	Waterloo	ADD2	Crosby	Crosby	Waterloo
ADD3	Merseyside	Merseyside	Liverpool	ADD3	Liverpool	Liverpool	Liverpool
PCODE	L45 8MM	L34 5TT	L22 6GG	PCODE	L23 6GT	L23 6GT	L22 6GG
HPHONE	01704-45464	01704-67738	0151-928-0088	HPHONE	0151-924-8989	0151-924-8989	0151-924-8767
DOB	31/01/45	09/01/43	03/05/75	DOB	02/05/62	03/10/70	01/02/47
START_DATE	02/09/69	02/09/69	01/02/98	START_DATE	03/01/81	18/09/87	05/05/94
JOB_DEPT	Production	Production	Sales	JOB_DEPT	Sales	Production	Admin
JOB_GRADE	2	2	5	JOB_GRADE	5	3	5
JOB_SALARY	18700	19000	3900	JOB_SALARY	5900	6500	7800
JOB_HOURS	35	35	27	JOB_HOURS	25	30	30
DAYS_SICK	10	09	10	DAYS_SICK	0	0	9
NAT_INS_NO	WW352920R	YY875658T	HJ870020G	NAT_INS_NO	GG902323R	HJ880213F	DE562376S
HOLS_TOTAL	28	28	28	HOLS_TOTAL	15	25	35
HOLS_TAKEN	14	09	10	HOLS_TAKEN	10	12	13

EMPLOYEE_NO	0022	0023	0024	EMPLOYEE_NO	0031	0032	0033
SURNAME	Wong	Owens	Hughes	SURNAME	Snell	Peat	Farley
FORENAME	Christine	Susan	Stephen	FORENAME	Peter	Fred	John
TITLE	Miss	Mrs	Mr	TITLE	Mr	Mr	Mr
ADD1	23a Devon Close	54 Wood Street	5 Rotten Row	ADD1	2 The Close	5 Geraints Way	2 Channel View
ADD2	Walton	Aintree	Southport	ADD2	Seaforth	Waterloo	Thornton
ADD3	Liverpool	Liverpool	Merseyside	ADD3	Liverpool	Liverpool	Liverpool
PCODE	L14 6TR	L9 8HY	L65 6YY	PCODE	L21 5RR	L22 6RD	L18 5FF
HPHONE	0151-525-3123	0151-523-0099	01704-78222	HPHONE	0151-931-2121	0151-928-0078	0151-924-7923
DOB	12/07/69	25/09/39	15/09/46	DOB	19/03/49	13/12/60	01/04/67
START_DATE	03/06/89	09/06/88	07/07/69	START_DATE	17/04/71	15/05/92	12/12/94
JOB_DEPT	Sales	Marketing	Accounts	JOB_DEPT	Production	Marketing	Production
JOB_GRADE	3	1	1	JOB_GRADE	2	2	2
JOB_SALARY	15000	29000	38000	JOB_SALARY	16000	14800	16300
JOB_HOURS	35	35	28	JOB_HOURS	40	35	40
DAYS_SICK	09	01	08	DAYS_SICK	03	09	10
NAT_INS_NO	GS676799K	WW780367F	GG566658L	NAT_INS_NO	RR234237T	QQ545454Y	TG090988T
HOLS_TOTAL	35	35	40	HOLS_TOTAL	35	35	35
HOLS_TAKEN	23	30	12	HOLS_TAKEN	12	21	18

Figure 30.2 *Part B*

EMPLOYEE_NO	0034	0035	0036	EMPLOYEE_NO	0037	0038	0039
SURNAME	Jackson	Low	Crowther	SURNAME	Jenkins	Pauling	Smith
FORENAME	Roy	Jane	Louise	FORENAME	Sheila	Jenny	Carol
TITLE	Mr	Mrs	Ms	TITLE	Mrs	Mrs	Ms
ADD1	3 Crane Street	5 Hart Street	45 Park Lane	ADD1	2 Cobham Road	3 Belham Road	32 The Byway
ADD2	Wavertree	Seaforth	Kirkby	ADD2	West Derby	Thornton	Crosby
ADD3	Liverpool	Liverpool	Liverpool	ADD3	Liverpool	Liverpool	Liverpool
PCODE	L13 5FD	L21 5RE	L31 4AS	PCODE	L13 8HU	L23 6TH	L23 4FR
HPHONE				HPHONE	0151-252-3409	0151-924-6512	0151-924-0071
DOB	12/12/54	16/01/65	12/09/76	DOB	30/09/50	27/02/51	29/04/61
START_DATE	15/01/95	17/01/95	08/05/95	START_DATE	12/10/71	13/12/75	10/02/93
JOB_DEPT	Production	Sales	Admin	JOB_DEPT	Personnel	Marketing	Production
JOB_GRADE	3	4	4	JOB_GRADE	1	2	1
JOB_SALARY	12300	8900	9550	JOB_SALARY	20500	17500	23000
JOB_HOURS	35	35	35	JOB_HOURS	35	35	35
DAYS_SICK	0	0	03	DAYS_SICK	4	0	0
NAT_INS_NO	YY354323C	CC676741V	FR566643D	NAT_INS_NO	FF342345R	HK090945R	JH890148F
HOLS_TOTAL	28	35	28	HOLS_TOTAL	28	28	28
HOLS_TAKEN	12	05	00	HOLS_TAKEN	28	15	28

Figure 30.2 *Part C*

Data verification

Data verification is a pre-input check to make sure that what is on a form is exactly what goes into the database. For the personnel database, it is a question of proof reading each record on the screen to check that it is exactly the same as what is on the form.

Data validation

Validation checks are checks that the database performs to make sure that the data is allowable. Databases will not allow you to put letters into a field which you have specified as numeric. Validation is performed by the actual database software.

QUESTIONS

A person tries to type a number into a field that has been specified as a character field. Will the computer accept it?

Using the database

Queries

Performing a query is sometimes referred to as searching or interrogating a database. Basically this involves extracting information from the database. For instance, you could make a request of the database to list the details of all personnel over a certain age. Suppose we don't want a list of every field in the database but only wanted a list of surnames and addresses, we could issue a command such as:

LIST SURNAME, ADD1, ADD2, ADD3, PCODE

Notice the list of the required fields is after the LIST command.

IT TASKS

Task 3

Write commands that would enable you to list the following fields (if your database commands are different, then use them):

1 a list of surnames, job departments and salaries for all employees
2 a list of surnames, their holiday totals and their holidays taken
3 a list of all employees' surnames, forenames and home telephone numbers.

Using search conditions

You may not want all the specified fields for each person to be listed. For example, you may just need the details on people in a certain department.

Suppose you wanted the surnames and salaries of the personnel in the production department. We could use a command similar to this:

LIST SURNAME, JOB_SALARY FOR JOB_DEPT = "Production"

Or, you might want to list the employee number, surname and job department for all employees earning over £15 000. You could use a command like this:

LIST EMPLOYEE_NO, SURNAME, JOB_DEPT FOR JOB_SALARY > 15000

Note that > is the symbol meaning greater than.

IT TASKS

Task 4

Write commands to perform the following searches and check that they work by producing a printout from the personnel database:

(a) the employee number, surname and department of staff working under 20 hours

(b) the names and addresses of all staff in the sales department

(c) the names and addresses of all the male employees (note you will need to think about how to do this)

(d) the surname, job department and grade of all the staff who have taken no time off sick

(e) the names, job departments and dates of birth of all staff who joined the company after 1/1/86.

Combining conditions

You can combine conditions using AND, OR and NOT. If you wanted to search the database for members of the production department who earned over £20 000 you could issue a command similar to the following:

LIST SURNAME, JOB_SALARY, NAT_INS_NO FOR JOB_DEPT ="Production".AND. JOB_SALARY >20000

If you wanted a list including people in the production department earning £20 000 exactly you would replace the last part >20000 by =20000.

Notice also that JOB_SALARY is a numeric field and you do not put inverted commas around the number. Inverted commas are placed only around character fields.

Adding new records to the database

Following expansion of the company, three new employees have been taken on. Add information about these to the database (this process of adding records to an existing database is called appending the database).

EMPLOYEE_NO	0037	0038	0039
SURNAME	Kent	Marshall	Hall
FORENAME	Colin	John	Peter
TITLE	Mr	Mr	Mr
ADD1	3 Hall Road	10 The Close	5 Bows Lane
ADD2	Seaforth	Thornton	Crosby
ADD3	Liverpool	Liverpool	Liverpool
PCODE	L20 9YU	L23 6RT	L23 5FD
HPHONE	0151-928-0087	0151-924-4546	0151-924-8976
DOB	30/09/69	20/10/73	21/09/77
START_DATE	22/04/99	12/5/99	13/5/99
JOB_DEPT	Production	Admin	Personnel
JOB_GRADE	5	4	5
JOB_SALARY	9000	11000	8500
JOB_HOURS	40	35	35
DAYS_SICK	0	0	0
NAT_INS_NO	FR232355H	GF802023F	HJ651023L
HOLS_TOTAL	28	28	28
HOLS_TAKEN	0	0	0

Deleting records

Julie Hughes and Steven Dawkins have left the company so their records need removing from the database. Perform this task and then explain how you did it.

Amending the database

Following the annual review of staff performance, the following staff have been promoted:

- Suzanne Sumner is now grade 3 and has a new salary of £8500
- Sean Murphy is now grade 2 and has a new salary of £14 700
- Margaret Gregson is now grade 1 and has a new salary of £17 800.

Also, the following amendments need to be made to staff records:

- Miss Margaret Gregson now becomes Mrs Margaret Hewitt
- John Ahmed has moved to the following address: 15 Forefield Road, Aintree, Liverpool, L9 7ET Phone 0151-546-2111.

It is the end of the month, so the holiday and days off sick records need amending. The following people have been sick or taken days off.

	Holidays taken this month	Days off sick this month
Sean Murphy	1	2
Margaret Gregson	5	
Simon Prescott	7	
Mark Johnston	2	
Stuart McGinley	1	3

Make all of the above amendments to your database.

QUESTIONS

How can the personnel department be sure that the personnel records are up-to-date?

Sorting and indexing

Sorting

Suppose we want to sort the personnel database into alphabetical order according to SURNAME. We could use the SORT command. With the SORT command a new file is produced which has the same contents as the original file but in a different order. Using the SORT command is quick but has the disadvantage that a new file is produced which takes up as much disk space as the original. Performing several sorts using a large database could mean that you could run out of disk space.

Using SORT you can usually sort on only one field. To sort a file into alphabetical order according to SURNAME you can use a command similar to this:

SORT ON SURNAME TO S1

SURNAME is the field we are sorting and S1 is the file name we are giving to the new sorted database.

IT TASKS

Task 5

Using the personnel database do the following:

1 Sort the file into alphabetical order according to SURNAME. Produce a printout showing the fields SURNAME and EMPLOYEE_NO to check that the sort has taken place.
2 Sort the file according to JOB_SALARY, with the personnel earning the most money at the start of the file (it is possible to sort in ascending or descending order; in this case it should be in descending order).

Indexing

Each record in a database is given a record number by the computer. This is not the same as the EMPLOYEE_NO. The record number is used to produce an index. Let's look at the first five records of the file.

Record number	SURNAME	FORENAME
1	Gregson	Margaret
2	Dawkins	Steven
3	Prescott	Simon
4	McGinley	Stuart
5	Ahmed	John

If these were to be placed in alphabetical order according to SURNAME the record numbers would need to be in the order 5, 2, 1, 4, 3. These record numbers are contained in an index and when displaying or printing out the list the computer uses this index to put things in the correct order. Indexing has the advantage that it does not eat up disk space, since only the index and the original database need storing.

Not all databases have an index facility. Check with your teacher so see if yours has.

You can index on a main, primary field, and then have another secondary index. So you could have employees in departmental order and then in alphabetical order of surname within each department.

IT TASKS

Task 6

Produce a list of personnel in alphabetical order according to surname:

(a) using a SORT

(b) using an INDEX, if your database can do this.

Forms and screens

Forms, or screen designs as they are often called, are used to allow the user to type data into the system. You can design boxes on the screen where the user can type in the data.

Reports

Reports are summaries of the data held on a database. They have a date and title, and contain neat columns of data. Reports are usually printed on paper.

Labels

Some databases allow you to print names and addresses from your database on self-adhesive labels to be used for mail shots. Some systems also allow the production of barcodes from the data in the database.

Comma separated variables

The file shown below, consisting of names and addresses, has been typed into a word-processor. Each of the items of data enclosed between quotes and separated by commas can be transferred directly to a database and the items correspond to the fields in the database. We can therefore export the data from the wordprocessor and import it into the database.

"Stephen","Doyle","12 Bancroft Rd","Crosby","Liverpool","L23 4ER"

"Norma","Prescott","3 Forest Rd","Formby","Merseyside","L31 OBQ"
"Jim","Jones","3 Foregarden Ave","Waterloo","Liverpool","L22 4RR"
"Frank","Moor","123 Edge Lane","Prescott","Merseyside","L13 5SE"

Comma separated variables (sometimes called comma delimited variables) are often used for merging data from a database into the gaps in a standard letter. This is called a mail merge.

If you are using an integrated package (i.e. one with a database, spreadsheet and word-processor all in one) then you will find the transfer of the data between the modules a lot easier.

Creating an information system using a database

The problem

To create an information system we must start with a problem to be solved. It may be that there is a manual system that needs replacing or it may be that an existing computer system is inadequate and needs improvement. For either of these, the processes involved in the design and implementation of a system are the same. It is very important to make a careful choice of the problem to be solved. If it is too ambitious then it will be hard to satisfy the assessment objectives and if it is too simple then all the objectives will probably not be met.

Always choose a topic that interests you or something you can find information about easily. Use friends or relatives to come up with problems they might encounter in their jobs. Often, the better projects are real projects that have been developed for an actual problem.

Make sure that the school or college has the equipment available to enable you to perform your project and that you will have enough time to complete it.

Initially you will be asked for a statement of the problem. Before stating what the problem is, it is best to write a short passage on the background of the organisation involved.

Research

If you are basing your project around an actual company or organisation, then you will need to find out about what it does and how it is done. The best way to do this is to produce a questionnaire (wordprocessed of course) and send it to your contact in the organisation concerned. When you get this back read it carefully and write down a list of interview questions which come to light from the questionnaire.

Try to arrange to see the potential users of your system.

Description of the existing system

1 The existing system
A description of the existing system along with its strengths and weaknesses should be included. Any manual documents should be copied and diagrams should be drawn to illustrate the flow of paperwork for the administrative procedures.

2 User requirements
The users will be more familiar with the problem to be solved than you will be, so it is important to ask them about the input, output and processing. Since you will be regarded as being more knowledgeable about what is technically possible, you should be able to make suggestions.

3 Constraints
The usual constraints of time and money always apply. Too much time may be needed to develop the new system or project. The user will need to be convinced that the benefits of the new system outweigh the costs of its introduction. For instance, the large volume of data that would need to be keyed in might prohibit the use of a large database. Alternative input methods such as barcoding and OCR could be looked into as an alternative to keying in.

4 The social implications of a new system
An appreciation of the effect of the new system on the work force should be considered. Many employees will be naturally sceptical about a new system. You will need to have some answers to their fears.

System design

Bearing in mind the constraints, an alternative to the original system should be developed, that will do as many of the things suggested by the user and yourself as possible. Sometimes, there may be several ways of solving the problem. Remember that the best solution to a particular problem isn't always the one that is chosen and that the choice is nearly always a compromise.

When designing your system you need to mention the following.

- Explain how the proposed system works, using diagrams rather than text wherever possible. The diagrams should include systems flowcharts and structure diagrams.
- Hardware and software requirements should be outlined, with reasons for their choice.
- Show how features have been designed. For instance, with a database you would need to mention how you arrived at the structure or with a spreadsheet you would mention how the format you have adopted was arrived at.
- Input and output need to be considered. Here you should look at the most appropriate form for the input and output. Methods of data capture can be included, along with the reasons for their choice.
- Information is needed about the choice of storage media along with justification.

Implementation

You need to give information about the implementation of a system, including:

- the method of implementation along with the reason for its choice (e.g. step-by-step, parallel running, etc.)
- how existing files are to be changed to the new file format, including how data will be keyed in (or the use of alternative methods such as OCR)
- how the new hardware and software are to be installed
- how the people who will be using the new system will be trained
- how the new system will be maintained –

what needs to be done and how often in order to keep the system up-to-date

- the social effects of the implementation of your system.

Documenting the system

Two levels of documentation are needed: one for the user and the other for the technical specialists.

User documentation

This should include:

- input and output formats
- sample runs to show the output
- error messages and what to do when things go wrong (e.g. data is sent to the printer without it being switched on)
- brief limitations of the system.

Technical documentation

This should include:

- the purpose of the system
- the requirements of the system
- the input and output formats
- the method of solution

- the further development potential (how the system could be improved or any extras which could be added on).

1 Debbie, an information technology manager says 'It's no use having a computerised database unless it is properly maintained.'
   (a) What does she mean by properly maintained?
   (b) What sort of tasks would be involved in maintaining the database?

2 In the 'personnel' database, we did not record a person's age but instead recorded their date of birth (DOB). Why isn't the age included?

3 Take a look at your parents' car insurance details to see what information is held.

Suppose a mistake was made by someone in the insurance company's office while keying the information in. What could be the consequences of such an error?

Things to do

1 Jane, who is a dentist, would like to install a computer system in order to provide information regarding her patients' teeth, their appointments, their treatment and how much their treatment costs.

   She decides to buy a Pentium PC with a 10GB hard disk and a laser printer.
   (a) What type of application software should she buy? Give reasons for your choice or choices.
   (b) Describe how the system could be used to handle the information for the various uses she has. Also mention the output she could expect from such a system.
   (c) What advantages are there in using an off-the-shelf application package rather than a tailor-made programmed package? What disadvantages might there be?
   (d) Give a possible advantage of the new system to each of the following groups of people:
   - receptionists
   - nurses
   - dentists
   - patients.
   (e) What possible disadvantage might there be in using the new system?

2 A company of estate agents, with a main branch in one town and several branches in nearby towns, is planning to change from a manual system to a computerised one.
   (a) The company plans to set up a computer file with details of houses that are for sale. This file will store the name of the owner, the address, the phone number and type for each house. Suggest **four** other fields that might be included on the file.

(b) Explain why some of the data in the fields in this file is stored in coded form.

(c) The file will store details of several thousand houses. People interested in buying any house should be able to obtain a printout of the details by simply calling in at a branch of the company. What type of store would be needed for the file? Give **two** reasons for your choice.

(d) Some of the fields in this file are of fixed length, others are of variable length.
   (i)   Give **one** advantage of using fixed length fields.
   (ii) Give **one** disadvantage of using fixed length fields.

(e) Describe the hardware the company will need to install in each of its branches and in the main office for the new computerised system.

(NEAB/WJEC Spec Option Q)

3 A company sells general hardware. It stores details of stock in a database.

For each item the database stores the following:
   Stock_no
   Description
   Location_code (aisle number)
   Supplier_code
   Reorder_quantity
   Minimum_stock_level
   Current_stock_level
   Lead_time (days)
   Date_of_last_delivery

(a) The database can be accessed using a special query language,
   e.g. List Stock_no,Description,FOR Current_stock_level less than 50.
   Write down a query command which would print out the description, for all the items that the company has more than 100 of in stock, with a Lead_time of less than 14 days.

(b) The company cannot function without the database. Which backup procedures should be used for the database files?

(c) The database file is very large. What method can be used to minimise storage requirements when archive copies are made?

(d) To be able to produce orders to be sent to suppliers, an additional database file is issued.
   (i)   What file would this be?
   (ii) What type of information would it contain?
   (iii) Copy and fill in the table below to show the structure of this file.

Field name	Field type	Size

(e) Describe, using any suitable method, the way in which the two files would be used to produce orders for all items where the Current_stock_level is below the Minimum_stock_level.

(NEAB/WJEC Spec Option Q)

4 A video-film club hires films to members. The club uses separate database files to store details about:
   films
   members
   films hired.

The table on the next page shows **part** of the **FILMS** database file.

Film number	Film name	Film category	Rating	Hire charge
0123	Mermaids	Comedy	15	£2.00
0124	JFK	Drama	15	£2.50
0254	Star Wars	Adventure	U	£1.50
0361	Mad Max 2	Adventure	18	£2.00
0422	City Slickers	Comedy	15	£1.25
0744	Die Hard 2	Adventure	18	£1.50
0813	Blackadder	Comedy	15	£1.50

Write down the instructions or steps that you might use if you wanted the FILMS database to display a list of adventure films which are rated 18 and cost less than £2.00 to hire.

(a) Choose suitable items of information for the MEMBERS database file from the list below.

Address of the club	Film name	Member's name
Original cost of film	Film number	Name of club manager
Membership number	Date of birth	Film category
Hire date	Phone number	Length of hire

	ITEM1	ITEM2	ITEM3	ITEM4
FILMS HIRED FILE				

(b) When new members join the video club they complete an application form. The form is used to enter information into the MEMBERS database file. Design a suitable form.

(NEAB/WJEC Spec Option R)

5 A company uses a computer to put buyers of second-hand cars in touch with people who are selling cars. It collects information from sellers by getting the sellers to complete a form. Buyers can then ring up and ask for a list of people who have the sort of car they want.

(a) Design a form for the input of information from a SELLER.   (5 marks)

(b) Describe clearly the processes required to get a list (in price order) of all Ford Escort cars less than 5 years old in the price range £3000 to £4000.   (5 marks)

(c) Explain why a manual card index might be better than a computer for a second-hand car dealer who usually has between 8 and 10 cars for sale.   (2 marks)

(SEG NT HT Spec)

IT TASKS

Task 7

Your local tourist board has decided to produce a database of attractions within a 20 mile radius of where you live. Some of the information they need would include:

- name of attraction
- location
- admission costs
- opening hours.

Design and produce a database to help them.

IT TASKS

Task 8

Use the *Guinness Book Of British Hit Singles* to compile a database which may be used by a person asking the questions in a music quiz. You need to hold as much information about each artist and their records as you can find.

Think about what questions might be asked using the database such as:
- What was the highest chart position of the record XYZ?
- What year did the group XYZ have a hit with VWX?
- Who had a hit with the song XYZ?

IT TASKS

Task 9

You have been asked to design an information system for a video library. Assume that the library has around 2000 members and 1400 videos, and that at present, it uses a manual system for recording details of members and videos.

It would be a good idea to arrange to visit a video library to see how such a system works. It might be hard to find a video library that uses a manual system, so try to find out how a manual school library system works, as the system will be similar.

IT TASKS

Task 10

One of the largest databases in the country is the Driver and Vehicle Licensing Authority (DVLA) database which contains the registration details of all the cars, motorcycles, lorries, etc. In addition to this information, it also contains the details of all the people who hold driving licences in the country.

Look at two documents: a registration document for a vehicle and a driving licence, and note the data that they contain.

You have been asked to develop a system that can be used to hold information about a fleet of company vehicles and their drivers. It is important to model this on the DVLA database and also put in some other information, such as the cost of the vehicles, service records, accidents, driver penalty points, etc.

Don't forget to fully document the system.

IT TASKS

Task 11

You have been asked to write an article on database packages for inclusion in a computer magazine. The article is aimed at the 14–18 years age group. You need to outline what a database is and how useful it can be. Also, you need to outline some of the facilities of the more popular database packages so that the reader can choose one.

IT TASKS

Task 12

Investigate and then develop and implement an information system centred around one of the following:
(a) a database of members of a health club
(b) a database of books held in a library
(c) a database of pupils in a school
(d) a database held by a mail order computer games company.

IT TASKS

Task 13

Investigate and then develop a system to hold information about the prices of branded goods at different supermarkets. This could be used by prudent shoppers so that they can go to different supermarkets and buy just those goods that were cheaper than anywhere else.

Fully develop and document the system.

Using database software

Describe how you would perform the following, using the database software you are going to use:

(a) load the database

(b) create a new database and design the structure

(c) save the structure and print it out

(d) add records to the database

(e) save the database

(f) go back to the structure and make changes, such as delete a field and insert a new field

(g) go back to the database and
    (i) edit a record
    (ii) delete a record

(h) perform a simple search (searching on a single field)

(i) search on several fields using the logical operators (AND, OR and NOT)

(j) produce a report containing selected fields

(k) change the format of a report.

A car stock list

A large second-hand car company keeps details of all its cars in stock using a series of records held in a filing cabinet. It is decided that the data should be transferred to a database held on computer.

Here is part of the file:

Make	Model	Price	Year	Type	Mileage
Nissan	Sunny 1.4L	£3 200	93	Saloon	24 000
Nissan	Sunny 1.4GL	£2 450	92	Saloon	35 000
Ford	Mondeo	£7 200	97	Saloon	34 000
Ford	Escort	£3 500	95	Saloon	56 000
Nissan	200SX	£5 495	95	Sports	34 000
Nissan	300ZX	£14 995	95	Sports	25 000
Nissan	Primera 2.0GL	£6 950	97	Saloon	19 000
Nissan	Micra 1.0L	£5 000	98	Saloon	23 000
Nissan	Micra 1.3GL	£4 950	97	Saloon	12 000
Ford	Probe (24v)	£12 995	98	Sports	5 000
Honda	Prelude (2.3)	£14 995	98	Sports	13 995
Honda	Civic	£7 995	96	Saloon	10 000
Honda	Accord	£12 999	97	Saloon	11 000
Ford	Probe (16v)	£9 999	97	Sports	6 000
Nissan	Sunny	£3 000	94	Estate	38 000
Mercedes	230	£20 000	97	Saloon	23 000
Nissan	Micra	£3 500	97	Saloon	40 000
Ford	Escort	£2 900	94	Saloon	56 000

1 Load your database software.

2 Create a structure for your database file (use only character and numeric fields), with suitable widths. When you are happy with your structure, save it and print a copy.

Skills Building

Skills for coursework

3 Enter the above data, verify it by proof reading and then save and print a copy.

4 Reload your database and make the following amendments:
- the Nissan Sunny for £3200 is actually a Nissan Sunny 1.4GLX
- the Mercedes 230 needs its price reducing to £17 995
- the Honda Accord is a 1998 model
- the Sunny estate needs its price reducing to £2500.

Make these amendments and save and then print a copy of the database.

5 The following cars have come in, so they should be added to the database:

Nissan	Micra	£4 500	98	Saloon	32 000
Ford	Escort 1.6	£6 000	96	Saloon	25 000
Nissan	Primera 1.6	£8 995	97	Saloon	4 000

Add them and then save the database.

6 The following cars have been sold so their details need deleting from the database.

Ford	Probe (16v)	£9 999	97	Sports	6 000
Nissan	Sunny 1.4GL	£2 450	92	Saloon	35 000
Nissan	Micra 1.0L	£5 000	98	Saloon	23 000

After deleting these records, save the database.

7 Sort the cars file
   (a) alphabetically according to make, with the As at the top of the file
   (b) numerically according to price, with the most expensive car at the top
   (c) using an index (if your database has one) according to make and then within this, according to price.

Produce a printout for each one to check that it has been sorted correctly.

8 Search for
   (a) details of all cars costing less than £3000
   (b) details of all Ford cars costing less than £7000
   (c) details of all cars costing between £5000 and £6000
   (d) details of all sports cars.

You should produce a printout to provide evidence that the search is correct.

Measurement and Control

Before reading this chapter you should look at Chapter 20, especially the section on pseudo-code. In this chapter we will look at monitoring, data logging and using computers for control.

Turtle graphics

In this section we will look at how you can use a series of instructions to move a turtle around on the screen of a computer. As the turtle moves, it can be instructed to leave a line behind it showing its path.

Turtle graphics is just one of the features of a programming language called LOGO. Ask you teacher how to load the LOGO software and get the turtle to appear on the centre of the screen. We can now instruct the turtle to move and leave a line drawn behind it to show its path.

Moving the turtle

When the turtle is facing a certain way, it can move only in that direction. To move in another direction you have to turn the turtle before moving it.

Let's now look at some of the commands:

FORWARD 30 moves the turtle 30 units forward. How far this is depends on the screen you are using. Notice also that a line is not drawn showing its path.
BACKWARD 10 moves the turtle 10 units backward.
PENUP raises the pen and stops the line being drawn.
PENDOWN puts the pen down so that a line is drawn behind the turtle.

Turning the turtle

The turtle is made to turn by giving it a direction of turn (LEFT or RIGHT) and an angle of turn in degrees. The angle is measured from

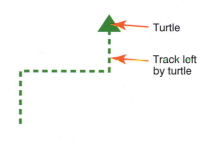

Figure 31.1 *With LOGO you control a movable turtle*

the line the turtle would take if it proceeded normally. Figure 31.1 helps explain this.

Here are some commands and explanations:

LEFT 90 turns the turtle to the left by 90 degrees.
RIGHT 90 turns the turtle to the right by 90 degrees.
CLEARSCREEN clears the screen.

Making a program

A program is a list of instructions arranged in a logical order that can be obeyed by a computer. We will now look at how to put some of the commands together that we have already learnt.

We can draw a square using the following program:

```
CLEARSCREEN
FORWARD 20
RIGHT 90
FORWARD 20
RIGHT 90
FORWARD 20
RIGHT 90
FORWARD 20
```

This method is tedious so there is an easier way:

```
REPEAT 4 (FORWARD 20 RIGHT 90)
```

The above instruction tells LOGO to draw four lines, each 20 steps long and to turn 90 degrees between lines.

Suppose we want to draw many squares. How do we do this?

Well, we can use what is called a procedure. This is a series of instructions to which we give a name. We can make up the procedure for the square like this:

TO SQUARE
REPEAT 4 (FORWARD 20 RIGHT 90)
END

Each time we refer to SQUARE it will repeat this section of program called a procedure. Sometimes what actually happens is not always what you think will happen. Take the following, for instance:

REPEAT 4 (SQUARE)

You might have expected this to draw the square and then go over it another three times. What actually happens is shown in Figure 31.2. Try to use the instructions with a piece of paper and pen, but when you do remember that it is important to know in which direction the turtle is pointing. What you are actually doing is performing a DRY RUN. A DRY RUN means working through a program with a pen and paper to see if it produces the expected results.

Figure 31.2

QUESTIONS

1 See if you can work out, using pen, paper and a protractor what happens in the following procedure.

TO PATTERN
FORWARD 50
RIGHT 150
FORWARD 60
RIGHT 100
FORWARD 30
RIGHT 90
END

Draw an accurate diagram of what you would see (assume that the pen is down).

2 Repeat the above pattern using the program:

REPEAT 20 (PATTERN)

Explain why it did not go over the drawing in the first question 20 times.

3 Write a LOGO program to draw an equilateral triangle on the screen with sides of length 50. (N.B. In an equilateral triangle, all the sides are the same length and all the angles are 60°.)

4 A polygon is a many-sided figure. All of the interior angles in a regular polygon are the same size and the sides are the same length. Write a series of programs to produce the following shapes:
(a) a square
(b) a pentagon (five sides)
(c) a hexagon (six sides)
(d) a heptagon (seven sides).

Things to do

1 The following instructions will draw a shape.

REPEAT 4 [FORWARD 5 RIGHT 90]
(a) Show clearly on squared paper the shape drawn.
(b) Write a similar list of instructions to draw a rectangle with sides of length 4 and 6.

(SEG IS FT)

2 A robot is used to retrieve fuel rods from a nuclear reactor. To get the rod labelled X, the following instructions could be given:

FORWARD 3
TURN RIGHT
FORWARD 1
TAKE

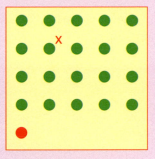

(a) The robot has an instruction (INPUT var) that allows numbers to be input into variables, which can then be used instead of the numbers indicated above. Write a program so that it will allow any rod to be retrieved. Make sure you clearly identify the use of your variables.
(b) Why would a robot be used for this job?

(SEG IS IT)

3 The pen on a graph plotter can be controlled by a computer using a simple set of commands which are stored as a program:

PEN UP
PEN DOWN
FORWARD x moves the pen forward x cm
RIGHT x turns x degrees to the right
LEFT x turns x degrees to the left
STOP

(a) You will need a protractor to measure the angles in the following program using the above commands:

PEN DOWN
FORWARD 10
RIGHT 90
FORWARD 10
RIGHT 90
FORWARD 10
RIGHT 90
FORWARD 10
STOP

Using a pen, paper, ruler and protractor, trace the shape that the plotter would draw using the above instructions.

(b) Write a program using the list of commands shown above to produce an equilateral triangle of side 15. (An equilateral triangle has equal sides and all the interior angles are 60°.)

(c) So that a series of instructions can be repeated, there are the following commands: REPEAT n TIMES

....
....
....
....

AGAIN

The dotted lines are used to represent the lines of commands that are repeated.
Write a program to draw a regular hexagon with sides of length 10 like the one shown in the diagram, using the REPEAT command.

4 A computer can control a turtle on the screen. When the turtle moves it leaves a line on the screen. Some of the commands are:

FORWARD steps
BACK steps
RIGHT angle
LEFT angle

For example, FORWARD 50 moves the turtle forward 50 steps in a straight line. RIGHT 45 turns the turtle 45° to the right.
Here are the commands which are needed to draw the S shape.

FORWARD 50 LEFT 90
FORWARD 50 LEFT 90
FORWARD 100 RIGHT 90
FORWARD 100 RIGHT 90

The turtle starts from the position shown in the diagram.
Arrange these commands in the right order to draw the S shape.

(NEAB/WJEC Spec Level P)

Monitoring physical quantities (temperature, pressure, etc.) using a computer

Monitoring temperature

If we wanted to look at how coffee cooled when placed in a polystyrene cup we could just use a stop clock and a thermometer and take a reading every minute over a period of an hour.

Doing it this way, we would need to sit with the whole apparatus for an hour and remember to take a reading of the thermometer every minute. Clearly this is tedious, even for one hour. If we needed to take more frequent readings over a longer period of time, we would probably give up.

Help is at hand though in the form of data logging (see Chapter 14). Here, we can use a

Figure 31.3 *Analogue-to-digital conversion is necessary with a temperature sensor*

computer (desktop or portable), an interface, suitable software and a temperature sensor to perform this experiment easily.

Once we have loaded the software and told the computer which sensors we have connected (some systems can do this automatically) we then need to tell the computer how frequently the measurements are to be made and over what period. We can then go away and do something else while the computer gets on with the job.

Most data loggers will record the data in the form of a table which can be imported into other software, such as spreadsheet or graphics packages for further work. You can usually display your readings graphically at the end of the experiment or while the experiment is taking place, since the readings are taken automatically by the sensor.

Logging

Logging interval
The logging interval is the frequency with which the individual readings are taken (i.e. per second, per minute, per hour, etc.). If you wanted to determine the average daily temperature you would probably choose to take a temperature measurement every hour. In one day you would have 24 separate measurements which could be added together and then divided by 24 to give the day's average.

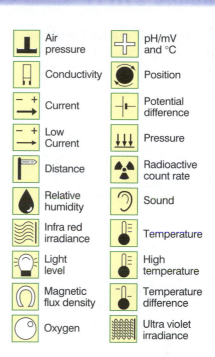

Figure 31.4 *The range of sensors available from Philip Harris Education, suppliers of data logging systems, sensors and control equipment*

Logging period
This is the time period over which the measurements take place. If you wanted to investigate the cooling of a cup of tea in different types of cup, you might choose a logging period of around one hour since this would be near the time taken for the drink to cool to around room temperature.

Figure 31.5 *The uses of sensors are limited only by your imagination*

Advantages of data logging

Data logging can be used for recording data about fast events that would happen too quickly for you to take readings manually. It can also be used for very slow events where recording them manually would be tedious and time consuming. Because the readings are taken automatically accurate measurements are made without human error and exactly at the right time.

IT TASKS

Task 1

Data logging

Here is a variety of tasks you can perform using data logging equipment. It is impossible to give exact instructions of how to use any particular piece of apparatus, because the instructions are different for different makes. This means you will have to find out from your teacher how to do the following:

1 Connect the sensor, interface and computer as instructed by your teacher.
2 Load the data logging software (if necessary).
3 Specify how frequently the readings are taken (most packages allow you to vary this from about one ten thousandth of a second to around 30 minutes).
4 Specify the total recording time (i.e. the total time over which the readings are taken). For most packages this can be from a fraction of a second to almost three weeks.
5 Display the data as a list on the screen.
6 Produce a display of the data plotted against time.
7 Save the data to disk for use later.
8 Plot the graph in real time so that, as a reading is taken, it is automatically plotted on the screen.
9 Export the previously saved data into other software packages such as spreadsheet or wordprocessing packages.

IT TASKS

Task 2

Temperature variation of water

Use data logging equipment to find out how the temperature of a glass beaker of boiling water varies with time when it is left to cool.

You will need to think about the following:
● how frequently the temperature reading needs to be taken and over what period
● what can be done to increase the time over which the water cools.
● try the experiment using different types of mug. Do tall, thin mugs keep the water hotter than short, fat mugs? Does the surface area in contact with the air matter? Try other, similar experiments.

Moisture content of soil

Monitor the change with time in the moisture content of the soil surrounding a house plant.
● What sensor or sensors will you use? (Hint: you will need to measure the moisture and any other physical properties on which the drying out of the soil depends.)

- How often does the data logger need to obtain a reading?
- Drying out is a slow process, so over what total time should the data logger operate? Why have you chosen this period?
- Explain exactly what you did and the reasons for doing it.

Conditions in a fish tank

Monitor the conditions in a tropical or marine fish tank over 24 hours.

You could use a variety of sensors such as:
- light
- temperature
- pH
- oxygen.

In a tropical or marine fish tank the temperature should be kept constant using the heater and the thermostat. From your readings, how successful was this system in keeping the temperature constant? You could try plotting physical quantities against each other rather than against time. For example, try plotting the amount of oxygen against the amount of light. Do they follow each other? Again fully document your experiment, paying particular attention to the use of the data logging equipment.

Wind chill factor

You may have heard the term wind chill factor being used by weather forecasters. We all know that, even on a warm day, it can feel a lot cooler if there is a wind.

One way of cooling a drink is to wrap a damp towel around the bottle and place it in a draughty place. The water evaporates and cools the bottle. Could we use this principle to make a device to give us a measure of the wind chill factor?

See what you can come up with and fully describe your solution.

Other examples of computer control

In this section we will look at how computers can be used to control devices and perform useful tasks.

Cold tea?

The problem
Make a system that warns you when your hot tea has cooled enough and is ready to drink. You should be able to cancel the alarm when you go to your drink.

Questions
- What temperature is the tea when it is cool enough to drink?
- What kind of a warning do you need?
- What will you use to tell the computer you have now received the warning and got your drink?

Solution
Tea at temperatures of around 55–70°C might be suitable for drinking. A buzzer would give a suitable warning. The buzzer would continue until a push button is pressed to cancel the alarm. The sensors may be connected to the interface along with a special module which is used for control. The buzzer is connected as number 6 and the push switch as input 1. If the temperature is less than 70°C the buzzer should be switched on. When the push button is pressed the buzzer stops. Using IF and WHEN, the computer tests the temperature and waits until the temperature condition is met.

Here is the control program:

WHEN TEMPERATURE IS
BELOW 70 THEN SWITCH ON 6
WHEN INPUT 1 IS ON
THEN SWITCH OFF 6

Here is another program which does the same thing

```
REPEAT FOREVER
IF TEMPERATURE IS
BELOW 70 THEN SWITCH
ON 6
AGAIN
```

Alternatively, both solutions can be built as procedures to give the same results:

```
BUILD teaalarm
WHEN TEMPERATURE IS
BELOW 70 THEN SWITCH
ON 6
WHEN INPUT 1 IS ON
THEN SWITCH OFF 6
END
```

or

```
BUILD teatwo
REPEAT FOREVER
IF TEMPERATURE IS
BELOW 70 THEN SWITCH
ON 6
AGAIN
WHEN INPUT 1 IS ON
THEN SWITCH OFF 6
END
```

Further work
1 If the freezer breaks down you need to know if the food has started to thaw out.
2 You have just put a bottle of warm cola in the fridge. You need a cold drink and want to know as soon as it's ready to drink. Make an alarm system.

Wake up

The problem
Make an alarm clock which switches on at dawn and switches off when you shout at it.

Questions
- How will the computer know if it is morning?
- How will the computer detect you have shouted at it?
- How loud do you need to shout to stop the alarm?
- What can you use to set the alarm?
- How could you tell that the alarm has been set?

Solution
The light sensor can measure the light level. When the light reaches a certain level the alarm will be switched on. A sound sensor is used to detect the voice. The sound level at which the alarm switches off should be set high enough so that it is not switched off by the alarm itself. Use the push switch to set the alarm and switch on a green light to indicate it is set. Connect the sound sensor and the module to the interface. Connect the light and sound sensors to the interface. The push switch is connected as input 1 and the green indicator lamp is connected as number 3.

Here is the control program. This program is written as a procedure.

```
BUILD alarm
REPEAT FOREVER
WHEN INPUT 1 IS ON
THEN SWITCH ON 3
WHEN LIGHT IS ABOVE 40
THEN SWITCH ON 6
WHEN SOUND IS ABOVE
80 THEN SWITCH OFF 6
SWITCH OFF 3
AGAIN
END
```

To make this procedure run, type the line below:

```
DO alarm
```

Further work
1 Make an alarm that tells you when you're playing your music too loud.
2 Make a burglar alarm that can be triggered by the noise level. The alarm sound can be on and off like a siren.

Shop

The problem
Make a buzzer for a shop that works when you go in and step on the door mat.

Questions
- What can you use to tell if the mat has been stepped on?
- What should the buzzer do – should it stay on all the time or should it switch off after a certain time?

- What should happen if another customer enters the shop?

Solution

Use a push switch to tell if the mat has been stepped on. If the push switch has been pressed the buzzer should be switched on. The buzzer should stay on for a few seconds then it should be switched off. Go back and check if the push switch has been pressed, in case another customer enters the shop. This will be repeated over and over. Connect the module to the interface. The buzzer is connected as number 6 and the push switch as input 1.

Here is the control program:

```
REPEAT FOREVER
WHEN INPUT 1 IS ON
THEN SWITCH ON 6
WAIT 20
SWITCH OFF 6
AGAIN
```

Alternatively, we can use a procedure called shop to do the same:

```
BUILD shop
REPEAT FOREVER
WHEN INPUT 1 IS ON
THEN SWITCH ON 6
WAIT 20
SWITCH OFF 6
AGAIN
END
```

To make this procedure run, type the line below:

```
DO shop
```

Further work

Make the buzzer produce an intermittent sound. As an alternative to the push switch it is possible to make a pressure 'switch' by attaching a near flat balloon to a pressure sensor. Use the same procedure as above but replace the lines that read:

```
WHEN INPUT 1 IS ON
THEN SWITCH ON 6
```

with

```
WHEN PRESSURE IS
ABOVE 20 THEN SWITCH
ON 6
```

You may need to experiment with the value of the pressure to make the buzzer work in the way that you want.

Lighthouse

The problem

Make a flashing warning light for a lighthouse.

Questions

- Which colour will you use for the warning light? Give your reason.
- What should the warning light do?

Solution

Use a red light, LED number 1, as red is a good warning colour. The warning light should come on for a second then go off for a second. This should repeat over and over. Connect the module to the universal interface.

Here is the control program:

```
REPEAT FOREVER
SWITCH ON 1
WAIT 5
SWITCH OFF 1
WAIT 5
AGAIN
```

Alternatively, you could build a 'procedure' called flash to do the same thing:

```
BUILD flash
REPEAT FOREVER
SWITCH ON 1
WAIT 5
SWITCH OFF 1
WAIT 5
AGAIN
END
```

To run this procedure type the line below:

```
DO flash
```

Further work

Use two flashing lights as the warning signal.

Go away

The problem

People keep ringing your door buzzer at night. Make a door buzzer that works only in the daytime.

Questions

- What will you use as a push button?
- How will the door bell know whether it is night or day?
- What should the light level be for the door buzzer to work – above 60, above 40 or something else?

Should the buzzer work:

1 when it is pressed or the light level is low?
2 when it is pressed or the light level is high?
3 when it is pressed and the light level is low?
4 when it is pressed and the light level is high?

When should the door buzzer stop buzzing – when you stop pressing it, after a few seconds or when you answer the door?

Solution

Use the push switch as the door push button. Use a light sensor to find out whether it is night or day. Trial and error will determine the most suitable light level for the buzzer to work. The door buzzer should work only if two conditions are met: if the push switch has been pressed and if the light level is high. The buzzer should be switched off a few seconds after the button has been pressed. Next go back and check if the push switch has been pressed again. This will be repeated forever.

Connect the light sensor and module to the universal interface. The buzzer is connected as number 6 and the push switch as input 1. Here is the control program:

```
REPEAT FOREVER
IF LIGHT IS ABOVE 50
AND INPUT 1 IS ON THEN
SWITCH ON 6
WAIT 20
SWITCH OFF 6
AGAIN
```

Alternatively you could use a procedure called buzzer:

```
BUILD buzzer
REPEAT FOREVER
IF LIGHT IS ABOVE 50
AND INPUT 1 IS ON THEN
SWITCH ON 6
WAIT 20
SWITCH OFF 6
AGAIN
END
```

Further work

Porch light

You want a light to come on at your front door whenever it is dark and switch off when it gets light. To save electricity, you also want to be able to switch the light off when you go to bed.

Welcome home

You want a light to come on at your front door when you arrive home at night. Obviously it doesn't come on during the day.

Modelling

Modelling coursework

There is a series of coursework tasks at the end of this chapter for you to choose. It is best to choose one that interests you. Ask your teacher if the task is a suitable one for you to do. You don't have to use any of the ones given and you could make up your own. Either way, you need to provide evidence for the modelling strand. To provide this evidence you need a fairly structured approach to the documentation. For this reason it is best for you to adopt a format along the lines shown below.

Identify

The first step is to identify the problem. You need to express clearly what the problem is for which you are trying to produce a model. You also need to say why you have chosen particular software rather than something else. Mention software you thought of choosing but you later rejected with reasons why you rejected it.

Analyse

At the analysis stage, you need to plan out your approach to the problem and also include any simplifications or assumptions you have made. Also include the variables you need to enter and the output you need from the system.

Design

When dealing with the design, you can describe what the model as a whole will look like and then go into greater detail. At this stage you can start to plan the layout of the spreadsheet if you are using one.

Use/implement

At this stage you provide evidence that you have produced some solution to the problem or are well on the way to getting nearer to a solution. Remember, it is very difficult and in many cases impossible to produce a perfect model. If you have had to alter your design for whatever reason then you need to say why you have altered it. Always include every piece of your work as evidence, even the parts which you did completely wrong.

You need to test your model. In some cases this will just be comparing some of the answers with those obtained using a calculator, but in others you may be able to test the system against reality. For instance, if you had to produce a model for the population growth in Britain over the last century, you could obtain actual figures and see how good your model is.

Evaluation

When you evaluate your model you need to say whether you are happy with it. Given more time, what further adjustments would you make to it? Could you have approached the problem in a different way?

Refinement

If you are unhappy with your model you can refine it. Sometimes you can name each version (attempt 1, attempt 2, etc.) until you get your final version. At the end you can include a final evaluation.

Modelling a supermarket queue

In this example we will look at the problem of making a model of a supermarket queue.

Figure 32.1

The way the model is written up is the same as that outlined before. When doing any coursework on modelling, make sure that you adopt a similar format.

Identifying the problem

Suppose we are opening a new supermarket. How do we decide how many tills or point-of-sale terminals to use? If the supermarket is part of a chain like Tesco, then past experience may help us. But if this is our first supermarket we haven't any others to make a comparison with. Some other method will need to be used.

Analysing the situation

Why do we need to get it right?

If we don't get the number of tills right the consequences could be:

1 either we could buy too many POS terminals and thereby waste money
2 or we could buy too few and cause long queues which might make the shoppers reluctant to shop at the store again.

What software do we need to use to perform this task?

Since we are trying to understand how a real system operates, we could use a spreadsheet.

We do need to think carefully about the problem before we start trying to design the spreadsheet. We are going to construct a model of the queue using numbers.

We need first to decide:

1 the inputs to the system
2 the calculations that need to be performed on these numbers
3 the outputs from the system.

The advantage of constructing such a model is that we can make changes to the inputs and see what effects they have on the output. For example, the supermarket owner/manager can immediately see the effect of altering the number of tills on the lengths of queues and the average waiting times.

What are the inputs to the supermarket model?

The inputs include:

1 how many people are waiting
2 how many POS terminals or tills there are
3 how long each person takes to be served. This will have to be an average time, since the time depends on the number of items the person is buying and the method of payment (e.g. credit card, debit card, cheque or cash).

Always produce the simplest model to start with. This will help you get a grasp of the problem and you can refine it later. Make sure that you include all your work if you are including a modelling/simulation project for your coursework.

Design

In this section we have to start designing our model. In this case we will be using a spreadsheet so we can either design it straight onto the spreadsheet or plan it on paper first. If you are designing the model straight onto the spreadsheet, make sure that you know enough about the commands to move things around if you need to alter them.

In this problem we can have a heading and then divide the spreadsheet into two parts for the inputs and the outputs. Calculations are performed on the inputs to produce the outputs. Figure 32.2 shows the design.

Figure 32.2 *Design of the model*

Suppose that there are 40 shoppers waiting to pay for the goods and there are 20 checkouts. Let us also assume that, on average, it takes a shopper two minutes to pass through the checkout. We will have to assume that the shoppers will distribute themselves equally in the queues. We can then calculate the average number of shoppers in each queue using the formula:

$$\text{average number of shoppers in each queue} = \frac{\text{number of shoppers waiting}}{\text{number of tills}}$$

Using our figures we get:

$$\text{average number of shoppers in each queue} = \frac{40}{20} = 2$$

Now, the last shopper in each of these queues will have to wait a time which is given by the following formula:

time last person in queue has to wait = average time for a person to go through the checkout in minutes × average number of shoppers waiting in each queue.

Using our figures we get:

$$\text{time last person in each queue has to wait} = 2 \times 2 = 4 \text{ min}$$

Now, the beauty of using a spreadsheet is the ease with which we can carry out the calculations. However, we must make sure that we link the outputs to the inputs using formulae.

Figure 32.3 shows the formulae that have to be used. You should be able to print your spreadsheet out showing any formulae placed in each cell. Produce this as evidence in your project.

Figure 32.3 *Spreadsheet showing the inputs, outputs and the formulae used to calculate the outputs*

Implementation

Implementation involves actually using the model. In other words we have to perform a simulation by putting in numbers to see what happens.

Figure 32.4 shows the effect of altering the inputs to the system. Try to use the model you have created to explore the effect of changing the variables and rules and to test hypotheses.

	A	B	C	D	E	F	G
1							
2							
3			*Model of a supermarket queue*				
4							
5	**Inputs**						
6	Number of shoppers waiting				50		
7	Number of tills				10		
8	Time for a shopper to pass through a checkout				2	min	
9							
10							
11							
12	**Outputs**						
13	Average number of shoppers in each queue				5		
14	Time the last person in the queue has to wait				10	min	
15							
16							

Figure 32.4 *Spreadsheet showing the effect of altering the number of tills*

Evaluation

We have to look carefully at the model we have produced. Maybe we could have made it better. Here we describe whether we are happy with the model, any improvements that could be made to it and whether it solves the problem that we started with.

Refinement

If the model is a good one, then no refinement is needed. If we need to alter the model in any way to reflect the real situation more accurately, then we need to say why and provide evidence of having done this, which would include printouts of the improved model. Obviously you could go on forever making changes and trying to get things right but there has to be a point where you stop. Finally, perfection is impossible to achieve especially if human behaviour is to be taken into account.

Break-even analysis

Beatbox is a new company set up by a brother and sister to manufacture small loudspeakers. They hope to sell the small speakers to people who want to attach their personal stereos or CD players to them, or who need speakers for multimedia applications.

They realise that things will be hard to start with so, to give themselves some light at the end of the tunnel, they would like to find out how many speakers they would need to sell to break even.

When a business is started, money has to be paid out for equipment, parts, premises, etc., before the company starts making the products. So money goes out of the business but there is none coming in. Once the product begins to be made and sold, the money starts coming back into the business. Eventually, when Beatbox has sold a certain number of loudspeakers, the company will break even. This point, called the break-even point, occurs when the money coming in from the sale of the loudspeakers balances the money that has been paid out. In other words, the company is neither making a profit nor a loss. There will be a certain number of loudspeakers for which this will occur. Once past this point, the sale of the speakers will start to produce a profit.

Break-even analysis is important when starting a business since the banks that lend the company money to start up will want to know when the borrower will start to make a profit.

In order to produce a model for break-even analysis, Beatbox needs to work out the fixed costs and the variable costs. The company's accountant tells the owners the following information.

Fixed costs

Fixed costs are any costs that do not depend on the number of loudspeakers sold. Fixed costs would include rent of buildings, rates, salaries and finance costs. It is important to note that fixed costs do not stay fixed forever. They are only fixed over the short term and over a certain range of production.

Variable costs

Variable costs are the costs that depend on the number of speakers produced. So, the costs of the parts which make up the speakers and the electricity used would be classed as variable costs.

Beatbox has worked out the following figures:

fixed costs = £1000
variable costs per speaker = £12.50
selling price per speaker = £18.00

Variable costs are the costs of making a certain number of speakers and sales revenue is the money which comes in when the same number of speakers is sold. So:

total cost of producing speakers = variable costs + fixed costs

variable costs = variable costs per speaker × number of speakers

sales revenue = selling price per speaker × number of speakers

We can now produce a table with the column headings shown below using spreadsheet software.

Number of speakers   Variable costs   Fixed costs   Total cost   Sales revenue

You will now perform a series of tasks which will determine the break-even point.

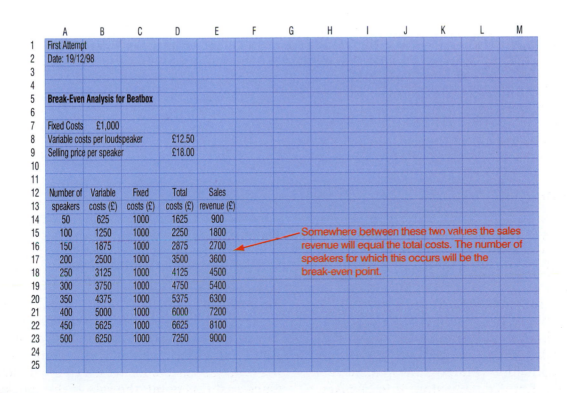

	A	B	C	D	E
1	First Attempt				
2	Date: 19/12/98				
3					
4					
5	**Break-Even Analysis for Beatbox**				
6					
7	Fixed Costs	£1,000			
8	Variable costs per loudspeaker		£12.50		
9	Selling price per speaker		£18.00		
10					
11					
12	Number of	Variable	Fixed	Total	Sales
13	speakers	costs (£)	costs (£)	costs (£)	revenue (£)
14	50	625	1000	1625	900
15	100	1250	1000	2250	1800
16	150	1875	1000	2875	2700
17	200	2500	1000	3500	3600
18	250	3125	1000	4125	4500
19	300	3750	1000	4750	5400
20	350	4375	1000	5375	6300
21	400	5000	1000	6000	7200
22	450	5625	1000	6625	8100
23	500	6250	1000	7250	9000
24					
25					

Somewhere between these two values the sales revenue will equal the total costs. The number of speakers for which this occurs will be the break-even point.

Figure 32.5 *Spreadsheet showing the inputs, outputs and the formulae used to calculate the outputs*

First attempt

The first attempt is used to obtain the very rough range that the break-even point could lie within.

In the first attempt to find the break-even point you can use numbers of speakers from 50 to 500 going up in steps of 50. Make sure that you key in all the information except that in the following columns: variable costs, total costs and sales revenue. You should work these out using suitable formulae and then copy them down the relevant columns. Check that your final model looks like the one in Figure 32.5.

The break-even point occurs where the sales revenue and the total costs are equal. As you can see there is no such value on our spreadsheet so we look for where the sales revenue goes from being smaller than the total costs to where it is greater. Looking at the spreadsheet you can see that this occurs between sales of 150 and 200 speakers. We need to investigate this region more closely to get a more accurate picture. We therefore produce a second spreadsheet just covering this area.

Second attempt

Produce another spreadsheet by altering the first one to go from 150 speakers to 250 speakers in steps of 10. Check with Figure 32.6 that you get the same values. It should reveal that the break-even point lies somewhere between 180 and 190 speakers.

Third attempt

Now repeat the process using the numbers of speakers from 180 to 190 in steps of one speaker.

What value do you get for the number of speakers to break even? What do you think you should do if it is not a whole number?

Check that your spreadsheet looks like the one in Figure 32.7.

Finding the break-even point graphically
We can find the break-even point graphically by plotting the sales revenue and total costs against the number of speakers sold. You can do this either using graph paper or get the computer to draw two line graphs like the one shown in Figure 32.8. The break-even point is where the two straight lines cross. The number of speakers sold to break even can be read from the graph.

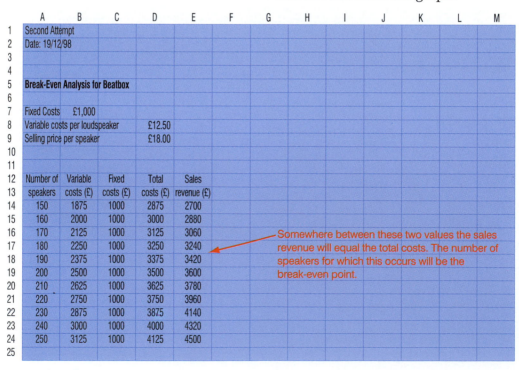

	A	B	C	D	E
1	Second Attempt				
2	Date: 19/12/98				
3					
4					
5	**Break-Even Analysis for Beatbox**				
6					
7	Fixed Costs	£1,000			
8	Variable costs per loudspeaker			£12.50	
9	Selling price per speaker			£18.00	
10					
11					
12	Number of	Variable	Fixed	Total	Sales
13	speakers	costs (£)	costs (£)	costs (£)	revenue (£)
14	150	1875	1000	2875	2700
15	160	2000	1000	3000	2880
16	170	2125	1000	3125	3060
17	180	2250	1000	3250	3240
18	190	2375	1000	3375	3420
19	200	2500	1000	3500	3600
20	210	2625	1000	3625	3780
21	220	2750	1000	3750	3960
22	230	2875	1000	3875	4140
23	240	3000	1000	4000	4320
24	250	3125	1000	4125	4500
25					

Somewhere between these two values the sales revenue will equal the total costs. The number of speakers for which this occurs will be the break-even point.

Figure 32.6 *Second attempt at finding the break-even point*

	A	B	C	D	E	F	G	H	I	J	K	L	M
1	Third Attempt												
2	Date: 19/12/98												
3													
4													
5	**Break-Even Analysis for Beatbox**												
6													
7	Fixed Costs	£1,000											
8	Variable costs per loudspeaker			£12.50									
9	Selling price per speaker			£18.00									
10													
11													
12	Number of	Variable	Fixed	Total	Sales								
13	speakers	costs (£)	costs (£)	costs (£)	revenue (£)								
14	180	2250.00	1000	3250.00	3240								
15	181	2262.50	1000	3262.50	3258								
16	182	2275.00	1000	3275.00	3276								
17	183	2287.50	1000	3287.50	3294								
18	184	2300.00	1000	3300.00	3312								
19	185	2312.50	1000	3312.50	3330								
20	186	2325.00	1000	3325.00	3348								
21	187	2337.50	1000	3337.50	3366								
22	188	2350.00	1000	3350.00	3384								
23	189	2362.50	1000	3362.50	3402								
24	190	2375.00	1000	3375.00	3420								
25													

Figure 32.7 *Third attempt at finding the break-even point*

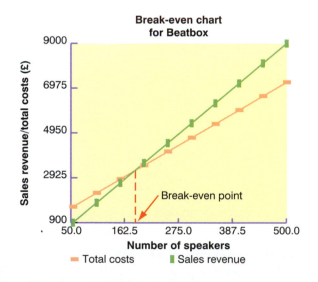

Figure 32.8 *Finding the break-even point graphically*

TEST YOURSELF

John enjoys woodwork and has decided to make a bird table for his parents. The table he makes is seen by his neighbours, who ask him if he can make them one. The word travels around and before long he has a book full of orders. He even starts to get the odd order from a garden centre.

He would like to speed up the construction of the tables by using more power tools. He has £400 in the bank, which he spends on the latest woodworking equipment. His variable and fixed costs are:

fixed costs (woodworking equipment) = £400
variable costs = £15.00 per bird table
selling price = £25.00 per bird table

Using a spreadsheet, work out how many bird tables he would need to sell before he breaks even.

IT TASKS

Task 1

Use a spreadsheet to solve a pair of simultaneous equations such as the pair:

$3x + 4y = 25$

$3x + 2y = 17$

There is a variety of ways you could approach this problem.
(a) You use the spreadsheet to set up a table for each equation and then use each table to plot a graph. Where the two straight lines cut, the x and y co-ordinates will give the solution to the above pair of equations.
(b) You could develop a method on the spreadsheet using trial and error.
(c) You could use matrices. Some spreadsheets have a function where you can solve simultaneous equations. See if yours has and find out how to use it.

IT TASKS

Task 2

Suzanne is 25 and lives at home with her parents. She is bored with her present job working in an office and would like a challenge. Her present job brings her in £150 per week.

She has just seen an advertisement in her local newspaper advertising a training course to become a driving instructor. Fees for the tuition and final examination are £1300. She can drive at the moment but does not have her own car. She therefore needs to buy a car with dual controls. Suzanne sees a car she likes and with the dual controls it will cost her £8000.

In order to get established Suzanne reckons she will need to undercut the fees charged by the other driving schools. She therefore decides to charge £12 per hour. To attract customers, she decides to advertise in the local paper and this will cost £30 per week. Also, her mother, who is at home all day, will answer the phone calls and make bookings and Suzanne will give her mother £20 per week for doing this.

Before giving up her job and going ahead with the venture she decides to work out how many hours she would need to work each week in order to break even. To do this she must work out her fixed and variable costs. This she has done and the following figures are obtained.

Fixed costs

Advertising in the local paper = £30.00 per week
Payment to her mother = £20.00 per week
Borrowing to buy the car and pay for tuition fees for course = £40.00 per week
Depreciation of the car = £80.00 per week

Variable costs

The only variable costs will be the running costs of the car. These include petrol, repairs, etc. She works out these variable costs to be 20p per mile. On average, in a one hour lesson she estimates that she will travel about 15 miles. Hence, the variable costs for one lesson will be 15 × 20p = £3.00.

Suzanne has asked for your help in making her decision.

You have your own computer and have told Suzanne that you will help her by making use of appropriate computer software.
1   Set up a model of the business and use your model to determine the number of lessons she would need to do each week in order to break even.
2   Suggest some improvements she might make and show them as printouts.
3   Write a brief report on the proposed business. Should she quit her job or stick with it? What do you think on the basis of your figures?

IT TASKS

Task 3

In mathematics you often come across equations such as:

$x^2 - x - 6 = 0$

We would normally solve this by factorisation like this:

$(x - 3)(x + 2) = 0$

giving values of $x = 3$ or -2.

Some equations are difficult to solve. For instance the quadratic equation:

$x^2 + 6x - 2 = 0$

has the solutions $x = 0.32$ or -6.32 to two decimal places, so we can't solve it by simple factorisation. We could however use a spreadsheet and try various values of x in the equation to see if we can get zero.

IT TASKS

Task 4

Here is an equation to solve using a spreadsheet. Do not try to factorise it because it cannot be factorised.

$x^2 - 8x - 6 = 0$

Now, you can use the same method to solve a cubic equation. With cubic equations, there are three solutions. See if you can find all the solutions for the following cubic equation:

$x^3 - 6x^2 + 3x + 10 = 0$

To give you a clue, all the solutions lie somewhere between −2 and +6.

You may also like to plot the equations using a graphics, curve sketching or spreadsheet package. Can you spot your solutions on the graph?

IT TASKS

Task 5

You are the promoter for a pop concert. You are going to organise a concert with a famous group or singer. You have certain overheads such as the costs of the group, singer, etc., as well as costs of rental of the hall, printing of tickets, security guards, refreshments, programmes, etc.

You are to produce a model of the business and simulate a variety of different situations, e.g. very few people turning up, a sell out concert, etc.

Produce a report showing examples of your model and explain any assumptions you made in making your model. Give a conclusion explaining how closely your model mimics the real situation and outline any improvements you could make.

IT TASKS

Task 6

In this task you will be required to solve a pair of equations simultaneously.

Here is the pair of equations:

$y = x^2 - 4x + 7$

$y = x + 1$

The first equation is called a quadratic equation and the second is called a linear equation. The solution to the simultaneous equations will be a value of x when put into either of the equations, that will give the same value of y. There are two such values of x for which this will happen and you, using a spreadsheet model will have to find them.

If you are submitting this task as part of your coursework, you need to make sure that you have fully documented both the initial problem and its solution. The structure of your solution should fall under the following headings:
- identify
- analyse
- design
- use or implement
- evaluate.

IT TASKS

Task 7

Explore a model of traffic flow at a crossroads with traffic lights. Find out the best timing of the north–south and east–west lights to minimise the queues of traffic for particular rates of traffic flows in each direction. Produce a brief report, including at least one printout to support your conclusions.

Model a set of temporary traffic lights, one at each end of some road works 100 m long. Only one line of traffic can pass, so the lights must be set to allow safe passage of traffic. Investigate the effect of different lengths of time on green on the length of queues for particular rates of traffic flows. Produce a brief report, including printouts of your model and of the queue for different values of variables.

(RSA Spec)

IT TASKS

Task 8

You have been asked to produce a model for electricity usage in a house over a year. Quantity of electricity is measured in a unit called a kilowatt hour (written as kWh). A 1 kWh appliance, such as a one bar electric fire, used for one hour would consume 1 kWh of electricity. Used for half an hour, it would consume 0.5 kWh. If you are unsure how to calculate amounts of electricity from the power of an appliance and the time it is used, consult your physics teacher.

Things to think about:
- Design a document on which you could record the names of the appliances owned and their power consumption.
- Use this document to collect the information.
- Interview the people who use the appliance, find out how long they use it for each week or month and then use this figure to work out the daily usage. You need to do this because not every appliance will be used each day.
- You will need to find the cost of a 1 kWh unit of electricity.
- Design a spreadsheet to model the situation with suitable column and row headings.
- You will need to calculate the total cost per day and the total cost per year.

Graphics Packages

Graphics

Graphics is a word used for all types of art-work, including line diagrams, bitmap images (made up of lots of tiny dots), photographs, graphs and charts.

Graphics packages

For most of us, graphics packages can mean just a simple paint package where you can draw line diagrams, flood fill, and produce a variety of shadings. You can also produce text in a variety of fonts and typefaces. These simple but very useful packages can be used as an alternative to specialist and more complicated desktop publishing packages. Producing diagrams is extremely difficult using a mouse so some professional artwork is hand drawn and then scanned into a graphics package. A great deal of professional artwork is now drawn with software packages which do not use a mouse.

Some graphics packages allow you to scan a photograph or diagram directly into the computer so that you can subsequently manipulate it in some way. Using special equipment and software it is possible to capture pictures from a television screen or from a video camera. The extra equipment needed to do this is called a video grabber. Digital cameras are very popular because you don't need a film and there are no developing costs. You can simply capture the photographs from the camera and then manipulate the images on the computer screen.

If you need to use pictures then you can use clip art.

Bit map and vector graphics

There are two formats that a graphics file can have: it can represent the image as a bit map or as a vector graphic.

A bit map file represents each dot or pixel on the screen as a single bit of information in a file. If the pixel is in colour, then additional bits will need to be stored. Many paint packages such as PC Paintbrush create bit mapped images. One of the main disadvantages of bitmapped images is that they are difficult to change because they have to be altered a pixel at a time.

With vector graphics, the lines are stored as equations inside the computer. They are expressed in vector format so they have a starting point, a length and a direction. The main advantage of vector graphics is that they are easy to change without any loss of resolution. With bit mapped graphics, if the image is enlarged, the number of pixels used stays the same. As a result of this the pixels move further apart and this makes the image look grainy. When a vector graphics image is enlarged, the number of pixels used to make up the image increases in proportion and the resolution stays the same.

CAD packages make use of vector graphics.

Clip art

For those without an artistic streak, the thought of having to draw pictures to be placed in an important document can bring on a cold sweat. Anyone who has tried to use a mouse to draw pictures using a paint or drawing package will know how hard it is. However, help is at hand with clip art. Clip art illustrations are copyright-free drawings which you can place in your documents. These documents could be wordprocessed, desktop published or could be a diagram drawn using a graphics package. Some clip art is shown in Figure 33.1.

Because clip art is accurately predrawn when imported into your documents, it gives a professional look to the documents. Disks

Figure 33.1 *Some holiday clip art*

Figure 33.2 *As well as importing clip art you can also import pre-stored photos*

containing clip art can be bought separately or as part of a graphics or DTP package. You can get special clip art packages and some have as many as one million images.

Presentation software

Pictures are able to communicate ideas and concepts to an audience much better than the written or spoken word alone. Presentations are used to sell products, services or just ideas to someone else. Good presentations use visual aids such as slides or transparencies on a projector. The visual aids are used to back up what the presenter is saying. Graphs are usually included in such presentations. If the work is displayed attractively, then the audience will be more able to digest the key points.

While a projector is needed for a large audience, for smaller audiences a rolling slide show can be produced on the screen of a computer.

Multimedia (hypermedia) presentations

Multimedia is sometimes called hypermedia. Multimedia presentations are useful for training since students can see demonstrations on-screen and can also interact with the software. It is hard to explain the capabilities of multimedia and you should look at different packages for yourself.

Colour

Colour printing is affordable if you use an ink-jet printer, but colour laser printers are expensive to buy. When producing graphics you need to decide whether they are to be printed out. It you do not have a colour printer then there is no point in worrying about colour when planning your design on the screen. You will find that much clearer graphics are produced on black and white printers if you use black and white on the screen.

Computer aided design

Computer aided design or CAD for short, is used by engineers, architects, etc. to produce high quality technical drawings drawn to scale. The sorts of diagram produced by these packages include plans of houses, maps, circuit diagrams, engineering drawings and 3-D plans of kitchens. Figure 33.5 shows a stairway design which has been produced using CAD.

Before computers were used, if a drawing needed a simple modification then it was often necessary to completely redraw it. Now, with the use of CAD software modifications can be made at the press of a button.

Architects can produce a plan view of a building and then immediately view it in three dimensions and even rotate it to see what it looks like from different angles. The most popular CAD package is AutoCAD, which is quite expensive, so you are unlikely to see it in schools. There is a cut down version available at a much lower price.

CAD images

Figure 33.3 shows a ray traced image and this is easily converted into a solid image which can be viewed from all angles by the computer.

Figure 33.3

Figure 33.4 *If you are artistic, then you can even produce graphic images like this one*

Computer graphics

Using sophisticated graphics packages the computer can be used to produce images like that shown in Figure 33.4.

Advantages of using CAD:
1 it saves a lot of time
2 it produces accurate scale diagrams
3 you can easily manipulate the images on the screen
4 you can produce drawings in 3-D, which is especially useful for diagrams of kitchens, gardens, buildings, etc.
5 images can be saved on disk and retrieved at a later date
6 drawings can easily be scaled up and down.

Figure 33.5 *Stairway design produced using CAD software*

Garden design software

Garden design software is one of the many specialist applications of design software and it allows gardeners to place their plants and features such as ponds, paths, terraces, etc. and see what they would look like. Using this software you can view the garden in 3-D and also from different angles. You can even see the garden in different seasons.

Figure 33.6 *A plan view of the garden.*

Screen shots taken from 'Geoff Hamilton's 3D Garden Design Software', published by Global Software Publishing

Figure 33.7 *This shows one of the many 3-D views of the same garden design.*

IT TASKS

Task 1

When people want to find you, it is handy to give them a map. Here is a map for you to copy.

Figure 33.8 *A map for you to draw*

Use appropriate software such as a painting, drawing or art package to perform the following tasks:

1 copy the map shown in Figure 33.8. Try to make it exactly the same and use a mouse to draw the roads
2 add the landmarks such as the Jolly Miller Pub, Peter Lloyd Sports Centre, etc.
3 add the text to your diagram, making sure that the size and font are suitable
4 add the boxes around the text as shown in the diagram
5 save your work using a suitable file name
6 print a copy of your map.

Now design and draw your own map, showing directions either to your house or to your school or college.

Things to do

1 (a) Explain what is meant by the abbreviation CAD.
  (b) Give three advantages of using CAD against performing the same task manually.

2 A friend of your family knows of your interest in computers and has asked you your opinion regarding buying a multimedia computer system.
  (a) What makes a multimedia system different from an ordinary computer system?
  (b) Describe two of the multimedia packages that you have used.

3 Many people find it easier to use clip art than use their own diagrams.
  (a) Explain what is meant by 'clip art'.
  (b) Why is it easier to use clip art?
  (c) What are the disadvantages of using clip art?

IT TASKS

Task 2

Pick one of the following, and use any graphics, paint or other package to help you with your design.
1 Design a package that could be used to hold a single golf ball. You will need to design the shape of the package and design the net.
2 You have been asked by a fabric manufacturer to come up with a new design for a fabric. Use appropriate software to do this.
3 A friend of yours is a question master in a local pub quiz. He decides that it would be nice to include a page of flags of different countries of the world in the quiz. The idea is that each contestant will be given a sheet with the flags on and the contestant has to write the name of the country underneath. If you do not have access to a colour printer then you could try taking a photograph of the screen. You could find the designs of the flags with an atlas such as the World Atlas held on CD-ROM.

IT TASKS

Task 3

Many companies use logos as part of their advertising. These logos are cleverly thought out and enable people to recognise the company or their products.

To see how important they are, can you draw the logos for the following companies:
- McDonald
- BT
- Acorn Computers
- the National Lottery.
- Shell
- the Bradford & Bingley Building Society
- Peugeot Cars

Choose a company which does not use a logo at the moment and design a logo for it using graphics software. You should include several designs, so that the company could choose between them. Also include a wordprocessed report outlining the ideas behind your logos.

IT TASKS

Task 4

You have been asked by the teacher of a local primary school to produce diagrams of a series of objects that can be coloured in by the pupils. Underneath each diagram will be the name of the object in large print so that the pupils can be taught to read.

Produce, using appropriate software, a series of suitable diagrams for this purpose. Remember that the diagrams will need to be quite large, otherwise they will be too difficult to colour in.

IT TASKS

Task 5

Look through a selection of clip art for any connected with transport, using a drawing, painting or graphics package. The clip art should be grouped into the following:
- road: cars, bicycles, vans, lorries and motorbikes
- rail: locomotives and carriages
- air: balloons, gliders, spacecraft, jets and helicopters
- water: pleasure craft, ferries, tankers, yachts and freight ships.

Produce an attractive display of clip art images under each of the above headings. A small piece of text should be added about each one.

IT TASKS

Task 6

A teacher in a junior school has approached you for some help in designing a sheet to be used by pupils for explaining the names and properties of certain shapes. The shapes they would like you to include are as follows:
- rectangle
- square
- rhombus
- parallelogram
- kite
- trapezium
- right-angled triangle
- equilateral triangle
- isosceles triangle.

Remember, as well as drawing these shapes, you have to name them and write a small piece explaining their properties.

You could try doing a similar task involving 3D-shapes, such as cuboids, cylinders, etc.

IT TASKS

Task 7

Produce a heart shape for a Valentine's card using the LOGO programming language. Fully document your solution by providing explanations of the methods you used to try to solve the problem. Evidence of your work should be provided in the form of program listings and screen dumps onto a printer. Include all your work, including the parts that you rejected. Now try to use an art package to do the same thing. What functions in the drawing package did you use? Make comparisons between the two ways of solving the problem. Which one was the easiest to use? Again, fully document your solution.

IT TASKS

Task 8

This task requires a knowledge of chemistry.

Using suitable software, produce a selection of hazard symbols (see Figure 33.9).

Figure 33.9

Using a selection of clip art images and the cut, paste and copy facilities, come up with repeating designs for one of the following:
- Christmas wrapping paper
- birthday wrapping paper
- wallpaper.

IT TASKS

Task 9

Produce a garden design using a painting or other suitable package. Remember that certain plants are in bloom at different times of the year so you could try to incorporate this fact in some way.

IT TASKS

Task 10

There is a variety of diagrams that can be used to describe a system, such as system flowcharts, structure diagrams and data flow diagrams. The diagrams make use of a variety of different shaped boxes. Some graphics packages have these boxes included with them as clip art.

Find out if your graphics package has any of these shapes; if not produce a selection and store each one in a separate file to be used later.

Finally, produce a systems flowchart (use the one on page 92 if you cannot make one up of your own) using your graphics package.

IT TASKS

Task 11

It is Christmas and the police are worried about people drinking and driving. There have been several fatal accidents involving people who have been drinking. Produce a poster which can be placed on pub walls outlining the horrors or the consequences of drinking and driving.

IT TASKS

Task 12

You have decided to sell your home computer or games console. Use DTP software to produce an advert for the system you are selling which will be placed on a school or college notice board. Try to make your design as eyecatching as possible by using special text effects, boxes and graphics.

IT TASKS

Task 13

Design and print a ticket for any one of the following:
- a disco
- a school concert
- a party for a special occasion
- a garden fete.

IT TASKS

Task 14

You have been asked by your local hospital to draw people's attention to personal hygiene. You decide to produce a series of posters. The sorts of topics you might consider could include:
- washing hands after using the toilet
- keeping food covered while it is left out.

Any health or hygiene message can be used. Go for a catchy phrase to help get your message across.

You have been asked to produce a picture of a birthday cake like the one shown in Figure 33.10 using a drawing/paint package.

Happy
Birthday
John

Figure 33.10

1 Load your software.
2 Draw a single candle with the flame at the top and save it to disk so that it can be copied as many times as you like.
3 Draw the rest of the cake.
4 Using suitable commands, copy and position the required number of candles on the top of the cake.
5 Select suitable fonts for the text and place the text in position on the diagram.
6 Save your design and then print it out.

Could you produce a better diagram of the cake shown? Have a go and print out your effort.

Skills Building

34 Exam Preparation

Revising

Most people think of revision as just reading notes and trying to remember them. This is true to some extent but there are some ways of revising more effectively. We will look at several ways of revising and some of the likely questions you would want to ask about revision.

Where should you revise?

Choose a room where there will be no distractions. Work at a table or desk, make sure that there is a bright light on the table and that the room is warm. Some students like to work in a local library. This can be quite a good idea but there can be distractions, such as people moving around. However, there won't be the other distractions that you may have at home such as brothers, sisters, radios and TVs. Try to work in silence. Your revision will be a lot more effective and you will not need to revise for as long (Figure 34.1).

You should make a timetable and decide how long to revise for, then you will have

earned your free time. Planned breaks in revision increase the amount of information you retain.

How often should you revise?

Revision should be a constant process throughout the years of your course (Figure 34.2). Try not to leave your revision to the few weeks before the exam. Divide your work into topics and then revise a topic at a time. Don't move on to a new topic until you have mastered the old one. It is better to have a thorough knowledge of a few topics than a skimpy knowledge of the whole syllabus.

When is the best time to revise?

Most people are at their peak early in the morning. Near exam time try to get up earlier. If you are on holiday then early morning is an ideal time, because you will have fewer distractions from other people in the house. Early evening is a good time, before you get tired.

Figure 34.1 *It is important to revise in the right surroundings*

Figure 34.2

What shall I revise?

Ideally it would be best if you could revise the whole syllabus. If you have difficulty with certain topics then you could leave them out but you will need to know the other topics really well.

Obtain a copy of your syllabus either by asking your teacher or by sending off to the examination board for their price list. The names and addresses of the examination boards are in the list of suppliers at the back of the book.

Using the syllabus to guide you, make a revision checklist of all the topics you need to study and tick them off as you complete your revision of each topic.

Syllabus and past papers

It will help a lot if you get your own copy of the examination syllabus. Since there are many different examination boards and sometimes different syllabuses even for the same subject with some examination boards, you should ask your teacher which board and syllabus you are following.

When you buy your own copy of the syllabus you will also be able to buy some copies of recent examination papers. You may also find that your local library or school library has copies of these publications. If you can't find them, ask the librarian in the reference section.

Near the time of the exam, check to see how much of the syllabus you have covered. Sometimes your teacher may not have time to cover the whole syllabus. If this happens, look at your syllabus to see which parts have been left out. You could then study the missing parts on your own. Having a set of past papers will enable you to see the way the exam is set out and familiarise yourself with the structure of the paper.

You can use the exam papers as an aid to your revision. Give yourself mock exams to see how your revision is going. Check your answers using this book or ask your teacher to have a look at them. Once you can answer most of the questions from the past papers, you will have nothing to fear about the actual exam.

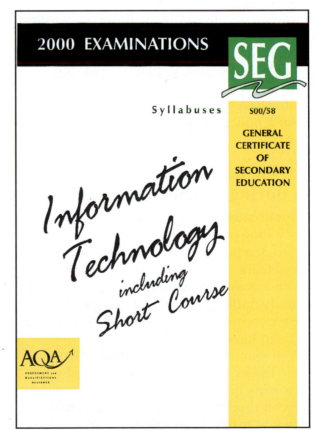

Reproduced with kind permission of SEG and AQA

Figure 34.3 *Get yourself a syllabus so that you know what to revise*

The exam

Before the exam

1 Collect the necessary equipment: two pens (in case one dries up); two pencils; a sharpener; a rubber; and a ruler. You may be allowed to use a flowchart template but check first. You might not be able to use one with the names of the boxes on it.
2 Always take a watch into the exam. There will be a clock in the room but if you are at the back you might not be able to see it.
3 Go to the toilet before the exam; this avoids the embarrassment of having to leave the room under supervision.
4 Check to see if you have to wear school uniform.

Things to check in the exam room

1 Check that you have the correct exam paper in front of you. Several different exams may be going on at the same time.
2 Check that there are no pages missing from the paper. It is not unknown for a page to be blank. If there is anything wrong with the paper, such as not being able to read the print, then you should ask for a new paper.

Use the knowledge you have built up during practical sessions

You will have built up your skills in using IT over a long period of time. You will also have had to demonstrate these skills when doing coursework.

Since many of the questions will be about actually doing certain tasks using IT the greater your experience the more knowledge you will have.

You should make sure that you demonstrate the experience you have gained when answering questions.

Even though you may have the knowledge you might have difficulty in answering questions and in the next section we will look at some important points when answering questions.

Answering questions

When answering examination questions it is important to know how much to write. You can sometimes tell this from the wording of the question. Here is a list of commonly used words that ask you to supply an answer.

At the top of the list only a single word or short group of connected words need be given. As you move down the list the amount of answer needed increases.

Simple answer required

Name
List
State
Give
Describe
Explain

More complex answer required (usually several sentences)

Use the mark scheme to help you

At the side of each section of an examination question there will be a number in brackets that tells you the number of marks for that part. Here is an example:

1(a)　List the three main parts of the central processing unit (CPU).　　(3)

There are 3 marks allocated for this part of the question and because it says 'list' in the question, this means that we only have to give a single word (or a few connected words) in answer.

A suitable answer would be:

Arithmetic and logic unit
Control unit
Main memory

Making sure that you understand the specialist terminology

There are many specialist terms used in IT. You may be asked about a specialist term in the exam. It is therefore important to be familiar with the meaning of these terms and also to be able to explain them to other people, including the examiner. You must be able to put these words into sentences.

Hints for the exam

The following list gives some hints on things you should do when actually taking the exam.

1 Always read the instructions on the front of the paper carefully. In particular, note the time you are allowed.

2 Time yourself. Don't spend too much time on a question that you can answer well at the expense of other questions.

3 Try to write neatly. The examiners have hundreds of scripts to mark and it is not worth risking annoying an examiner by making her waste time deciphering an untidy script.

4 Only do what the question asks. If it asks for two reasons, make sure that you give two: not three or one. Always check that, in an answer to a question with two parts, you have not written similar answers to both parts. If you have, you will only obtain marks on one of them.

5 Use the mark scheme at the side of the questions as a guide to how much you should write. If there are, say, two marks, there must be two points you need to mention in order to get both marks.

6 After you have answered a question, read the question through again to make sure that you have not missed part of it out.

SEG GCSE Syllabuses 2000: Information Technology

Summary of the Subject Content

(The italic text is **not** part of the Subject Content for the GCSE Short Course in Information Technology).

A Candidates should be able to demonstrate skills in, and show knowledge and understanding of, the use of **IT** to gather, store, process and present information. These should be developed through appropriate activities in a variety of contexts for a range of purposes, including:

(i) The identification of the data input, storage, output, processing and feedback needed by an information system.

(ii) The need to take into account the audience when presenting information, including visual impact, readability, *detail, complexity,* content and organisation.
The use of text fonts, styles and sizes, clip art, charts and graphs, *borders, tints and shading,* landscape, portrait and other views.

(iii) Automatic and manual methods of data collection, data capture, data preparation and input, including questionnaire design, OMR and bar code readers.

(iv) The plausibility and accuracy of data, methods of error detection, including verification techniques (including double entry) and validation techniques (including check digits, range checks, *type checks and table look-ups),* their use *and limitations.*

(v) Techniques for data manipulation, searching (including compound searches using AND, OR *and NOT)* and sorting, including ascending *and descending.*

(vi) The purpose and use of data and information structures, including numeric and alphanumeric data, formulae, files, records, fields, key fields and codes.
Types of file access, including direct and sequential.

(vii) The purpose and use of models, the reasons why models are used, and the capabilities and limitations of models.
How rules govern the operation of a model, the circumstances under which the rules governing a model should be changed *and modifying or creating suitable procedures and programs to model situations.*

(viii) The use of sensors to measure physical variables, the use of actuators to change physical conditions, operating a control system by use of a control language, and the role of feedback in determining the actions taken by a control system.

Reproduced with kind permission of SEG

Figure 34.4 *Page from the SEG syllabus*

A number of terms are shown below. For each term write a short sentence containing the word.
1 imported
2 encrypted
3 proof-read
4 backup copy
5 virus checker.

As with all examinations, you have to convince the examiner that you know the correct answer. Even if you know the correct answer but fail to express yourself clearly, the examiner will not be able to give you the marks. The examiner cannot guess what you meant to say.

Here is an example of an examination question:

Explain why accounts are prepared using a spreadsheet.

- You can correct mistakes easier by deleting or overwriting
- The spreadsheet automatically re-calculates totals when you change any of the figures and this saves you time.

Here is another examination question:

Name an application that uses MICR.

Here you are not expected to write a sentence.

If you had been asked to explain an application which uses MICR then you would have been expected to go into detail. You should use the marks allocated as a guide to how much to write.

Things to do

Examination Questions

Here is a variety of recent examination questions covering material present on all the examination boards' syllabuses

Chapter 1

1 CD-ROMs have become widely available.
   (a) Give two reasons why CD-ROMs help with learning. (2)
   (b) Give one disadvantage of using a CD-ROM in a classroom. (1)
       (MEG June 1998 HT Short course P2 q6)

2 (a) Give two reasons why CD-ROMs are used to store encyclopaedias. (2)
   (b) One type of information stored on a CD-ROM is text. Give two other types of information stored on a CD-ROM. (1)
       (MEG June 1998 FT Short course P1 q8)

Chapter 2

1 State two ways in which Information Technology can be used in the kitchen. (2)
       (MEG June 1998 FT Short course P1 q8)

2 Microprocessors are used to control many devices, e.g. washing machines.
   (a) What is a microprocessor? (2)
   (b) Name two different devices controlled by microprocessors. (2)
   (c) Give three different kinds of sensors that could be used in an automatic washing machine. (3)
       (WJEC June 1998 FT Full course P2 q7)

3 There is now an increasing number of 'message pads' (PDAs) available in computer shops. These message pads use the screen for direct input. Data can either be entered by ordinary handwriting using a special stylus (or pen) or by pressing the keys of a 'simulated' keyboard.
   (a) (i) What is one advantage and one disadvantage of using ordinary handwriting as a means of data input. (4)
       (ii) How do the manufacturers attempt to overcome the disadvantage you have highlighted? (2)
   (b) When a special connection kit is purchased the PDA can be linked to an ordinary computer. Give two reasons why people might want to link their PDA to an ordinary computer. (4)
   (c) More expensive PDAs have an inbuilt fax/modem and can be used for 'tone dialling'. What is:
       (i) a fax/modem? (3)
       (ii) tone dialling? (2)
       (NI Spec Paper 97 P3 q23)

Chapter 3

1 Each piece of hardware in the table below is either an input, output or storage device. For each, put a tick in the correct box. As an example, a keyboard is an input device and so a tick is placed in the Input column.

Device	Input	Output	Storage
Keyboard	✓		
(a) Hard disk drive			
(b) Scanner			
(c) Speaker			
(d) Ink-jet printer			
(e) CD-ROM drive			
(f) Heat sensor			
(g) Microphone			

(7)
(NEAB 1998 Paper 1 Tier F Full Course q1)

2 You have been asked to choose a printer for the school office where an integrated package is being used. Explain four factors you would consider before making your choice. (3)
       (NI Spec Paper 97 P1 q1)

Chapter 4

1 Given below is a list of **nine** pieces of hardware.
   (a) For each one, say if it is an **input device**, an **output device** or a **storage device**. The first one is done for you.

Hardware	Type of device
Keyboard	input
(i) Hard disk drive	....
(ii) Scanner	....
(iii) Mouse	....
(iv) Dot-matrix printer	....
(v) CD-ROM drive	....
(vi) Heat sensor	....
(vii) Ink-jet printer	....
(viii) Concept keyboard	....
(ix) Optical disk drive	....

(9)

(b) A computer system has two types of memory called RAM (random access memory) and ROM (read only memory). Give **one** example of the use of each of them. (2)

(NEAB FT Short course June 1998 q1)

2 Most computer systems have immediate access store (IAS) and backing store.
(a) Give two limitations of immediate access store which make backing store necessary. (4)
(b) Explain how ROM differs from RAM. (2)
(c) With reference to an application, explain how EPROM might be used. (2)

(NI June 1998 P3 q1)

3 Magnetic tape is one medium used for backing store.
(a) Name two others. (2)
(b) Give the approximate storage capacity for a high density floppy disk. (2)
(c) Explain the term backup. (2)

(NI June 1998 P3 q1)

4 Many early computers had a word length of 1 byte. However, now a word length of 32 bits or more is common.
(a) What is a 'bit'? (2)
(b) Explain why a 32 bit machine is considerably faster than a 1 byte machine. (2)
(c) Explain how the characters in the word 'FRED' could be held using 32 bits. (3)

(NI June 1997 P3 q4)

5 Which two of the following items is suitable for storing large amounts of data:

scanner	barcode	magnetic strip
CD-ROM	mouse	hard disk

(MEG FT Full course June 1998 P3 q3)

6 A computer has two types of memory, RAM and ROM.

(a) (i) What does RAM stand for?
(ii) What does ROM stand for? (2)
(b) Give two differences between RAM and ROM. (2)
(c) Give one use of RAM. (1)
(d) Give one use of ROM. (1)

(NEAB FT Short course P2 q3)

7 The following specification for a microcomputer appeared in a magazine.

200 MHz Processor

16Mb RAM
(Upgradable to 64Mb)

2.1 Gb Hard disk

1.44 Mb Floppy Disk

8x CD ROM drive

(a) Name the two backing store devices that the computer uses. (2)
(b) Which type of disk in the advertisement allows the fastest access to data? (1)
(c) The RAM can be upgraded from 16 MB to 64 MB.
(i) What is RAM? (1)
(ii) What is it used for? (1)
(iii) Give one advantage when upgrading the RAM to 64 MB. (1)
(d) Give one advantage to the user of a computer having a CD-ROM. (1)

(WJEC FT Full course P2 June 1998 q4)

Chapter 5

1 (a) Which three of the following tasks are carried out by all operating systems?
A transferring data to a printer
B allocating storage space on a disk
C positioning text in a wordprocessing document
D finding a database record
E accepting keyboard input
F adding colour to a drawing on screen.

(b) Describe an additional task which would have to be carried out by a multiuser operating system.

(c) What is a multitasking operating system?

(NEAB 1998 Paper 2 Tier H Full course q1)

2 The design of the user interface of an application is very important. The two screens shown are from a package which allows customers to choose and book a holiday.

(a) Describe three ways in which the user interface has been kept consistent in the two screen designs. (3)

(b) (i) In what ways does the design limit the choice a user can make? (2)

(ii) Why has the package been designed in this way?

(c) Describe two changes you would make to the design which would make the interface easier for customers to use. Explain why these changes would help the user. (2)

(d) Sometimes holidays are fully booked for the dates required. A message is displayed on the screen to tell the user the holiday is not available.

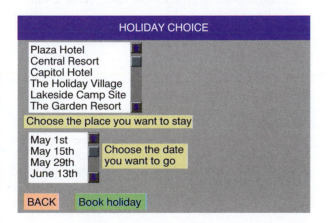

(i) Where on the screen should this message appear? (1)

(ii) Why is this position most suitable? (1)

(iii) How could the user's attention be drawn to this message? (2)

(NEAB 1998 Paper 2 Tier H Full course q7)

3 Computers have become more user friendly with the development of graphical user interfaces.

(a) Give **four** features of a graphical user interface. (4)

(b) Give **two** possible future developments to user interfaces. (2)

(WJEC HT Full course June 1998 P2 q5)

4 Ann has bought some new software. Give three items of documentation that came with it. (3)

(WJEC FT Full course June 1998 P2 q3)

5 An *operating system* is a program.

(a) Name **two** tasks the operating system does. (2)

(b) Name **one** operating system used by computers. (1)

(c) Microcomputers can carry out *multitasking*. Give the meaning of the term multitasking. (1)

(WJEC FT Full course June 1998 P2 q8)

6 The tourist information office in a holiday resort wants an information system to allow people to find out about attractions in the area. The manager must decide whether to produce the system using an existing database package or to have a program written in a suitable computer language.

(a) Give two advantages of producing this system using an existing database package. (2)

(b) Give one advantage of writing a program for this application. (1)

(NEAB FT Full course P2 q6)

7 Most computers have an icon-based graphical user interface (GUI).

(a) What is an icon? (2)

(b) Give two reasons why computers have this type of interface. (4)

(c) What peripheral device is commonly used with this interface? (1)

(NI June 1997 P1 q8)

8 (a) What is meant by a windows environment? (2)

(b) Give two advantages of using a windows environment compared with a command line environment. (2)

(MEG FT June 1998 P3 q9)

Chapter 6

1 (a) Name two ways in which text can be input to a computer. (2)

(b) Give one example where each of the following is used:
  (i)   barcode reader; (1)
  (ii) magnetic ink character reader (MICR); (1)
  (iii) optical mark reader (OMR). (1)

  (WJEC FT Full course June 1998 P2 q2)

2 Data stored in a computer system is often coded.

(a) (i) Give two advantages of coding data. (4)
   (ii) Give one disadvantage of coding data. (2)

(b) Give three considerations when designing a coding system. (3)

  (NI June 1997 P3 q14)

Chapter 7

1 Last year a school stored all the examination marks for year 7 on a computer. Each examination had a maximum of 100 marks. At the end of the year, some pupils' examination marks were wrong when printed out. To try to stop this happening again, the headteacher has decided to use data validation.

(a) Explain what is meant by data validation. (3)

(b) Explain how each of the following methods of data validation could be used in this situation.
  (i)   Presence check (2)
  (ii) Range check (2)

  (NEAB FT Short course June 1998 q6)

2 The Human Resources department of the APEXAN manufacturing company keeps a file of employee records on a computer.

This is part of the file:

Employee number	Family name	First name	Sex	Number of years employed
0127	Ryan	Jean	F	15
2971	Hussain	Sabina	F	200
5234	Ryan	Pauline	F	5
1253	Mercadal	Jean	F	7
1074	Razaq	Fazal	M	11

(a) The contents of a field in one record cannot be correct.
  (i)   Draw a circle around the error. (1)
  (ii) Explain why the contents cannot be correct. (1)
  (iii) Tick one box to show the type of validation check that could detect the error.

Tick **one** box

Check digit	☐
Range check	☐
Type check	☐
Table look-up	☐
Double entry verification	☐

(1)

  (iv) Describe in full a validation check that could detect this error. (4)

  (SEG FT Full course P2 June 1998 Part q2)

3 Explain why each of the following checks would be used to validate the entry of data into the record shown below:

Customer name: Miss Susan McGinn
Stock number: 4556216
Order quantity: 14

(a) Character or type check (2)
(b) Range check (2)
(c) Check digit (2)

  (NI June 1998 P3 q12)

4 Text prepared using a wordprocessor can have its spelling checked using a spellchecking facility. When this is activated each word in the prepared text is checked against a dictionary of over 50,000 words.

(a) How can a spellchecker confirm the correct spelling of a word? (2)

(b) Certain rejected words may be correctly spelt. Describe, with examples two distinct cases when this could occur and describe how a spellchecker could accommodate such words for future reference. (4)

  (NI Spec Paper 97 P3 q1)

5 Tony studies GCSE Business Studies at Hightop School. As part of his course, he collects data on breakfast cereals eaten by students.

(a) Give **two** ways he could collect the data. (2)

(b) The software used by Tony to set up the file allows him to validate the data. What is validation? (1)

(c) A sample of Tony's file is shown below.

Student Number	Form	Cereal
24	10A	Cornflakes
14	11C	Bran Flakes
21	10B	Rice Krispies

To ensure that every pupil's data is input, Tony makes use of a hash total. Calculate the *hash total* for the above sample. (1)

  (WJEC FT Full course P2 June 1998 q9)

Chapter 8

Accession No.	Title	Author	Publisher	Date of publication
1324	Computer Studies	Waites, N	BEP	1994
1333	Computing	Waites, N	BEP	1992
1325	Business GNVQ	Callaghan, P	BEP	1993
1272	Compilers	Mak, R	Wiley	1991
1174	Computer Graphics	Foley, J	Addison-Wesley	1990
1024	C Programming	Michie, D	Pelican	1989

1 A school has computerised its library. Some of the information from the book file is shown in the table above.
(a) State how many *records* are shown above. (1)
(b) State how many *fields* are shown above. (1)
(c) Name the *key field*. (1)
(d) Why is a key field required? (1)
(e) The librarian wants the file *sorted* into *descending* order according to the *date of publication*. Complete the following table to show the result of the sort.

Title	Date of publication
Computer Studies	1994

(f) Explain why the librarian would need to:
(i) *delete* a record from the book file; (1)
(ii) *add* a record to the book file. (1)

2 Tape streamers are becoming an increasingly popular form of backup. What is a tape streamer?
(2)
(NI Spec 1997 P1 q13)

3 (a) Define the following terms and give an example of each:
(i) Verification; (2)
(ii) Validation. (2)
(b) Some of the files on a computer system have fixed length fields while others have variable length fields.
(i) Give one advantage of using fixed length fields. (1)
(ii) Give one advantage of using variable length fields. (1)

(iii) A variety of field types can be found in a database system, for example, numeric field. Name two other types of field that could be found in a database. (2)
(c) Some of the fields within files are coded, for example, B-Boy, G-Girl. Give two advantages of coding data. (2)
(WJEC HT Full course P2 June 1998 q10)

4 Serial, sequential, indexed sequential and direct (random) are four methods of file organisation commonly used. Complete the table below to show which method can be used with magnetic tape and which method can be used with magnetic disk.

Method	Magnetic tape	Magnetic disk
Serial	Yes	
Sequential		
Indexed sequential		
Direct (random)		Yes

(6)
(NI P3 June 1997 q1)

5 The following record structure for a datafile has been set up:

Field name	Field length	Field type	Key field
Name	30	Character	No
Address	25	Character	No
Membership number	6	Numeric	Yes
Telephone number	13	Alphanumeric	No
Date joined	8	Date	No

(a) How many fields does each record in this file contain? (1)
(b) Explain why only 'Membership number' is a key field. (2)
(c) Give one reason why it is important to specify the field type. (2)
(NI P1 June 1997 q2)

6 A company which has been in existence for some time has accumulated a number of datafiles for its business. They are now considering replacing these datafiles with a database.

(a) Explain what is meant by a database. (3)

(b) Give two reasons why a database might be preferred to datafiles. (4)

A database management system (DBMS) is a program that provides an interface between the operating system and the user and simplifies access to the data.

(c) Give two other functions provided by the DBMS. (4)

(NI P3 June 1997 q3)

Chapter 9

1 Tick **two** applications which use batch processing.

Monitoring a patient's heartbeat ☐
Producing electricity bills ☐
Air traffic control system ☐
On-line cinema seat reservation system ☐
Clearing cheques ☐
Recording the temperature in an experiment ☐

(2)

(MEG HT June 1998 P4 q3)

Chapter 10

1 An estate agent decides to store the pictures of the houses on the hard disk of the computer in a compressed form.

(a) (i) Give two advantages of using compression in this situation. (2)

(ii) Give one disadvantage of using compression in this situation. (1)

(NEAB HT Full course P1 June 1998 Part q6)

2 Sound, as most people hear it, is not capable of being stored or processed by a computer system in its natural form; it needs to be changed to a more suitable representation. An analogue to digital converter (ADC) performs this task.

(a) Using the axes below draw a typical sound signal before and after conversion. (2)

Most modern computers have a speaker built into the system but in some cases the quality of sound is poor.

Before conversion   After conversion

(b) Explain how the sound quality could be dramatically improved by adding extra hardware. (3)

(c) Describe two applications where computer-generated sound might be used. (4)

(NI P3 June 1998 q13)

Chapter 11

1 The IT coordinator at Ballyhouse High School has a budget to spend on CD-ROMs. The school has five stand-alone CD systems in the library. Two of the systems are Mac based and the others are PCs.

The following titles are available from a supplier's catalogue:

The Oxford English Dictionary of Quotations	PC only	£50
Hutchinson's Encyclopedia	PC only	£30
The Guinness Disk of Records	Mac/PC	£40
1000 colour Clip Art images	Mac/PC	£90
Chess Coacher	Mac only	£25
The Bible and Bible Lands	Mac/PC	£30
Multimedia Space Encyclopaedia	PC only	£60
The life, time and music of Mozart	Mac/PC	£30
A Hard Day's Night	Mac only	£30
Shakespeare Complete Works	Mac/PC	£40
Asterix Learn French	Mac only	£30
101 games and leisure pursuits	PC only	£40
Musical Instruments	PC only	£30
The Sunday Times	Mac/PC	£100
Microsoft Art Gallery	Mac/PC	£40
The Tortoise and the Hare	Mac/PC	£40

The coordinator has been conducting a survey to find the most popular and relevant titles.

You have been invited to choose **four** titles for the library and say why each has been chosen. Give your choice and reasons below:

(NI Spec Paper 97 P1 q19)

Chapter 12

1 The system flowchart below shows how a supermarket point of sale system works.

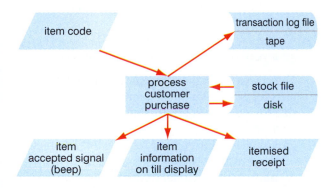

(a) How would the item code normally be input into the system? (2)
(b) Give two reasons why an item accepted signal is used in this situation rather than an item rejected signal. (2)
(c) These are the fields in the stock file:

>   item code
>   type
>   description
>   size
>   quantity in stock
>   minimum stock level
>   reorder quantity
>   supplier code

Which field in a stock record would be changed when an item is sold? (1)

SUPERSAVERS
High Street
Manchester
M50 9ZZ

20th June 1998

To:

Bulk Grocery Supplies

Fax 0161 888 2740

Please deliver:

Type	Description	Size	Quantity
bargain brand	baked beans	450g	20 cases

(d) The stock file is also used by an automatic reordering system. This produces orders like the one shown above. Another file called the supplier file is used. Give three fields the supplier record will have to contain to allow the order to be produced.

(e) The transaction log file is kept on tape.
  (i) What data would be written to the transaction log file? (1)
  (ii) What is the purpose of this file? (1)
  (NEAB HT Full course P2 June1998 q4)

Chapter 13

1 A group of doctors in a medical centre wants to computerise their existing filing system. Analysis, design, implementation, testing and evaluation will all be stages in the production of their information systems.

At which of these stages does each of the following take place?
(a) Setting up a database of their patients
(b) Looking at which tasks to include in the new system
(c) Collecting information about how other doctors tackled this problem
(d) Producing a testing plan for the new system
(e) Planning the layout of a letter to the hospital
(f) Entering test data for the accounts spreadsheet
(g) Reviewing how well the patient database works
(h) Working out the record structure for the patients' database
  (NEAB 1998 Paper 2 Tier H Full course q2)

2 When a new computerised system is suggested, a full analysis of user requirements has to be carried out. Describe the methods which can be used to find out about an existing system and what will be needed in the new system. Discuss the advantages and disadvantages of the methods used.
  (12 marks)
  (NEAB 1998 Paper 2 Tier H Full course q10)

3 During systems analysis it is important to find out as much as possible about the existing system. This is called fact finding.
(a) Describe four methods often used for fact finding. (8)
(b) Describe two activities carried out during the design stage of systems analysis. (4)
Three methods that could be used to implement a new system are:
  • direct,
  • phased,
  • parallel.
(c) Explain each of these three methods. (6)
  (NI June 1998 P1 q18)

4 Jane is employed as a systems analyst by a software house. She has been asked to produce a

computerised system for a holiday company. Describe briefly what is involved during the following stages of her work on the new system:
(a) analysis   (2)
(b) design   (2)
(c) implementation   (2)
(d) maintenance.   (2)

(WJEC HT Full course P2 June 1998 q7)

5 A video games shop has decided to use a spreadsheet to help with its finances. The tasks listed below have to be carried out during the development of this system:
A entering all the existing data for the income and expenditure of the shop
B working out the spreadsheet structure
C looking at the present system to see how it works
D finding out if the new system works
E setting up the spreadsheet
F reviewing how well the system works
G making a test plan.

Using the letters A to G from the list of tasks, answer the following questions.
(a) Which one of these takes place during the analysis stage?
(b) Which two of these take place during the design stage?
(c) Which one of these takes place during the testing stage?
(d) Which two of these take place during the implementation stage?
(e) Which one of these takes place during the evaluation stage?

(NEAB FT Short course June 1998 q9)

6 A new system is to be introduced into a school for pupils to pay for their dinners using computer cards. Describe the steps taken in the analysis and design of this system.

(MEG HT Full course P4 q9)

Chapter 14

1 Sensors can be attached to a computer system and used to collect data. In a geography investigation, students are studying how temperature varies during the course of 24 hours. A sensor is connected to a computer to take readings.
(a) What do we call this method of data capture?
                                                (1)
(b) (i) What kind of sensor should be used?   (1)
    (ii) Why is this sensor needed?   (1)

(c) (i) How often should a reading be taken? (1)
    (ii) Why is this a suitable interval?   (1)
(d) How could this data be presented in a report on the investigation?   (1)

(NEAB FT Short course June 1998 q10)

2 A computer at a regional weather centre gathers information from remote weather stations.

The computer at the regional weather centre contacts the computer at each remote weather station and downloads the information that has been recorded.
(a) Using terms from the following list, complete the flowchart shown to show what the computer at the regional weather centre does.
     Save regional weather file.
     Download information.
     Add information to regional weather file.

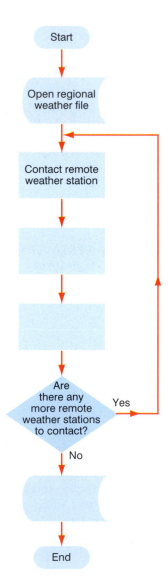

(b) Draw and label a diagram showing the computer at the regional weather centre communicating with the computer at a remote weather station using modems and the telephone network   (2 marks)

(c) If the regional weather centre cannot contact a remote weather station, processing is halted and has to be restarted.

(i) Tick **two** boxes to show why this is a shortcoming of the IT system.

	Tick two boxes
Information is not recorded at remote weather stations during the winter.	☐
Remote weather stations are solar powered.	☐
Restarting the system wastes time as the same information may be collected from the same remote weather stations on several occasions.	☐
The information available is not collected if part of the system is faulty.	☐
The system cannot be restarted.	☐

(2 marks)

(ii) Using terms from the following list complete the two sentences.

> monitoring and evaluation
> systems analysis and design
> systems investigation
> the holidays
> user training

The shortcoming was built into the IT system during ....
The shortcoming would be detected during ....
(2 marks)

(d) Discuss the advantages and disadvantages of using this IT system.   (6 marks)
(SEG Paper 3 Higher tier June 1998 Full course q7)

Chapter 15

1 The ISDN (Integrated Services Digital Network) is now widely available.

(a) Describe **two** applications for ISDN.   (6)

Three network configurations (topologies) commonly used are: **star**, **bus** and **ring**.

(b) Show the cabling configuration for each of these networks.

(i) **star**

(1)

(ii) **bus**

(1)

(iii) **ring**

(1)

(c) Complete the table below to indicate a ring, bus or star network configuration as appropriate.

Network Configuration	Advantage	Disadvantage
	Easy to add more stations without disrupting the network	The whole network goes down if the main cable fails at any point
	If one cable fails the other stations are not affected	Costly to install because of the length of cable required
	No dependence on a central computer or fileserver	Unusable if a single station fails

(3)

(d) Apart from sharing resources give **two other** benefits that a network of computers would provide. (4)

(e) Explain the following network terms:
   (i)   LAN
   (ii) WAN
   (iii) node
(6)

(NI June 1997 P3 q6)

2 The Internet is a large worldwide network of linked computers. Give three different uses of the Internet. (3)

(WJEC FT Full course P2 June 1998 q5)

3

The diagram above shows a LAN (local area network) which is used in an office.

(a) Fill in the table to show **two** differences between this network and a WAN (wide area network).

	LAN	WAN
Difference 1		
Difference 2		

(4)

(b) Give **two** advantages to the **office staff** of having the network rather than the same number of separate computers. (2)

(c) Give **one** disadvantage to the **office staff** of having the network. (1)

(NEAB FT Full course P2 June 1998 q7)

Chapter 16

1 Rashid enjoys playing computer games. He often downloads demonstration versions of games from the World Wide Web. One day he discovers his computer system is producing lots of error messages. Several important data files have disappeared. His computer has a virus.

(a) What is a computer virus? (2)

(b) Suggest how the virus may have got into Rashid's computer system. (2)

(c) How can Rashid remove the virus from his computer system? (1)

(d) What precautions can Rashid take to help prevent more viruses getting into his computer? (1)

(NEAB Foundation tier June 1998 P2 q4)

2 Give **two** ways that data in a computer file can be protected from being seen by unauthorised people.

(MEG FT Full course P3 June 1998 q11)

3 (a) Give one example of how a virus can affect a computer. (1)

(b) Give one way a virus can be removed. (1)

(MEG HT Full course P4 June 1998 q2)

4 Newspapers often mention the terms computer virus and computer **hacking**.

(a) (i) What is a computer virus? (1)

   (ii) How can a computer virus be detected and prevented? (2)

(b) (i) What is computer hacking? (1)

   (ii) Give **one** way 'hacking' can be prevented. (1)

(WJEC SC HT June 1998)

Chapter 17

1 (a) Describe two ways the Data Protection Act tries to protect individuals from the misuse of personal data held on computer. (2)

(b) Other than the misuse of personal data, describe two ways in which information technology has created problems for the individual. (2)

MEG FT Full course June 1998 P3 q12)

2 'It is easier to misuse data when it is held in electronic form'. Discuss this statement. (4)

(MEG June 1998 P4 Higher tier Full course q13)

3 A life insurance company stores information about its customers on a large database.
(a) Give **three** fields, other than **name** and **address**, which might be included on the file.
(b) The insurance company, as a data user, must obey the rules set out in the Data Protection Act. Give **four** rules that data users must obey.
(c) Give **two** rights the Data Protection Act gives to the customers.

(NEAB 1998 Paper 1 Tier H Full course q4)

4 Mrs. Brown is divorced with two children. She has recently returned to full-time education and is in the final year of a science degree. She has taken out student loans of £5000. She regularly plays squash at the local sports centre. She does not have any credit cards. She rents a council house from her local authority.
(a) Using only the information given above, write down four facts about Mrs. Brown which are likely to be stored in a computer database. (4)
(b) Explain clearly the difference between information and data. (2)

(NEAB HT Full course June 1998 P1 q2)

Chapter 18

1 Computer software is covered by the Copyright, Designs and Patents Act (1988) and is protected for a number of years. Give **three** ways by which this Act may be broken. (6)

(NI P3 June 1997 q9)

2 (a) Name the Act of Parliament which is intended to protect software from being stolen or illegally copied. (2)
(b) Explain the following terms:
  (i) hacking (3)
  (ii) virus (3)

(NI P1 June 1998 part q6)

Chapter 19

1 The widespread use of IT has had a great impact on today's society. One benefit that the increased use of IT has brought, is the creation of some new jobs.
(a) Give **three examples of jobs** that have been created by the introduction of IT. (3)
(b) Describe briefly **three other** possible benefits that this increased use in IT has brought. (3)
(c) Personal information, stored electronically, is potentially easier to misuse than that kept in paper files. Give **two** reasons why this is true.

(NEAB FT Short course June 1998 q11)

2 Discuss the issues raised by the use of IT in society. Your answer should cover a number of different areas, taking into account the environmental, ethical, moral and social effects. You should highlight possible disadvantages as well as advantages.

(NEAB 1998 Paper 1 Tier H Full course q10)

3 Describe how computers might be misused giving rise to legal and moral problems. (4)

(MEG HT P2 June 1998 P2 q11)

4 Explain the drawbacks of using robots in manufacturing cars. (4)

(MEG HT P4 June 1998 q12)

Chapter 20

1 (a) What is a robot? (2)
(b) Give two advantages of using robots for various tasks. (4)
(c) Describe a situation where it would be almost impossible to do a particular task without a robot. (2)

(NI Spec 1997 P1 q13)

2 Sensors can be attached to a computer system and used to collect data. In a geography investigation, students are studying how temperature varies during the course of 24 hours. A sensor is connected to a computer to take readings.
(a) What do we call this method of data capture? (1)
(b) (i) What kind of sensor should be used? (1)
  (ii) Why is this sensor needed? (1)
(c) (i) How often should a reading be taken? (1)
  (ii) Why is this a suitable interval? (1)
(d) How could this data be presented in a report on the investigation? (1)

(NEAB 1998 Tier F Short course q10)

3 A computer controlled hopper is used to fill bottles. The bottles are placed on the conveyor which moves them under the hopper where they are filled.

The operator can use these instructions.

MOVE   Moves the conveyor one position
FILL   Opens the valve, fills the bottle, and
       closes the valve.
START Indicates the beginning of the program.
END   Indicates the end of the program.

(a) Write the instructions to fill these **three** bottles.

START

....
....
....
....
....
....
....

END

(3)

(b) (i) Explain why the computer system shown
        cannot be used to fill the bottles **automatically**. (1)
    (ii) Describe the additional **hardware** needed
         so that the computer system could fill the
         bottles automatically. (2)
    (iii) In this context, explain what is meant by
          feedback. (2)

(c) Tick **one** box to show the **type** of operating
    method used.

	Tick **one** box
Batch	☐
Library	☐
Joystick	☐
Real time	☐
Serious	☐

(1)

(d) Discuss the advantages and disadvantages of automated manufacturing. (6)
(SEG Paper 3 Higher tier, June 1998 Full course q5)

Interface

Sensor

Heater

Material

4 A science class uses a computer to investigate the heat transfer through various materials. For this they need an interface, analogue sensors and a heater. The front of the material is heated and the sensors measure the heat at the front and at the back of the material.
(a) Give two reasons why an interface is needed. (2)
(b) Explain the difference between an analogue signal and a digital signal. (3)
(c) Explain how the computer could be used to assist in plotting a graph showing the heat input and output over a period of time. (4)
(NI June 1997 p1 q18)

5 Betterview prepares lenses for spectacles and contact lenses in their own laboratory. The conditions in the laboratory must be continuously monitored.

Humidity, temperature and dust must be kept constant to ensure that lenses are produced properly.

Conditions are computer controlled.
(a) Explain how regular measurements of temperature could be recorded by the computer. (4)
(b) Explain how the computer controls the humidity, temperature and dust measurements to stay within certain limits. (4)
(c) The measurements of humidity, temperature and dust are stored regularly in a computer file.

Describe how data that is stored in the computer could be processed to present and compare readings. (4)
(d) Describe TWO sensible analyses that could be performed on this stored data. (4)
(London HT Short course June 1998 p2H q2)

6 A company breeds large numbers of fish for fish farms. The young fish will only grow if they have enough oxygen. A computer system is used to control the amount of oxygen in the tanks. Sensors in the tanks detect the amount of oxygen in the water. A pump connected to the computer system can be used to pump oxygen into the tanks.

Explain how monitoring **and feedback** can be used to make sure that the fish have enough oxygen.
(NEAB 1998 Paper 1 Tier H Full course q7)

Chapter 21

1 The widespread use of computers has led to a reported increase in illnesses and health hazards associated with them. Some doctors are becoming worried by this development.

Describe one health hazard or illness specifically associated with using computers and suggest how it can be prevented.
(WJEC HT Short and Full course June 1998 q4)

2 A school secretary sits in front of a computer all day. Give two pieces of advice which should help prevent medical problems. (2)
(MEG FT P1 June 1998 q9)

3 Computer monitors can be high, medium or low resolution and must conform to a certain standard to protect their users.
(a) The level of resolution is measured in pixels. What is a pixel? (2)
(b) List and explain two potential dangers to people who use monitors. (4)
(c) Explain one other health problem associated with the use of computers. (2)
(NI Spec 1997 P1 q13)

Chapter 22

1 A school has its own internal network which consists of terminals or computers linked to a fileserver. The network has other hardware devices linked to it which may be used by the pupils. It is not possible to access the Internet from this network.

(a) Give **two** *other* hardware devices you would expect to find linked to this network. (2)

(b) The school is considering producing an electronic newsletter on the Internet, to advertise the school. The school has telephone lines and computer systems (*computer, disk drive and printer, wordprocessing, database and spreadsheet software*) but would need **additional** extra hardware and software to access the Internet.

   (i) Give **one** extra hardware device the school must have in order to access the Internet. (1)

   (ii) Give **one** extra item of software the school must have in order to access the Internet. (1)

   (iii) Give **one** advantage *to the school* of advertising on the Internet. (1)

   (iv) Give **one** disadvantage *to parents* of accessing an electronic newsletter on the Internet. (1)

(c) Every day more and more uses are being found for the Internet. Give **two** ways the Internet could be used by the police to combat crime. (2)

(d) In addition to the Internet we have other types of communications systems. One of these is broadcasted information.

   (i) Name **two** broadcasted communication or information systems. (2)

   (ii) Give **one** problem that can occur with broadcasted systems. (1)

   (WJEC FT Short course June 1998 q8)

2 A company has branches all over the world and uses electronic conferencing to communicate with its employees.

(a) Describe electronic conferencing.

(b) Give two benefits to the company and its employees of using electronic conferencing. (2)

   (MEG June 1998 P4 Higher tier Full course q7)

3 One reason for the increase in popularity of teleconferencing is the potential for it to save companies substantial amounts of money.

(a) Explain the term teleconferencing. (3)

(b) Give two ways that teleconferencing could help to save money. (4)

(c) Apart from the computer system name three items of hardware needed for teleconferencing. (3)

   (NI 1998 p3 q9)

4 In the future many homes will have access to the *Internet*.

(a) What is the *Internet*? (1)

(b) Users of the *Internet* electronic mail service need a personal address, for example: info@wjec.co.uk. Once on line, what are the main stages involved in sending a short electronic message? (3)

(c) Briefly describe **four** other, different services provided through the Internet. (4)

(d) 'Traditional newspapers will be replaced by electronic editions.' Discuss why this is likely to happen. Explain the advantages and disadvantages of such a development. (11)

   (WJEC HT Full course June 1998 P2 q11)

Chapter 23

1 An expert system can be used to give medical advice.

(a) Give **one** other example of an expert system. (1)

(b) Give **one** benefit of using this expert system. (1)

   (MEG June 1998 P4 Higher tier Full course q8)

2 A spreadsheet is used to process data about the number of cars using two car parks over a year.

	A	B	C	D
	Month	**Car park A**	**Car park B**	**Most popular car park**
1				
2				
3	January	120	145	if (B3>C3, 'A', 'B')
4	February	140	135	
5	March	174	201	
6	April	134	120	
7	May	167	130	
8	June	278	290	
9	July	290	315	
10	August	312	289	
11	September	216	290	
12	October	213	278	
13	November	126	178	
14	December	78	98	

(a) Cell D3 shows how the most popular car park for January is calculated. After typing the formula in cell D3, describe a quick way of putting a similar formula into D4 to D14. (2)

(b) Describe how a chart or graph is created to show the use of car parks over a period of one year. (3)

(c) (i) Give one different situation which can be modelled using a computer. (1)

(ii) Give two reasons why a computer model would be useful in this case. (2)

(MEG June 1998 P2 Higher tier Short course q3)

3 A farmer uses insecticide to control insects that attack the crops. The farmer uses software to model the relationship between these three factors:

● the size of the insect population
● the volume of the insecticide used
● crop yield.

(a) Describe three other factors that could affect the relationship modelled. (3)

(b) The farmer describes one of the rules built into the model like this:

'As more insecticide is applied, more insects die.'

(i) Explain why the farmer's description is not always accurate. (2)

(ii) **T** is the total size of the insect population. **V** is the volume of insecticide used in litres. **N** is the number of insects killed. 1 litre of insecticide can kill 300 insects. Complete this table. Two rows have been done for you.

T	V	N
1300	4	1200
800	1	
1000	3	
700	3	700
400	2	

(iii) Using the terms from the following list, complete the sentence to show the exact rule built into the model.

$T > V*300$
$T = V*300$
$N = V*300$
$N = T$
$N = V$

IF.......... THEN.......... ELSE.......... (3)

(c) Write down in words a **different** rule that would be built into this model. (2)

(d) Explain how you could compare the accuracy of a model. (2)

(SEG Paper 3 Higher tier Full course June 1998 q5)

Chapter 25

1 Most banks now have automatic teller machines (ATMs) on the outside of their branches.

Banks issue customers with a plastic card so that they can use the ATM.

They also give customers personal identification numbers (PINs).

(a) Give the name of ONE data item that **must** be stored on the plastic card. (1)

(b) State the reason why each customer is given a PIN. (2)

(c) Give TWO benefits **to the bank** of this cash machine system. (2)

(d) Give TWO benefits **to the customer** of this cash machine system. (2)

(e) State ONE problem that the customer might find with using a cash machine. (2)

(f) Some bank customers can now carry out bank transactions from home. State ONE way in which a customer's home computer can be connected to the bank computer system to carry out bank transactions. (1)

(g) Charlotte is a customer who uses the home banking facilities. She wants to find out how much money she has in her bank account.

(i) When Charlotte accesses the bank system, a welcome screen appears. Part of the screen is shown below.

Name the TWO items that Charlotte will have to enter if she wants to use the home banking facility. (2)

(ii) The screen at the top of page 322 then appears.

Name TWO services that should appear on the menu for home banking services. (2)

(iii) Name a service that is not available through the Safe and Friendly Bank home banking system. (1)

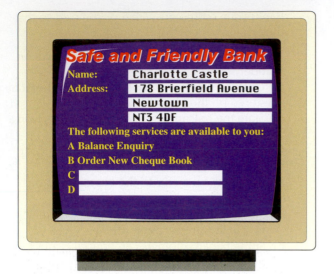

(h) Give TWO advantages to a bank customer of using the home banking facility rather than visiting the bank. (2)

(i) Give TWO disadvantages to a bank customer of using the home banking facility rather than visiting the bank. (2)

(EDEXCEL Paper 2F June 1998 Full course)

2 A bank gives a cheque book and a cheque guarantee card to a customer who has a current account.

(a) Tick **two** boxes to show the information **printed** on a cheque before it is filled in.

Tick **two** boxes

The bank's sort code. ☐
The date the cheque is filled in. ☐
Who is to be paid. ☐
The amount to be paid. ☐
The customer's account number. ☐
(2)

(b) Tick **one** box to show how information on a cheque is **input** to a computer.

Tick **one** box

Using CD-ROM. ☐
Using voice recognition ☐
Using Magnetic Ink Character
    Recognition (MICR) ☐
Using a heat sensor. ☐
Using mark sensing. ☐

(c) (i) State one item of information that must be printed on a cheque after it has been filled in and **before** it is input to a computer. (1)

(ii) Explain why this must be done. (1)

(d) The cheque guarantee card can be used to withdraw money from a cashpoint or an Automated Teller Machine (ATM).

(i) Write these steps in order to show what happens when money is withdrawn from a cashpoint.
Step 1: The amount of money is entered.
Step 2: The card is returned and the money is paid out.
Step 3: The personal identification number (PIN) is entered.
Step 4: The card is inserted. (1)

(ii) Explain why a PIN is entered. (1)

(iii) Using a term from the following list, complete the sentence.

actuator
barcode
hologram
graph plotter
magnetic stripe

The cashpoint reads information from the .... on the cheque guarantee card. (1)

(iv) Describe three other tasks that can be done using ATMs. (3)

(e) Describe three other uses for a cheque guarantee card. (3)

(SEG Paper 3 Higher tier Full course June 1998 q1)

3 Many supermarkets use a bar code system as shown below.

7 33809 00039 0

(a) Give two items of data contained within a bar code. (2)

(b) Give one advantage to the customer of using a bar code system in the supermarket. (1)

(c) Give one reason why the price of a product is not included in a bar code. (1)

(d) Supermarket customers are allowed to pay for their shopping in several ways. Name four different ways they could pay for their shopping. (4)

(e) Many supermarkets and shops now encourage customers to have loyalty cards, as shown in the illustration below. Loyalty cards allow customers to earn points every time they spend money in the supermarket.

(i) Give **one** benefit *to the customer* of using such a loyalty card. (1)

(ii) Give **one** benefit *to the supermarket* in having a loyalty card scheme. (1)

(WJEC SC HT June 1998 q2)

Chapter 27

1 A secretary is writing a letter to a client using a wordprocessor.

(a) A letter can be made more attractive by including pictures and other graphic images. Tick two boxes to show how these can be input into a wordprocessor.

Tick **two** boxes

Line art can be drawn using a pencil.	☐
Pictures can be copied from a clip art gallery	☐
Graphic images can be input using a scanner.	☐
Bar charts can be input using a flowchart.	☐
Photographs can be scanned using a tracker ball.	☐

(2)

(b) Describe **two** other ways a wordprocessor can be used to make a letter more attractive to a client. (2)

(c) The secretary wants to send a personalised letter to several clients using mail merge. Describe what must be done **before** a mail merge can be run. (3)

(SEG HT Full course P3 June 1998 q4)

2 A software company sends information to its customers by personalised letter. These letters are created using mail merging.

(a) Describe the processes involved in mail merging. (3)

(c) The company is considering using electronic mail to send information to its customers. Describe the process of sending and receiving electronic mail. (3)

(MEG HT P4 June 1998 q10)

3 You have a friend who wants to buy a word-processing package. He has asked for your advice. Assume that all wordprocessing packages will allow you to enter, edit, save and print text and change margins. Give four other features your friend might need in his new wordprocessing package. Explain why he might need each of the features.

(NEAB FT Full course P2 June 1998 q2)

4 Office staff now use computers for wordprocessing.

(a) Text can be formatted when using a word-processor. Give two examples of formatting. (2)

(b) Give two advantages of using a wordprocessor compared to using a manual typewriter. (2)

(c) Give two ways in which office staff have been affected by the introduction of word-processors. (2)

(MEG FT P3 June 1998 q6)

Chapter 28

1 Chris is a receptionist at one of the Betterview shops. He uses spreadsheet software to produce an appointment sheet for the opticians who work in his branch of Betterview. He makes one spreadsheet that contains details of the appointments for all three opticians.

(a) Give TWO reasons why Betterview use spreadsheet software for this task. (2)

(b) Appointments on a Monday are made from 10 a.m. to 4 p.m. An appointment lasts for twenty minutes. Each optician has a lunch break for forty minutes. Design a suitable spreadsheet that Chris would use for the appointments on Monday. (6)

(c) State TWO other tasks for which Betterview might use spreadsheet software. (2)

(London FT Full course P2F June 1998 qA3)

2 A group of friends who live in the North East of England regularly go to pop concerts. Next year they are planning to go to five concerts. Not everyone wants to go to all of the concerts. Below is part of the spreadsheet that is used to work out the cost for each trip. This is produced once it is known how many people will be going to each concert and the cost of the tickets.

	A	B	C	D	E	F	G
1	Group	Venue	Travel costs	No. of	Travel costs	Cost of	Total cost
2			for car	people in	for 1	1 concert	of trip for
3				the car	person	ticket	one person
4							
5	Oasis	London	£60.00	4	£15.00	£20.00	£35.00
6	Spice Girls	Birmingham	£40.00	4	£10.00	£18.00	£28.00
7	Blur	Newcastle	£15.00	3	£5.00	£17.00	£22.00
8	Hanson	Manchester	£30.00	2	£15.00	£15.00	£30.00
9	Peter Andre	Glasgow	£40.00	2	£20.00	£15.00	£35.00

(a) The travel cost for the car trip to Manchester was wrongly entered. The cost should have been **£35 not £30**. Which **cell** in the spreadsheet must be changed?

(b) Which **two other cells** would change automatically as a result of this change? (2)

(c) What **formula** would be in the cell E5? (1)

(d) Name **one** other cell, in another column, that contains a **different** formula. (1)

(e) Last year the friends used a calculator to work out their costs. Give **three advantages** of using a spreadsheet like the one given above, compared with their own manual method. (3)

(NEAB FT Short course June 1998 q8)

3 A keen music enthusiast hopes to purchase a new stereo music system. To help her choose the best of five different systems (A, B, C, D or E) she uses her computer. First she makes a list of the features of a system which are important to her. Following this she allocates a weighting to each feature where a value of 9 is an extremely important feature and a value of 2 is less important. The completed list is shown below.

Feature	Weighting
Purchase cost	5
Control layout	7
Sound quality	9
Range of features	6
Ease of operation	5
Size of speakers	4
Remote control	9
Colour	2

She then ranks each system according to each of the above features and allocates a numerical score of either 5, 4, 3, 2, 1 where 5 is the best and 1 is the worst.

The spreadsheet on page 325 was set up to model this situation:

(a) Which of the five systems would she purchase? (1)

(b) Which system is placed last? (1)

(c) What formula does cell E18 contain? (3)

(d) Which cells would need to be selected to produce the chart shown below? (2)

(e) (i) Suppose the music enthusiast changed her mind about the importance of the size of speakers and decided to award this feature a weighting of 9 instead of 4. Explain how the spreadsheet could quickly show the overall effect of this change. (3)

(ii) Explain what effect this might have on her choice of system to purchase. (3)

(NI P3 June 1997 q21)

4 A garden centre uses a spreadsheet to work out the cost of producing plants and how much they should be sold for.

(a) Shade in the cell which shows the cost of compost for a lavender plant. (1)

(b) The formula used to work out the selling price in G3 is

=F3*1.5

Write down the formula which is needed in each of the cells below.

(i) I7

(ii) F3 (2)

(c) (i) Which cell would you change to find the effect on the profit of selling more pear trees? (1)

(ii) Which cells would change as a result? (2)

(NEAB HT Full course P2 q3)

	A	B	C	D	E	F	G	H
1								
2				System Ranking where 5 = the best and 1 = the worst				
3	**Feature**			A	B	C	D	E
4	Purchase cost			3	5	2	1	4
5	Control layout			4	5	2	1	3
6	Sound quality			4	3	5	1	2
7	Range of features			3	5	4	1	2
8	Ease of operation			4	5	3	1	2
9	Size of speakers			4	1	5	3	2
10	Remote control			1	3	5	4	2
11	Colour			2	5	3	4	1
12								
13				Score obtained by each system				
14	**Feature**		**Weighting**	A	B	C	D	E
15	Purchase cost		5	15	25	10	5	20
16	Control layout		7	28	35	14	7	21
17	Sound quality		9	36	27	45	9	18
18	Range of features		6	18	30	24	6	12
19	Ease of operation		5	20	25	15	5	10
20	Size of speakers		4	16	4	20	12	8
21	Remote control		9	9	27	45	36	18
22	Colour		2	4	10	6	8	2
23								
24				146	183	179	88	109

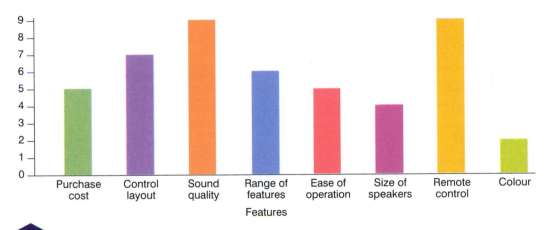

Question 3, page 324

Question 4, page 324

	A	B	C	D	E	F	G	H	I
1	Type of plant	Cost of pot (£)	Cost of compost (£)	Weeks to reach full size	Weekly cost of keeping plant	Total cost of plant	Selling price of plant	Number of plants sold	Total profit (£)
2	Rose	0.30	0.15	16	0.05	1.25	1.88	150	93.75
3	Pear Tree	0.70	0.75	52	0.05	4.05	6.08	75	151.88
4	Pansy	0.02	0.02	4	0.08	0.36	0.54	325	58.50
5	Lavender	0.08	0.10	12	0.04	0.66	0.99	125	41.25
6	Holly	0.15	0.20	16	0.04	0.99	1.49	147	72.77
7								Total profit	418.15

Chapter 29

1 The Head of Drama has produced the outline shown below to advertise the school musical.

> Toptone School
> presents
> its
> Annual Musical
> 'Oh What a Lovely War'
> Performances
> Thursday, Friday, Saturday
> 17th–19th of July
> Tickets on sale in the School

The IT teacher has used his desktop publishing package to produce the poster shown:

(a) Give four changes made to the original poster by the IT teacher. (4)

(b) Before printing out the final poster, the IT teacher used the spellchecker facility of the desktop publishing package.
　(i)　Why would the IT teacher use a spellchecker? (1)
　(ii)　Describe how a spellchecker works. (2)

(c) In addition to wordprocessing and desktop publishing software the Head of Drama could use other software to help with the musical.
　(i)　Name **one** other *different* type of software which would be used to organise, administer or present the musical. (1)
　(ii)　What would this software be used for? (1)
　　　　　(WJEC FT Short course June 1998 q2)

2 A man has decided to sell all his golfing equipment. He plans to advertise the items he has for sale. He will put copies of his advert in the local shops and in the golf club. Below is a copy of the advert he has produced using a DTP (desk top publishing) package.

> FOR SALE – GOLF EQUIPMENT
> For sale FULL set of golf clubs, 10 irons, 4 woods and a putter.
> All clubs are in excellent condition and carry a well known brand name.
> Also for sale golf trolley, umbrella, golf shoes (size 9) and 100 golf balls. £150 for a quick sale.
> Telephone Dave Brown on 565656.

Describe **five different features** of a DTP (desk top publishing) package that he could use to improve the advert. Give a reason why each **feature** might be used. (10)
　　　　　(NEAB 1998 Tier F Short course q3)

Chapter 30

1 A pupil database contains two data files. The structure of the two files is shown below.

Pupils	**Subjects**
Pupil number	Subject code
Surname	Subject name
Forename	
Date of birth	
Address 1	
Address 2	
Address 3	
Contact phone number	
Home phone number	
Subject code 1	
Subject code 2	
Subject code 3	
Subject code 4	
Form	

(a) Why is it better to store the data in two separate files, rather than keeping it all in one file?
(1)
(b) Why is date of birth stored rather than age? (1)
(c) To find all the pupils in the same form a search can be carried out. In this database package searches take the form

<fieldname><comparison><value>

A search for surname = 'Robinson' would find all pupils with the surname Robinson. Write down the search you would carry out to find all the pupils in the Form called 7B. (3)
(d) The Head Teacher wants to be able to send personalised letters to the pupils' parent or guardian. What extra field would be needed to allow the letters to be produced? (1)
(*NEAB FT Full course Paper 2 June 1998 q9*)

Chapter 32

1 (a) A hospital uses a fleet of ambulances. The hospital uses a computer-based model of the surrounding area to decide which ambulance should go to an emergency.
  (i) This is part of the map of the surrounding area the model displays. The numbers are the average time in minutes for an ambulance to travel that section of the map. Which ambulance should be sent to the emergency? (1 mark)

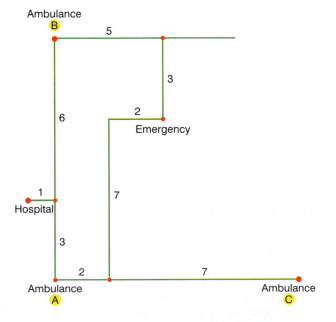

  (ii) Tick two boxes to show the information the model should provide to help the hospital decide which ambulance to send.

Tick two boxes

The time it will take for each
  ambulance to get to the emergency. ☐
The distance each
  ambulance will have to
  travel to get to the emergency. ☐
The name of the patient. ☐
The amount of petrol the
  ambulance will use. ☐
An indication of whether
  the medical supplies carried
  will allow an ambulance to
  deal with the emergency. ☐
(2 marks)

  (iii) The model has to make some assumptions about the ambulances. For example, the model assumes that all the ambulance drivers are fully trained.
  Describe two other assumptions the model would make. (2 marks)
(b) A spreadsheet is used to manage the medical supplies carried by an ambulance. This is part of the spreadsheet:

	A	B	C	D	E
1	Description of item	Unit cost	Quantity		
2	stretchers	707.50	2	1415.00	
3	bandages	2.00	50	100.00	
4	medicines	5.50	40	220.00	
5					
6			Total value =	1735.00	
7					

  (i) Write a formula that will work out the value in cell D3. (1)
  (ii) Write a formula that will work out the value in cell D6. (1)
  (iii) Complete these sentences, using the terms from the list.

a byte
a cable
a formula
a matrix
a number
text

Cell B2 contains ....
Cell C6 contains ....
The value of .... may be recalculated when the value of a number in a cell is changed. (3)

(iv) It is decided to reduce the total value of the medical supplies carried by an ambulance to below £1400.
Explain how the spreadsheet could be used to decide what medical supplies will be carried. (3)

(c) The computer-based model and the spreadsheet are separate information systems. The hospital wants to integrate all its information systems. A systems analyst is asked to carry out a **feasibility study**.
Complete the sentences, using terms from the list.

buildings
costs
problems
reports
stores

The systems analyst finds out what the .... are by talking to users.
The systems analyst looks at all the possible ways of integrating these information systems and works out the .... of each option.
The systems analyst .... the findings of the feasibility study to management. (3)

(SEG Spec Paper June 1998 Foundation tier Full course P2 q2)

2 Betterview, a firm of opticians, used to keep **manual** records of the sales of each of the eight shops.

A computer model was needed to give an improved breakdown of financial details and to predict future profits, based on previous sales, with greater accuracy.

Betterview now uses a spreadsheet to record the sales information. Part of this spreadsheet is shown below.

	Branch 1 Predicted sales	Branch 1 Actual sales	Branch 2 Predicted sales	Branch 2 Actual sales
Number frames sold	1832	2546	7712	6775
Original buy-in price £	36342	41454	53156	47651
Final profit (pre-tax) £	27124	31239	36453	29987

(a) Explain what is meant by *computer model*. (1)
(b) Describe THREE features of spreadsheet software which make it suitable for computer modelling. (6)

(c) (i) Using the information shown above, describe TWO features of the relative performances of the two branches of Betterview.
(ii) Betterview wants the spreadsheet to report automatically about the relative performances of the branches.
Describe how the spreadsheet could be extended to do this. (4)

(London HT Full course P2H June 1998 qA3)

Chapter 33

1 A school has recently bought a new graphics package. The package has tools that carry out various tasks. Five of the different tools that are available in the graphics package are given below. Explain clearly the purpose of each.
(a) Freehand drawing (1)
(b) Pre-defined shapes (1)
(c) Text (1)
(d) Copy (1)
(e) Palette (1)

(NEAB 1998 Tier F Short course q2)

2 'CAD – computer aided design is one of the most widely used commercial applications of computer graphics.'
(a) Name two different applications of CAD programs. (2)
(b) Give three features/facilities you might expect a CAD program to contain. (3)

(WJEC HT Full course P2 June 1998 q2)

3 Drawing packages have many different tools with which to draw.
(a) Name **four** tools commonly found in a drawing package. (4)
(b) Describe a feature of a computer aided design (CAD) package that you would not normally find in a drawing package. (3)

(NI P1 June 1998 q11)

Full course Higher tier questions

1 A large health centre decides to replace its manual information system with a network of computers.
(a) Give **three** advantages a network of computers could give the health centre rather than using stand-alone computers. (3)
(b) (i) Suggest a suitable *general purpose* software package that could be used by the health centre accountant. (1)

(ii) Give **two** different uses for this software in the running of the health centre. (2)

(c) One of the doctors requests that an *expert system* should be used to help with medical diagnosis.
  (i) What is an expert system? (2)
  (ii) State **three** benefits an expert system might give patients or doctors. (3)
  (iii) Give **two** drawbacks of using an expert system. (2)

(d) Give **two** different datafiles that could be used by the doctor in the treatment of patients. (2)
(WJEC HT Full course June 1998 P2 q3)

2 A software company sends information to its customers by personalised letter. These letters are created using mail merging.
(a) Describe the processes involved in mail merging. (3)
(b) The company is considering using electronic mail to send information to its customers. Describe the process of sending and receiving electronic mail. (3)
(c) Describe the relative benefits and drawbacks of using electronic mail to order and pay for goods. (4)
(MEG June 1998 P4 Higher tier Full course q10)

3 Satellites are widely used in communications. Most satellite dishes are permanently fixed to receive signals from just one particular satellite, but some are capable of rotating to receive signals from different satellites. This is achieved by using a microprocessor linked to a motor to rotate the dish, analogue sensor to evaluate the signal received and the principle of feedback to maintain the strongest signal possible.

(a) What is a microprocessor? (3)
(b) What item of hardware is needed to allow the microprocessor to process the signal from the analogue sensor? (2)

This control system uses the principle of 'feedback'.
(c) Explain the principle of feedback. (3)
(d) Give two reasons why feedback is necessary for most control systems. (4)
(e) Apart from television communication give one other purpose for which satellites are used. (2)
(NI 1997 P3 q20)

4 Complete Bedroom Design is a firm which makes, designs and installs bedroom furniture.

The firm uses information technology methods to:
- produce a catalogue of equipment and prices
- design the best arrangement of bedroom furniture
- help with financial matters and stock control.

(a) A two-way communication link is necessary between the main office and the design staff, who spend a lot of time away from the office with customers.
  (i) Name a piece of computer software that staff need to make this communication possible.
  (ii) State a use for this piece of software. (4)

(b) Name THREE other types of software that Complete Bedroom Design needs, apart from your answer to (a)(ii).
Describe a use for each type of software you have given. (6)

(c) The senior management of Complete Bedroom Design decide to change to the use of information technology methods to perform the payroll calculations for all their staff.
Some staff are part-time and some are full-time.
  (i) They intend to buy new hardware to record and input automatically the working times of all the staff into the computer system. State the name of ONE piece of hardware that would be suitable for this task.
  (ii) Describe TWO advantages to the firm of making this change,
  (iii) Describe TWO disadvantages to the firm of making this change. (9)
(London June 1998 Full course HT P2H qB1)

5 During systems analysis it is important to find out as much as possible about the existing system. This is called fact finding.
(a) Describe four methods often used for fact finding.

Systems diagrams are used in documentation to convey the overall design of a system. These diagrams often show the processes that are performed on the data and the devices and storage methods used. Shown on page 330 is an incomplete systems diagram for processing electricity payments and bills.
(b) Complete this diagram using the list below. You need only use the letters A to F to represent your choice.
  A Sorted Payments Transaction File
  B Master File

C   Payments Transaction File
D   Input using keyboard
E   List of Invalid Entries
F   Update Program

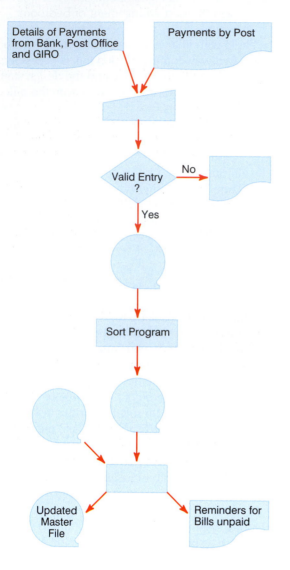

(NI P3 June 1998 q20)

6 Computers will not function without an operating system.
(a) What is an operating system? (1)
(b) Give **three** functions of an operating system. (3)
(c) A multi-access, multi-tasking operating system is installed on a large computer which is also used for batch and real-time transaction processing. Give the meaning of the following:
(i)   multi-access; (1)
(ii) multi-tasking; (1)
(iii) real-time transaction processing; (1)
(iv) batch processing. (1)
(WJEC June 1998 HT Full course P2 q6)

7 An estate agent is going to transfer all the details of her houses for sale from paper files to files stored on a computer.
(a) Suggest an input device she would need to buy to input the pictures of the houses into the new computerised system. (1)

The estate agent decides to store the pictures of the houses on the hard disk of a computer in a compressed form.
(b) (i)   Give two advantages of using compression in this situation. (2)
(ii) Give one disadvantage of using compression in this situation. (1)
(c) Give three reasons why it may be easier to misuse data when it is stored on the computer system rather than when it was stored on paper. (3)
(NEAB HT Full course June 1998 P1 q6)

Full course Foundation tier questions

1 A school is going to buy a number of laptop computers for pupils to borrow and use at home. Give **three** problems that this may cause? (3)
(MEG Foundation tier Full course P1 q15)

2 Ben and Shaazia run a small firm supplying computer hardware and software. They have a small shop and a mail order business.

Customers can:
● call at the shop
● fill in forms from the catalogue
● ring up to make an order.
(a) Each item of hardware and software in the shop has a bar code on it. The bar code is a unique identifier to a piece of hardware or software.
List THREE pieces of information that will be stored in the computer file for this item of hardware or software. (3)
(b) Give TWO reasons why Ben and Shaazia use bar codes on their goods. (2)
(c) When customers ring up with their orders, Ben uses a screen input form to collect details of:
● the customer
● their order
● the method of payment.
New customers are given a customer number. Existing customers are asked to give their customer number. Ben uses a different screen

input form for the new customers. Give TWO reasons why Ben uses a **different** form for new customers. (2)

(d) Design a screen input form that Ben could use for **new** customers ordering computer goods from the mail order catalogue. (7)

(e) Ben and Shaazia own a business that sells computer hardware and software.

   (i) They need to know from which parts of the country most of the mail orders come. Name the data item that must be stored so that they can identify these parts of the country.

   (ii) Ben and Shaazia want Fernando to join the management of the business. Fernando says that he wants to see information about the sales made during the last year. Describe, in detail, how a computer system could be used to present this information to Fernando. (5)

(EDEXCEL Foundation tier June1998 P2F qB2)

3 When a new computerised system is developed it is important that it is properly tested and documented.

(a) A package processes examination marks. When the marks are input they have to be validated with a range check. Marks are allowed if they are in the range 0 to 100. Give **three** numbers you would use to test the range check worked correctly. Explain why you would carry out each of your tests. (6)

(b) Documentation supplied with a system should provide instructions for normal use. Describe **three** other topics which should be included in the user guide. (3)

(NEAB June 1998 FT Full course P2 q10)

4 A computer company uses mail order to sell its goods. A new computerised system is to be introduced.

(a) Describe **two** steps involved in implementing the system. (2)

(b) Describe **two** items of documentation which would be supplied with the system. (2)

(c) Describe **two** verification methods the company could use when the data is entered into the computer. (2)

(d) Give **two** reasons why the company uses codes to store data about the goods being sold. (2)

(e) Describe **two** methods used to ensure that the data is not accidentally lost. (2)

(MEG June 1998 P3 Foundation tier q14)

5 A new system is to be introduced into a school for pupils to pay for their dinner using computer cards. Describe the steps taken in the analysis and design of this system. (6)

(MEG Foundation tier Full course 1998 P3 q17)

6 An *operating system* is a program.

(a) Name **two** tasks the operating system does. (2)

(b) Name **one** operating system used by computers. (1)

(c) Microcomputers can carry out *multi-tasking*. Give the meaning of the term multi-tasking. (1)

(d) Computer hardware can be linked up to form *networks*. Draw a diagram of a network you are familiar with. (4)

(e) Give **two** advantages a network has over a number of stand-alone computers. (2)

(f) Networks create security problems because of the increased number of users sharing the system. Give **three** security measures to make the system more secure. (3)

(WJEC FT Full course June 1998 P2 q8)

7 Under the terms of the Data Protection Act, give **four** legal obligations of any company storing personal data on a computer file.

(WJEC FT Full course June 1998 P2 q10)

8 The Silsden Tennis Club is having a dance to raise funds.

(a) The Secretary uses desk top publishing (DTP) software to design a poster to advertise the dance. Complete the sentences using terms from the list.

    clip art
    columns
    fonts
    pixels
    sizes

    DTP software helps the Secretary lay out text and graphics in .... on the poster. DTP software allows the Secretary to use different .... and .... for the text on the poster. The Secretary can import .... into the DTP software. (4)

(b) The Secretary prints the poster on a laser printer. Tick one box to show why a laser printer is used. (1)

Tick **one** box

A laser printer costs less to
  buy than a dot-matrix printer. ☐

A laser printer costs less to
run than a dot-matrix printer. ☐
A laser printer is environmentally
friendly. ☐
A laser printer prints good quality
text and graphics. ☐
A laser printer prints good quality
text but cannot print graphics. ☐

(c) Name one hardware device that is useful for
DTP, other than a keyboard, a disk drive, a
monitor, a mouse, a printer and a processor.
Describe what the hardware device is used
for. (2)

(d) When the Secretary bought the computer, it
was supplied with an operating system and
some utility programs.
(i) Tick **two** boxes to show the tasks done by
an operating system. (2)
(ii) Tick **two** boxes to show the tasks done by
utility programs (2)

Enters information into
a database. ☐
Displays a screen saver
when the computer is not
being used. ☐
Formats a floppy disk. ☐
Cleans the computer room. ☐
Alerts the police when
burglars break into the
computer room. ☐

(e) The computer was also supplied with a user
manual.
(i) Complete the sentences, using terms from
the list. (2)

dictionary
hardware
index
puzzle
tripod

You can also use the .... in the
manual to help you find the information
you want.
You may have to read the section on setting up the .... before you can
use the computer.
(ii) Tick three boxes to show the features of a
good user manual.

Tick **three** boxes

The language used should
be easy to understand. ☐

The manual should be large. ☐
The manual should have a
picture on the front cover. ☐
There should be a word search
at the end of each chapter. ☐
There should be no missing
instructions. ☐
It should be easy to find the
information you want. ☐
(3)

(f) Some Tennis Club members believe that the
Secretary should not use information technology. Tick three boxes to show why the Secretary
should not use information technology.

Tick **three** boxes

Silsden is a thriving market
town with a flourishing
textile industry. ☐
The Tennis Club has twelve members. ☐
Multimedia is an application
of information technology. ☐
The hardware and software
needed cost more than £2500. ☐
None of the Tennis Club's members
can use information technology
except the Secretary. ☐
When the fibre-optic cable
has been laid, the Secretary can
send E-mail to other tennis clubs. ☐
(3)

(SEG Full course Foundation tier Spec Paper 2 q1)

9 Members of a library are given a membership
card when they join the library.

The membership card has a bar code on it.

Anytown
Library
Membership Card
▌▎▌▌▎▌▌▎▎▌▌▎
HU P00043085 4

(a) Tick three boxes to show which of these
statements are true. (3)

Tick **three** boxes

The number printed under the bar
code is also stored in the bar code. ☐
Different members have the same
number on their membership cards. ☐
Every member has a different number
on their membership card. ☐

The member's address is stored in
the bar code. ☐

Bar codes can be read into the
computer without the need for
data preparation. ☐

The library computer would
understand the bar code on
a can of baked beans. ☐

(b) When a member borrows a book, either the
bar code on their membership card is read
into the computer using a bar code reader, or,
the librarian types the number on the card
into the computer.
Tick three boxes to show which of these statements are true. (3)

Tick **three** boxes

Librarians can tell if a member
has not returned all the books
they borrowed by looking at
their membership card. ☐

It is faster to use a bar code
reader than to type the number
into the computer. ☐

The librarian could make a
mistake typing in the number. ☐

The bar code reader is almost always
accurate. ☐

Bar code readers are too expensive
to be used in libraries. ☐

The librarian types the number into
the computer if the bar code
reader is not working. ☐

It is faster to type the number into
the computer than use a bar
code reader. ☐

(c) The bar code has a check digit in it.
Tick three boxes to show which of these statements is true. (3)

Tick **three** boxes

When you work out the check
digit on a bar code, you should
always get the same answer. ☐

When a bar code is read, the check
digit is worked out. If it is correct
then the computer assumes that
the bar code has been
read accurately. ☐

The number under the bar code
does not contain the check digit. ☐

If you know the check digit, you can
find out the information stored
in the bar code. ☐

Different bar codes will have the
same check digit. ☐

Every bar code has a different
check digit. ☐

(d) Every book in the library has a different bar
code on it.

Anytown
Library Book
HU 06256 12

(i) When a member borrows a book from the
library, the bar code on their membership
card and the bar code on the book are
read into the computer. Explain why both
bar codes are read. (2)

(ii) When a member returns a book, only the
bar code in the book is read into the computer. Explain why only the bar code in
the book is read. (2)

(e) Several bar code readers are connected to the
library's computer. The librarian can use the
computer to send electronic mail while it is
reading bar codes. Tick three boxes to show
the types of operating method the library
computer uses. (3)

Tick **three** boxes

on-line ☐
virtual reality ☐
batch ☐
multi-tasking ☐
multi-access ☐
gateway ☐

(SEG Full course Foundation tier Spec Paper 2 q6)

Short course Higher tier questions

1 The Internet is often called the 'information
superhighway'. Every day new uses are found for
the Internet.

(a) A mail order company usually sends its customers a printed catalogue. Now it is
considering using the Internet to advertise its
goods in an electronic catalogue.
Many of the company's customers already have
telephone lines and computer systems (computer, disk drive and printer, wordprocessing,
database and spreadsheet software) but would
need **extra** hardware and software to access
the electronic catalogue using the Internet.

(i) Give **one** extra hardware device the customer must have in order to access the Internet. (1)

(ii) Give **one** extra item of software the customer must have in order to access the Internet. (1)

(iii) Give **one** advantage to the company of advertising on the Internet. (1)

(iv) Give **two** disadvantages to the customer of accessing an electronic catalogue using the Internet. (2)

(b) Once they are able to access the Internet, the customer can use it to access many different services. Give **one** other different service that they could access on the Internet. (1)

(c) Every day more and more uses are being found for the Internet. Give **four** ways the Internet could be used to help the police combat crime. (4)

(d) In addition to the Internet we have other types of communications systems. One of these is broadcasted information.

(i) Name **two** broadcasted communication or information systems. (2)

(ii) Give **one** problem that can occur with broadcasted systems. (1)

(WJEC SC HT June 1998)

2 A computer system is to be set up in a school laboratory.

(a) Identify two safety issues which must be considered. (2)

(b) Describe two sensors which could be attached to the computer to collect data from experiments. (2)

(MEG June 1998 HT Short course P2 q10)

3 Describe how computers might be misused giving rise to legal and moral problems. (4)

(MEG June 1998 P2 Higher tier Short course q11)

4 Discuss the advantages and disadvantages of using information technology in shopping. (6)

(MEG June 1998 P2 Higher tier Short course q14)

5 Describe how information technology can be used to design the layout of a computer room. (3)

(MEG June 1998 P2 Higher tier Short course q13)

Short course Foundation tier questions

1 The widespread use of IT has had a great impact on today's society. One benefit that the increased use of IT has brought, is the creation of some new jobs.

(a) Give three examples of jobs that have been created by the introduction of IT. (3)

(b) Describe briefly three other possible benefits that this increased use in IT has brought. (3)

(c) Personal information, stored electronically, is potentially easier to misuse than that kept in paper files. Give two reasons why this is true. (2)

(NEAB June 1998 FT Short course q11)

2 Computers can be used in science laboratories to collect data from experiments.

(a) Give three reasons why computers are used in this way. (3)

(b) Give one example of an experiment in which data-logging is used. (1)

(c) Describe how information technology is used to create a report on the experiment. (4)

(d) What type of printer should be used to give high quality output. (1)

(MEG FT Short course June 1998 P1 q16)

Glossary

Access   To obtain data from a computer.

Actuators   Hardware devices, such as motors, which react according to signals given to them by the computer.

ADC   See Analogue-to-digital converter.

Applications package   A program or a set of programs to carry out a particular application, such as accounts or payroll.

Algorithm   A set of rules that gives a sequence of operations for solving a problem.

ALU   See Arithmetic and logic unit.

Analogue computer   A computer that works on data represented by some continuous physical quantity such as electric current.

Analogue-to-digital converter   ADC. A device that changes continuously changing quantities (such as temperature) into digital quantities.

Application   What a computer can be used to do.

Archiving   Storing copies of important files for back-up or reference purposes.

Arithmetic and logic unit   Part of the central processing unit. It performs all the arithmetic and logic operations.

Artificial intelligence   The science of developing computers that 'think' like humans.

ASCII   American Standard Code for Information Interchange. A code for representing characters in binary.

Assembler   A program that converts assembly language into machine code.

Assembly language   Low-level language where one programming instruction corresponds to one machine code instruction.

Automation   The automatic control of a process or system without requiring a human operator.

Backing store   Memory storage outside the CPU. It is non-volatile which means the data does not disappear when the computer is switched off.

Backup file   A copy of a file which is used in the event of the original file being corrupted (damaged).

Barcode   A code formed by lines on the side of goods, luggage, etc.

Barcode reader   An input device used to scan a series of lines (called a barcode).

BASIC   A high-level programming language.

Batch processing   A method of processing where programs are run in batches and data is processed in batches.

Baud rate   A data transmission rate: the number of bits per second.

Bit   Binary digit, 0 or 1.

Bitmap   An image represented by patterns of tiny dots called pixels.

Bitmap graphics   Graphics formed by a pattern of pixels. The whole picture is stored as a series of dots.

Buffer   A storage area where data is temporarily stored. Printers have buffers so that the data can wait to be printed while the user gets on with something else.

Bug   A mistake or error in a program.

Byte   The amount of memory needed to store one character, such as a letter or a number. See also kilobyte, megabyte and gigabyte.

C++   A general purpose programming language which is easier to understand than assembly language but runs almost as fast. It is a development of the programming language C.

CAD   Computer aided design. A method of using the computer to produce technical drawings.

CAL (computer assisted learning)   The process of using computers for the instruction, training or testing of learners.

CD-ROM   Compact disk – read only memory.

Cell   An area on a spreadsheet in which data may be placed produced by the intersection of a column and a row.

Central processing unit (CPU)   The computer's brain. It stores and processes data. It has three parts: the arithmetic and logic unit, the control unit and the memory.

Character   Any symbol that you can type from the keyboard.

Check digit   A number placed after a string of numbers to check that they have all been correctly input to the computer.

Chip   An integrated circuit etched onto a thin slice of silicon.

Clones   The name given to computers that are copies of the original IBM Personal Computer.

COBOL   A high-level programming language used mainly in business because of its good file handling facilities. COBOL is an abbreviation for COmmon Business Orientated Language.

Compiler   Software that converts a high-level language program into machine code.

Configuration   The hardware that is needed to set up a certain computer system.

Continuous stationery   Stationery in continuous sheets, for use, for example, with a dot matrix printer. It may be pre-printed with company logos, etc.

CPS   Characters per second. A measure of the speed of data transfer between hardware devices.

CSV   Comma separated variables. A way of holding data so that it can be transferred into databases or spreadsheets.

Data   Information in a form that a computer can understand.

Database   A series of files stored in a computer which can be accessed in a variety of different ways.

Data capture   The way the computer obtains its data for processing.

Data compression   Taking files on a disk and using software to reduce their size so that they take up less space on the disk.

Data logging   A system that automatically collects data over a certain period of time. Remote weather stations use data logging.

Data processing   Doing something with raw data to produce some form of useful output.

Data Protection Act 1998   A law that restricts the way personal information is stored and processed on a computer.

Debugging   Removing all the errors from a program.

Decollate   To separate the sheets of continuous stationery.

Desktop publishing   Software that can be used to combine text and pictures on a screen to produce neat looking posters, newsletters, brochures, etc.

Digital computer   A computer that works on data represented by numbers. Most ordinary computers are digital.

Directory   A list of the names of programs and files stored on a disk. The directory enables files to be retrieved from backing store by the operating system.

Disk   A storage medium used to hold data.

Document   A text file produced by a word-processor.

Documentation   The paperwork that accompanies an information system explaining how the system works. The manuals that accompany a program.

DOS   Disk operating system. A program that tells a computer how to work. Controlling data storage on the disk drives is one of the many tasks it performs.

Dot matrix printer   An impact printer that produces characters by using a print head with either 24 or 9 pins that punch through a ribbon onto the paper.

DPI   Dots per inch. The term is used to describe the resolution of printers. A 600 DPI laser printer will produce a sharper image than a 300 DPI printer.

Dry run   Writing down the results of each program step manually to check that the program is correct.

e-mail   Electronic mail. E-mail messages and documents can be created, sent and read without the need for them to be printed out.

EDI   Electronic data interchange. A network link that allows companies to pay suppliers electronically without the need for paper invoices and cheques.

Edit   Change something stored on a computer.

EFT   Electronic fund transfer. The process of transferring money electronically without the need for paperwork or the delay that using paperwork brings.

EFTPOS   Electronic fund transfer at point of sale. Where electronic fund transfer takes place at a point of sale terminal.

Electronic mail   See e-mail.

Encrypt Sensitive files can be encrypted, which means coding them. To be read they have to be decoded.

EPOS Electronic point of sale. A computerised till which can be used for stock control.

Ergonomics The science of the correct design of working equipment and the working environment.

Execution errors Errors detected during the running of a program.

Evaluation The process of determining the quality of software or hardware.

Expert system A program that behaves in the same way as a human expert in a specialist field.

Fact finding The investigation of a system prior to performing a feasibility study.

Fax A machine capable of sending and receiving text and pictures along telephone lines.

Feasibility study A study carried out by experts to see what type of system is needed before a new system is developed.

Fibre optics Thin strands of glass along which light signals pass for communication purposes.

Field A space in a database used for inputting data. For instance, you could have fields for surname, date of birth, etc.

Field check A check performed by a computer to see if the data is the right type to be put into a field. It would be able to check that only numbers are entered into numeric fields.

File A collection of related data; for example, a student file would contain details of all students in a school.

File server A network computer used for storing all the users' programs and data.

Flat-file database A database that is able to use only one file at a time unlike a relational database, which is able to use two or more files at a time.

Floppy disk A magnetically coated disk used to store data. The 3.5 inch disk is inside a hard case.

Flowchart or Flow diagram A chart or diagram used to break down a task into smaller parts.

Font A style of type.

FORTRAN A high-level programming language.

Gateway The connecting computer link that translates between two different kinds of computer networks.

Generation of files Every time a file is updated, a new generation of the file is produced.

Gigabyte Roughly 1000 megabytes.

GIGO Garbage in garbage out. It means that if you put rubbish into a computer then you get rubbish out.

Grammar checker A program (usually part of a wordprocessing package) that checks a document for grammatical errors and provides suggestions for the corrections.

Graph plotter A device that draws by moving a pen. It is useful for scale drawings and is used mainly with CAD packages.

Graphics Diagrams, charts or graphs either on the screen or printed out.

GUI Graphical User Interface. A way of allowing users to communicate with a computer that makes use of icons and pull-down menus. Windows is a GUI and Macintosh computers use a GUI.

Hacker A computer expert who tries to break into a secure computer system.

Hard copy Printed output from a computer which may be taken away and studied.

Hard disk A rigid magnetic disk which provides more storage and faster access than a floppy disk.

Hard drive A unit containing a hard disk.

Hardware The components of the computer system that you can actually touch. These would include the visual display unit, processor, printer, modem, etc.

Hash total A meaningless total of numbers used to check that all the numbers have been entered into the computer.

Hexadecimal A number base system used by computers. Hexadecimal numbers use a number base of 16, compared with the number base of 10 that we normally use.

High-level language A programming language where each instruction corresponds to several machine code instructions.

Icons Symbols displayed on the screen in the form of a menu.

Immediate access store   Storage in the memory of the central processing unit.

Impact printer   Any printer that relies on a character pressing against an inked ribbon for its operation.

Implementation   The process of converting to a new system.

Information   What we get from a set of data.

Information retrieval   The process of recovering information after it has been stored.

Information technology   The application of a combination of computing, electronics and communications.

Ink-jet printer   A printer that works by spraying ink through nozzles onto the paper.

Input   Data fed into a computer for processing.

Integrated circuit   Semiconductor circuits inside a single crystal of semiconductor.

Interactive   A program or system that allows the user to respond to questions from the computer (and vice versa) and immediately acts on the answers.

Interface   The hardware and software used to enable devices to be connected together (e.g. an interface would be needed to connect a joystick to a computer).

Internet   A worldwide computer network of networks. The Internet forms the largest connected set of computers in the world.

Interpreter   A program that converts a high-level language into machine code. An interpreter is different from a compiler because it translates each instruction and then carries it out. Compilers translate the whole of the program first and then carry out each instruction separately.

Interrogation   The process of getting information from a file.

Invoice   A bill.

Joystick   An input device used instead of the cursor keys or mouse as a way of producing movement on the screen.

K   Short for kilobyte or 1024 bytes. Often abbreviated as KB. A measure of the storage capacity of disks and memory.

Keyboard   A computer keyboard consists of the standard typewriter keys plus calculator keys and some special keys.

Key-to-disk   A way of inputting data directly into a computer and onto disk using the keyboard.

Kimball tag   A piece of card with holes punched in it which represents a code. When something is bought, the card is removed and input to a computer. It is used mainly in clothes shops for stock control.

LAN   Local Area Network. A network of computers on one site

Laptop   A portable computer small enough to fit on your lap. Laptop computers use rechargeable batteries.

Laser printer   A printer which uses a laser beam to form characters on the paper.

LOGO   A simple computer language which enables a 'turtle' to move according to the instructions given to it.

Loop   A sequence of steps in a program which repeats.

Low-level language   A programming language very similar to the machine language of the computer. Each low-level instruction can easily be converted into a machine code instruction.

Machine code   The language the computer can understand without it being translated. Each type of computer has its own machine code.

Magnetic ink character recognition (MICR)   A method of input that involves reading magnetic ink characters on certain documents. MICR is used on cheques by banks.

Magnetic media   Media such as tape and disk where the data is stored as a magnetic pattern.

Magnetic stripe reader   A device that reads the data contained in magnetic stripes, such as those on the back of credit cards.

Magneto optical disk   A disk that combines the technologies of magnetic media and CD-ROM to produce a disk looking like a CD-ROM but with the difference that you can read and write to it, and data on it can be erased

Machine readable   Data that can be input directly into a computer without any data preparation. For example, the magnetic ink characters on cheques are machine readable.

Mainframe   A large computer system with many dumb terminals attached.

Mainstore   Memory inside a CPU.

Master file   The main source of information and the most important file.

Medium   The material on which data can be stored, such as magnetic disk, tape, etc.

Memory   An area of storage inside silicon chips. ROM and RAM are two types of memory.

Merge   To combine data from two different sources.

Megabyte (MB)   Roughly one million bytes (1 048 576).

Megahertz (MHz)   One million cycles per second. The speed of the internal clock which controls the speed of the pulses in the computer is measured in megahertz. Chip design and clock speed determine the overall performance of the CPU.

Microcomputer   A cheap but relatively slow computer that is able to work only on one program at a time. The memory is usually limited.

Modem   MODulator/DEModulator. A modem converts data from a computer into a form that can be passed along a telephone wire and vice versa.

Monitor   Another name for a VDU.

Mouse   An input device which, when it is moved over a table, moves a cursor on the screen. Buttons on a mouse are pressed to make a selection from a menu.

MS-DOS   Microsoft Disk Operating System. An operating system used by personal computers.

Multi-access system   A system which allows many different users to access a computer 'simultaneously'. Each user appears to have sole access because of the speed of the CPU, although in actual fact the time is being shared amongst the users.

Multimedia   Software that combines more than one medium for presentation purposes, such as sound, graphics and video.

Network   A group of computers which are able to communicate with each other. See also LAN and WAN.

OCR   Optical character recognition. A combination of software and a scanner which is able to read characters into a computer.

OMR   Optical mark reader/recognition. A reader that detects marks on a piece of paper. Shaded areas are detected and the computer can understand the information contained in them.

On-line/off-line   When a device is under the control of the computer it is said to be on-line, otherwise it is off-line.

Operating system   The software that controls the hardware and also runs the programs.

Output   The results from processing data.

Package   Sometimes called an applications package. A set of programs, with documentation, used to perform a task or a set of tasks.

Peripheral   A device connected to and under the control of a CPU.

PIN   Personal identification number. The secret number that needs to be keyed in to gain access to a cash dispenser.

Piracy   The illegal copying and use of software.

Privacy   The rights of individuals to decide what information about them should be known by others.

Programmer   A person who writes computer programs.

Protocol   A set of standards that allow the transfer of data between computers on a network.

Pseudocode   A combination of English and a programming language used to express the flow of a program.

RAM   Random access memory. A fast temporary memory area where programs and data are stored while the computer is switched on.

Range check   A data validation technique which checks that the data input to a computer is within a certain range.

Real time   A real time system accepts data and processes it immediately. The results have a direct effect on the next set of available data.

Record   A set of related information about a thing or individual. Records are subdivided into fields.

Relational database   A database that consists of several files. It is possible to use a single file and access data in several of the other files.

Remote sensing   The process where sensors are connected via communication lines to a main computer.

Robot   A machine or device that has been programmed to carry out some (usually mechanical) process automatically.

ROM   Read only memory. Computer memory that cannot be changed by a program.

Run time error   An error detected during the running of a program (e.g. division by zero).

Screen dump   A printout of what appears on the screen.

Search   To look for an item of data.

Sensors   Devices which measure physical quantities such as temperature, pressure, etc.

Serial access   Accessing the data in sequence. The time it takes to locate an item depends on its position.

Simulation   The imitation with a computer program of some system (e.g. aircraft flight) or some phenomenon that can be described mathematically (e.g. how the economy of the country works).

Smartcard   A plastic card which is 'intelligent' because it contains its own chip.

Software   The programs used in a computer.

Source documents   The original documents from which the data is taken.

Spellchecker   A program usually found with a wordprocessor which checks the spelling in a document and suggests correctly spelt words.

Spreadsheet   A software package which consists of a grid used to contain text, numbers or formulae. Spreadsheets are often used to produce financial predictions.

Syntax error   An error reported by a computer due to the incorrect use that contradicts the rules governing the structure of the language.

Systems analyst   A person who studies the overall organisation and implementation of an IT system.

Tape   Magnetic media used to store data.

Telecommunications   The field of technology concerned with communicating at a distance (e.g. telephones, radio, cable, etc.)

Terminal   A computer on a network, or a keyboard and VDU connected to a mini or mainframe computer.

Test data   Data used to test a program or flowchart for logical errors.

Thesaurus   Software which suggests words with similar meanings to the word highlighted in a document. Thesauruses are found mainly with wordprocessors.

Time slice   The time given to a terminal.

Toner   Tiny black plastic particles used by laser printers as the 'ink'.

Trace   A check performed by a computer program, where it follows the program, writing down the line numbers of each step as it is carried out. Tracing is useful for checking the logic of a program.

Tracker ball   An input device which is rather like an upside down mouse.

Transaction file   A file on which all the transactions (items of business) over a certain period of time are kept. A transaction file is used to update a master file.

Translator   A program used to convert a program written in a high- or low-level language into machine code.

Turnaround document   A document produced by a computer, filled in manually and then used as the input to the computer.

UNIX   An operating system used in multi-user computing.

Update   The process of changing information in a file that has become out of date.

User   A person who uses a computer.

Validation   A check performed by a computer program to make sure that the data is allowable.

VDU   Visual display unit. The screen on which data is displayed. Also called a monitor.

Vector graphics   Graphics which are defined using co-ordinate geometry. They are easy to scale (make bigger or smaller) without any loss of resolution.

Viewdata   A computer-based information retrieval system such as Teletext or Prestel, which uses screen messages to display information.

Virtual reality   Computer technology which creates a simulated multidimensional environment for the user.

Virus   A nasty program that has been created to do damage to your computer system.

Visual display unit   See VDU.

Voice recognition   The ability of a computer to 'understand' spoken words by comparing them with stored data.

WAN Wide area network. A network where the terminals are remote from each other and telecommunications are used to communicate between them.

WIMP (Windows Icons Menus Pointing devices) The graphical user interface (GUI) way of using a computer rather than typing in commands at the command line.

Windows A commonly found graphical user interface (GUI).

Wordprocessor A wordprocessor allows text to be typed and displayed on a VDU and to be edited before being printed out.

Write-protect notch A notch on a 3.5 inch floppy disk or on an optical disk which, when opened, will not allow data to be stored on the disk.

Names, Addresses and Internet Sites

Equipment Suppliers

For data logging systems, sensors and control equipment used in Chapter 31 contact

Philip Harris Education
Lynn Lane, Shenstone, Lichfield
Staffordshire WS 14 OEE
Tel 01543 480077

'The Weather Reporter' fully automatic data-logging weather station is available from

AU Enterprises Ltd
126 Great North Road, Hatfield Herts AL9 5JZ
Tel 01707 266714

The World Development Database is available from

Worldaware
The Centre for World Development
Education
1 Catton Street, London WCIR 4AB
Tel 0171 831 1746

For Weather Satellite Systems contact

Timestep
PO Box 2001, Newmarket CB8 8XB
Tel 01440 820040

Dartcom
Powdermills, Postbridge, Yelerton
Devon PL20 6SP
Tel 01822 88253

Model Builder, Expert Builder and Energy Expert, as mentioned on pages 183–185, can be obtained from

National Council for Educational Technology
Milburn Hill Road, Science Park
Coventry CV4 7JJ
Tel 01203 411418

Examination Boards

NEAB
Northern Examinations & Assessment Board
12 Harter Street, Manchester M1 6HL
Tel 0161 953 1180

OCR
Head Office
1 Regent Street, Cambridge CB2 1GG
Tel 01223 552552

AQA (SEG)
Southern Examining Group
Stag Hill House, Guildford, Surrey GU2 5XL
Tel 01483 506506

Edexcel
Stewart House, 32 Russell Square
London WC1B 5DN
Tel 0171 393 4444

CCEA
Northern Ireland Council for the Curriculum,
Examinations and Assessment
Clarendon Dock,
29 Clarendon Road
Belfast BT1 3BG
Tel 01232 261200

WJEC
Welsh Joint Education Committee
245 Western Road, Cardiff CF5 2YX
Tel 01222 561231

Useful Internet sites for GCSE Information Technology

The PC technology guide
Excellent, but a little advanced, guide to removable storage:

http://www.dircon.co.uk/pctechguide/16storage.htm

For information about printers, scanners etc.:

www.epson.co.uk

For information about notebooks, palmtops, PDAs etc.:

www.sharp.co.uk

For information about monitors, LCD displays etc.:

www.phillips.com

For information about speech recognition:

www.Free.Speech98.com

For the latest information about backup devices such as the Zip or Jaz drives:

www.iomega.com

To see some computer generated graphics, try the following sites:

http://www-graphics.stanford.edu/demos/

http://www.bergen.org/ATC/images

http://tqd.advanced .org/3543/

For further information about commercial flight simulators try the following:

http://www.quadrant-systems.co.uk.welcome.htm

To see real-time satellite pictures from the Meteostat satellite try the following:

http://www.btinternet.com/~thetford.weather/weather/satmen.htm

For a free demo of simulation software which allows you to experiment with electricity, mechanics and sound:

www.crocodile-clips.com/education/

For information about geographical information systems contact:

www.erdas.co.uk

www.mapinfo.com

www.intergraph.com

The Old (1984) Data Protection Act

The Data Protection Principles

The principles state that:

1 The information to be contained in personal data shall be obtained and personal data should be processed, fairly and lawfully.
2 Personal data shall be held only for one or more specified and lawful purposes.
3 Personal data held for any purpose or purposes shall not be disclosed in any matter incompatible with that purpose or purposes.
4 Personal data held for any purpose or purposes shall be adequate, relevant and not excessive in relation to that purpose or those purposes.
5 Personal data shall be accurate and, where necessary, kept up to date.
6 Personal data held for any purpose or purposes shall not be kept for longer than is necessary for that purpose or purposes.
7 An individual shall be entitled:
   (a) at reasonable intervals and without undue delay or expense
      (i) to be informed by any data user whether he holds personal data to which that individual is the subject
      (ii) to have access to any such data held by a data user; and
   (b) where appropriate, to have such data corrected or erased.
8 Appropriate security measures shall be taken against unauthorised access to, or alteration, disclosure or destruction of, personal data and against accidental loss or destruction of personal data.

Data subjects and data users

Everyone, whether we like it or not is a 'data subject', because organisations and companies, called 'data users', hold personal details about us on their computer systems. The worrying thing about this is that, because of the power of and the ease of communication between computers, this data can be transferred from one computer to another at the press of a button. This means that data collected by one computer user can be transferred to other users, who can use the information for completely different purposes.

The Data Protection Act gives us the right to see our personal data kept on a computer and to get it corrected if it is wrong. It also gives us the right to complain to the Data Protection Registrar if we don't like the way the data is collected or the way that it is used.

How does a data user register?

If a data user holds personal data on a computer and does not fall into one of the categories covered by the exemptions, then the user must register their use. To do this a registration form is filled in. This may be obtained from any main post office. The form is filled in with the following:

- details of the personal data held
- the purposes to which this data is put
- how the data was originally obtained
- the people to whom the information may be passed
- any different countries where the data may be transferred.

There is a fee for registration, which is currently £70.

What happens if an organisation doesn't register?

If an organisation does not register its use of personal data or it provides false information to the registrar, then the organisation may be fined up to £5000 in the magistrates court or an unlimited fine in the high court.

Is compensation payable?

If a person suffers damage because the data held about them is inaccurate or if the data is unlawfully passed to someone else, then that person may be able to claim compensation. The amount of the money to be paid is decided by the courts on the basis of the severity of the damage done.

Are there any exemptions?

Not everyone has to register their use of personal data, so, if you hold your address book or your Christmas card list on your home computer, you can sleep at night.

The following use of personal data is exempt. In other words, you do not need to register your use of personal data if your use falls into any of the following categories:

1 when the data held is being used only in connection with personal, family or household affairs, or for recreational use

2 where the data is being used only for preparing the text of documents

3 where the data is being used only for the calculation of wages and pensions or for the production of accounts

4 where the data is used for the distribution of articles or information, e.g. unsolicited mail (i.e. mail that advertises goods or services that you have not asked for)

5 where the data is held by a sports club or a recreational club which is not a limited company.

Your rights as a data subject

You have the right to see any details about you held on computer. To see the details, you need to send a letter.

The organisation has to respond to your request and may send a form for further details about you to aid identification or it may send the data in the form of a letter or a computer printout. An organisation is able to make a small charge for providing the information.

You do not, however, have the right to see all the information held about you. You may be denied the information if it is being used for any of the following purposes:

- the prevention or detection of crime
- catching or prosecuting offenders
- collecting taxes or duty (e.g. VAT)
- medical or social workers' reports in some instances.

Index

Page references in *italics* indicate illustrations

ABS (antilock braking system) 166
actuators 25, 163
ADC (analogue–digital conversion) 80, 107–8
amendments to databases 67, 260–1
analogue data 79–80, *79*
analogue–digital conversion (ADC) 80, 107–8
ancestral file system 65–6, *65*
animation 204
antivirus software 129
applications software 36–7
archiving of files 130
arithmetic and logic unit 9
ASCII (American Standard Code for Information Interchange) 77, 78
assemblers 39, *39*
assembly language 37–8, 39
autofill 232
automated teller machines (ATMs) 147, 148, 208–9
Avon Cosmetics 121–2

backing storage 7, *7*, 29, 30–2, 78
backup files 65
backups 31, 32, *32*, 65, 130, 131
bandwidth 123
Bankers' Automated Clearing Service (BACS) 208
banking and IT 206–9
barcodes and barcode readers 16, 45, *46*, 200–1, *200*, *201*
BASIC 38
batch processing 73–4, 91
biometric testing 147, *147*
bit map graphics 292
body scanners 205, *205*
bold text 251
boot program 30
borders 231, 250
break-even analysis 284–7
browser software 121
bubble-jet printers 22–3, 23, *23*
buffers 163
bullets 251
Bulmer Ltd, HP (case study) 190–3

bus topology 116, *117*
bytes 29

C++ 38
cables 119, 123
CAD (computer aided design) 203, 294, *294*
CAL (computer aided learning) 83
cameras
    crime prevention and detection 148, 154, 199–200, 210
    digital 21, 247
car park management systems 210
car safety 166
cash cards 146, 147, *147*
cash dispensers 147, 148, 208–9
cashless society 156–7
CD-R 32
CD-ROMs 31, 83
cells, spreadsheet 229, *229*, 230, 231, *231*
central processing unit (CPU) 7, *7*, 9–10, *10*, 75
character type checks 55
check digits 56
cheque clearing 207–8, *207–8*
chips 12, 29
client computers 117
clip art 222, 251, 292–3
clipboard 251
closed-loop control 164
COBOL 38
codes
    data collection 43–4
    pseudo- 165
    system design 99
colour
    desktop publishing 247, 250
    graphics 293–4
    printers 23, 247
    spreadsheets 232
columns
    desktop publishing 247, 249, *250*
    spreadsheet 229, *229*
comma separated variables (CSV) 78, 262
command-driven interfaces 35
compilers 38, 39, *39*
compression, data/files 79, 123
Computer Active 212

computer aided design (CAD) 203, 294, *294*
computer aided learning (CAL) 83
computer games 155, 183
computer magazines 212
Computer Misuse Act (1990) 149–50
computers
    digital and analogue 79–80
    drawbacks of use 8
    physical security 128–9
    and privacy 135
    reasons for using 7–8
    types of 10–11, *10*
    see also hardware
concept keyboards 14–15, *15*
connectors 119
control, computer
    equipment 161–4
    examples 277–8, 277–80
    LOGO 271–2
    open and closed-loop 164
    process 164–5, 191–2
    pseudo code 165
    robots 160–1
control signals 10
control totals 55, *55*
control units 9
Copyright, Designs and Patents Act (1989) 149
coursework 211–12
    examination boards 213–16
    software 211, 212–13
CPU *see* central processing unit
credit cards 146–7, *146*, 147, 201
crime
    computer 146–50
    prevention and detection 154, 157–8, 198–200
cropping 250
CSV (comma separated variables) 78, 262
custom dictionaries 56
cutting 251

DAC (digital–analogue conversion) 80
data 1
    loss of 128, *128*
    security 130–1
data analysis 67

data capture 44
  automatic 47–8
  methods 44–7
  turnaround documents 48–9
data checking 131
  consequences of errors 53
  and direct input methods 58, 58
  reasons for errors 53
  types of error 57
  validation 55–7, 99, 259
  verification 53–4, 99, 259
  wordprocessed documents 57–8
data collection
  coding data 43–4
  data capture 44–9
  data used for other purposes
    139–40
  design of forms 42–3, 43
  see also data logging
data controllers 138, 139
data duplication 63, 63
data flow diagrams 88–9, 89, 90
data logging 106, 166–7, 274–5
  advantages 108, 276
  weather reporting 106–108, 106,
    107, 108
  see also data collection
data preparation 99
data presentation 82–4, 241, 241
data processing 1, 1, 8
  batch 73–4, 91
  multi-access 74, 75, 75
  multitasking 74–5
  real-time 73
  transaction 75
Data Protection Act (1998) 137–9
Data Protection Act (1984) 344–5
Data Protection Registrar 140, 143
data signals 10
data storage 29–32
  see also databases
data subjects 139, 140–1
data transfer 77, 108
  ASCII files 77
  between wordprocessors 78
  compression 79, 123
  and data protection 139–40
  digital and analogue data 79–80,
    79
  file conversion 77
  networks 115–24
data users 139
databases 64
  additions 67, 260
  amendments 67, 260–1
  comma separated variables 262
  data entry 256–7
  data validation 259
  data verification 259

DBMS 64
deletions 67, 260
design 255–6, 256
field lengths 61–2, 66
file access 65
file organisation 64
file processes 66–8
file types 65–6
indexing 261–2
manual systems 63
parts of 61, 62
record design 61, 62, 62
searching 67, 259–60
sorting 67, 261
and spreadsheets 240–1, 241
and system design 262–4
DBMS (database management
  system) 64
debit cards 20, 146, 147, 201–2
debugging 38
deletions 67
desktop publishing (DTP) 246, 246
  advantages 248
  basic techniques 249–50
  equipment 246–7
  features 247–8, 247, 250–1
  terms used in 251
  when to use 248–9, 249
diagnosis, illness 205
dictionaries 56
digital cameras 21, 247
digital data 79–80, 79
digital versatile disks (DVDs) 32
digital–analogue conversion 80
digitisers 16
direct access files 65
disk failure 130
disks 30–1, 32, 83, 130, 131
dot-matrix printers 23, 23
drawing 222, 250
driving licences 2, 154, 154
dry runs 272
DTP see desktop publishing
dumb terminals 72
DVDs (digital versatile disks) 32
DVLA (Driver Vehicle Licensing
  Authority) 2, 198

e-mail 122, 177, 203, 222–3, 222
EDI (electronic data interchange)
  124, 177, 191, 202
EFTPOS (electronic fund transfer
  at point of sale) 20, 147,
  201–2
electrical signals 25
electronic offices 176–9'
electronic point of sale (EPOS) 16,
  20
embedded graphics 247, 248

employment patterns and IT 153,
  156
encryption 131
encyclopaedias 83
Energy Expert 184, 184, 185
environmental issues 155
EPOS (electronic point of sale) 16,
  20
EPROM (erasable programmable
  read-only memory) 30
errors see data checking
ethical issues 156
examination boards 213–16
examinations 302–5
Expert Builder 184, 184
expert systems 184
exporting 108
  see also data transfer
eyestrain 171

fax 177
feasibility studies 96–7
feedback 164
fields 61, 61, 62, 255
  key 62
  length 61–2, 66, 66
  sorting 67
file handling packages 78
file servers 117, 119
files 61, 61
  accessing 65
  compression 79, 123
  conversion 77
  design 61–2, 99
  interrogation 67, 259–60
  manipulation 67–8
  organisation 64
  protection 130–1
  transfer between wordprocessors
    78
  types 65–6
  updating 66–7
fingerprints 199
fire protection 129
fixed length fields 66, 66
flight simulators 185–6, 186
floppy disks 30–1, 30, 32, 130,
  131, 131
flowcharts, systems 90–2, 90, 91,
  92
fonts 220, 247, 250, 251
formatting 220, 232
forms (database) 262
forms (questionnaire), design of
  42–3, 43
formula, spreadsheet 229, 230
FORTRAN 38
frames (DTP) 247, 250, 251
fraud 146, 147–8

games, computer 155, 183
garden design software 295, *295*
gateways 115, 123
geographical information systems (GIS) 67–8
gigabytes (GB) 29
GIGO (garbage in, garbage out) 8
grammar checkers 221, *221*
grandfather–father–son principle 65–6, *65*
graph plotters 24–5, *24*, *25*
graphical display units 22
graphical user interfaces (GUIs) 35–6, *35*
graphics 82, 292
  clip art 292–3
  colour 293–4
  computer aided design 294, *294*
  desktop publishing 247, *248*, 250
  formats 292
  garden design 295, *295*
  presentations 293
  TV/video 204
graphics tablets 16
graphs 233, *234*
greenhouses 165–6
GUIs (graphical user interfaces) 35–6, *35*

HP Bulmer Ltd (case study) 190–3
hacking 137, 149, 150, 156
handshakes 123
hard copy 82
hard disk drives 31, *31*, 78, 130
hardware 7, 99, 202–3
  desktop publishing 246, 247
  wordprocessing 219
hash totals 55, *55*
headers 251
health and safety 171–2
hierarchical networks 117–18
high-level computer languages 38, 39
HTML (Hypertext Markup Language) 121
humidity sensors 163
hypermedia *see* multimedia
hypertext 120–1

identity cards 154
illness diagnosis 205
immediate access store (IAS) 9, 30
importing 108, 222, 232
  see also data transfer
indexing 221, 261–2
information 1
  misuse of 137
  see also data

information superhighway 155
information systems 1–4, 87
  Bulmer's case study 190–1
  components of 7–12
  describing 87–92
  input and output 14–25
  social effects 152–8
information technology (IT)
  banking 206–9
  crime prevention and detection 157–8, 198–200, 210
  effects of 152–5, *153*
  issues raised by 155–8
  medicine 205–6
  music industry 203–4
  pollution monitoring 210
  supermarkets 200–3
  traffic control 209–10
  TV/video industry 204
ink-jet printers 22–3, 23, *23*, 249
input 1, *1*, 14, 98–9
input devices 7, *7*, 11–12, 14–22, 161–3, *162*
insertions 67
Integrated Services Digital Network (ISDN) 119
integrated software 37
integrity of data 131
intensive care 206
interactive systems 72
interfaces 160–1, 163, *163*
  user 35–6
Internet 120, 178
  social and ethical considerations 156
  voicemail 19–20
  World Wide Web 120–2
Internet service providers (ISPs) 20, 119–20, *120*, 121
interpreters 38, *39*
interrogation, file 67, 259–60
ISBN (International Standard Book Number) 56
ISDN (Integrated Services Digital Network) 119
IT *see* information technology
italics 251

Jaz drives 32
joysticks 15
justify 251

kerning 251
key fields 62
keyboards 14–15, *15*, 172
kilobytes (KB) 29
Kimball tags 19, *19*

labels, address 262

landscape mode 233, *234*
languages, computer 37–8, 165
LANS (local area networks) 115, *115*, 191
laser printers 22, *22*, 23, 24, 247
laser scanners 200–1, *200*
  see also barcodes
LCDs (liquid crystal displays) 11, 22
leaders (DTP) 251
length checks 56
light pens 16
light sensors 162, *162*
line topology 116, *117*
liquid crystal displays (LCDs) 11, 22
local area networks (LANS) 115, *115*, 191
logging *see* data logging
logging interval 275
logging period 275
LOGO 38, 40, 271–2
London examination board 214–15, 342
lookup tables 56–7, 238–9, *238*, *240*
low-level computer languages 37
loyalty cards 136–7, *136*

machine language/code 37, 38, 39
macros 221, 232
magazines, computer 212
magnetic ink character readers (MICR) 17–18, 45, *45*
magnetic media storage devices 30–1, *30*, *31*
magnetic strip readers 16, *16*
magnetic tape 31, *31*
mail merge 221, 262
main store (memory) 29–30
mainframe computers 11, 202
Major Incident Room Index and Action Management (MIRIAM) 199, *199*
manipulators 160, *161*
master files 65, 66
measurement taking *see* data logging
medicine and IT 205–6
megabytes (MB) 29
memory (main store) 29–30
menu-driven interfaces 35
mercury tilt switches 161, *162*
merging 67
MICR (magnetic ink character reader/recognition) 17–18, 45, *46*
microcomputers *10*, 11
microphones 19–20, 204
microprocessors 12

MIDI (musical instrument digital interface) 84
mini computers 11
MIRIAM (Major Incident Room Index and Action Management) 199, *199*
Model Builder 183
models and modelling 181–2, 281
  3-D 182, 199
  break-even analysis example 284–7
  inflation 182
  predator/prey example 186–7
  queue example 281–4
modems 80, 118, *118*, 121, 123
monitoring 274–5
  see also data logging
monitors *see* VDUs
moral issues 156
mouse 15, 246
multi-access *74*, 75, *75*
multimedia 82–4, *83*
  presentations 293
multiprogramming 34, 74–5
multitasking 34, 74–5
multiuser software 34
music industry and IT 203–4
musical instrument digital interface (MIDI) 84

NEAB examination board 216, 342
network cards 119
networks 99, 115
  advantages 115–16
  bandwidth 123
  costs 123–4
  disadvantages 116
  e-mail 122
  electronic data interchange 124
  file access 123
  handshakes 123
  Internet 119–22
  ISDN 119
  local area (LANs) 115
  modems 118
  Open Systems Interconnection 122
  part of 118–19
  protocols 123
  speed of access 123
  topologies 116–18
  wide area (WANs) 115
nodes 116
Northern Ireland GCSE 215, 342
notebook computers *10*, 11

OCR examination board 215
OCR (optical character readers) 17, 20, 46

offices
  electronic 176–9
  office design 172
OMR (optical mark readers) 18–19, *18*, 45
on-line help 213, *213*, 222
on-line systems 73
Open Systems Interconnection (OSI) 122
open-loop control 164
operating systems 34–6, *34*, 38–9
optical character readers (OCR) 17–18, 20, 46
optical disk 31–2
optical mark readers (OMR) 18–19, 45
organ transplants 205
OSI (Open Systems Interconnection) 122
output 1, *1*, 14, 98
output devices 7, *7*, 12, 22–5

palmtop computers *10*, 11
parallel running 100
parity checks 56–7
passwords 130–1
pasting 251
patient records 206
payment cards *see* debit cards
peripheral devices 12
personal data 137, 138–9, 140–1
personal digital assistants (PDAs) *10*, 11
personal identification number (PIN) 147
pH sensors 163
phantom withdrawals 148
photographs 222, 250
PIN (personal identification number) 147
piracy of software 149, 156
Police National Computer (PNC) 2, 157, 158, 198–9
pollution 155, 210
portrait mode 233, 234
position sensors *162*, 163
pregnancy and VDUs 171
presence checks 55
presentation of data *see* data presentation
presentations 193, 293
print preview 222, 232
print servers 117–18
printers 22–4, *22*, *23*, 247, 293
privacy 135, *135*, *136*, 156
procedures 272
process control 164–5, 191–2
processing 1, 9
  see also data processing

programming languages 37–8
programs 7, 37, 271–2
  see also software
proof-reading 54, 57, 58
protocols 123
proximity sensors 162, *162*
pseudo-code 165
punched cards 19
push switches 162, *162*

queue modelling 281–4

RAM (random-access memory) 30
random files 64, 65
range checks 55
read-only memory (ROM) 29–30
real-time processing 73
recording studios 204
records 61, *61*
  design 62, *62*
remote sensing 48
  see also sensors
repetitive strain injury (RSI) 171
reports, database 262
revision for examinations 302–3
ring topology 116, *116*
robots 25, *25*, 160–1, 164
ROM (read-only memory) 29–30
rows, spreadsheet 229, *229*
RSI (repetitive strain injury) 171

sales-based ordering 202
satellites 109
scanners 20–1, 247, *247*
school management system 2–4, *3*, *4*
screen designs 262
searches, database 67, 259–60
security 128
  files 130–1
  and integrity 131
  physical 128–9
  software 129–30
security cameras 148, 154, 199–200
security files 65
  see also backups
SEG examination board 213–14, 342
sensors 22, 47, 48, 161–3, *162*, 164, *275*
  use in hospital 164
  weather reporting 107, *107*
sequential files 64, 65
serial files 64, 65
server computers 117
shelf labelling 202
simulations 182, 185
  examples 192

expert systems 184
flight simulators 185–6, *186*
games 183
see also models and modelling
smart cards 148–9, 154
smart terminals 72
social issues 156
    cashless society 156–7
    effects of IT 152–5
    Internet 156
software 7, 34, 99
    applications 36–7
    browser 121
    and coursework 211, 212–13
    desktop publishing 246, 247–51
    file handling 78
    graphics 292–5
    multimedia 83, 293
    network 118
    operating systems 34–6, 38–9
    piracy and theft 149, 156
    programming languages 37–8
    security of 129–30
    spreadsheet 229–42
    wordprocessing 219, 220–3
sorting databases 67, 261
sound 83–4
sound cards 80, 83–4
sound recording 203–4
sound sampling 80, *80*, 204
sound sensors 162, *162*
special effects, TV 204
speech recognition 19, 46–7
speeding, vehicles 210
spell checkers 56, 58, 220–1, 232,
    251
spreadsheets 229, *229*, *230*, 282,
    285
    building tips 232
    for business decisions 235, 285
    calculating maximum volumes
        235–8, *237*
    calculations 230–1, *231*
    cell referencing 231, *231*
    creating databases 240–1, *241*
    documenting 242
    entering data correctly 229–30
    features of 231–2
    graphs 233, *234*
    IF function 232–3, *233*
    lookup tables 238–9, *238*, *240*
    mathematical operators 232,
        232
    printing 233, *234*

testing 242
star topology 116–17, *118*
stepper motors 163–4, *163*
stock control 202, 203
storage of data *see* data storage
structure diagrams 87–8, *87*, *88*
style sheets 247
supermarkets 200–3, 281–4
syllabuses 212, 303
synthesisers 204
systems analysis 96, 262
    analysis phase 97–8, 263
    documentation 100–1, 264
    fact finding research 96, 263
    feasibility study 96–7
    system design 98–9, 263
    system evaluation 101, 263
    system implementation 99–100,
        263–4
    system testing 99
systems flowcharts 90–2, *90*, *91*,
    92
systems software 34–6, *34*, 38–9

tables, wordprocessor 222
tailor-made software 37
tape streamers 32, 130
tasks 1, *1*, 87
technical documentation 101, 264
telecommunications 72, 119
teleconferencing 119, 178–9
telephones 21
teletext 178
television industry and IT 204
teleworking 155, 179
temperature
    protection from extremes of 129
    sensors 107, 162, *162*, 274–5
templates 222, 247, 251
terminals 72, 73
Tesco (case study) 200–3
theft
    computer 128–9
    software 149, 156
thesaurus 221
3-D modelling 182, 199
TIFF 251
timesharing *74*, 75, *75*
top-down approach 87–8, 165
topologies, network 116–18
touch screens 16
touch sensitive pads 15, *15*
touch tone telephones 21
tracker balls 15

tracker pads 15, *15*
traffic control systems 209–10
transaction files 65, 66
transaction log files 65
transaction processing 75
transcription errors 57
transfer of data *see* data transfer
translation programs 36, 38–9, *39*
transposition errors 57
turnaround documents 48–9, *48*
turtle graphics 271–2

updating files 66–7
user guides 100, 264
user interfaces 35–6
utility programs 36

validation 55–7, 99, 131, 259
variable length fields 66, *66*
VDUs (visual display units) 22,
    171, 172, 247
vector graphics 292
verification 53–4, *54*, 99, 131, 259
video digitisers 20
video industry and IT 204
videoconferencing 119, 178–9
virtual reality 84, *84*
viruses 129–30
visual display units (VDUs) 22,
    171, 172, 247
voice output 25
voice recognition 19, 46–7
voicemail 19–20

warehouse systems 203
weather reporting 105–9, 210
websites 121–2
wide area networks (WANs) 115
WIMP 36
wizards 222
WJEC examination board 216, 342
word-count 222
wordprocessing 219
    advantages 219–20
    choosing software 223
    compiling e-mail 222–3, *222*
    file transfers 78
    hardware and software 219, *219*
    software features 220–2, *220*
World Wide Web (WWW) 120–2
WYSIWYG 220, 251

Zip files/drives 32, 79
zoom facility 222